AF564396

The Humayun Nama

Praise for *The Humayun Nama*

'India's first woman-nama.'
– **Irwin Allan Sealy**

'A rare window into the Mughal world, seen through the eyes of the fascinating Gulbadan Begum. Ruby Lal's masterful introduction breathes fresh life into this royal memoir, revealing the Emperor Humayun not just as a ruler, but as a brother. This edition is bound to become a classic for scholars and casual readers alike.'
– **Sam Dalrymple**

'Gulbadan Begum's *Humayun Nama* is one of the most remarkable histories of the Mughal world, written from within the imperial household and attentive to the textures of everyday life at court. A Mughal chronicle unlike any other. Read through Annette Susannah Beveridge's meticulous translation, and alongside Ruby Lal's illuminating introduction, this new edition traces a lineage of three women bound by a single text across centuries.'
– **Aanchal Malhotra**

Also by Ruby Lal

Tiger Slayer: The Extraordinary Life of Nur Jahan, Empress of India

Vagabond Princess: The Great Adventures of Gulbadan

Empress: The Astonishing Life of Nur Jahan

Coming of Age in Nineteenth-Century India: The Girl-Child and the Art of Playfulness

Domesticity and Power in the Early Mughal World

The Humayun Nama

Gulbadan Begum

An Annotated Scholarly Edition of
Annette Susannah Beveridge's 1902 translation
of Gulbadan Begum's *Humayun Nama*

With an Introduction by Ruby Lal

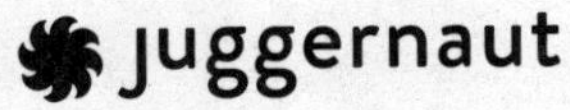

JUGGERNAUT BOOKS
C-I-128, First Floor, Sangam Vihar, Near Holi Chowk,

New Delhi 110080, India

First published by Juggernaut Books 2026

Written by Gulbadan Begum

Originally translated in English by Annette Susannah Beveridge and first published in 1902 by the Royal Asiatic Society in the United Kingdom

10 9 8 7 6 5 4 3 2 1

P-ISBN: 9789353456177
E-ISBN: 9789353452131

Typeset in Time New Roman by R. Ajith Kumar, Noida

Printed at Saurabh Printers Pvt. Ltd.

For Ananya, Aashna, Fanny

For Gudden and Reena

For Prabhakar and Gyan

TABLE OF CONTENTS

INTRODUCTION
GUARDIANS OF HISTORY

SURREY, 1899

A fifty-seven-year-old deaf Victorian woman was hard at work in her study on a 12-acre property in Haslemere, in southwest Surrey, 39 miles outside of London. Nearly 650 feet above sea level, Pitfold had been built as a small cottage nearly a hundred years earlier when its owner, a local hairdresser, added a front and a turret. It had an old garden and an ancient barn that had been converted into a billiard-playing and dancing room.

She had settled there with her husband and children in late 1894 after decades of adventure, grave losses and learning a complex of politics, the best of literature and several languages, including Latin, German and Bengali. Dependent on trumpets for hearing, she was now engrossed in reading a book written in Persian, a language she began learning formally in 1892 – a remarkable decision given that she couldn't hear its sound.

She diligently gardened, digging, planting and working on the aesthetics and layout. Two statues of the Buddha stood on each side of the door leading to the garden. At Pitfold, two of her children grew to adulthood, two had died earlier. There too, she joined the local chapter of the National League for Opposing Woman Suffrage.[1]

---

[1] William Henry Beveridge, *India Called Them* (London: George Allen and Unwin Ltd., 1947), p. 351.

George Bernard Shaw spent his honeymoon at Pitfold when the property was sublet for the summer of 1895. Becoming friends with him later, she debated him, expressing her firm opinions on the topics of the time. 'Perhaps the cleverest lady and the wickedest in her opinions that I have ever met,' he inscribed in his book *The Perfect Wagnerite*, a gift for her.[2]

What preoccupied this well-built, gentle-eyed, sharp-nosed woman was neither the expansive view of her property nor entertainment, dialogue or engagement in local politics. Entertaining friends and animated discussions were activities on the side. By the late 1890s, she was obsessing over a sixteenth-century princess. Her name was Gulbadan Begum, or Lady Rosebody, as she liked to call her. Gulbadan, the beloved daughter of Babur, the patriarch of the magnificent Mughals of India, a dynasty founded by conquest in the early sixteenth century, was also the first and only woman historian of the Empire.

For nearly five years, Annette Susannah Beveridge had been enthralled by Princess Gulbadan's extraordinary writing. Annette's husband Henry Beveridge, whom she had married in India, had chanced upon the Princess's work in the British Museum in London. At the time, Henry had been absorbed in his own undertaking, an English translation of the first official history of the Mughal Empire, the voluminous *Akbar Nama*, commissioned by the third Mughal emperor Akbar, Gulbadan's nephew. While conducting research in the British Museum, Henry came across Gulbadan's work, classified in the manuscript catalogue as Or. 166 and mentioned it to Annette.

Earlier, Annette had consulted the works of several historians of the Mughal Empire in her English translation of Friedrich August Graf von Noer's German book on Emperor Akbar. Count Noer had written his work based on an English translation of H.M. Elliot and John Dowson's compilations of the *Akbar Nama* and on an

[2] William Henry Beveridge, *India Called Them* (London: George Allen and Unwin Ltd., 1947), p. 350.

English translation by Lieutenant Chalmers of a manuscript at the Royal Asiatic Society, the latter based on an abridged version of the Persian. Clearly, Annette had some Persian skills already in the late 1880s, when she translated Noer's *The Emperor Akbar* and revised it in part with Henry's help.[3]

In 1890, their youngest child, Herman, had passed away due to seizures and a high fever. In 1893, Letty, their eldest daughter, died after a five-day struggle with influenza. Knowing that languages were Annette's forte, Henry thought that advancing her Persian would be a welcome distraction for his bewildered and broken wife.

So, this grieving Victorian woman of steely temperament began to work with this relatively new language. Her tryst with Persian, meant to help her heal after the tragic death of her beloved daughter, became a lifelong passion. At once ahead of her time yet deeply moored in its moralities, Annette had been enthralled by learning and ideas, the very attributes she shared with Princess Rosebody: a passionate witness, a playful writer and a Mughal loyalist.

And then there was India, the princess's home and the land where Annette and Henry had lived for two decades. They met in Barisal in Bengal, traveled through vast spans of the subcontinent, discussed books, took positions on politics and laws surrounding the British Raj and brought up their four children. Letty was given an Indian middle name: Laetitia Chintamani ('Jewel of Thought') Beveridge.

The imprints of India were manifold. Annette's connection with India's women had begun in her late twenties. Now, three decades later, she was engaging with one of the Mughals, the lead thinker of the most distinguished court of Asia.

3 Friedrich August Graf von Noer; Annette Susannah Beveridge, translated and in part revised, *The Emperor Akbar, A Contribution Towards the History of India in the 16th Century* (Calcutta: Thacker, Spink & Co.; London, Trübner & Co.1890).

UNITARIAN STOURBRIDGE, RADICAL LONDON, 1842–1872

Born in winter 1842 in Stourbridge, a small town west of Birmingham, Annette Akroyd grew up Unitarian in religion, a pathway that emphasized the oneness of God, which could coexist with rational thoughts and science. She was radical in politics – a predecessor of a new generation of impressive and accomplished women, such as Beatrice Webb and Gertrude Bell. Her father, William Akroyd, was a self-made man of the rising English middle class, 'an early Victorian with a post-Georgian outlook.'[4] Sarah Walford, her mother, was the daughter of a livery stable keeper and the first funeral director of Stourbridge. Having given birth to six children, Sarah passed away in 1849. Annette's father remarried a woman named Jemima – 'Mama' to Annette and her siblings.

The Sunday Tribune, Wikimedia Commons

Annette Susannah Ackroyd

[4] William Henry Beveridge, *India Called Them* (London: George Allen and Unwin Ltd., 1947), p.75.

'Physically a tiny creature,' Annette, her father's favorite, was 'upright as a ramrod and every inch of her radiated pure energy and indomitable will.'[5] At eighteen, she was determined that she wanted higher education. Her father strongly endorsed her desire. There were no university degrees available for women, but Bedford College in London admitted them for higher education. In 1860, she enrolled at Bedford, where she learned mathematics from Richard Holt Hutton, the first editor of *The Spectator*, and attended lectures on Greek literature and Latin. Three years later, when she returned to Stourbridge, armed with accolades and certificates, there was nothing on offer for this energetic person. Chapel, Sunday school, balls and social engagements did not entice her, nor did the prospect of looking for a husband. In 1869, her father passed away, and Jemima decided to live separately from Annette and her siblings. Annette's life changed. She often spent time with her two sisters. They had a modest inheritance, no regular career, but the world was open before her.

Bedford, though nondenominational, had a strong Unitarian influence. British Unitarians had a special interest in India and embraced members of the Brahmo Samaj, a monotheistic reform movement founded in Calcutta in 1828 by Raja Ram Mohan Roy and Dwarkanath Tagore, Rabindranath Tagore's grandfather. Annette became acquainted with many reformers, among them Keshab Chandra Sen, the head of one of the branches of the Samaj.[6]

---

[5] William Henry Beveridge, *India Called Them* (London: George Allen and Unwin Ltd., 1947), p. 78.

[6] There is a great deal of scholarly writing on the Brahmo Samaj. For general introduction to the movement and its history, David Kopf, *The Brahmo Samaj and the Shaping of the Modern Indian Mind* (Princeton, NJ: Princeton University Press, 2015); Kenneth Jones, *Socio-Religious Reform Movements in British India* (Cambridge: Cambridge University Press, 1989). On Keshab Chandra Sen, there is extensive work. For general sketch of his life, Gouri Prasad Mazoomdar, *A Glimpse of the Life of Keshub Chunder Sen* (Calcutta: Thacker, Spink & Co., 1912); and Tapan Raychaudhuri, 'Sen, Keshub Chunder (1838–1884),' Oxford Dictionary of National Biography (Online; Oxford University Press, 2004). For deeper reading of the subject of reform, Sumit Sarkar, *Essays of a Lifetime: Reformers, Nationalists, Subalterns* (SUNY series in Hindu Studies; SUNY Press, 2018).

While teaching as a volunteer at a London college, Annette started to read Sen's eloquent speeches. He had come to London in 1866 and was warmly received by Unitarians for his attempt to incorporate Christian theology within the framework of Hindu thought. Annette was curious about Sen's call to women of England to help educate women in India without trying to proselytize them. They needed 'an unsectarian, liberal, sound, [and] useful education,' he said in a fiery speech at a meeting of the Victoria Discussion Society on 1 August 1870. Annette was not at the gathering, but she heard about it. She went to listen to Sen's next address at Stanford Street on 14 August. He had just returned from a private interview with Queen Victoria. Annette was, as her son later remarked, 'in Keshab's net.'[7]

---

[7] William Henry Beveridge, *India Called Them* (London: George Allen and Unwin Ltd., 1947), pp. 84, 85.

Andhra Patrika, Wikimedia Commons

Keshab Chandra Sen

While enthralled by Sen, her decision to go to India was mindful and unhurried, and she prepared for her journey with characteristic meticulousness. She met more visitors from India. She reviewed her plans with Mrs Aubrey, to whom she often went for advice. And she began to learn Bengali from a man named Krishna Kumar Gupta.

On 25 October 1872, she boarded *Xantho*, a steamer bound for Calcutta.

A MARRIAGE OF TWO MINDS IN VICTORIAN INDIA, 1872–1893

While aboard the ship, Annette met Mrs Goldie, a Scottish woman traveling to see her recently widowed son-in-law, Henry Beveridge. After studying at Edinburgh Academy, the University of Glasgow and Queen's College, Belfast, Henry passed the public exams for the Indian Civil Service (ICS). He left for India in 1857. Allotted the Bengal cadre, he served as a judge in many of its districts.

Determined to work with Keshab Chandra Sen, Annette arrived in Calcutta in mid-December 1872, a few days after her thirtieth birthday. Teaching girls in India was on her mind. She stayed initially with Manmohan Ghose, a well-known lawyer. She met Henry Beveridge, courtesy of Mrs Goldie, but she would have met him even without the latter's involvement, as he was a close associate of her Bengali tutor Krishna Kumar Gupta. Henry quickly became a supporter in Annette's teaching venture. Among the first on her list of contributors, he gave a large donation for the school she wanted to establish – 100 rupees and an additional ten rupees per month, though he had some family responsibilities and not much discretionary income.

As the months passed, Annette sensed a chasm between Sen's public positions on the status of women and his private life. Sen's life story was extraordinary. Born into a Vaishnava *vaidya* (physician) caste in Calcutta, he had a Westernized education. In

1858, he joined the Brahmo Samaj. In 1862, Debendranath Tagore, a Brahmin, initiated Sen as the organization's first non-Brahmin teacher. Subsequently, a group of more radical thinking Brahmos, as they were called, aligned with Sen and rejected traditional Hindu practices such as caste hierarchy and distinctions. While rejecting missionary Christianity, Sen experimented with religious practices (a personal synthesis of Christian and Hindu elements) and became increasingly indifferent to social reform. In 1878, he married his thirteen-year-old daughter to the fifteen-year-old crown prince of a British princely state in a traditional Hindu marriage ceremony. This apparent approval of child marriage, and what his comrades regarded as idolatry, led to Sen's abandonment by many of his followers.

Annette was surprised when she met Mrs Sen, the 'wife of the great apostle of women's emancipation in India … ignorant of English and covered with a barbaric display of jewels, playing with them…. like a foolish petted child.' In a public meeting addressed by Sen, there were only three women among the 2,000 attendees. In 1873, amidst a host of administrative and funding problems, Annette opened one of the earliest all-female boarding schools for girls, the Hindu Mahila Vidyalaya. Sen joined the committee formed to launch her school, but soon resigned. Newspapers aligned with him criticized Annette for her intervention in women's education. Her critiques of India mounted, and she moved away from the idea of working closely with Sen. 'For the first time I realized how uncivilized are their notions about women,' she observed.[8]

What Sen embodied was typical of the visionary men of his time: experimental, politically radical and socially conservative. This was a vital historical detail that Annette had missed. Henry urged her to try to understand a reformer's complex sociopolitical situation. 'I fancy Keshub is a good man but the leader of a party is always to a certain extent its slave…. I venture to suggest to you as a matter of

---

[8] William Henry Beveridge, *India Called Them* (London: George Allen and Unwin Ltd., 1947), pp. 89, 90.

policy that you should keep in as far as possible with Keshub and his party.'[9] But Annette and Sen parted ways.

Annette continued her work with the help of Henry and her other Indian allies: reformer Durga Manmohan Das and Maharani Swarnamoyee, the great philanthropist and queen of Cossimbazar. Friends, including High Court judge Mr John Budd Phear and his wife Mrs Phear, helped her, too, with the latter serving on her school board. Yet, it remained an uphill task. Back home in East Worcestershire, the local paper, the *Brierly Hill Advertiser*, celebrated her work: 'Among the most hopeful plans for societal regeneration in India … the education of the women … has been projected by Miss Annette Akroyd … throwing herself into the work with all the characteristic energy and self-devotedness of her father …'[10]

The Sunday Tribune, Wikimedia Commons

Annette Akroyd with the students of Hindu Mahila Vidyalaya, 1875

9 William Henry Beveridge, *India Called Them* (London: George Allen and Unwin Ltd., 1947), pp. 99, 100.

10 William Henry Beveridge, *India Called Them* (London: George Allen and Unwin Ltd., 1947), pp. 92.

Meanwhile, Annette and Henry grew close. They exchanged courteous letters when he was on judicial assignments and other related travels. He was concerned about her school and the ongoing difficulties. They wrote about the social reform movement in India, about Mrs Goldie and about Henry's memories of Scotland. Yet they often disagreed on politics, reform and colonial rule.

Although he initially addressed her as 'my dear Miss Akroyd,' Henry gradually began to use more intimate forms of address, such as 'My dearest....' He began concluding his letters with 'yours affectionately.' In proposing marriage to Annette on 13 March 1875, he wrote a candid message saying that he could not promise her 'a brilliant future … I don't think I will ever get much higher in the service than I am now … I fear [I shall] be at daggers drawn with some of my superiors … [and] always be looked upon as an unsafe man ... I am also resolved to stick to India, and probably the most unpopular part of it – Eastern Bengal …'[11]

[11] William Henry Beveridge, *India Called Them* (London: George Allen and Unwin Ltd., 1947), pp. 106, 107.

Henry and Annette in March 1875

India Called Them, Wikimedia Commons

They married soon thereafter, on 6 April 1875, in a Calcutta registration office under a new law, the Act of 1872, which provided the option of civil marriage, as Henry objected to a church marriage. Annette closed her school and began a new role as the wife of a district officer in Bengal, attending to her duties at home and raising children amidst long separations from Henry. Annette valued her new role as wife and mother – very much in keeping with nineteenth-century Victorian family values. The epistolary was to be a form of communication the couple would never leave. Stacked in boxes, nearly 200 of their letters, including many to their children, close friends and literary colleagues, are housed in the British Library in London.

Theirs was a household of books. Henry's *The District of Bákarganj: Its History and Statistics*, a gazetteer-cum-history that he was working on at the time, was the subject of extended discussion, as were books by William Makepeace Thackeray, Indian dailies such as the *Brahmo Public Opinion*, Alfred Lord Tennyson's poems, Plutarch's *Marcus Cato* and Seneca's *De Constantia Sapientis*.

Their daughter, Laetitia Santamani, was born in Rangpur in July 1877, in a house frequented by cobras. In the same house, their son William Henry was born two years later. He was called *bhaiya* or *bhai* ('brother'), an affectionate form of address for a son in many parts of eastern India. In 1880, when Henry moved to Bankipur near Patna, an easier to access station compared to his earlier posts, their daughter, Annette Jeanie, or Tutu, was born. Annette would later give birth to Herman, her fourth child.

Amidst long separations, Annette brought up her children: in Rangpur, on the banks of the Ghangot and the Teesta River (now in Bangladesh); in Bankipur; in Darjeeling; in Mussoorie in the Himalayas; and in Shillong in the Assam Hills. She would travel with her children on treacherous journeys to see Henry, feeling embittered at being apart from him. The trip from Rangpur to Darjeeling, for example, took five days. Rangpur was not on a railway line. They started their journey on a *palki* (a palanquin or cushioned and covered carriage) and continued it on a horse-drawn *tonga*. Their servants had been sent ahead of them. 'Rain, rain, rain,' she wrote on 6 September 1877.[12]

Strong of character, Annette and Henry both held firm opinions. Henry was not ambitious, as he had indicated to Annette. Part of this had to do with his holding views that were unpopular among the high and mighty of the colonial regime. His sympathy for Indians was clear. He travelled a great deal, was a dedicated worker and read voraciously. He never focused on promotions or attractive postings. A year into his marriage with Annette, he completed *The District of Bákarganj*. A decade later, while Annette was busy with their home and children, Henry published *The Trial of Maharaja Nanda Kumar, Narrative of a Judicial Murder*, in which he dived into a century-old dispute about an East India Company–appointed tax collector, Nand Kumar, who leveled corruption charges against Governor General Warren Hastings. Henry's possibilities dwindled even further. His postings were tough. There were two furloughs during which he spent time in England, while Annette stayed on in India with the children.

He loved his children and was keenly interested in their life. He argued with Annette against Sunday school but agreed in the end with her view that it would give the children another community. But the management and expenses of their home and the sicknesses and challenges of nurturing children were Annette's business. Civil disagreement always remained central in their relationship, a rare feature in a nineteenth-century colonial marriage. Yet, as their son William later wrote: '… it may be surprising to learn from her letters how submissive she was to my father in India, how she trembled at his frown, and sat up all night to answer his reproof.'[13]

Then came 1883. Annette and Henry differed openly on the Ilbert Bill proposal, which was to enable senior Indian officers of

---

[12] William Henry Beveridge, *India Called Them* (London: George Allen and Unwin Ltd., 1947), p. 155.

[13] William Henry Beveridge, *India Called Them* (London: George Allen and Unwin Ltd., 1947), p. 374.

the ICS to try British people in criminal cases in their jurisdiction. Prior to this bill, Europeans and British people appeared before a British or White magistrate; if one was not available in the area, the case would be led where a British magistrate was present. The first Indian had qualified for the ICS in 1864, and by the 1880s, there were several senior Indian officers in the districts. The bill caused an uproar among Europeans, especially in Calcutta, the seat of the British government. Many British men and women protested, carrying out a campaign in the newspapers in India and in Britain.

To Annette, the problem with the proposed change was that it would allow British women to be tried by Indian magistrates. In a letter to *The Englishman*, she wrote that she was not afraid to assert that her feelings were shared by all English women in India. 'It is not pride of race that dictates this feeling,' she wrote 'but the pride of womanhood.'[14] How could the government subject English women to the jurisdiction of those who, in her view, had not done much for their own women? To Henry, she wrote that as an Englishwoman, she would 'call uncivilized a people which cares about stone idols, enjoys child marriage and secludes its women and where at every point the fact of sex is present in the mind.' Exposing English women to the jurisdiction of Indian judges was 'an insult' not to 'pride of race' but to 'the pride of womanhood,' she declared.[15]

Historians have reviewed Victorian as well as late colonial attitudes and the manner in which systems of power played out in the thinking of privileged white persons.[16] Scholars have

---

[14] William Henry Beveridge, *India Called Them* (London: George Allen and Unwin Ltd., 1947), p. 228.

[15] T.C.A. Raghavan, 'The Whispering Past,' *Open*, 11 August 2023, https://openthemagazine.com/cover-stories/the-whispering-past/; Retrieved 14 June 2025.

[16] See, for example, Pat Barr, *The Memsahibs: The Women of Victorian India* (London: Secker and Warburg, 1976), pp. 188, 189; Mrinalini Sinha, *Colonial Masculinity: The 'Manly Englishman' and the 'Effeminate Bengali' in the Late Nineteenth Century* (Manchester: Manchester University Press, 1995), pp. 58–60; M.A. Scherer, '*Woman to Woman*: Annette, the Princess, and the Bibi,' *Journal of the Royal Asiatic Society*, Third Series, Vol. 6 (July 1996), pp. 197, 209; also, M.A. Scherer, 'Annette Akroyd

simultaneously considered the work of a panorama of women missionaries, social activists, theosophists, Orientalists, teachers, doctors and reformists, signalling a mixed and complex history of race, class and gender in colonial India and of the 'burdens' that English women carried.[17]

As to Annette's response to the Ilbert Bill, her liberal friends, both in India and in England, were dismayed. Henry was a supporter of the Ilbert Bill – a minority among the British. He didn't think it necessary to press Annette on her views even though he disagreed with them.

Scientism – with the added sanctity of domestic life that was at the heart of Annette's views – infused the convictions of people of this era. The remarkable evolution of science from the sixteenth century through the Enlightenment and the Industrial Revolution brought substantial economic, ideological and political changes in the nineteenth century. It marked a pivotal transformation in Western civilization, which its ideologues frequently contrasted against the earlier, more rudimentary phase of the so-called Dark Ages, and strengthened the belief that the Western world's civilizing mission alone could enlighten darker times, places and peoples. With the objective of uncovering new peoples and territories, scientists diligently gathered data, scrutinized and categorized various plant and animal species and human skulls as they sought to map the planet's vast diversity. Botany, anthropology, hydrography,

---

Beveridge: Victorian Reformer, Oriental Scholar' (Unpublished PhD dissertation, The Ohio State University, 1995) Chapter II. I discuss the nature of Annette's translation and the wider ethos of Scientism. Ruby Lal, 'Historicizing the *Harem*: The Challenge of a Princess's Memoir,' *Feminist Studies*, Vol. 30, no. 3 (Fall/Winter 2004), pp. 590–616.

[17] Kumari Jayawardena, *The White Woman's Other Burden: Western Women and South Asia during British Rule* (New York: Routledge, 1995). Also, essays in part two of Antoinette Burton's, *Empire in Question: Reading, Writing, and Teaching British Imperialism* (Durham, NC: Duke University Press, 2011), a volume that looks at unusual Victorian encounters with India and Indians, such as Mary Carpenter's role in 'colonial reform' in India, as reflected especially in her *Six Months in India* (1866).

mapmaking and geology were tools in the exploration of foreign lands, keys to the representation of little-known people.[18]

The *other* – non-white, different – appeared darkly in this triumphalist vision, in which the institutions, practices, traditions, belief systems and men and women of the West were seen as true, rational humans. Those of the non-Western world were perceived as backward and yet to be civilized. Annette Beveridge's public opposition to the Ilbert Bill of 1883 and her views on Sen's position on Indian women were in accord with these views. These robust contradictions, unquestioned stances and deep commitment to causes she thought urgent made Annette the person she was – forceful, clear-headed and determined.

In January 1893, at the end of Henry's ICS tenure, the Beveridge family left India. Henry went home via Italy, where he had promised to see his brother. Annette went on her own with her son and two daughters. Her deafness was very advanced, and she was still grieving the loss of her youngest son, Herman. Henry cut short his time in Italy and joined his family in February, eager to be with them as they began a new life in England. Then, in April of 1893, Letty died.

Amidst layers of loss, the scholarly Annette gradually emerged – an 'imperious lady,' strong-minded yet soft, as her contemporaries observed.[19] She held on to her Victorian views, but other worlds now completely absorbed her. Curious and deeply observant about a bookish princess, she began to create another life for herself.

At that time no one knew anything about Gulbadan or her chronicle of her times. Annette gradually uncovered her remarkable history.

---

[18] For an introduction to writing on science and the nineteenth century, which is a vast field of debate and literature, Catherine Delmas, Christine Vandamme and Donna Spalding Andréolle, *Science and Empire in the Nineteenth Century: A Journey of Imperial Conquest and Scientific Progress* (Cambridge: Cambridge University Press, 2010).

[19] William Henry Beveridge, *India Called Them* (London: George Allen and Unwin Ltd., 1947), p. 374.

POWERHOUSE PRINCESS

In 1868, the British Museum purchased Gulbadan's manuscript from the widow of Colonel William Hamilton, who had brought back nearly a 1,000 manuscripts from Lucknow and Delhi. These became part of the Delhi collection, which included 1,957 Arabic, 1,550 Persian and 157 Urdu manuscripts, representing what remained in 1858 of the famed Mughal Imperial Library – the items that had not been gifted, sold or seized during constant raids and incursions, beginning with Nadir Shah's invasion of Delhi in 1739. India's British colonial government acquired the collection, estimated at 4,700 volumes, at a sale in 1859. In 1867, they acquired another 1,120 less valuable items.[20] The trunks holding the lesser items from the Delhi collection ended up in the India Office Library in London and contained Gulbadan's book.

The princess's work was in the catalogue of the manuscript collections that Charles Rieu, the legendary Keeper of Oriental Manuscripts at the British Museum, set about making in 1871.[21] Busy digging the collections for his translation of the voluminous *Akbar Nama*, Henry chanced upon Gulbadan's work. At the time, he didn't know that the story of the production of the *Akbar Nama* and Gulbadan's work were intertwined.

Writing in real time, the princess captured the gritty and fabulous daily lives of ambitious men, subversive women, brilliant eunuchs, devoted nurses, gentle and perceptive guards, captive women and children who died in war zones, royal gatherings, feasts, messy arguments between Mughal men and women and their joys and sorrows.

Gulbadan was sixty-four when she wrote her unique book, the *Ahval-i Humayun Badshah* or *Life Conditions of Emperor Humayun*,

---

[20] https://www.bl.uk/collection-guides/the-delhi-collection; Retrieved 14 June 2025.

[21] Charles Rieu, *Catalogue of the Persian Manuscripts in the British Museum,* Vols I–III (London, British Museum, 1879, 1881 and 1883).

popularly called the *Humayun Nama*.[22] The book that we have today is small by comparison with the large books of Gulbadan's era. There is no frontispiece or margin. The pages, which include blank flyleaves, are impossibly thin, 229 by 140 millimetres per leaf. There are eighty-two folios, or pages, with approximately fifteen lines on each page. The state of the paper and the writing style date the text to the seventeenth century.

The language of Gulbadan's girlhood and of her kith and kin and elder generations was Chagatay Turkish – called so to distinguish it from modern Turkish, to which it is only distantly related – and the language in which her father wrote his memoirs, the *Baburnama*, which she read. Much later, in 1594, her father's memoirs were translated into Persian at Akbar's court. While she wrote her *Ahval* in Persian, the language of the court, among the Mughal family, and its wider circles by this time, there are Turkish and Hindavi words – from which modern Hindi evolved – to be found.

Like her migratory ancestors, from Timur (Tamerlane) and Chingiz Khan through Babur, the landscape of her childhood was fluid, dynamic and flooded with awe-inspiring ancestresses. Gulbadan arrived in India in 1529, at age six. She was the first Mughal girl to travel in a royal caravan across the dangerous Khyber Pass and the massive river Indus on the way to being reunited with the militarily victorious Babur. As she came of age in mansions by the river Yamuna, strong women peopled her world.

Her poised and reserved Aunt Khanzada had been captured by her father's ardent foe and kept as booty in war, married to the

---

[22] For a critical analysis of the history of the production of Gulbadan's book, and Annette Beveridge's translation, Ruby Lal, *Domesticity and Power in the Early Mughal World* (Cambridge: Cambridge University Press, 2005), especially Chapter 3. For Gulbadan's biography in relation to the political scandal surrounding her book, Ruby Lal, *Vagabond Princess: The Great Adventures of Gulbadan* (New Haven and London: Yale University Press, 2024). For an analysis of Mughal texts and literary genre, Taimiya R. Zaman, 'Instructive Memory: An Analysis of Auto/Biographical Writing in Early Mughal India,' *Journal of the Economic and Social History of the Orient*, Vol. 54, no. 5 (2011), pp. 677–700.

enemy for over a decade. Her mother Dildar Begum had given birth to five children and generously shared her daughter, the princess, with her co-wife, the woman of Babur's affection. Gulbadan grew up with a biological and a guardian mother, a big clan with multiple generations and many staff members. There were no splendid permanent palaces then. Rather, it was a garden society: much of life and its activities, including get-togethers and strategic discussions, took place outdoors.

Perennial warfare was part of young Gulbadan's environment. She witnessed the turbulent exile of her brother Humayun, the second Mughal Emperor and father of Akbar. She was married during this period to her second cousin, a man named Khizr Khwaja Khan, a grandee of Humayun's court. She doesn't write much about her husband, except for a couple of difficult conversations with him in the context of momentous political events. With Khizr, she had a son who is mentioned in her memoir. In the late 1540s, when Humayun lost his territories to Sher Shah, the Afghan ruler, her family was driven out of Agra. She escaped to Kabul. From the splendor of the Afghan mountains, she returned a decade later to Hindustan, the land of her girlhood and youth.

After the robust itinerant years spent between Afghanistan and North India, in the mid-1570s, Gulbadan came to live in the newly built red sandstone harem in Fatehpur Sikri, just outside Agra. New regulations, including the seclusion of generations of women in grand new quarters, were put in place by her nephew Akbar, the third Mughal Emperor.

Unaccustomed to such restraint, the princess, a highly influential matriarch by this time, devised a plan to travel to western Arabia for the annual Muslim pilgrimage. She organized older and younger harem women and led them across the waters of the Indian Ocean and the Red Sea. From behind the red sandstone walls to the Prophet's land in Arabia, it was the first collective pilgrimage of women from a sixteenth-century Muslim court.

Gift in honor of Madeline Neves Clapp; Gift of Mrs. Henry White Cannon by exchange; Bequest of Louise T. Cooper; Leonard C. Hanna Jr. Fund; From the Catherine and Ralph Benkaim Collection 2013.307

A Man Dips His Hand into a Cauldron as Ladies of the Harem Stand in Amazement: A Page from a Manuscript of Religious History, c. 1600. Mughal India. Gum tempera and gold on paper; page: 31.6 x 20.4 cm (12 7/16 x 8 1/16 in.). The Cleveland Museum of Art.

Five years after Gulbadan returned from Arabia, around 1587, Emperor Akbar made an important announcement: he commissioned a comprehensive history of his empire. The first state-sponsored (hence official) record of Mughal glory, it would be unmatched in scope. For this massive undertaking, he asked servants of the State and old members of the family to record their memories of Mughal rule. There was one woman among the invited writers: the enormously accomplished Gulbadan, now sixty-four, a unique witness, partaking in the ventures of her kin, along with her own grand initiatives. The invitation produced stunning results.

Gulbadan was an influential family member, a learned and impressive library owner and an astute and highly regarded elder in her community. While it was normal for aristocratic women to be literate, her reputation was unmatched. She was one of the best sources that Akbar could have asked to contribute to his royal volume.

In the first portion of her two-part book, Gulbadan explores her father's daily life. We see the dynamic facets of his wanderings in Afghanistan and Hindustan, his desperation and longing during wars and victories and the messy early years of Mughal rule in Hindustan. We also find rare, nuanced and complex accounts of Mughal domestic life – especially in comparison to how those issues are discussed in other chronicles. We meet the young Gulbadan in Kabul, dazzled by the news of the curiosities of Hind, traversing the Khyber Pass to begin a new life in Agra in the aftermath of her father's Hind victories.

In the second part, she devotes substantial space to her favored half-brother Humayun's exile and kingship. We glean fabulous details of his desert wedding to Hamida, and her legendary prenuptial negotiation in which she argued why she couldn't marry Humayun even though he was a king. We learn about Mughal women lost in wars and the debacle in the Battle of Chausa, in which Gulbadan's favorite six-year-old niece was lost, and about Akbar's birth amidst the harsh circumstances of his parents' itinerant life, senior women's feasts at Humayun's accession and Gulbadan's brother Hindal's wedding. The princess animates the lost world of the court in camp in a personal way that no other chronicler of the time approaches.

Lady Rosebody, so long 'shrouded in silence,' mesmerized Annette. In June 1898, in a long essay published in the *Calcutta Review*, she introduced Gulbadan's extraordinary writing to the world. Colloquial playfulness in her work, thronged by women, escorts, gifts, reception ceremonials, feasts, 'hazy points of kinship and intermarriage,' granular details of wars and internecine politics spoke to the vigor of observation of the princess. Annette added some thoughts on Gulbadan's pilgrimage to Mecca. On the 'next item of the doings of Gulbadan,' wrote Annette, there was something 'quite quaint and singular in the fact that the woman who had lived through so much … should now devote herself to literature!' The *Calcutta Review* essay would serve as the basis of her introduction to the translation of the princess's memoir, which Annette intended to finish soon. But there was a problem: the 'defective manuscript,' as she called the *Ahval*.[23]

Then kept in the British Museum (presently in the British Library), Gulbadan's chronicle breaks off mid-sentence on folio #82, as she describes the 1553 blinding of her stepbrother. Is this Gulbadan's *ellipsis*, an abridgement of a well-known scene, or someone else's alteration? Did Gulbadan write more? Even as Annette painstakingly translated the work into English – and thought highly of the content and tone of the princess's work – her notes, revisions, emendations and letters do not suggest that she knew that Gulbadan's book was the first and only prose chronicle by a woman. In the words of a modern translator of Gulbadan, it was '… one of the first works ever written by a woman' not only from the Mughal dynasty, but from the sixteenth-century Muslim courts,

[23] Annette Susannah Beveridge, 'Life and Writings of Gulbadan Begam (Lady Rosebody),' *Calcutta Review*, No. CCXII (April 1898), pp. 345–72. Citations above on pp. 345, 346, 347.

including Ottoman Turkey, Safavid Iran and beyond.[24] Henry and Annette ardently searched for a second copy and puzzled over the lack of duplicates, but perhaps never realized that manifold layers of action surround the void in Gulbadan's book.

There is no separating the void and the content in the making of Gulbadan's book. In my recent biography of Gulbadan, *Vagabond Princess: The Great Adventures of Gulbadan*, I unearthed the immense hullabaloo surrounding Gulbadan's extended stay of over four years in Arabia from 1577 to 1581.[25] Sultan Murad III of Turkey, then sovereign of the Holy Lands, issued several eviction orders against her, five of which are preserved in the National Archives in Istanbul.[26]

---

[24] Wheeler M. Thackston, *Three Memoirs of Homayun* (Costa Mesa, California: Mazda Publications, 2009), p. xii. Alongside Gulbadan's chronicle, Thackston also translates and provides commentaries on the memoir of Bayazid Bayat, Mughal officer and Jawhar, royal water-carrier. This translation is presented in easy English that gestures to Annette's work – 'Mrs. Beveridge's admirable edition and translation.'

[25] Ruby Lal, *Vagabond Princess: The Great Adventures of Gulbadan* (New Haven and London: Yale University Press, 2024). Much of the discussion that follows in this section is from this book. I include other required references.

[26] N.R. Farooqi used these orders as part of his broader investigations on Ottoman–Mughal relations; see also, his, 'Six Ottoman Documents on Mughal-Ottoman Relations During the Reign of Akbar,' in Iqtidar Alam Khan (ed.), *Akbar and His Age* (New Delhi: Northern Book Center, 1999), pp. 209–222; and 'An Overview of Ottoman Archival Documents and their Relevance for Medieval Indian History,' in *The Medieval History Journal*, Vol. 20, no. 1 (2017), pp. 192–229. I consulted the copies of the orders preserved in the National Archives in Istanbul with the help of Alexis Wick, historian of the Red Sea, who also helped with close translations of these edicts. The registers (fully digitalized) are housed at the archives of the office of the president (formerly and still often known as the Ottoman archives of the office of prime minister, the Başbakanlık Osmanlı Arşivi, BOA) Muhimme Defterleri, vol. 35, folio 292, farman no. 740; A_{DVNSMHM_00035_00149; Muhimme Defterleri, vol. 35, folio 292, farman no. 741; A_{DVNSMHM_00035_00149; Muhimme Defterleri, vol. 39, folio 160, farman no. 349; A_{DVNSMHM_00039_00082; Muhimme Defterleri, vol. 39, folio 238, farman no. 471; A_{DVNSMHM_00039_00121; Muhimme Defterleri, vol. 43, folio 54, farman 107; A_{DVNSMHM_00043_00030; Muhimme Defterleri, vol. 62, folio 205, farman no. 457; A_{DVNSMHM_00062_00119. A fuller discussion of these orders appears in later chapters of this book.

The Ottomans of Turkey had been masters of Egypt and parts of Arabia since 1517. For them, the prominence and public activities of Gulbadan and her companions were cause for concern. Ordinary folk stared at and crowded around the Mughal visitors in all sorts of places: near the Great Mosque, in markets and at fountains. The excitement – 'disturbance,' in Murad's terms – spread to areas far beyond the sacrosanct precincts of Mecca and Medina, to Karbala, Qom and Mashhad, key Iranian Shi'a cities where they travelled.[27]

The Mughal women's constant visibility and unwavering public commitment was 'indecorous.' But the issue was more dire. What irked Murad was Gulbadan's protracted distribution of *sadaqat*, a word he used in all his orders. 'Voluntary' or 'beneficent' donation does not capture the word's depth. Also translated as right, privilege, grant or gift, the word exemplified a moral position of justice, righteousness and graciousness associated with hospitality and assistance for the needy. In public spaces and in the house of God, gifts and donations were welcome. Food was seen as 'the most essential form of assistance.' Words of solace and 'small kindnesses' mattered. 'Guard yourself against Hellfire even by giving half a date, and if you have none to give, speak a kindly word.'[28]

Sadaqat was seen as the highest form of giving in Islam: it elevated the giver, and was the very *source* of the legitimacy of

---

[27] 'Abd al-Qadir Badauni; George S.A. Ranking, W.H. Lowe and Sir Wolseley Haig (trans and eds), *Muntakhabu-t-Tawarikh* (1884–1925; rpt Delhi, 1986), Vol. II, pp. 216, 217. Qom in northwest Iran, also a center of ancient Zoroastrianism; Karbala, 62 miles southwest of Baghdad, home of Husain's tomb, the Prophet's martyred grandson. A major oasis along the Silk Road, Mashhad lay to the northeast in Persia. According to Farooqi, a report said that Akbar desired to have the *khutba* read in his name in the sacred city of Mashhad; N.R. Farooqi, 'Six Ottoman Documents on Mughal–Ottoman Relations During the Reign of Akbar,' in Iqtidar Alam Khan (ed.), *Akbar and His Age* (New Delhi: Northern Book Center, 1999), p. 190.

[28] Amy Singer, *Charity in Islamic Societies* (Cambridge: Cambridge University Press, 2008), p. 67.

Ottoman rule in Arabia. Murad, and his forefathers before him, had voiced a claim on the Arab lands as *protectors and servitors of all*: townspeople, farmers, Bedouins, visitors and pilgrims. Imperial protection especially mattered in a land with agricultural scarcity, water shortages and competing political and religious networks.

The Mughal women quickly became the subject of popular discussion. They disbursed *sadaqat* among the poor from faraway lands and from Arabia.

As 'Servitor of the Holy Cities,' Murad had the responsibility of taking care of all the people of Arabia. His authority hinged on that. The year Gulbadan landed in Arabia – 1577 – saw acute grain shortages. The Sultan faced a severe shortage of resources. According to an Ottoman source, he even struggled to find funds to take care of the falling bookcases in the library in Medina.

The self-assured Princess Gulbadan, her almond-shaped eyes lined with kohl and strands of grey in her hair, was resolute in making donations. Worse, the very presence of the harem women spoke of the might of Emperor Akbar. The Mughal's bid to project himself as a great, pious ruler was vividly on display.

'Send them back,' ordered the Sultan. From 1578, the orders kept coming. Mughal women were indulging in 'strange activities,' Murad wrote in 1580 to the Sherif of Mecca, a key political–religious authority.[29] 'Stop the distribution of alms,' ordered Murad. 'Send them back.'[30] But the women stayed and continued giving, finding fulfilment in benevolence.

There was no word from Akbar in response to Murad's charges, even though the Red Sea and the Indian coast were in constant contact. It was after Murad's fifth eviction order that Akbar sent a senior courtier to escort Gulbadan back to India.

In March 1580, the women boarded *The Swift One* and headed south from Jeddah. Near the port of Aden, their ship was wrecked. Following the rescue operations, Gulbadan and her companions

[29] *Muhimme Defterleri*, Vol. 39, Folio 160, Farman No. 349, issued on 13 February 1580.

[30] Ibid.

stayed in Aden for another seven difficult months. Nevertheless, they were reluctant to leave, as Murad's edicts and a stray entry in Akbar's imperial history show.

That Murad commanded the expulsion of the Mughal women was a blow for the Mughal Emperor. His aunt's pilgrimage was meant to elevate his status as the great Islamic monarch, vital to his bid to be the millennial sovereign. According to scriptural predictions, in 1591, an Islamic messiah would inaugurate a new epoch of peace and prosperity. Like the Ottoman Turkish Sultan and many other Islamic monarchs and saints, Akbar dreamed of being declared the long-awaited *Mahdi*, or Renewer who would banish evil and usher in a just world order.

Whichever philosophical basis for his sovereignty appealed to Akbar the most – the 'Perfect Man' of Philosopher Al-Arabi, the scriptural notion of the *Mahdi*, or the concept of divine light – all converged in the belief that he was an agent of God who would maintain the 'rhythm and balance of the cosmos.'[31]

By 1577, Akbar was getting closer to his *Infallibility Decree*, the pronouncement that made him the supreme arbitrator in civil and ecclesiastical matters. As a godlike king, he would be the final authority on any opposition to his imperial dictates and commands. In these audacious times, he needed the blessings and support of elders like Gulbadan.

Like other Muslim monarchs of the time, no Mughal emperor made the pilgrimage. As heads of their respective domains, they had to stay away from such risky adventures to safeguard their lands and people. Women from royal families often made the pilgrimage, thus accruing blessings for the entire dynasty. A royal Mughal women's pilgrimage would consolidate Akbar's standing as a great and blessed Muslim Emperor.[32]

---

[31] A. Azfar Moin, *The Millennial Sovereign: Sacred Kingship and Sainthood in Islam* (New York: Columbia University Press, 2012), p. 9.

[32] For greater details of these events, Ruby Lal, *Vagabond Princess: The Great Adventures of Gulbadan* (New Haven and London: Yale University Press, 2024).

Perhaps for this reason, Akbar's official history, the *Akbar Nama*, refused to record the details of what the royal women did. Instead, we find sanitized descriptions celebrating the homecoming of the royal aunt, an esteemed pilgrim – not someone who had infuriated the then ruler of Mecca and Medina.

Do these events explain the mysterious break in Gulbadan's chronicle? Akbar had commissioned Gulbadan to write about the empire, and to include memories of olden times that would elevate him. She would surely highlight her nephew's permission for her pilgrimage, which was as important to him as it was to her. But in so doing, she would describe other things as she saw them, in tune with the rest of the folios. The very virtues of movement would be celebrated, Arabia would be recalled and the women's distribution of *sadaqat* would be highlighted.

The incidents in Arabia likely affected the princess's book, which she wrote upon her return. What would the lost pages of Gulbadan's book look like? This is a question I have asked since I first consulted the manuscript. My obsession with the void in her work prompted me to write my recent biography of Gulbadan, *Vagabond Princess: The Great Adventures of Gulbadan*.

Nineteenth-century progressive thinker, writer and educationist Maulana Shibli Nomani (1857–1914) was certain that Gulbadan's book covered Akbar's reign. Annette noted in her *Calcutta Review* that Abul Fazl, Akbar's official historian, likely 'read it and despised it.'[33]

Royal scribes routinely prepared copies of important royal and non-royal works. Bayazid Bayat, a medium-rank Mughal officer, known to the royals for two generations, was also asked to record his memories. Nine copies of his work survive, including one he sent to Gulbadan. 'It was very rare that fewer copies were made,' notes a distinguished Mughal historian.[34]

---

[33] Annette Beveridge, 'Life and Writings of Gulbadan Begum,' *Calcutta Review*, No. CCXII (April 1898), p. 345.

[34] Irfan Habib, 'Persian Book Writing and Book Use in the Pre-printing Age,' *Proceedings of the Indian History Congress*, Vol. 66 (2005–6), p. 522.

In 1898, Annette was in correspondence with J. Bloch, the philology secretary of the Asiatic Society of Bengal, about her upcoming translation. In a letter to her on 14 June 1898, he expressed concern about the solo manuscript. 'The Rule is that no work should be published of which the Editor has not got three independent MSS. I fancy, your edition is based on one MS. only [*sic*]. Nevertheless, I do not see any reason why this Rule should be adhered to so strictly … and I shall try to move Council to revoke its previous resolutions.'[35]

IN SEARCH OF THE PRINCESS'S BOOK

Upon the publication of her essay in the *Calcutta Review*, Annette's editor wrote to her that her article was 'the best thing' to appear in the journal 'for a long time.' With the payment she received, Annette bought herself a bracelet and had it inscribed, 'Gulbadan 1898.'[36]

Compliments poured in. Annette relished Judge Phear's praise that arrived from India. This was the High Court judge in Calcutta whom Annette had known in her early days there. It was rare for Henry to commend Annette's work, even though he wrote hundreds of loving letters to her. After the essay's publication, he congratulated her. Famous Orientalist Nikolay Katanov of Kazan University wrote to her, and included a photo of himself in the letter.

By 1899, Annette was hard at her work on her translation. Page after page of her typed translation that I consulted in the British Library shows her unfailing meticulousness: remarks in the margins, sections crossed out, words rethought and folio numbers of the Persian manuscript added, removed and added back in again. Annette made cross-references to important lines, wrote long notes to herself explaining the events and the order of their appearance in other Mughal documents and noted spelling errors. She added:

---

[35] Letter in Mss. Eur. C. 176/182.

[36] Mss. Eur. C. 176/143; Letter dated 13 and 18 June 1898, from Annette to Tutu.

'Necessary Emendations.'[37] Henry wrote to their daughter Tutu that Annette was ill from working too hard. He would take her on a trip upon the Rhine.

The void in Gulbadan's chronicle continued to trouble Annette. Having consulted the British Museum copy closely, she wrote that the manuscript was 'rebound (not recently, I believe), plainly, in red leather … The folio that stands last is out of place, an error apparently made in the rebinding.'[38]

In July 1899, Henry was getting ready to take a trip to India. He missed the places he knew, his connections, the books and bazaar vendors, and he wanted more materials on Akbar. He planned to visit the emperor's tomb in Sikandra, outside Agra, but was just as keen to see if he could find another copy of Gulbadan's book for Annette. Henry toured several towns and corresponded with booksellers and scholars. The Sir Salar Jung Library in Hyderabad had the best manuscript collections of Indo-Persian and Urdu history and literature. Henry was hopeful that he might discover another copy of Gulbadan's memoirs there, but his conversations and research led to nothing. Instead, he found a fine copy of the princess's father Babur's memoir – christened the *Haiderabad Codex* – which he later lent to Annette. This was a copy of Babur's manuscript, probably made in the first half of the seventeenth century in the library of Emperor Shah Jahan. She used it as a key source for the collation of the various versions of the *Baburnama*, another masterpiece translation of the first Mughal's memoir, when she was in her eighties.[39]

---

[37] Mss. Eur. C. 176/221. The pages of Annette's lined notebook are not numbered. I have given a sense of her thorough work with the help of the pages of her notebook with the heading, 'Gul-Badan Begim's Humayun-nam; Translation Of.'

[38] Annette S. Beveridge (trans.), *The History of Humayun: Humayun Nama by Gul-Badan Begum* (1902; rpt Delhi: Low Price Publications, 1994), p. 79.

[39] Annette Susannah Beveridge (trans.), *Babur-nama (Memoirs of Babur) of Zahiru'd-din Muhammad Babur Padshah Ghazi* (1921; rpt Delhi, 1997).

India Called Them, Wikimedia Commons

Annette had been reading Babur's memoirs in English. She was astonished that the first English translators of the *Baburnama*, William Erskine and John Leyden, had not mentioned Gulbadan's memoir and seemed to have no knowledge of its existence. She saw immediately that their translation would benefit greatly from reading the princess's work. 'The fact of her [Gulbadan's] authorship has escaped even from the serried ranks of Professor Blochmann's biographical statements. Mr Erskine had not seen her book,' she wrote in her *Calcutta Review* essay, 'or his account of the families of Babar and Humayun would have been fuller and more exact … many of her anecdotes are … hers only; they have not been quoted, and no use has been made of the lights she throws on some hazy points of kinship and intermarriage.'[40]

For seven months, Henry toured towns and cities in India,

---

[40] Annette Beveridge, 'Life and Writings of Gulbadan Begum,' *Calcutta Review*, No. CCXII (April 1898), p. 345.

corresponded with and interviewed scholars and booksellers and parsed the catalogues, to no avail. In Makhan Lal and Co., a Delhi bookstore, he felt he came close to finding the book. It turned out to be ewer-bearer Jawhar's memoir, written at the same time as the princess's work. Again, at the Rampur Reza Library, well-known – then and now – for Persian and Arabic manuscripts, Henry had no luck. Even in other cities such as Bombay, Bhopal, Aligarh, Allahabad, Patiala, Lucknow and Bankipur, no one seemed to have a copy. In his *Darbar-e Akbari*, the Urdu writer Muhammad Husain Azad, author of *Ab-e Hayat* ('Elixir of Life'), had mentioned the princess's work, calling it a 'monument of Gulbadan Begam's abilities…' 'But when I saw him,' wrote Henry in an essay he published about his search in the *Journal of the Royal Asiatic Society of Great Britain and Ireland*, 'he denied all knowledge of it … I was disappointed in the main object of my journey ... to find another copy of Gulbadan Begam's memoirs, so as to supplement the imperfect copy in the British Museum.'[41]

Back in London, Annette had lunch with a Muslim man (unnamed in her papers), who claimed to have 400 manuscripts in his possession. Such meetings sometimes led to rare books, and Annette initially suspected that he might have a copy of Gulbadan's memoir in his collection, but ultimately she had no luck. She worked steadily on and completed her translation based on the only known copy, then in the British Museum.

In January 1901, as Queen Victoria was dying, Annette, now fifty-eight, made a pioneering contribution to history. 'I congratulate you heartily on the completion of Gulbadan and I have no doubt that the book will be well received by the pundits…,' wrote E.G. Browne, a Cambridge scholar and renowned expert in Persian

[41] Henry Beveridge, 'Notes on Persian MSS. In Indian Libraries,' *Journal of the Royal Asiatic Society of Great Britain and Ireland* (January 1901), pp. 69–85; citations on pp. 74, 83.

literature, especially of the history of Iran.[42] The Royal Asiatic Society published the first English translation of Gulbadan's work in their Bibliotheca Indica series. On its acceptance for publication, M.S. Thight from the Royal Asiatic Society editorial board wrote to Annette that Gulbadan's book is 'a volume of unique interest.... a little history.' 'It is but a little thing, but you, who care for the young, will be glad that they shall have the help,' Thight added.[43]

Established by an eminent Sanskrit scholar, Henry Thomas Colebrook, the society was known for its scholarly interest and publications in science, literature and the arts of Asia. Henry and Annette were both members. Another publisher, Sampson Low, was attracted to Annette's translation, and the editor there suggested that she set the Persian manuscript alongside the English translation. While she didn't publish with Samson Low, Annette ensured that Gulbadan's Persian manuscript was included at the back of her 1902 English translation, *The History of Humayun (Humayun-Nama) by Gul-Badan Begum*.[44]

---

[42] Mss. Eur. C. 176/182–s3; Letter dated 13 December 1901.

[43] Mss. Eur. C. 176/195–6; Letter dated 9 January 1901.

[44] A favorable review ran in *The Spectator* – 'The slightly sentimental tone of the comments is not inappropriate in a woman editing another woman's memoirs,' it noted, as it praised Annette's work. In India, the *Pioneer of Allahabad* reviewed her book favorably, and this was mentioned in the Royal Asiatic Society annual meeting. There was as well a 'flattering notice' in Lahore's *Civil and Military Gazette*. M.A. Scherer, 'Annette Akroyd Beveridge: Victorian Reformer, Oriental Scholar' (Unpublished PhD dissertation, The Ohio State University, 1995), pp. 67, 69, 500.

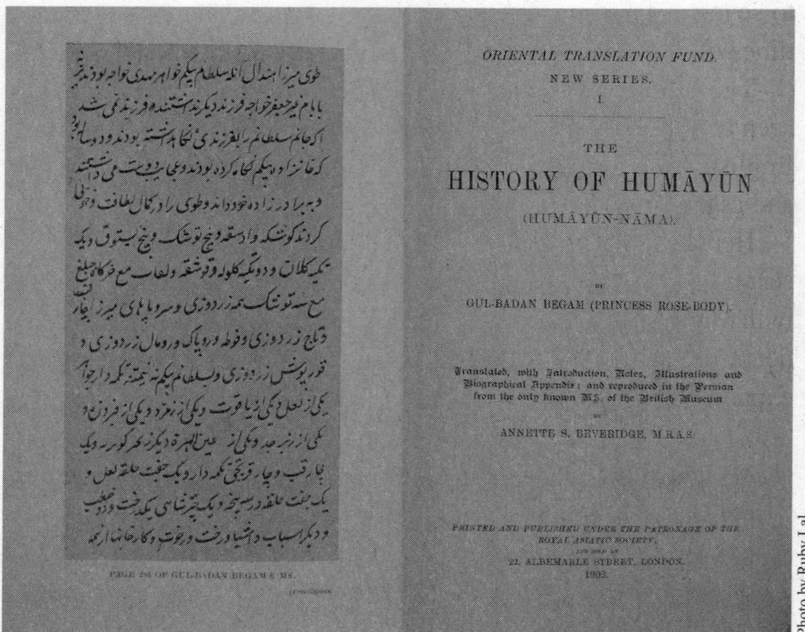

ORIENTAL TRANSLATION FUND.
NEW SERIES.
I.

THE
HISTORY OF HUMĀYŪN
(HUMĀYŪN-NĀMA).

BY
GUL-BADAN BEGAM (PRINCESS ROSE-BODY).

Translated, with Introduction, Notes, Illustrations and Biographical Appendix; and reproduced in the Persian from the only known MS. of the British Museum

BY
ANNETTE S. BEVERIDGE, M.R.A.S.

PRINTED AND PUBLISHED UNDER THE PATRONAGE OF THE ROYAL ASIATIC SOCIETY,
AND SOLD AT
22, ALBEMARLE STREET, LONDON.
1902.

Photo by Ruby Lal

Front page of translation

THE HUMAYUN NAMA

Gulbadan's prose chronicle was written in cursive or *nasta'liq* Persian script, which few could read in the nineteenth century and fewer can read now. Thanks to Annette's English translation, it became available to a much wider audience. Interested English readers gained access to Gulbadan's account of bartered women, children lost to war or sickness, women arguing with kings, sour-faced men and grim-eyed women, kind eunuchs, Afghans and Iranians looking longingly to Al-Hind (the land beyond the river Indus) and the adventures of Mughal women among wars, tents, movement and mansions. Gulbadan's visual, visceral world featured brocade tents, rhubarbs, decadent picnics and royal gifts. These are among the best-translated sections of Annette's 1902 achievement. The introduction, based upon Annette's *Calcutta Review* essay, runs to seventy-nine pages, and is a major statement about the life and times of Gulbadan.

The tenor of Annette's translation is complex. This can be seen at times in her literal paraphrasing in an attempt to find exact English equivalents of Persian words that have complex histories and associations.

Here is a passage in which Gulbadan describes the marriage of the second Mughal emperor, her brother Humayun. This conversation with Maham Begum, his mother, takes place two years after Babur's death (1532), at a time when Humayun was trying to retain and expand his father's territories in India.

> My lady, who was Maham Begam, had a great longing and desire to see a son of Humayun. Wherever there was a good-looking and nice girl, she used to bring her into his service. Maywa-jan, a daughter of Khadang (? Khazang), the chamberlain (*yasawal*), was in my employ. One day (after) the death of his Majesty *Firdaus-makani*, my lady said: 'Humayun, Maywa-jan is not bad. Why do you not take her into your service?' So, at her word, Humayun married and took her that very night. Three days later Bega Begam came from Kabul. She became in the family way. In due time she had a daughter, whom they named 'Aqiqa. Maywa-jan said to Lady (*Aka*) Maham Begam, 'I am in the family way, too.' Then my lady got ready two sets of weapons, and said: 'Whichever of you bears a son, I will give him good arms.' … [She] was very happy, and kept saying: 'Perhaps one of them will have a son.' She kept watch till Bega Begam's 'Aqiqa was born. Then she kept an eye on Maywa-jan. Ten months went by. The eleventh also passed. Maywa-jan said: 'My maternal aunt was in Mirza Ulugh Beg's *haram*. She had a son in the twelfth month; perhaps I am like her.' So they sewed tents and filled pillows. But in the end everyone knew she was a fraud.[45]

[45] Annette Beveridge, 'Life and Writings of Gulbadan Begum,' *Calcutta Review*, No. CCXII (April 1898), pp. 112, 113; Gulbadan Banu Begum, *Ahval-i Humayun Badshah*, British Library Ms.Or.166, fo. 21b–22a.

The first line of the passage quoted above tells us that in the Mughal world, as elsewhere in that time, it was the role of younger wives to produce heirs. At a later stage, they would instruct younger wives in such responsibilities. Elder women advised the young, and the young carried forward the name of the dynasty by birthing children. Reproduction was of no small consequence. Maywa-jan and her desire fit a tradition, in which the birth of royal children was deeply longed for. The task was especially crucial in the time of Babur and Humayun when the risk of the fading of the Mughal ruling family was real: Babur faced political threats in Central Asia, and Humayun encountered massive Afghan challenges in Hindustan. In this context, Maham made the point about male heirs. She looked for wives for Humayun for the momentous task of birthing heirs to the throne.[46] In her discussion of the aforementioned episode, Annette portrays Maham Begum as follows:

> Maham Begam was a clever woman, and both as wife and as widow made herself felt in her home. Lady Rosebody lifts the *parda* and shows us the Empress-mother busied in duties not often thus disclosed to the outside eye. In telling the story, which for the sake of its many special points we quote in full, she has no air of being indiscreet, and is, as may be seen, quite matter-of-fact.[47]

The phrase 'a clever ... Empress-mother,' in Annette's translation, does not capture the role of a senior woman with wisdom, status and authority. Nor does it show that she would have seen it as her duty to advise and guide her younger women kinsfolk, and to sustain the name and honor of her lineage. The attribution of cleverness to Maham Begum seems hasty, especially as Annette notes the rich

---

[46] For an elaboration of these points, Ruby Lal, *Domesticity and Power in the Early Mughal World* (Cambridge: Cambridge University Press, 2005).

[47] Annette Beveridge, 'Life and Writings of Gulbadan Begum,' *Calcutta Review*, No. CCXII (April 1898), pp. 353, 354.

projection of plural, overlapping circles of intimates and authorities in Gulbadan's memoir – the 'hazy points of kinship and marriage,' as she noted early on.

Gift in honor of Madeline Neves Clapp; Gift of Mrs. Henry White Cannon by exchange; Bequest of Louise T. Cooper; Leonard C. Hanna Jr. Fund; From the Catherine and Ralph Benkaim Collection 2013.338

A princess reclining on a terrace with attendants, c. 1730–1740. India, Mughal, 18th century. Gum tempera and gold on paper; page: 20.6 x 30.6 cm (8 1/8 x 12 1/16 in.). The Cleveland Museum of Art.

Indeed, according to Gulbadan, a striking trait of the early Mughal domestic world was that kinship networks were extended to form new familial communities. The talk of royal blood remained, but the idea of intimate relationships was also accommodated around practices such as wet-nursing and fostering of children. Many wet-nurses and their husbands became influential in the Mughal court. Their many-sided duties show layered notions of family trees, kinship and the affairs of the monarchy itself.

'My Lady,' for *Akam*, found throughout the translation, poses a similar challenge. Annette ponders its meaning: the 'Turki Aka is used as a title of respect from a junior to a senior. It has also the sense [of] "elder brother", which makes application to a woman doubtful. Babur uses the word … and Mr. Erskine [a contemporary scholar of Annette Beveridge] suggests to read "my Lady" [*sic*].'[48]

It is difficult to find an equivalent word for *akam* in English. A poised translation is not about equivalence, but rather about transferring tonality and texture from one language to another, which Annette does effectively in many instances. A phrase such as 'My Lady,' however, tends to blur the tone of affection and respect in the original and evokes associations with elevation and romance from the late medieval European knightly tradition. *Aka,* a Turki word (used for men), is very close in essence to *khanum* or *begum*. Reverence, privileged status and deference (associated with enhanced age) are marked characteristics of all these terms.

Readers familiar with Persian might also ask questions about the word '*havasak*' in the translation cited earlier. In the last line of the passage, Annette uses the word 'fraud' for the Persian *havasak*. While Annette interprets *havasak* as a pejorative, Maywa-jan's craving, or deep desire, for a child is hardly unexpected given the Mughal politics of marriage and reproduction.

Finally, a word on the title of Gulbadan's book, the *Ahval-i Humayun Badshah*, rendered *Humayun Nama* in English. Over the last two decades of studying Gulbadan's writing, I have learned that it was noticeably different from anything that other official chroniclers or servants of the king produced at the time.[49] Other writers tended to favor genres such as *tarikh* (annals, histories and chronological narratives); *tazkireh* (biographies and memoirs); *nameh* (biographies, exemplary accounts, aside from histories,

---

[48] Annette S. Beveridge (trans.), *The History of Humayun: Humayun Nama by Gul-Badan* Begum (1902; rpt Delhi: Low Price Publications, 1994), pp. 89, 90, f.n. 4.

[49] Ruby Lal, *Domesticity and Power in the Early Mughal World* (Cambridge: Cambridge University Press, 2005); *Vagabond Princess: The Great Adventures of Gulbadan* (New Haven and London: Yale University Press, 2024) provide the bulk of my thinking discussed on Gulbadan's *Ahval-i Humayun Badshah.* For the list of the sources used for the compilation of the *Akbar Nama*, see Abu-l Fazl 'Allami,' Henry Beveridge (trans.), *The Akbar Nama of Abu-l-Fazl* (1902–39; rpt Delhi, 1993), Vol. I, Introduction, especially, pp. 29–33, including footnotes.

epistles and accounts of exemplary deeds); *qanun* (normative accounts or legal texts); and *vaqi'at* (narratives of happenings, events and occurrences).[50] The title that Gulbadan chose was different: *ahval*, meaning conditions, states, circumstances or situations.[51] Does this title animate a different conception of what a history of the times should be?

Gulbadan read the masters of poetry, Jami and 'Ali Sher Nawa'i, whom her father adored. She grew up on the fabulous allegorical tales of Sadi's *Rose Garden* and his *Bustan* or *The Orchard*, with chapters on justice, mercy, love, humility, contentment and education. She memorized the Quran. She took auguries from Hafiz. She likely saw the colorful visual folios of the *Tuti-Nama*, or the *Tales of the Parrot* – India's *One Thousand and One Nights* – produced in her nephew Akbar's atelier.

She is bound to have seen, after she came back from Kabul in the late 1550s, the masterly paintings of the *Hamzanama*, the Epic of Hamza, being created in Akbar's atelier, which displayed the valour of the uncle of Prophet Muhammad.[52]

She read memoirs, including her father's *Baburnama*. As mentioned earlier, Bayazid Bayat sent her a copy of his *Tazkireh-i Humayun va Akbar*, a history of the reigns of Humayun and Akbar from 1542 to 1591, which she kept in her library. She likely read ewer-bearer Jawhar's portrayal of Humayun, composed in a 'shaky and rustic' Persian, in the words of Hermann Ethé, who catalogued it for the British Library.[53] Gulbadan would have loved Jawhar's

---

[50] For the meanings of the words, S. Haim (ed.), *Dictionary English-Persian Persian-English* rev. ed.; F. Steingass, *A Comprehensive Persian-English Dictionary*, 2nd ed.; and S. Haim, *Shorter English Persian Dictionary*, 3rd ed., s.v. 'tarikh,' 'tazkireh,' 'nameh,' 'qanun' and 'vaqi'at.'

[51] Steingass, *Persian*; Haim, *Shorter Dictionary*, s.v. 'ahval.'

[52] Henry Blochmann (ed.) and H.S. Jarrett (trans.), *The A-in-I Akbari* (1873, 1894; rpt Calcutta, 1993), Vol. I, p. 115.

[53] Hermann Ethé, *Catalogue of Persian Manuscripts in the Library of the India Office*, Vol. 1 (Oxford, 1903), p. 222.

intimate book, but it is hard to say at what stage she read it, or Bayat's book, both concurrent with her own. She inscribed her name on her copy of courtier Khwandamir's book about Humayun's ordinances and buildings.[54]

She would have known the didactic texts and famous books of advice such as the *Akhlaq-i Nasiri* and the *Qabusnama*, both ubiquitous in Islamic courts. Rumi's *tenth-century masnavi,* an epic poem, was a cherished work. The *Shahnama*, Firdawsi's *Book of Kings*, a monument of poetry and history, and thousands of other books were in the harem and the imperial library, where they were regularly read aloud to Akbar.[55]

None of these works served as a literary model for Gulbadan's writing, which differed from most court chronicles of her time. For one thing, her work has no didactic charge; it falls outside the prevalent 'mirrors for princes' genre, which emphasizes pragmatic guidance and the role of rulers as moral exemplars.

Instead, the wide world and its people were her books. Her knowledge germinated from gardens, tents, pavilions, caravans, ships, rivers, oceans, deserts, camels, mosques, water fountains, hills, mansions and the red sandstone harem, as well as from the people around her. Women in history – Scheherazade, the heroine of *One Thousand and One Nights*; her daring grandmother Isan Daulat; and

---

[54] For Persian and English editions of Bayazid Bayat, Jawhar and Gulbadan, Wheeler M. Thackston, Three Memoirs of Homayun (Costa Mesa, California: Mazda Publications, 2009). Khwandamir wrote his *Qanun-i Humayuni* (also called *Humayun-nama*), in 1534 under Humayun's patronage. The author spent time at the court of 'Abdul Ghazi Sultan Husiyn bin Mansur bin Bayqura, the ruler of Herat (1468–1505), and in Khurasan and Persia, before joining Babur in 1528. He spent his last days in the court of Humayun. Khwandamir's memoir is, by his own claim, an eyewitness's account of the rules and ordinances of Humayun's reign, accompanied by descriptions of court festivities and of buildings erected by the *padshah* (king). See Beveridge's note on Gulbadan's ownership of this work, Annette S. Beveridge (trans.), *The History of Humayun: Humayun Nama by Gul-Badan* Begum (1902; rpt Delhi: Low Price Publications, 1994), pp. 76, 78.

[55] Henry Blochmann (ed.) and H.S. Jarrett (trans.), *The A-in-I Akbari* (1873, 1894; rpt Calcutta, 1993), Vol. I, p. 110.

her strategic Aunt Khanzada – were her books. Experience was her book. Crossing the Khyber Pass in a caravan at the age of six; being a young woman in exodus to Kabul; and her time as a sagacious woman lodged in the harem all informed her writing. Indoors and outdoors, as well as upon the seas, her own body was her experience. Experience is in the body. Memory is *embodied.* She commenced writing from embodied memory and from events as she saw and thought of them. She created tapestries of court life, domestic life, political intrigues and ceremonies as she interpreted them.

Gulbadan brings to life a stretch of the Mughal world that is very different from that of the official histories and much of the subsequent historiography. First, chronologically speaking, it evokes a powerful impression of an empire that is not already known or made, a political formation taking unsteady steps from infancy to maturity. Second, in terms of domestic conduct and emotional life, her work provides much food for thought on the less tangible (and less documentable) aspects of Mughal history. Finally, on the question of history (and empire) itself, the *Ahval* serves as a symbol of how official history came to be written as part of the construction of an empire.

Translation is a rich and generative process. Gulbadan's history offers a unique sixteenth-century documentation of places, restraints and beauties and the nature of conflict and solidarity. The itinerant Mughals come to life amidst multi-valent notions of duty, sexuality, celebration, joy, loss and grief. Gulbadan and Annette guide us through the dense relations in which women of the nobility engaged in special ways in the daily business of living and the public–political affairs that were conducted in tents and courts.

An outstanding feature of Annette's translation is Appendix A – at the back of the translation – in which she systematically presented a remarkable collection of biographical notices of 203 Mughal women – servants, wives, concubines, mothers, grandmothers and women of other royal and non-royal families connected with the Mughals. She wrote long narrative paragraphs for each of these

Caravan of Good Fortune

Molly Crabapple

entries with sources for the basis of the detail and the problems of collation. Acutely attentive to facts, Annette provided evocative mini-portraits of Mughal and non-Mughal women. It is a wide-ranging compilation, given the scant information available and the difficulties of assembling information on women in Mughal and Islamic sources of the early modern world.

Both by convention and patriarchal mores, women tended to be unnamed in the male-authored chronicles and histories. Many women shared the same name – there is more than one Dildar, Ayesha, Maham, Khanzada and so on. Family trees are complex, with multiple marriages, and kinship structures wind around multiple families. A society in which men had children by several wives, and where children were reared by women who were not their mothers, such as Gulbadan and her brother Hindal, poses difficulties in the collation of evidence and translation of text. Even in the brevity of the passages, Annette animates how women lived: when, who and whether they married or remarried, as well as their political and social engagements.

An invaluable history of women and a sort of cluster biography, Annette's long appendix is a dazzling source that sits behind a dazzling source.

Books and chronicles from centuries past are precious gifts. Holding onto their words, line by line, we can dive into the beauty and torment of human history. These rare materials offer us a portal to another time. In Gulbadan's writings, we can see the lives of those almost always left out of official records. But who decides what makes a great book? Whose interpretation proclaims a book marginal? Is it settled that if a work is incomplete or has a void, it is defective? If so, then Geoffrey Chaucer's *Canterbury Tales*, Jane Austen's *Sanditon*, Mary Wollstonecraft's *Maria* or *The Wrongs of Women* and Ralph Ellison's *Juneteenth* would not be among the great books.

Annette's English translation was published in 1902, making Gulbadan's stellar book widely available. Even so, it was relegated to the margins of history – to mere footnotes in volumes on Mughal politics, war, economy and agrarian histories. In an important 1976 book on the sources of Akbar's reign, the author added a single footnote on Gulbadan: 'I have not included a study of the *Humayun Nama* of Gulbadan Begam in this chapter though it falls in the same class of ["Minor Historical"] works as the three mentioned above. The reason is that I feel I have practically nothing to add to what its translator, Mrs. Beveridge, has said in her introduction to the translation.'[56]

Annette's contribution is remarkable, and the untold story of how her life and experiences brought her to Gulbadan's book and how she went about translating it is as important as it is compelling. My hope is that an intellectual portrait of Annette, featuring her work, alongside a reissue of her translation, will connect today's readers to a remarkable Victorian-era scholar who ensured a Mughal princess's inimitable document of her dynasty survived. I also hope that they will see a connection between Gulbadan and Annette.

I was the first scholar to decisively engage the princess's rarely consulted Persian chronicle and bring it to the attention of the academy in the US, the UK and India with my first book, *Domesticity and Power in the Early Mughal World*, thanks to Annette Beveridge, whose translation I chanced upon in an old bookstore in Mughal Delhi. Later, in London, I went directly to Gulbadan's Persian

[56] Mukhia's reasons for not including Gulbadan's memoir in his monograph stem partly from the fact that he distinguishes between major (political, administrative and emperor-centered) and minor sources (of royal women, servants and so on), privileging the 'hard politics' of the former against the 'soft society' of the latter. The presumption of the supposedly central character of some sources, as opposed to the peripheral (or minor) status of others, derives in this case from a belief that despite limitations, certain texts like the *Akbar Nama* are authentic because they were based on 'official documents as well as memoirs of persons involved in, or witness to, the events.' Mukhia is not alone in this belief in the 'authenticity,' hence 'reliability,' of these sources. Harbans Mukhia, *Historians and Historiography during the Reign of Akbar* (New Delhi: Vikas Publishing House, 1976), pp. xvi, 154n1, 71. See also, Ishtiaq Husain Qureshi, *Akbar: The Architect of the Mughul Empire* (1978; rpt Delhi: Idarah-i-Adabiyat-i-Delli, 1987), pp. 2, 6.

writing and restored erased female figures, their experiences and histories in a plural and itinerant Mughal setting – what many have called the first feminist history of the Mughal Empire and of the dynamic harem world. A line thus connects my scholarship with Gulbadan's and Annette's stories.

Oblivion and erasure are themes that have been at the core of my work since I began my career as a historian. I explore not only what happened in the past, and why certain figures do not take centre stage in Mughal history, but also how women, girls, ordinary people, ambiguous figures (eunuchs, concubines, wet nurses), spaces (harem, gardens, tents) and multiple forms of desire are *made* deviant, redundant or obscure in history. The fact is that scholars are largely complicit in how history is designed, presented, *made* available and preserved. We are the guardians of history. The question is how we preserve translations, map histories of production and investigate erasures. These are subjects I have carried forward in all my books and essays.

A NOTE TO THE READER

The private papers of Annette and Henry Beveridge housed in the British Library under the library catalogue MSS. EUR C.176 are at the centre of my introduction to Annette Beveridge's intellectual world and her work on the Mughals. The Beveridge collection is large comprising letters, notes, articles, photographs and memorabilia distributed in several boxes with supplementary numbers, which I reference in the required sections. My work on the Persian manuscript of Gulbadan Banu Begum, the *Ahval-i Humayun Badshah*, at the British Library Ms.Or.166, started in the late 1990s and led to the publication of *Domesticity and Power in the Early Mughal World* (2005). That book and my recent biography of Gulbadan, *Vagabond Princess: The Great Adventures of Gulbadan* (2024), provide the bulk of my thinking here. Annette and Henry's eldest son wrote a book on their life and times, *India Called Them* (1947), which is especially useful for the intimate life of the Beveridge family in India and England. All other documents, books, essays and published writings by Annette and Henry Beveridge related to Gulbadan's memoir are referenced in the required places.

Annette Beveridge's translation of Gulbadan's work is in the public domain and was reissued in print by Low Price Publication in India. In 2009, Wheeler M. Thackston brought out an English translation of Gulbadan that places her work amidst the memoir of a Mughal officer and that of a royal water-carrier. *Three Memoirs of Homayun*, the triple translation, is in easy English, suitable to modern ear, with some gestures to Annette's work – but without discussion of features such as her spectacular Appendix A, or a critical engagement with the liveliness of her Victorian English and her candor. As noted earlier, an outstanding feature of Annette's translation is its Appendix A, in which she systematically presented a remarkable collection of biographical notices of 203 Mughal women – and women of other royal and non-royal families connected with the Mughals. She wrote long narrative graphs for each of the 203 entries, providing sources for the basis of the order of names and facts, and the problems of collation. It's an impressive and expansive compilation, given the difficulties of assembling information on women in the sources of the early modern world. Annette's contribution is stellar, but the untold story of her translation and her link to Gulbadan is as important as it is absorbing. Hence, at the initiative of Yale University Press, this relaunch of Annette's translation of Gulbadan's book, with my introduction to the translator, connects readers to the remarkable woman who ensured a vital piece of history survived.

Along with the licensing department of the British Library, I tried to obtain information on the rights-holder for Annette Beveridge's estate, but to no avail. I had hoped to include a few pages from Mss. Eur.C 176-221 to show Annette's detailed work on her translation of Gulbadan's book, the thorough and repeated edits, work on chronology and emendations.

Page numbering in the index follows the pagination of the 1902 edition.

In the introduction, the translation of Gulbadan's Persian manuscript is mine unless noted otherwise. There is no standard system for transliterating Persian into English. I have used the modified version of the *International Journal of Middle East Studies* (IJMES) system, developed by Layla S. Diba and Maryam Ekhtiar for their edited volume, *Royal Persian Paintings*: *The Qajar Epoch, 1785–1925* (New York, 1998). I have retained the common English form of all well-known names of persons, places and Persian texts. Thus: *Baburnama* and *Akbar Nama*, rather than *Baburnameh* and *Akbarnameh*; Agra rather than Agreh; and Begum/Beg rather than Bigum/Biyg.

DRAMATIS PERSONAE

The following figures appear in the princess's memoir. This list is arranged alphabetically by first name. Additional names are provided to show Gulbadan's wider relationships and those involved in the production of her chronicle, even though many of these names here do not appear in her writing. Wherever known, I provide birth and death dates for the listed figures.

ABUL FAZL (1551–1602)

Abul Fazl was the son of Shaikh Mubarak, a man with humble beginnings, who later became renowned for his expertise in philosophy and the Islamic sciences. After his early learning with his father, Abul Fazl joined Akbar's court in 1574 and became known for his forceful debates with the jurists in the *Ibadat Khana.* Emperor Akbar selected him to write the first official history of the Mughal court, the three volume *Akbar Nama*, including the imperial gazetteer, the *Āīn-i Akbari*. Meant to be a contribution towards the making of *Akbar Nama*, Gulbadan wrote her work at the behest of Akbar.

ABUL BAQA

Amir Abul Baqa, well-versed in Unani medicine, was also a close confidant of Emperor Babur. He advised both Babur and Humayun during important political and personal moments in their lives as kings.

'ABD-AL QADIR BADAUNI (1540–1605)

A courtier in Akbar's court and a committed Sunni Muslim, he disapproved of the emperor's eclectic policies and politics. A prolific translator of many Sanskrit and Persian works, he wrote his history, the *Muntakhab-ut-Tawarikh*, in hiding. The work contains extraordinary materials about the times and is a valuable counter to the panegyric *Akbar Nama* of Abul Fazl.

AKBAR (1542–1605)

Born in October 1542 in Amarkot (now in Sindh province, Pakistan), Akbar was one of the greatest emperors of India. Son of Hamida Banu Begum and the second Mughal king Humayun, he succeeded to the throne at the age of thirteen. A contemporary of Elizabeth I, he reigned for four decades, extending Mughal power over the greater part of India and secured the northwest frontier by recapturing Kabul and Kandahar. A humanist who remained dedicated to Islam, he took an active interest in other religions and denominations. His court drew world attention and attracted a wave of aristocrats and creative people from Persia, Afghanistan and Central Asia. At the heart of Akbar's success was his pluralist outlook.

'ASAS

Khwaja Muhammad 'Ali 'Asas, a devoted ally of Emperor Babur, supported him in many critical times and was the first to follow when he renounced wine. He appears at various entertainments in Babur's and Gulbadan's accounts. His last known role was as caretaker of Babur's tomb.

'ASKARI (1516–1557)

'Askari was the son of Babur and Gulrukh Begum and the blood brother of Prince Kamran. After participating in the early Mughal conquests of India, Babur appointed him governor of Sambhal. He died in 1557 while on Hajj.

ATUN MAMA

She was an intimate assistant of Babur's mother. In 1501, Atun walked on foot from Samarkand, the city Babur had then lost, for days in the snow to be reunited with the Mughals. She was left behind because there was no horse for her to ride. A legendary figure, Gulbadan mentions her many times and includes her in the list of women who attended her brother Hindal's wedding feast.

BABUR (1483–1556)

The first Mughal king, Babur – poet, wanderer, the author of the *Baburnama* – descended from Central Asian heroes: Chingiz Khan (1167–1227) on his mother's side and Timur (1336–1405) on his father's. Babur's paternal grandfather had parceled out his empire to his sons. It was over these possessions – provinces controlled by uncles or cousins of varying degrees – that Babur fought with close and distant relatives for much of his life. During a protracted struggle for the coveted city Samarqand (Timur's capital), Babur lost the territory his father bequeathed to him. By about 1504, he was driven to Kabul; eventually, in 1526, he defeated Ibrahim Lodi of Delhi and inaugurated Mughal rule.

BAYAZID BAYAT

Bayazid Bayat first emerged in the pages of Mughal history when he accompanied Bairam Khan to Kabul in late 1545. From aboard his ship, he sent a letter to Gulbadan when she was stranded in Aden. He was among the officers Emperor Akbar asked to record their memories for the *Akbar Nama*, which led to Bayazid's *Tazkireh-i*

Humayun va Akbar – a history of the reigns of Humayun and Akbar from 1542 to 1591.

BEGA BEGUM (1511–1581)

The senior-most wife of the second Mughal king, Humayun, and mother of their first child, al-Aman (who died in Badakhshan soon after his birth). Bega was captured in 1539 by Sher Shah in the Battle of Chausa – where she also lost her daughter ‘Aqiqa – and later returned to the Mughals. Famous in history as Hajji Begum, she was honour thus in the aftermath of a pilgrimage she undertook to western Arabia in 1564–65, a decade before Gulbadan led the royal women’s group there.

BUWA BEGUM (D. 1528)

Mother of Sultan Ibrahim Lodi of Delhi, whom Babur defeated in the Battle of Panipat. She was responsible for poisoning Babur. On her enforced journey to Kabul, she drowned herself in the Indus River.

BIBI MUBARIKA

Bibi Mubarika was the daughter of Malik Shah Mansur, chief of the Yusufzai tribe of Pashtuns. She was the fifth wife of Babur, the first Mughal Emperor. Their marriage in 1519 established friendly relations between the Mughals and the Yusufzais. Along with her co-wife Maham Begum and stepdaughter Gulbadan, Mubarika was among the first women from the Kabul household to travel to Hindustan in 1529 in the aftermath of Babur’s victory over Delhi and Agra. Frequently mentioned by Gulbadan, with whom she shared a playful relationship, she was fondly called *Afghani Aghacha* or ‘the Afghan lady’ by the princess.

BAIRAM KHAN (1501–1561)

Of Persian origin, Bairam Khan was a skilled military commander and a powerful statesman who served during the reigns of Humayun and Akbar. He is remembered for his role as Akbar's regent during his boyhood years, as well as his chief mentor, adviser and most trusted ally. As Akbar began to robustly take charge of the affairs of his empire, he dismissed Bairam in 1560. Bairam was murdered en route to Mecca.

BIBI FATIMA (B. 1490s)

A wetnurse of Humayun, she played significant roles, such as the *ordu-begi* (an armed woman/warrior of Humayun's harem) and envoy in an important political marriage of the emperor. Some sources indicate that in the early part of Akbar's reign, she may have served as the *sadr-i anas* or the superintendent of the harem. Gulbadan mentioned her repeatedly, as did Bayazid Bayat.

DILDAR BEGUM

Dildar Begum's ancestry is not discussed in contemporary records. Her marriage to Babur took place between 1508 and 1519 (these years of the *Baburnama* are missing from the manuscripts) and she came to the Kabul household as his second wife. She gave birth to Gulrang, Gulchihra, Hindal, Gulbadan and Alwar (the last of the five children died in childhood). She shared Hindal and Gulbadan with her senior co-wife Maham Begum. (The emperor had other wives in his boyhood. He divorced one and others had died.) Gulbadan discusses several episodes of Dildar's fine intervention and firm speech, fondly calling her mother *Acam* in Turkish.

GULBADAN BEGUM (1523–1603)

Gulbadan Begum, daughter of Dildar and Babur, travelled to Agra from Afghanistan at the age of six and a half, after her father had made substantial conquests in the region. An unusual witness to the emerging Mughal monarchy – from its inception in the early conquests by Babur to its majesty in the reign of Akbar – she recorded what she had seen in her memoir, *Ahval-i Humayun Badshah* (literally, conditions in the time of Humayun Badshah). Popularly called the *Humayun Nama*, this unique piece of writing, the only example of prose by a Mughal woman, is the best document for Mughal domestic life and the character of the empire as it was taking shape. From the Fatehpur Sikri harem, she led the *haraman* on an unprecedented group pilgrimage to Mecca, braving treacherous seas and unknown territories – including a year in Aden on the Red Sea after their ship was wrecked. My book, *Vagabond Princess: The Great Adventures of Gulbadan*, centers her life and adventures, including the scandal that ensued due to her presence and actions in Ottoman territories.

GULRUKH BEGUM

As with Dildar, Gulrukh's family background is not mentioned in the contemporary records, nor the date of her marriage to Babur, which likely took place between 1508 and 1519 (these years of the *Baburnama* are missing from the manuscripts). She bore Shahrukh, Ahmad and Gul'izar (all three died young), and Kamran and 'Askari.

HAMIDA BANU BEGUM (1527–1604)

It is difficult to precisely chart Hamida Banu's family tree, but sources suggest that she was a descendent of a renowned saint. Prominent as the revered mother of Emperor Akbar, she fits well the trajectory of Mughal women who animated royal circles with their presence, support and wisdom born of age. She married Humayun, the second Mughal king, at Pat in the summer of 1541 and gave birth to Akbar in 1542 while the royals were in exile. Hamida surfaces frequently in Mughal sources, especially in the *Akbar Nama*. She sought forgiveness on behalf of Prince Salim, future Jahangir. She did not join the party of senior women pilgrims that her close ally, Gulbadan Begum led, likely staying back to support Akbar.

HARKHA BAI (1542–1623)

Daughter of Raja Bharmal, the Kachwaha ruler of Amer, she was the first Rajput Hindu woman to marry Emperor Akbar. She gave birth to Prince Salim. Ennobled later in Akbari histories as *Maryam-uz-Zamani*, she lived into her son's reign.

HINDAL (1519–1551)

Son of Babur and Dildar Begum, he was born in Kabul as his father was on his way to conquer the regions across the river Hind. Taking his birth as a good omen, Babur named him Hindal – of Hind – and commemorated it in his memoir. He was placed in the care of Babur's senior wife, Maham Begum, as was his younger sister Gulbadan. By age nineteen, he emerged as a strong contender for the newly emerging Mughal throne in India. Eventually, he pledged allegiance to Humayun and remained faithful to him till 1551, when he died fighting for the Mughals against Kamran's forces.

HUMAYUN (1508–1556)

Humayun was born in March 1508 in Kabul, the son and successor Babur, founder of Mughal rule in northern Hindustan. Humayun inherited in 1530 an empire that was still in the making: the Afghans and the Rajputs were restrained but not subdued after his father's victories at Panipat (1526), Khanua (1527) and Ghaghara (1529). His biggest challenge came from the Afghan Sher Shah Suri, who had consolidated power in Bihar and Bengal. Sher Shah defeated Humayun in Chausa in 1539 and at Kannauj in 1540, expelling him from northern India. After years of exile, during which time he married his beloved Hamida Banu, who gave birth to Akbar, Humayun regained Kabul and eventually returned to Hindustan. He ruled again from 1555 to 1556.

ISAN DALAT KHANUM

Babur's maternal grandmother, she married Yunas Khan Chagatai, the Great Khan of the Mughals, around 1456. She gave birth to three daughters and bravely shared the vicissitudes of her husband's career, being taken captive by his enemies four times. Sagacious and far-sighted, she was revered for her good judgment. Towards the end of her life, she lived in a garden-house in Andijan.

JAWHAR AFTABCHI

Jawhar is known for his valiant act of saving Emperor Humayun from drowning during the Battle of Chausa. He accompanied the exiled Humayun to Sind and Persia, then to Hindustan. He wrote the *Tazkirat-ul-Vaqi'at*, a candid account as a witness of Humayun's reign, in response to Akbar order of 1587.

KAMRAN (1512–1557)

Son of Babur and Gulrukh Begum, he had a contested relationship with his half-brother Humayun. After Humayun returned from the Battle of Chausa, Kamran refused to place his troops under Humayun's command. Kamran forcibly took Gulbadan during the Mughal clan's forced relocation to Kabul, and when Humayun left for Sind and eventually to Persia. By 1545, Humayun took over

Kabul. Although Humayun resisted the pressure to put his rebellious brother to death, he was persuaded that something needed to be done and so he had him blinded. Humayun banished him to Mecca where he later died. Later, two of his daughters accompanied Gulbadan on the pilgrimage to Mecca.

KHANZADA BEGUM (1478–1545)

Khanzada Begum, born in 1478, was Babur's formidable sister. Accounts of her life emerge in her brother's and niece Gulbadan's accounts. She is lauded in the chronicles for the 'sacrifice' she made by marrying Shaibani Khan Uzbek to establish peace between the Mughals and the Uzbeks. She came back to her family ten years later and acquired immense respect, as discussed and underlined by Gulbadan. Her rendering of Khanzada's special status, the *akeh-janam*, 'my dearest *akeh*,' marks a privileged status with enhanced age and deference. Her nephews, Babur's sons, regularly sought her out as an elder. Khanzada's guidance to Babur's fighting sons on reading their name in the Friday sermons, called the *khutba*, is memorable, a striking statement of how senior women collaborated in promoting kings.

KHWAJA KALAN

Among Babur's prominent men, he served in the right wing of the armed forces that fought against Ibrahim Lodi and played an important role in the takeover of Agra. After the victories, he was assigned the task of taking bounties of Hind for the royal household. Kalan served for a few years in Hindustan and then returned to Kabul. Fond of him and reliant on Kalan, Babur was loath to see him leave and sent him poems that he wrote in Agra.

MAHAM BEGUM

An influential senior wife of Babur and mother of the second Mughal Emperor Humayun, her ancestry is unknown. Babur met her in 1506 in Herat, and they were married soon afterward. After Humayun, she had four other children, all of whom died. She took over Hindal and Gulbadan from her co-wife Dildar. Gulbadan is the best chronicler of her guardian mother's life events.

MAHDI KHWAJA

The third husband of Khanzada Begum, Babur's powerful sister, he was in the emperor's service and served in the left wing of the armed forces against Ibrahim Lodi. It is unclear when his marriage with Khanzada took place or what the nature of the relationship was. At the instigation of Babur's senior courtier, Nizam-al Din Barlas, he attempted to win over Mughal courtiers to secure the nomination for the Mughal throne. But the entire saga ended terribly.

MURAD III, OTTOMAN SULTAN OF TURKEY (1546–1595)

From 1574 until his death in 1595, Murad III ruled the Ottoman Empire that included among other places in Arabia – the holy cities of Mecca and Medina, as well as Egypt to the north. He ordered the eviction of Mughal royal ladies that went on a pilgrimage under the leadership of Princess Gulbadan. His charge was that the royal visitors as well as the caravans of Hind had overcrowded the holy cities. But the story was more complicated, as this book shows with the help of his eviction orders are preserved in Turkey.

NIZAM-AL DIN BARLAS (KHALIFA)

Along with his wife, he received the six-year-old Gulbadan in Aligarh in 1529, when she arrived there from Kabul. His brother was married to Babur's half-sister, and he and the emperor were friends of long standing. Initially he was opposed to Humayun's accession to the throne, but eventually endorsed his rule.

RUQAYYA BEGUM (D. 1626)

One of the longest-living matriarchs of the Mughal Empire, she was the first wife of Emperor Akbar and also his first cousin, a Mughal princess by birth. She had no children of her own but raised Akbar's grandson Khurram. As a senior Mughal woman, she was instrumental in forging peace between Akbar and her stepson Jahangir, paving the way for his accession to the throne. Ruqayya was an important Mughal guide for Mihr-un-nisa when she came to the harem. Jahangir wrote fondly of Ruqayya in his memoirs and recorded her death. Her burial place is i the Garden of Babur (Bagh-e-Babur) in Kabul, Afghanistan.

SALIMA SULTAN BEGUM (D. 1613)

Salima was the granddaughter of Babur. In 1557, she accompanied Gulbadan and Hamida Banu to Agra and she was married shortly after that to Akbar's regent Bairam Khan. After Bairam's death 1561, Salima married her first cousin Akbar. A senior wife of Akbar, she was central in pleading forgiveness on behalf of Prince Salim and wielded much influence in his eventual succession to the throne. She was one of the senior women who accompanied Gulbadan on the Hajj. Along with Ruqayya, she guided Mihr-un-nisa – future Mughal co-sovereign Nur Jahan – upon her arrival in the harem. There is some uncertainty about the date of her death, but Jahangir records it 1613 in Agra. Mentioned repeatedly as a cultured and wise woman, Jahangir notes particulars of her birth and descent, her marriages and her death.

SHER SHAH (D. 1545)

Founder of the Suri dynasty in Bihar, he was born Farid Khan. A brilliant strategist and a gifted administrator, he defeated the second Mughal emperor Humayun in the 1540s, which led to the migration of the Mughal clan to Kabul and Sind. His monetary, fiscal and administrative reforms were the bedrock for Mughal rule in Hindustan.

The History of Humāyūn
(Humāyūn-Nāma)

طوی میرزا هندال آنکه سلطانم بیگم خواهر مهدی خواجه بودند بغیر
بابام غیر جعفر خواجه فرزند دیگر نداشتند و فرزند نمی شد
اکه جانم سلطانم را بفرزندی نگاه داشته بودند و دو ساله بود
که خانزاده بیگم نگاه کرده بودند و عجایب دوست می داشتند
و به برادرزاده خود دادند و طوی را در کمال لطافت و خوبی
کردند کوشکه و ادسقه و پنج توشک و پنج لیستوق و یک
تکیه کلان و دو تکیه کلوله و قوشقه و لعاب مع خرگاه جلیغ
مع سه توشک همه زردوزی و سروپاهای میرزا چار
و تاج زردوزی و فوطه و روپاک و رومال زردوزی و
قور پوشش زردوزی و سلطانم بیگم نه نیمتنه تکمه دار جواهر
یکی از لعل و یکی از یاقوت و یکی از زمرد و یکی از فیروزه و
یکی از زبرجد و یکی از عین الهره دیگر از بحر کوریه و یک
چار قب و چار قربیجی تکمه دار و یک جفت حلقه لعل و
یک جفت حلقه در سه پنجه و یک چیز شاهی یکدرخت و دو خطیب
و دیگر اسباب و اشیا و رخت و رخوت و کارخانها از همه

PAGE 28b OF GUL-BADAN BEGAM'S MS.

[Frontispiece.

Page 28b of Gul-Badan Begam's MS.

The History of Humāyūn (Humāyūn-Nāma)

Gul-Badan Begam (Princess Rose-Body)

Translated, with Introduction, Notes, Illustration and Biographyical Appendix; and reproduced in the Persion from the only known MS. of the British Museum

Annette S. Beveridge, M.R.A.S.

MY HUSBAND
Who set my feet upon the Persian way,
and has strewed it
with open-hearted largesse of help and counsel.

A.S.B.
November, 1901

PREFACE

It was in October, 1900, that the late Mr. F.F. Arbuthnot made arrangements with me for the publication of this volume. It has now to put forth bereft of his guidance. I can but trust that he would have given to the finished work the welcome with which he greeted the small portion I was able to show him in print. It is natural to feel towards him what he has expressed in his dedication of the Assemblies of *Al Ḥarīrī* to Chenery, and to hope he may be glad of the fulfilment of this piece of his work.

The little history which is reproduced in this volume has few, if any, compeers, in as much as it is the work of a Musalmānī, and lights up her woman's world. She writes colloquially and without pose, and is unaffected and spontaneous. For these reasons I have tried to make an accurate copy of her text, and to preserve her characteristics of orthography and diction; and this the more that the British Museum MS. may be her very own, unique, and autographic. With a few chosen exceptions, I have reproduced all her deflections from common rule without comment; my additions to the MS. are limited to a few *iẓāfats* and other signs of which example is given at some place in the MS.

Princess Rose-body has rendered one essential service to history, by giving precise details of relationship in her own and some contemporary families. Up till now, however, no use has been made of her information, and her book has remained, both in India and Europe, a literary *pardanīshīn*.

The Biographical Appendix, which I have modelled in admiration of Professor Blochmann's in his *Aīn-i-akbarī*, will, I hope, be of use to future writers. It is the outcome of the notes of several years, but it is incomplete and over brief. Nevertheless, it discloses the elements of many a romantic story.

One of an author's most agreeable final touches is the expression of thanks to those who have helped his book on its way. My obligation to my husband is too great to be told. I am much indebted to Mr. A. G. Ellis for his unfailing kindness during the long and pleasant time of my work in the British Museum, and to my friends Mr. E. H. Whinfield and Mr. W. Irvine for the expression of their opinions on several perplexing points. As I have said in writing of the plates, I owe all my illustrations but one to Mr. Bourdillon, B.C.S..

The printing of a book so full as is this one of unfamiliar names and of diacritically-marked letters entails a heavy tax upon proof-readers and compositors. I wish to express my sense of this, and to thank Messrs. Billing, their proofreaders and their compositors for what they have done to accomplish a difficult and tiresome task. My thanks are indeed due and are offered to Messrs. Drugelin for the patience and skill with which they have dealt with Persian copy from my untrained hand.

I now venture to express, in Mr. E. Granville Browne's words, the thought which haunts all who make a book, and to beg my critics to listen to their plea:

'Now, seeing that to fail and fall is the fate of all, and to claim exemption form the lot of humanity a proof of pride and ranity, and somewhat of mercy our common need; therefore let such as read, and errors detect, either ignore or neglect, or correct and conceal them, rather than revile and reveal them.'

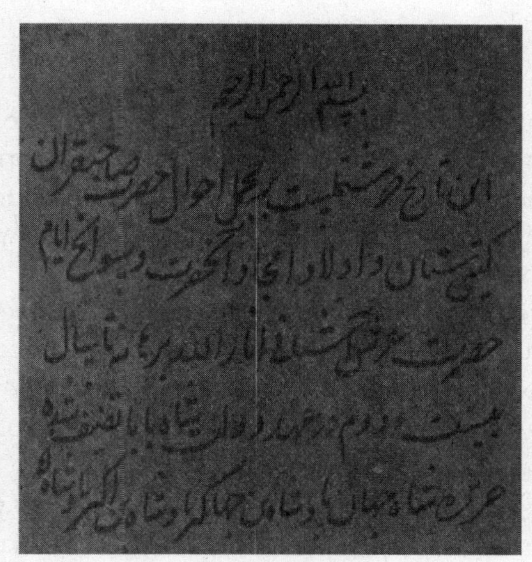

Autograph note of Shāh-Jahān

NOTE ON THE ILLUSTRATIONS

The page of the MS. selected for reproduction in Plate I. contains several words which I have found difficult, and concerning which explanation will be welcomed. It and Plate No. II. make silent protest against printing, and plead that the sun best shows the grace and beauty of manuscript.

With the exception of the first illustration, all the plates are photographic reproductions from a splendidly illustrated Persian MS., entitled the *Tārīkh-i-khāndān-i-tīmūriya,* which is the choicest volume in the library with which Maulvi Khūda-baksh *Khān Bahādur* has enriched the city of Patna.[1]

The Emperor Shāh-jahān appears to have paid R.8,000 for the illustrations in the volume. The MS. itself is of older date, and Mr. Beveridge has found in it some portions, at least, of the *Tārīkh-i-alfī.* The title-page is wanting.

The volume has a further distinction, inasmuch as it bears on an opening page an autograph note of Shāh-jahān. This is reproduced (as Plate No. II) on the opposite page, and by its charm and grace is worthy of that royal fount of creative beauty.

The pictures of Bābar's devotion of himself and the triad connected with the birth of Akbar are admirable; they repay close attention and enlargement under a glass.

---

[1] A copy of the Maulvī's catalogue (published while he was Chief Justice in Hydarābād) is in the British Museum, and may be consulted for some details of the book. (p. 110) Mr. Beveridge also gives some particulars about it in the *R.A.S. Journal,* January, 1901, p. 81.

I am indebted for these picture, first to Mr. Beveridge who, when he examined this *Tārīkh* in 1899, thought of my book, and, secondly, to Mr. Bourdillon, the then Commissioner of Patna, who most kindly photographed them for us.

TRANSLATION OF SHĀH-JAHĀN'S NOTE

In the name of God, the Merciful, the Compassionate.

This history, which contains an abridgment of the affair of Majesty, *Ṣāḥib-qirān Gītī-sitānī* (Timur), and of his glorious descendants, and of the events of the days of *'Arsh-āshyānī'* (Akbar)—May God make clear his proof!—down to the twenty-second year of his reign, was written in the time of Shāh Bābā (Akbar).

Signed: Shāh-jahān Pādshāh, son of Jahāngīr Pādshāh, son of Akbar Pādshāh.

INTRODUCTION

PART I

BIOGRAPHICAL ACCOUNT OF THE PRINCESS AND HER FAMILY[1]

SECTION I.—UNDER BĀBAR

Gul-badan Begam (Princess Rose-body) was a daughter of Ẓahru-d-dīn Muḥammad Bābar, in whom were united the lines of highest Central Asian aristocracy—namely, that of Tīmūr the Tūrk, through his son Mīrān-shāh; and that of Chingīz the Mughal, through his son Chaghatāi. He was born on February 14th, 1483, and succeeded to his father's principality of Farghāna when under twelve. He spent ten years of early youth in trying to save his small domain from the clutch of kinsmen, but, being forced to abandon and the task, went southwards in 1504 to Afghānistān, where he captured Kābul from its Arghūn usurpers.

Prineess Gul-badan was born somewhere about 1523 and when her father had been lord in Kābul for nineteen years; he was master also in Kunduz and Badakhshān; had held Bajaur and Swat since 1519, and Qandahār for a year. During ten of those nineteen years he had been styled *pādshān*, in token of headship of the house of Tīmūr and of his independent sovereignty. To translate *pādshāh,*

[1] In selecting from the mass of Material which. without discursiveness, might have been included under the above heading, only that has been used which concerns the begam or is in touch with her interest and sympathies.

This Introduction corrects several errors which occur in an article on the life and writings of the begam, and which was published by me in the *Calcutta Review*, April 1898.

however, as is often done, by the word *emperor* would give a wrong impression of Bābar's status amongst rulers at height of his rising fortunes. Nevertheless, Gul-badan born the child of a strong and stable chief, and of one was better followed in war than his nominal domains would allow, because his army was drawn for the most part from tribes not under his government, and was not territorial and of Kābul but personal and inherited.

Bābar says that he cherished the desire to conquer beyond the Indus for nineteen years. At the date of Gul-badan's birth he was engaged in the attempt, and succeeded when she was about two and a half years old. He then became the first Tūrkī sovereign in Hindūstān, and the founder of its miscalled Mughal dynasty.

If the princess had first seen light in London instead of in Kābul, she would have had Henry VIII for king, the slumbers of her birth-year might have been troubled as men marched forth at Wolsey's will to fight and lose in France. Her personal vicissitudes were the greater she was a Tīmūrid and Tūrk. She spent her childhood under her father's rule in Kābul and Hindūstān; her girlhood and young wifehood shared the fall and exile Humāyūn; and her maturity and failing years slipped past under the protection of Akbar.

Her mother was Dil-dār Begam—the Heart-holding Princess—of whose descent, it is noticeable to observe, neither her husband nor her daughter gives any information. This peculiarity of omission she shares with Māham, the wife of Bābar's affection and the mother of his heir; and with Gul-rukh, the mother of Kāmrān and 'Askarī. All three ladies are spoken of by our begam with the style befitting the wives of a king; all were mothers of child and for this reason, if for no other, it seems natural that something should be said of their birth. Bābar frequently mentions Māham, and calls her by this name *tout court.* Dil-dār's name occurs in the Tūrkī version of the Memoirs but not in the Persian, and she is there styled *āghācha i.e.,* a lady, but not a begam, by birth. Gul-rukh is, I believe, never named by Bābar. This silence does not necessarily imply low birth. It may be an omission of the contemporarily obvious; and also it may indicate that no one of the three women was of royal birth, although all seem to have been of good family.

Three Tīmrids had been Bābar's wives in childhood and youth. These were: 'Āyisha, who left him before 1504 and who was betrothed to him when he was five; Zainab, who died in 1506 or 1507; and Ma'sūma, whom he married in 1507 and who died at the birth of her first child. Māham was married in Khurasan, and therefore in 1506; Dil-dār and Gul-rukh probably considerably later, and after the three royal ladies had passed away from the household. The next recorded marriage of Bahar is one of 1519, when a Yusufzāi chief brought him his daughter, Bībī Mubārika, as the seal of submission. She had no children, and was an altogether charming person in the eyes of those who have written of her.

To return now to Dil-dār. She bore five children, three girls and two boys. The eldest was born in an absence of Bahar from Kabul and in Khost. This fixes her birth as occurring somewhere between 1511 and 1515. She was Gul-rang (Rose-hued), named like her sisters from the rose; then came Gul-chihra (Rose-cheeked); and then Abū'n-nāṣir Muḥammad, the Hindāl of history, who was born in 1519; next was Gul-badan (Rose-body); and last a boy, whom his sister calls Alwar, a word which looks like a sobriquet drawn from the Indian town. He died after the migration of the household to Āgra, and in 1529.

Princess Gul-badan was born some two years before Bābar set out on his last expedition across the Indus, so her baby eyes may have seen his troops leave Kābul in November, 1525, for the rallying-place at Jacob's Village (*Dih-i-ya'qūb*). It is not mere word-painting to picture her as looking down from the citadel at what went on below, for she tells of later watching from this view-point which would give the farewell glimpse of the departing army, and, as weeks and years rolled on, the first sight of many a speck on the eastern road which took form as loin-girt runner or mounted courier.

We who live upon the wire, need a kindled imagination to realize what it was to those left behind, to have men-folk go to India. With us, fancy is checked by and books, and has not often to dwell on the unknown inconceivable. To them, what was not a blank was probably a fear. Distance could have no terrors for them, because they were mostly, by tribe and breeding, ingrain nomads; many of them had come from the far north and thought the great mountains or the desert sands the desirable setting for life. Such experience, however, would not to understand the place of the Hindūs, with its heat rains, strange beasts, and hated and dreaded pagans.

It is not easy to say wherein lies the pleasure of animating the silhouettes which are all that names, without details of character, bring down from the past. Perhaps its roots run too deep and close to what is dear and hidden in heart, for them to make way readily to the surface in speech. But it is an undoubted pleasure, and it is what make agreeable to linger with these women in Kābul in those hours when our common human nature allows their thoughts and feelings to be clear to us. Sometimes their surroundings are too unfamiliar for us to understand what sentiments they would awaken, but this is not so when there is news of marches, fighting, defeat, or victory. Then silhouettes round, and breathe, and weep or smile.

Bābar left few fighting men in Kābul, but there remail a great company of women and children, all under nominal command and charge of Prince Kāmrān, who himself a child. His exact age I am not able to down, for Bābar does not chronicle his birth, an omission which appears due to its falling in one of the gaps of Memoirs. Bābar left the city on November 17th, and joined on December 3rd by Humāyūn at the Garden Fidelity (*Bāgh-i-wafā*). He had to wait for the boy, and was much displeased, and reprimanded him severely. Humāyūn was then seventeen years old, and since 1520 had been governor of Badakhshān. He had now brought over his army to reinforce his father, and it may well be that Māham had something to do with his delayed march from Kabul. She could have seen him only at long intervals since she had accompanied Bābar, in 1520, to console and settle her child of twelve in his distant and undesired post of authority.

Shortly after the army had gone eastwards, disquieting news must have reached Kābul, for three times before the middle of December, 1525, Bābar was alarmingly ill. What he records of drinking and drug-eating may explain this; he thought his illness a chastisement, and set himself to repent of sins which were bred of good-fellowship and by forgetfulness in gay company; but his conflict with them was without victory. He referred his punishment to another cause than these grosser acts, and came to regard the composition of satirical verses as a grave fault. His reflections on the point place him near higher moralists, for he says it was sad a tongue which could repeat sublime words, should occupy itself with meaner and despicable fancies. 'Oh, my Creator! I have tyrannized over my soul, and if Thou art not bountiful to me, of a truth I shall be numbered amongst the accursed.' These are some of the thoughts of Bābar which lift our eyes above what is antipathetic in him, and explain why he wins the respect and affection of all who take trouble to know him.

Not long after January 8th, 1526, a messenger would reach Kabul who took more than news, for Bābar had found manuscripts in the captured fort of Milwat, and now sent some for Kāmrān, while he gave others to Humāyūn. They were valuable, but not so much so as he had hoped, and many were theological. This and other records about books remind one that they were few and precious in those days. How many that we now rank amongst the best of the sixteenth century had not yet been written! There was no *Tārīkh-i-rashīdī,* and the very stuff of the *Tūzūk* was in the living and making.

On February 26th Humāyūn created news which would be as welcome to Māham as it was to Bābar, for he was successful in his first expedition on active service. This occurred at Ḥiṣār-firoza, and the town and district were given to him with a sum of money. News of the victory was despatched to Kabul from Shābābād; and immediately after Bābar's record of this in the Memoirs, there occurs a passage of varied interest, although it seems to European ears a somewhat strange commemoration of a detail of toilette: 'At this same station and this same day the razor or scissors were first applied to Humāyūn's beard.' Bābar made an entry in June, 1504, of the same act accomplished for himself. It was one which Turks celebrated by festivity. The entry quoted above is made as though by Bābar, but it is followed by an explanation that it is inserted by Humāyūn in pious imitation of his father's own. Humāyūn did this in 1553-4, shortly before he set out to recover his father's lost domains in Hindūstān. The date is fixed by his statement that he made the interpolation when he was forty-six.[1]

Humāyūn's little victory would be dwarfed by the next news of the royal army, for April 12th, 1526, brought the battle of Panipat and the overthrow of Ibrahim *Lodī Afghān,* the Emperor of Hindūstān. The swiftest of runners would carry these tidings to Kābul in something under a month. On May 11th Bābar distributed the treasures of five kings, and left himself so little that he was jestingly dubbed beggar (*qalandar*). He forgot no one, but sent gifts far and wide to kinsmen and friends, and to shrines Loth in Arabia and ʿIraq. Kābul was specially remembered and a small coin sent for every soul within it. Gul-badan tells what was given to the ladies, beginning with the great begams, the aunts of frequent mention. It was certainly a wonderful day when the curiosities and splendid things of Hind were unpacked for their inspection, and very welcome, too, would be the amīr who escorted the precious caravan. He was Bābar's friend, Khwājā Kilān, who had extorted a most unwilling leave from India on the ground that his constitution was not suited to the climate of that country, a delicate assumption of blame to his own defects which it is to be hoped he conveyed to the ladies as a reassurance. After the gay social fashion of the time,

[1] There is a point of great interest about this note of Humāyūn and Mr. Erskine's translation of it. I venture to refer readers who take interest in the Memoirs, as a book, to my article on the Tūrkī text of the Memoirs (*Royal Asiatic Society's Journal,* July, 1899), which contains information gathered from some sources which were not at Mr. Erskine's disposition, and which suggest that another reading is allowable to the concluding words (not mentioned in this text) of Humāyūn's interpolation.

no doubt he helped the ladies to run day into night in the tale-telling they loved. It appears probable that there was no such complete seclusion of Tūrkī women from the outside world as came to be the rule in Hindūstān. The ladies may have veiled themselves, but I think they received visitors more freely, and more in accordance with the active life of much-travelling peoples, than is the case in Hindu or Moslim houses in India at the present day.[1]

The little Gul-badan will have had her present with the rest, and probably, like some others, it was chosen by her father specially for her. He sent a list with the gifts so that each person might receive what he had settled upon. This he is said to have done both in allotting the jewels and the dancing-girls, the latter of whom are mentioned as sent to the great begams. Their novel style of dancing ranks them amongst the 'curiosities of Hind,' but nothing is said about their views of presentation to foreign ladies in Kabul. Certainly Gul-badan will have seen them dance, and she will also have enjoyed the joke played off by Bābar from Āgra on an old dependent called ʿAsas (night-guard).

This and all the begam's stories are left for her to tell, as she does later in this volume.

There came with the gifts an injunction which calls out the remark, that at all crises Bābar gave expression to religious feeling and performed due devotional ceremonies. He had desired Khwāja Kilān to arrange for the ladies to go out of the city to the Garden of the Audience-hall, so that they might there make the prostration of thanks for the success of his arms. They were to go in state, and to remain some days. He must have sighed as he planned an excursion so much to his liking and in which he could not share. The act of thanksgiving would be done under a summer heaven, in an enchanting June garden, of which the snowy hills were the distant

[1] I remember Muḥammadan gentleman astonishing me by a story of a Musalmānī: child who died of the shock to her propriety when she was taken out from the *ḥaram*. He was an 'English-educated' man, and the child was his sister.

girdle. Our princess will have gone out with the rest, and with theirs her small figure, bravely attired, will have bowed forehead to the earth in thanks to the Giver of Victory. Tender thoughts will have travelled to the absent, and especially to him who loved his Kābul as Bābar did.

It is remarkable in him that, longing to return home as he did, he should have had endurance to remain and fight on in Hindūstān. His constitution was assuredly not suited to its climate. His men hated it; his closest friend had left it; Humāyūn and other intimates were soon to follow the khwāja on leave; but he resisted all influences, even when he had become so homesick that he wept at sight of fruit from Kābul. Only love of action, desire to be great, and capacity for greatness, could have held and upheld him at his self-chosen post. It cannot be called a small matter on which the history of hundreds of years turns, and yet it was but the innate quality of one man, and that man very human. Bābar stood fast, and India had Akbar and his splendid followers and all the galaxy of their creations in sandstone and marble.

When Gul-badan was about two years old, and therefore shortly before her father left Kābul, she was adopted by Māham Begam to rear and educate. Māham was the chief lady of the royal household and mother of Bābar's eldest son; she was supreme, and had well-defined rights over other inmates. Perhaps this position justified her in taking from Dil-dār two of her children, Hindāl and Gul-badan, as she did in 1519 and 1525. Before 1519 Māham had lost four children younger than Humāyūn; they were three girls and a boy, and all died in infancy. So it may have been heart-hunger that led to the adoptions she made, or they might be the outcome of affection for Bābar (it is said she was to him what ʿĀyisha was to Muḥammad), which determined her, if she could not rear her children for him, at least to give him his children with the stamp of her love upon them. In some cases which are mentioned by Bābar, adoptions were made by a childless wife of high degree from a slave or servant, but no such reason seems behind those from Dil-dār. She is spoken of in terms which preclude the supposition that (as Ḥaidar puts it in another place,) she was outside the circle of distinction.

The story of Hindāl's adoption is briefly this: In 1519 Bābar was away from Kābul on the expedition which gave him Bajaur and Swat, and which brought into the royal household Bībī Mubārika *Yusufzāi.* On January 25th he received a letter from Māham, who was in Kābul, about a topic which had been discussed earlier between them—namely, the adoption by her of a child of which Dildār expected the birth. Now she repeated her wishes and, moreover, asked Bābar to take the fates and declare whether it would be a boy or girl. Whether he performed the divination rite himself, or had it done by some of the women who were in camp with the army, (he speaks of it as believed in by women,) it was done, and the result was announced to Māham as promising a boy. The rite is simple: Two pieces of paper are inscribed, one with a boy's name and one with a girl's, and are enwrapped in clay and set in water. The name first disclosed, as the clay opens out in the moisture, reveals the secret. On the 26th Bābar wrote, giving over the child to Māham and communicating the prophecy. On March 4th a boy was born, to whom was given the name of Abū'n-nāṣir with the sobriquet of Hindāl by which he is known in history and which is perhaps to be read as meaning 'of the dynasty of Hind.'[1] Three days after birth he

[1] The account of the adoption of Hindāl is given in much abbreviated form both by the Persian and English versions of the Memoirs. The latter has, indeed, an error which is not borne out by the Persian; *i.e.,* it states that several children had been born in 1519. The correct statement is that several had been borne by Māham younger than Humāyūn. The Tūrkī text of Kehr and Ilminsky has a longer account, with curious details which may have been omitted on revision of the Memoirs by Bābar himself in later copies, or may have been omitted by the Persian translator. The former is the more probable suggestion, because if the full passage had occurred in the Elphinstone Tūrkī text used by Leyden and Erskine, it could not have escaped both these careful workers. (This MS. is unfortunately not forthcoming for consultation.) The point is of interest as bearing on the history of the Tūrkī texts. It makes for the opinion that Kehr's source was one of the early copies of the Memoirs, since the passage is one which from its domestic nature would be less likely to be added to, than omitted from a revised version.

was taken, whether she would or no, from Dil-dār to be made over to Māham.

It is clear that Dil-dār objected; and although the separation could not have been so complete where the real and adoptive mothers are part of one household as it is under monogamous custom, it was certainly hard to lose her firstborn son in this way. She had still her two elder girls. Gul-badan was born four years later and removed from her care at the age of two, by which date, it may be, she had her son Alwar. In after-years Dil-dār, as a widow, lived with Hindāl, and she had back Gul-badan while the latter was still a young and unmarried girl.

Bābar was separated from his family for over three years after he left Kābul in 1525. The tedium of waiting for news or for his return was broken for the ladies by several interesting home events, and by several items of Indian news which must have stirred the whole community in Kābul. On August 2nd, 1526, Māham gave birth to a son who was named Fārūq, but he too died in babyhood and his father never saw him. In December, 1526, there occurred to Bābar what must have roused anger and dread in all Kabul, for he was poisoned by the mother of Ibrāhīm *Lodī Afghān.* How Bābar conveyed the news of this to his people at home can be seen, because he has inserted the letter he wrote to allay anxiety, as soon as recovered strength permitted. Gul-badan has given the main points of the crime. She observes that Bābar had called the 'ill-fated demon,' mother, and had shown her kindness, a sectional view which leaves out the Afghān mourner, Buw'ā Begam, whose son had been defeated and killed, his dynasty overthrown, and herself pitied by the man on whom she tried to avenge herself. Her fate is worth commemorating. She was first put under contribution—*i.e.*, made over for the exploitation of her fortune to two of Bābar's officers—and then placed in the custody of a trusty man for conveyance to Kābul. Perhaps she dreaded her reception there, for she contrived to elude her guards in crossing the Indus, threw herself into the water, and was drowned.

The letter above-mentioned is full of what one likes in Bābar. He quotes, 'Whoever comes to the gates of death knows the value of life,' and says, with thanks to Heaven, that he did not know before how sweet a thing life is. Here, too, he shows that he felt the tie which bound him to the Power in whose hands are the issues of life and death. He, his daughter, and his cousin and literary compeer, Ḥaidar Mīrzā *Dughlāt,* frequently express religious sentiment; and here Bābar exhibits the human graces of kind thought and solicitude to lessen the anxieties of his distant household and people. He forced himself to live again, in words, the horrible experiences of which he wrote while still in retirement, and four days[1] only after their occurrence.

Three months later Kābul had news of an uplifting victory, inasmuch as it had been won from men of alien faith, whose overthrow was a plenary religious duty to the Moslim. It was fought on March 13th, 1527, against Hindū Rājpūts under Rānā Sangā, and at Khānwa, on the skirts of the yet uncrowned hill of Sīkrī. It was preluded by dread amongst the Musalmāns, and by solemn acts which should make them more worthy to be the tools of Heaven and to enforce the stern belief that in battle with the pagan there was vengeance of the cause of God. Men declared repentance for sin and took oaths of abstinence; gold and silver drinking-vessels, probably of Persian handicraft and artistic beauty, were broken up

---

[1] This letter bears date December 26th, 1526, and thus provides a detail which is of use when considering the probable time of composition of the Memoirs. Was a copy of the letter kept? Did the original return from Kābul? The impression given by points of evidence is that the book was written down in present form later than the date of this letter. There are in the beginning of it statements which refer its composition or revised version to 1528. The same point is raised by letters of 1529 to Humāyūn and Khwāja Kilān, the date of which may indicate progress in the composition.

All the letters share another ground of interest, which is that, having been composed in Tūrkī, they have been preserved in Tūrkī in the Persian translation. This may be an act of pious deference. The Memoirs were certainly altogether in Tūrkī, but they were not addressed to individuals as were the letters. It is a fact of interest, and open to pleasant interpretation.

and given to the poor; wine was poured out upon the ground, and some was salted into vinegar. Where the libation of penitence was offered, the earth was dedicated to the uses of an almshouse with chambered well. So strengthened, the Musalmāns went into the fight and made great slaughter of valiant foes.

The victory was followed by change in the personnel of Bābar's army, which had long been wearying for home and murmuring against Hindūstān. This was especially so amongst Humāyūn's Badakhshīs, who were accustomed to short service of one or two months, and it was now almost sixteen since they had left even Kābul. Only promise of immediate leave to follow had induced some men to stay for this one fight, and they had been told that when it was over, all who desired it should have freedom to go. Many amirs had given 'stupid and unformed opinions' against remaining in Hindūstān at all, and down to the humblest followers these views had found acceptance. As has been said, nothing would persuade Bābar's closest friend to stay with him, although before his final decision was acted on, his master had called a council, and had expressed himself with directness and vigour.

'I told them that empire and conquest could not exist without the material and means of war; that royalty and nobility could not exist without subjects and dependent provinces; that by the labour of many years, after undergoing great hardships, measuring many a toilsome journey, and raising various armies—after exposing myself and my troops to circumstances of great danger, to battle and bloodshed, by the Divine favour I had routed my formidable enemy (Ibrāhim), and achieved the conquest of numerous provinces and kingdoms which we at present held. And now, what force compels, what hardship obliges us, without visible cause, after having worn out our life in accomplishing the desired achievement, to abandon and fly from our conquests, and to retreat to Kābul with every symptom of disappointment and discomfiture? Let anyone who calls himself my friend never henceforward make such a proposal; but if there is any among you who cannot bring himself to stay, or to give up his purpose of return, let him depart. Having made this fair and reasonable proposal, the discontented were of necessity compelled, however unwillingly, to renounce their seditious purpose.'

After the Rājpūt defeat the time came for the promised leave, but there is no mention in the Memoirs of a general exodus. Humāyūn went with his Badakhshīs, and also, as he seemed 'uncomfortable,' Mahdī[1] Khwāja, Khānzāda's husband. He, but not only he, had been through one hot season in the plains and another was approaching,—a discomposing fact, and one to wing the fancy and the feet to Kābul. He, however, left his son Jaʿfar in his government of Etāwa, and returned to India himself in 1528.

Humāyūn said farewell on April 16th, 1527, and betook himself to Dihlī, where he broke open the treasury and stole its contents. If he had needed money to pay his men, his act might have taken different colour and have been leniently described; but he had had lavish gifts in money and kind from Bābar, and had been allowed to keep the great diamond which the Rānī of Guāliar had given him as the price of family honour and which, there is good ground to believe, is the *Koh-i-nūr.* Treated as he had been, his act was a crime, and base and mean. Perhaps it may be set to the credit of the older Humāyūn that the record of his theft has survived 1553-4 and his then perusal and annotation of his father's Memoirs. By that time he had suffered many painful consequences of his own acts, and may have concurred with his father's judgment on his younger self. Bābar was extremely hurt by his unexpected conduct and reproached him severely. There was enough now known of Humāyūn's character to awaken doubt of his fitness to rule, and to need all his father's great affection to veil and forgive. From Dihlī he returned to Badakshān, and is next heard of in the autumn of 1528, when he announced the birth of his first-born son, Al-amān. Al-amān was the child of that Bega (*Ḥājī*) Begam of whom the

[1] There are difficulties in tracing the descent of this man, which are discussed in the Appendix. *Cf.* Index, *s.n.* Muḥammad Mahdī.

histories all speak, when in 1539 she is captured by Shīr Shāh at Chausa.

Together with the news of Al-amān's birth came that of a marriage of Kāmrān with a daughter of Sulṭān 'Alī *Begchik.* Bābar sent congratulatory gifts to both sons in response; and he has included his covering letter to Humāyūn in his text. It is frank, fault-finding, and affectionate. It objects to the name given to the child; it urges action: 'The world is his who exerts himself'; it objects to Humāyūn's complaints of the remoteness of Badakhshān, and tells him that no bondage is like the bondage of kings, and that it ill becomes him to complain. It attacks Humāyūn's spelling and composition, and ends this topic with words good to quote: 'You certainly do not excel in letter-writing; and you fail chiefly because you have too great a desire to show off your acquirements. For the future, write unaffectedly, clearly, and in plain words, which will give less trouble to writer and reader.' Some remarks about Kāmrān have a coming interest; Bābar faintly praises him as a worthy and correct young man, and enjoins favour for him, without a hint of suspicion that it could ever be in Kāmrān's power to show favour to Humāyūn. Humāyūn is also desired to make friends with Khwāja Kilān and with Sulṭān Wais of Kūlāb. He failed with the khwāja, who on Bābar's death joined the worthy and correct Kāmrān. Humāyūn kept on better terms with Sulṭān Wais (*Qibchāq Mughal*), and at a later date owed much to his daughter, the inimitable Ḥaram (Khurram), who stands up in history bold, capable, haughty, and altogether strongly outlined.

Something must now be set down about Bābar's third adult son, who was a younger full-brother of Kāmrān and is known in history by his sobriquet of 'Askarī, which indicates a camp as his birthplace. Neither his birth nor Kāmrān's is mentioned in the Memoirs, as we now have them,—an omission which other sources allow to be explained by their falling in one of the gaps of the book. 'Askarī was born in 1516 (922H.), and during a period of storm and of camp life. His name first occurs in the Memoirs as having presents sent to him after the battle of Pānīpat, when he is classed with Hindāl, as suited their ages of nine and seven, and they received various gifts, and not, like their two seniors, sums of money. In 1528 he was in Multān, but there is no entry of an appointment, perhaps because it would fall in the gap which extends from April 2nd to September 18th. On the latter day he was received, in home fashion, by his father in his private apartments at Āgra, and then, having spent till December 2nd with him, he was furnished with munitions of war for a campaign in the eastern districts. Special injunctions were given to the officers to consult with him as to the conduct of affairs. The interest of these details is their relation to the boy of twelve. Few years were needed in those days to support military command. Humāyūn had gone to Badakhshān at eleven; Bābar had been a fighting king at twelve. Boy chiefs were common when fathers were so apt to die by violent means; so were baby figure-heads of armies such as that few-monthed Persian baby who (like an angel's semblance on an ancient battleship) led his father's army for Humāyūn's help in 1544.

On December 12th other signs of dignity were bestowed on the boy ʿAskarī: not only a jewelled dagger, a belt, and royal dress of honour, but the insignia of high command, the standard, horse-tail, and kettle-drums; excellent horses, ten elephants, mules and camels, the equipage of a royal camp, and leave to hold a princely court and sit at the head of a hall of state. The small boy's mind is clear to us about the horses, for where is the child of twelve whom they would not delight? But what was in it about the elephants? and how did he look when he inspected their bulky line?

He bade farewell to his father on the 21st,—the Emperor being in his bath, a statement which exhales the East,—and after this, though there are many details of his campaigning, nothing of living interest is set down in the Memoirs about him. In the future he was Kāmrān's shadow, and displayed a loyalty to mother-blood which was natural under the difficulty of being loyal to Humāyūn, but which made him a Tīmūrid foe to his house, who initiated nothing and walked always in the bad path marked out for him by the 'worthy and correct' Kāmrān.

Coming back from this excursion into the future, to the simple topic of Bābar's presents to his children, there can be mentioned a set which is quite delightful in its careful choice and appropriateness. It was sent to Kābul in 1528 for Hindāl, and consisted of a jewelled inkstand, a stool inlaid with mother-of-pearl, a short robe of Bābar's own, and an alphabet. What could be better for the royal schoolboy of ten?

In 1528 an order was issued which brought about an event of extreme importance to the ladies in Kābul,—namely, that they should migrate to Hindūstān. There was delay in the execution of the royal command; and having regard to the number of ladies, the difference of opinion as to the advisability of going at all, discussion as to the details of the journey, and also remembering that (as the facts about the migration come out in the Memoirs,) there would be many who thought their family interest might be better served by remaining in Kābul, it is not remarkable that there was delay in starting the cavalcade.

The migration was amply dictated to many of the party by Bābar's wish to see his own people again; but it is clear that the enforced *levée en masse* of the ladies was a result of considerations of policy and peace. The city was full of women who, by birth or marriage, were attached to various branches of the Tīmūrids, and there was conflict of aims and palpable friction. It may well be that Kāmrān's government provoked unrest, because he was the son of a mother of less birth than were very many of the resident begams of Kābul.

The Emperor was put in full possession of the state of affairs by a letter from Khwāja Kilān which reached him in camp on February 6th, 1528, and which was brought by a servant who, in addition to the written words, gave him all the news of Kābul by word of mouth. Bābar replied to the khwāja on February 11th by that letter which those who know the time and writer rank amongst the truly interesting epistles of the world. The tenor of the khwāja's own is clear from it, and in part reply the Emperor writes:

'You take notice of the unsettled state of Kābul. I have considered the matter very attentively and with the best of my judgment, and have made up my mind that in a country where there are seven or eight chiefs, nothing regular or settled is to be looked for. I have therefore sent for my sisters and the ladies of my family into Hindūstān, and, having resolved on making Kābul and all the neighbouring countries and districts part of the imperial domain, I have written fully on the subject to Humāyūn and Kāmrān. … Immediately on receiving this letter you will, without loss of time, attend my sisters and the ladies of my family as far as the Nīl-āb (Indus); so that, whatever impediments there may be to their leaving Kābul, they must, at all events, start out within a week after this arrives; for as a detachment has left Hindūstān and is waiting for them, any delay will expose it to difficulty, and the country, too, will suffer.'

Who were these seven or eight chiefs in Kābul? Not men! The fighting chiefs were almost all in India; even Mahdī had rejoined the army before the date of this letter. Bābar's word 'sisters' is a guiding light, and it does not altogether exclude the influence of the men who, though in Hindūstān, were in touch with Kābul and its friction and intrigues. First of sisters was Khānzāda, who had certainly a holding for her support; and who had influence of birth and personal, as having sacrificed herself in her earlier marriage to secure Bābar's safety. She was now the wife of a man, Mahdī Khwāja, who, if the story told of him by the author of the *Ṭabaqāt* is true even in gist, was such as to suggest him as a possible successor of Bābar to the powerful and sensible Khalīfa. There was, since her husband was with Bābar and all great ladies had been left in Kābul, Shahr-bānū, Khānzāda's half-sister, wife of Khalīfa's brother, Junaid *Barlās,* and mother of a son. There was also, it is probable, another of ʿUmar Shaikh's daughters, Yādgār.[1]

Besides Bābar's sisters *de facto,* there were others of courtesy. Such was Sulaimān's mother, whose anxieties for his future were, however, about to find happy end by his reinstatement in 1530 in his hereditary government of Badakhshān. There were the families of three men of Tīmārid birth, grandsons of Sulṭān Ḥusain Mīrzā *Bāyqrā,* all of whom were in India, and all of whom were men of high pretension. They were,—Muḥammad Sulṭān Mīrzā, the arch-rebel of the future; Qāsim Ḥusain Sulṭān Mīrzā, son of an Uzbeg father; and Muḥammad-zāman Mīrzā, son of Ḥusain's son, Badīʿu-z-zāman. There were in Kābul the people of Yādgār-nāṣir also, Bābar's half-nephew. These instances will suffice to show the reality of the elements of unrest which conflicting family interests and jealousies might and did foment in Kābul; they do not include the many others furnished by Bābar's personal circle, and by his numerous and influential aunts.

Two Tīmūrid ladies, Fakhr-jahān and Khadīja, both paternal aunts of the Emperor, had gone to Hindūstān so early as November, 1527. With whom they went or why they went is not recorded. The first was the wife of a Tīrmīzī sayyid, member of a religious family with which royal alliance was frequent, and she would find relations of her husband in the army. The second, Khadīja, has no man mentioned as her husband, an omission by Bābar and Gul-badan which surprises, and which the chance word of another writer may easily fill up. Perhaps these aunts joined their nephew in response to his invitation of April, 1526, that kinsfolk and friends would

[1] Of the two others who are the complement in girls of his family, it is safe to say that they were absent. Mihr-bānū was the apparently contented wife of an Uzbeg Sulṭān, and Ruqaiya, who, like Mihr-bānū, had been spoil of battle and an Uzbeg wife, was recently dead. Bābar says she died just when he was making the entries about her parentage at the beginning of the Memoirs. This can hardly have been before 1528, because an appointment mentioned on the same page is recorded on its occurrence as made in 1528.

come and see prosperity with him. They brought their children, and were met outside the city by Bahar on November 23rd, and by him conducted in a lucky hour to their assigned palace[1] in Āgra.

Fakhr-jahān and Khadija stayed eleven months, and were bidden good-bye before their return journey to Kābul on September 20th, 1528. After all, Khadija did not go, having affairs of her own to detain her, and this delay allowed the Emperor to pay her another of the Friday calls which he habitually made, during the time of his occupation of Hindūstān, on his elder kinswomen. On the 17th three sisters of Fakhr-jahān and Khadīja arrived in the suburbs and were welcomed. From all these Bahar could hear the news and gossip of Kābul, and thus add to the impressions which led to his order for the begams to join him in India.

Apropos of the aunts of frequent mention, it may be said that both Bābar and Ḥaidar convey the opinion that deference to elder women was a permanent trait of their age and set. Comings and goings of aunts are set down; houses and incomes provided; advice is sought; troubles are carried to them for sympathy; they are ambassadors of peace; their nephews vie with one another as to who shall entertain them; in short, both the *Tūzūk* and the *Tārīkh* indicate distinct deference to women of an elder generation.

A good deal about the exodus of the ladies can be gleaned from Bābar and from our princess, who now comes on the scene in her small person of five or six. The order for it was given at latest in 1528; this is clear from the royal letter to the khwāja and from the fact that Māham started in January, 1529. Bābar heard on March 22nd that all had really left Kābul, which news, taken with the arrival of the main cavalcade three months after her, suggests that Māham started first and travelled quickly, as being of a small company, and that the rest set off in detachments, as they and their transport were

[1] Readers who are interested in the Tūrkī and Persian texts of the Memoirs, will like to have attention drawn to the fact of there being a record of this episode in one of the fragments attached to Kehr's MS., and that this varies in detail from his text and from the Persian source of the Memoirs.

ready. The whole party would get off between January 21st and the end of February; this can be surmised, because the letter of March 22nd would be about a month in reaching Bābar. Most of the journey would be made by horse-litter, and some perhaps by palki with bearers. Men frequently dropped down the Kābul River on rafts, being thus able to do in twelve hours what ten marches covered; but one cannot suppose the ladies would make this adventurous journey, which was attended by risk even when people did not fall off the raft after potations, as some of Bābar's companions had done. Probably the road taken was that by But-khāk (Dust of Idols) and Jagdalik, and by Jalālābād and the Khaibar; but there is no certainty, because there is no information.

Gul-badan travelled with Māham in advance of her sisters, and thus had experiences all her own and a reception by her father unalloyed by numbers. Her liveliness would while away the tedium of the five months' travel, and help to distract Māham's sad thoughts from the loss of Fārūq, her youngest born. Unfortunately, she sets down nothing about the journey until near its end. Letters between the Emperor and the travellers were frequent. One of the couriers, named Shīrak (Little Lion), who was despatched by him on March 5th, carried not only letters to Māham, but was entrusted with a copy of the Memoirs which had been made to send to Samarqand.[1]

On April 1st, and at Ghāzīpūr, Bābar heard that the ladies had been met at the Indus on February 19th by their military escort under his master-of-horse, and by this amir convoyed to the Chanāb. This might fitly be told of Māham's party, for there are other records of covering the distance to the Indus in about a month.

On the 22nd a servant of Māham brought letters to Arrah from her whom he had left at the Garden of Purity (*Bāgh-i-ṣafā*), near

[1] This is the earliest recorded copying of the Tūrkī text. This Samarqand MS. and its descendants (if any) may have been written up subsequently; but the points of this early transmission to Central Asia of a copy and the variations of the Hussian texts from those found in India, are worth consideration. There is an unexplored MS. in Bukhārā. of high reputation.

Pind-dādan Khān, and this is the last such entry. Māham reached Āgra on June 27th, and Bāhar met her outside the city at midnight.

Gul-badan gives amusing particulars of her own arrival, all of which she shall be left to tell. She followed Māham into Āgra on the 28th, not having been allowed to travel with her through the previous night. Then she saw her father. Of him she can have kept only a dim memory, and it is likely enough she would stand in some awe of him and his deeds, but no word he has written suggests that a child needed to fear him, and she soon experienced 'happiness such that greater could not be imagined.' Happy child! and happy father, too! who recovered such a clever and attractive little daughter. It is not only her book that lets us know she had a lively mind, but the fact of its composition at an age when wits are apt to be rusted by domestic peace. Only a light that was strong in childhood would have burned so long to guide her unaccustomed pen after half a century of life, and only a youth of happy thoughts and quick perceptions have buoyed her, still gay and vivacious, across the worries and troubles of Humāyūn's time.

There were pleasant days after the coming to Āgra, when Bābar took Māham, and the child also, to see his works at Dholpūr and Sīkrī. He had always been a builder and a lover of a view, a maker of gardens and planter of trees. Much of the scenery of his new location displeased him; he thought the neighbourhood of Āgra 'ugly and detestable' and 'repulsive and disgusting,' words which do not now link well with that Āgra which he and his line have made the goal of the pilgrim of beauty. It is difficult to go back in fancy to the city without a Tāj, with no Sikundra near and with Sīkrī uncrowned.

Dholpūr and Sīkrī had much to show of work done by the orders of the Emperor,—'my royal father,' as Gul-badan generally calls him, using the home word *bāba* invariably. At Sīkrī, amongst other buildings, was that in which she says he used to sit and write his book, *i.e.,* the *Tūzūk.* There, too, the great battle which had been fought in 1527 will not have been ignored to ears so sympathetic as Māham's. Perhaps here the little girl first learnt dimly what it was to be a Ghāzī, and to fight on the side of Heaven. She says that when these excursions had been made, and three months after her own arrival had sped by, the begams, with Khānzāda as their chief, came within meeting distance of the capital, and that the Emperor went out to welcome them. There is nothing of this in the Memoirs, which are silent after the arrival of Māham as to the doings of the royal ladies. The reunion was soon to be clouded by anxieties and loss.

A brief return in the story of Humāyūn must be made here. In the summer of 1529 he heard in Badakhshān of his father's failing health, and, without asking leave, set off for India. He passed through Kābul, and there, to Kāmrān's surprise, met him, who had just come up from Ghaznī. The two conferred, and persuaded the ten-years-old Hindāl, who was under orders for Āgra, to take up the government of Badakhshān. Humāyūn then continued his march, and arrived in Āgra without announcement to his father.

He came to the presence just when, by a coincidence which Māham may have helped to bring about, his parents were talking of him. It would be natural for the mother, who cannot have been ignorant of her son's coming, to stir gentle thoughts of him and to warm his father's heart towards him before they met, and by this to break the shock of the unpermitted absence from duty.

Bābar was greatly angered by the desertion, which in truth placed Badakhshān in difficulty by withdrawing both troops and control. Its consequences were important, and caused him profound regret. To stand fast across the mountains and to push out the royal holdings beyond the Oxus from the vantage-ground of Badakhshān was a cherished dream, and one which he had taken steps through both Humāyūn and Kāmrān to realize. He wished Humāyūn to return to his post, but the latter, while saying he must go if ordered, was not willing to leave his people again. Bābar then asked Khalīfa to go, but this request was evaded, and there is much to arouse surmise that Khalīfa saw in it the act of someone who wished him absent from the scene of crisis now foreseen as near. In his objection to leave Āgra, affection for his old master would be a natural factor; another was his own supreme influence, the sequel of his character and of Bābar's recent failure in health; and springing from his power was, perhaps the dominant factor of his objection to leave,—a disposition to supplant Humāyūn in the succession by a ruler of less doubtful character.

The fate of Badakhshān was decided by its bestowal on its hereditary chief, Sulaimān Mīrzā, *Mīrān-shāhī,* now a boy of sixteen, while Humāyūn's youthful *locum tenens* was ordered to come to India. Humāyūn betook himself to the idle enjoyments of his *jāgīr* of Sambhal, and was there, in a few months, attacked by illness which threatened life and which led to the remarkable episode of Bābar's self-sacrifice to save him. The narrative of this stands in all the histories and need not be repeated, but for the sake of making our princess' details clear, it is as well to state what was the rite performed by Bābar.

There was and is in the East belief that if offering be made of the thing most precious to the suppliant, and if the offering be accepted, Heaven will give the life of a sick man in exchange. The rite observed is simple: first prayer of intercession is made; then the suppliant walks three times round the sick man's bed. Of Bābar's sincerity there is no doubt; in mind and heart he gave himself; he felt conviction that, after the circuits, he had borne away the illness. Humāyūn was restored and Bābar died,—a return from the gate of death and an entry there which might have occurred without Bābar's rite, but none the less was the self-sacrifice complete because he believed in its efficacy and was willing to die.

His health worsened rapidly after this and he made ready to go. Marriages were arranged for Gul-rang and Gul-chihra; the amirs were addressed; Humāyūn was counselled and named to the succession. Bābar died on December 26th, 1530. 'Black fell the day,' says his daughter; 'we passed that ill-fated day each in a hidden corner.'

The question of Khalīfa's wish to supersede Humāyūn is of great interest. It is written of by Niẓāmu-d-dīn Aḥmad, in the *Ṭabaqāt,* who had the story he retails from his father, Muqīm, an old retainer of the Court. Abūl-faẓl repeats the main statement, which is that Khalīfa had had thoughts of superseding Humāyūn by Muḥammad Mahdī Khwāja, the husband of Khānzāda Begam.[1]

A few of the many points involved in Niẕāmu-d-dīn's story find fitting entry here. Bābar must have been long conscious of the fact that he was not so strong as before be faced the Indian climate; he did not send for Humāyūn; be wished him to leave when be came unasked; be bad ʿAskari: in the full dignity of a commander near him; as he lay dying, be was fretfully anxious for Hindāl's coming; he and Khalīfa were friends of many years' testing; both knew the faults of Humāyūn; if Khalīfa had planned to set the latter aside, it is likely that the thought was not altogether absent from the mind of Bābar; it is not credible that Khalīfa should have regarded a supersession as practicable, if he had no acquaintance with the Emperor's doubts as to Humāyūn, and without knowing that these were shared by others than his master and himself, for the nomination would be made by Bābar and to his chiefs.

Muḥammad Mahdī Khwāja is one of those men about whose birth and descent particulars are looked for with the sure hope of success in the search. Yet nothing is said on the topic by Bābar or by Gul-badan. When he first appears on the scene (in the Persian version, and presumably also in the Elphinstone text), he is not introduced, as it is customary for Bābar to introduce, with some few words indicating family. This omission may be a result of forgetfulness bred of familiarity, or it may be, and most probably is, that he himself first met Muḥmmad Mahdī at a date which falls in one of the gaps of his book.[2]

---

[1] Neither of the sources thus describes Mahdī, but a somewhat full consideration of the several Mahdīs of the time allows no other than the husband of Khānzāda to be understood by the name Mahdī Khwāja of the two sources. *Cf.* Appendix, *s.n.* Muḥmmad Mahdī.

[2] This omission, and perhaps some others, are straws pointing to the existence, at some time, of material which would fill the gaps.

Niẓāmu-d-dīn's statements must have some corn of truth, and they imply that by birth, as well as by marriage and military rank, Mahdī was a man who, without outrage, might be raised still higher. There are hints which make it seem probable that he was a Tirmīzī sayyid and the son of a Tīmūrid mother. The suggestion of Tirmīzī parentage is supported by the burial of Abū'l-maʻālī *Tirmīzī* in the place of interment of Mahdī and Khānzāda.[1]

It has suggested itself to me as possible that Khalīfa's plan of superseding Humāyūn was meant to apply only to Hindūstān, or at least to a part of Bābar's dominions. Abū-saʻīd had partitioned his lands amongst his sons; provinces so varied as Bābar's seem to demand division even more than his grandfather's had done. We look back to Bābar across Akbar's Indian Empire, and may not give sufficient weight to the fact that Dihlī and Āgra were not the centre or the desired heart of Bābar's. He wanted Farghāna and Samarqand and much more beyond the Oxus, and he had taken decisive steps towards securing his object through both his elder sons, and had given them charge and work of extension in those countries. Kābul was the true centre of his desired empire, and to force the Uzbegs back in widening circle was his persistent wish.

If Mahdī or any other competent man had ruled in Dihlī, by whatever tenure, this would not necessarily have ruined Humāyūn,

---

[1] It is singular that both Khalīfa and Mahdī disappear from prominent place with the death of Bābar. From Gul-badan it is known that the latter was living at the time of Hindāl's marriage with his sister Sulṭānam in 1537, because she names his gifts to the bridegroom. A good deal of search has failed to disclose other particulars of action or death of either man after Humāyūn's accession. Khalīfa's brother, Junaid (like Mahdī, a brother-in-law of Bābar), fought faithfully for Humāyūn till his recorded death. Khalīfa was older than Junaid, and the impression given by the early part of the Memoirs is that he was older than Bābar. The difficulty of the obvious interpretation of the silence about Khalīfa's later life is, that he withdrew support from Mahdī's promotion, and it is distinctly said of Humāyūn by Badayunī that he was made emperor by the concurrence of Khalīfa. So there would be no ground for a conspiracy of courtly silence about him. He was probably dead before the exile of the Tīmūrids from India in 1540, because his wife Sulṭānam was with the royal household, and made her pilgrimage shortly after the exodus to Sind.

or have taken from him the lands most coveted by Bābar. All Bābar's plans and orders were such as to keep Humāyūn beyond the Hindū-kush, and to take him across the Oxus. The dislike of the royal army to Hindūstān was a large factor in the question of centralizing government there, and so too would be the temptations to indolence afforded by its climate and customs, to which it was easy to foresee from Humāyūn's life in Sambhal that he would readily succumb.

Kābul was made an imperial domain by Bābar's written command to both elder sons, and his own words leave one in doubt as to his further intentions about it. To whom Hindūstān would have been given if Humāyūn had obeyed orders and had held fast in Badakhshān, there is nothing to show, but weight is due to the gist of the story of the supersession. Kāmrān declared that Kābul was given to his mother Gul-rukh, and Humāyūn gave it in fief to Kāmrān at his accession. There is mist over the scene from which only the accomplished facts emerge. Humāyūn came to India; he was Māham's son; she was there; Khalīfa let Mahdī fall; Humāyūn's personal charm reasserted itself over Bābar's anger, and he became Emperor of Hindūstān and all the imperial domains.

Child though Gul-badan was at her father's death, she must have been impressed by the events that preceded it: Alwar's death; her own accident at Sīkrī; her father's premonitions and dervish-moods; Humāyūn's sudden arrival and the anger it caused; his illness and the dread for his life; her father's awe-inspiring rite and its bewildering success; her sisters' marriages, which could not be joyful; the haunting suspicion of poison; the end and the blank,—all too much for so short a time in strange scenes and in a disabling climate.

Following the death came the forty days of mourning, and of good works and gifts at the tomb in the Garden of Rest at Āgra. Sīkrī furnished a part of the endowment for its readers and reciters, and Māham sent them food twice daily from her own estate. The tomb was put under the guardianship of a man whom our begam calls Khwāja Muḥammad ʿAlī ʿ*asas* (night-guard), and who may be he that 'never killed a sparrow,' and may be Māham's brother. If so, he will be heard of again under other and widely different circumstances in 1547. As is well known, Bābar's body was conveyed to Kābul, and there laid to rest in the spot chosen by himself.

SECTION II—UNDER HUMĀYŪN

In Bābar's history the man holds the interest and lifts the eyes over his shortcomings to his excellence. No character demanding admiration attracts interest to Humāyūn, but yet his story is one which it needs a master-hand to unfold. A Tolstoi could depict his faults and merits; his qualities and defects rolled a tide of retribution over him and those bound to him as surely and visibly as it does over Anna Karénine and her associates. From the historic standpoint, Mr. Erskine has told the tale in a way to hold his readers, and it befits this humble introduction to build up only such framework as will support details, some of which concern the ladies of the time, and others of which may interest readers who are not Orientalists.

In order to realize how fully the fate of the ladies was involved in that of the Emperor, it must be remembered that his occupation of Hindūstān was unrooted, military and the sport of war. When we in Britain have to lament a reverse of arms, we do it in safe homes and we brace ourselves to what will come next, in the familiar surroundings of the daily tradesman, the usual postman, and the trivial comforts of the hearth. Even Colonials had a refuge under the flag at measurable distance from their outraged homes in 1899-1900. But when the Tīmūrids were defeated in 1539-40, and driven from Āgra and Dihlī and Lāhōr, there was no refuge open to all. Their head, Humāyūn, had none; a brother took his last. Like the Israelites, he and his followers then wandered in deserts and hungered and thirsted; dwelt in strange lands, pursued and attacked, exiled and humiliated. The course of events was less historic than biographical, was individual and not national. There were no nations behind Bābar and Humāyūn; there were only ruling families who came and went as they could or could not get the upper hand of other houses; and there was the dumb mass whom the earth nourished, and labour of whom fed, in luxury of life and strength of alien arms, whatever dynasty had just struck hardest.

An enumeration of the chief events of the downfall of Humāyūn and of his years of exile will give our required framework. He became Emperor in December, 1530. In the next year Kāmrān took possession of Lāhōr and the Panjāb, in addition to his grant of Kābul, and he was allowed to remain in possession of these wide and potential lands. In 1533 there were rebellions of the 'mīrzās.' By 1535 Gujrāt had been overrun, and in 1537 was lost. Years of indifference fostered the growth of Shīr Shāh *Afghān's* power, and there were campaigns against him in Bengal, which began well and ended ill. There was growing indignation against Humāyūn's character and private life, and this culminated in the attempt to set him aside for Hindāl in 1539. Through months of indolence and folly, he dropped oil on his own descending wheels, and practically abdicated the throne; finally, there were the crushing reverses of Chausa on June 27th, 1539, and of Kanauj on May 17th, 1540. Then came the flight of the Tīmurīds to Lāhōr, and their exodus from the lands that had been theirs east of the Indus.

Māham was spared the worst of these misfortunes; she died before Hindāl's marriage, which Jauhar places in 1537. Her son had certainly addicted himself to drugs before her death, but his worst lapses into sloth followed it, and it was after 1537 that the pace of his descent became rapid. Much can be learned from our princess of the reaction of outside events on the inner circle, and she gives details which could only be gathered in that circle. This is particularly so as to Hindāl's rebellion and the home conference about it, and about the murder in his name, but not by his act, of Humāyūn's favourite, Shaikh Bahlūl. Gul-badan, like the good sister she was, makes excuses for her brother, and those who have not her bias of affection, can add others and stronger. Hindāl was nineteen, a good and successful young general; he was supported by men of rank and age, some of whom had come from Gaur, and had seen Humāyūn's army perishing in that sink of fever and corruption, and Humāyūn buried within its walls. There was no ruler in Hindūstān; Shīr Shāh was between Humāyūn and the capital. The 'mirzās' were lifting up their heads again, and a chief was needed. Hindāl was perhaps always the best of Bābar's sons in character, and certainly so when Humāyūn had become the changeling of opium. He had the Friday prayer (*khuṭba*) read in his own name; and on his behalf, Nūru-d-dīn Muḥmmad, a son-in-law of Bābar and grandson of Sulṭān Busain *Bāyqrā,* murdered Shaikh Bahlūl. The motive of the crime appears to have been desire to place the death as an impassable barrier between the royal brothers.

The news of Hindāl's rebellion stirred Humāyūn to move from Gaur. His march to Āgra was broken off tragically by the rout at Chausa, where he lost 8,000 of his best Tūrkī troops by sword or river. Here Maʿsūma was widowed, and here a terrible blank was made in the royal household by the loss of several women. Bega's (Ḥājī Begam) capture is known to all the histories, and so, too, is her return to Humāyūn. Shīr Shāh promised safety to all women found in the camp, and there is no reason to doubt that he did his best for them. But there had been fighting round their tents before his guards arrived, and some of Humāyūn's amīrs had perished in trying to defend them. It came about that there were losses of women and of children as to whose fate no word was ever heard again. Amongst them was ʿĀyisha *Bāyqrā* the wife of Qāsim Ḥusain Sulṭān Mīrzā. The next name in our begam's list takes us far back. It is that of Bachaka, a head-woman servant (*khalīfa*), and one such and so named had escaped from Samarqand with Bābar's mother in 1501. The one lost at Chausa had been a servant in Bābar's household, and may have been she of the memorable siege. Next are named two children, a foster-child and Bega's ʿĀqīqa of six years old. Two of Humāyūn's wives of low degree also disappeared.

When Humāyūn had been rescued from the river by a lowly water-carrier, he made way to Āgra, and there had a conversation with Gul-badan about the loss of ʿĀqīqa. The princess was then seventeen years old, and a comment of his, which she sets down, lets it be known that she is now a married woman. Humāyūn told her he did not recognise her at first, because when he went away with the army (1537) she wore the *tāq,* and now wears the *lachak.* The *tāq* is a cap, and the *lachak,*—a wife's coiffure—is a kerchief folded crossways, tied under the chin by two corners, and capable of much more elaboration and ornament than this simple description would lead one to suppose. This is Gul-badan's nearest approach to informing her readers of her marriage, and she never mentions her husband as such. He was her second cousin, Khiẓr Khwāja Khān, *Chaghatāi Mughal,* and of the line of the Great Khāns. His father was Aiman Khwāja, and his mother a cousin of Ḥaidar Mīrzā *Dughlāt.* One ancestor was that Yūnas whose fate as a chief of nomads was in such entertaining contrast to his taste as a lover of cities and books. Khiẓr had many other noteworthy kinsfolk, but to tell of them would lead too far afield. It is useful, however, to say that Gul-rang and Gul-chihra had married two of his uncles, and that his brother Yasīn (Ḥasan or Aīs)-daulat, the Fair Sulṭān, became the husband of Kāmrān's Ḥabība. He had two other brothers in India, namely, Mahdī and Mas'ūd. Their father and one at least of them came from Kāshghar to Āgra just after the death of Bābar.

Shortly after this interview Humāyūn took the field against Shīr Shāh, and Kāmrān, deserting his post, left Āgra and led off his 12,000 troopers towards Lāhōr. Under his escort went an immense convoy of women and helpless people, and he wished to take Gul-badan also. She was extremely unwilling to go and only partially resigned herself when she saw that it was Humāyūn's will. She bewailed herself as parting from those with whom she had grown up, and no uninitiated reader could guess that she was going with her father's son. She was a clever and attractive girl whose society was welcome to all her brothers, but in Kāmrān's wish to take her now there is something more. It is possible that he who liked her, thought of her safety; it is probable that, as he had attached two of her husband's brothers, Yasīn-daulat and Mahdī, and perhaps the third, Masʿūd, he desired to have Khiẓr too. Gul-badan's departure from the home circle was perhaps her first adventure into the foreign world as a married woman. By going when she did and under the Escort of Kāmrān's strong force, she was spared a terrible journey which her mother and the rest of the royal party made under care of Hindāl, with foes in front and behind, and at great peril.

There now followed that amazing battle at Kanauj, in which 40,000 men in armour fled, without a gun fired, before 10,000. Here again, as at Chausa, the deaths in the river were appalling, and here again the Emperor was saved by a lowly man. Again the remnant made its way to Āgra; but, says Ḥaidar, 'we made no tarry; broken and dispirited, in a state heart-rending to tell, we went on to Lāhōr.' Their road took them to Sīkrī, of which the memories and witness to Bābar's genius for living must have rubbed salt into the wounds of their spirit. Many ladies had remained in Āgra, and Humāyūn spoke to Hindāl of the difficulty of getting them safe to Lāhōr, and confessed that he had often regretted not killing ʿAqīqa with his own hand. Ḥindāl combated the suggestion, born of defeat, that a mother and sisters should be killed, and himself fought his way through country folk and Afghāns, and convoyed them safe to Lāhōr.

Here was a mighty gathering of Tīmūrids and their following, and five months slipped by in uncertain counsels and fruitless talk. The four brothers met often to discuss plans, and it seems that the emptiness of this in practical result lay in what was in the mind of Kāmrān and made him object to every course proposed. He wished to make terms for himself with the daily approaching victor, and to keep Lāhōr and the Panjāb; but if this could not be, he meant to hold fast to Kābul and keep Humāyūn out of it. The fief of Kābul had been granted to him by Humāyūn; Humāyūn therefore could resume it. That he would now do so was Kāmrān's expectation; so, when Humāyūn proposed to go to Badakhshān, Kāmrān would not hear of it, because the road thither lay through Kābul, and once in that beloved city, it was highly improbable that Humāyūn would move further.

On October 30th, 1540, something decisive had to be done, for Shīr Shāh had crossed the Biah and might appear at any hour. 'It was like the Day of Resurrection,' says our princess; the confusion was extreme, and, like the simile, impossible for us to realize. It has been said that 200,000 souls left Lāhōr in flight on that day; an overtax of all resources of transport.

Happily for the fugitives, the Rāvī was fordable, but the Chanāb required boats and the Jhelam was in flood. Many episodes unfolded themselves in the *duāb* of the Rāvī and Chanāb. Ḥaidar Mīrza took his departure for Kashmīr, hoping to secure in it a royal retreat; Ḥindāl and Yādgār-nāṣir deserted and went south for Multān; Humāyūn was urged to put further mischief out of Kāmrān's power by his death; he refused,—a refusal which would be upheld in the *ḥaram,* ever faithful to the injunctions of Bābar, and knowing these better than the real risks caused by Kāmrān's disloyalty. Penetrating everything was the irritation aroused by Kāmrān's opposition to the royal march for Kābul,—irritation which diffused itself and barely missed a sequel of bloodshed.

The depression and gloom of the men who were the responsible leaders of the fugitive mob must have been deep and painful; but what was in the minds of their dependents,—the ordinary troopers, the helpless women, the comfortless children, and the camp-followers?

There were many striking scenes in the lives of Bābar and Humāyūn, but none more dramatic than that in which the latter's flight through the Panjāb ended. A little west of the Jhelam, at Khushāb, the road runs through a ravine of an outlying spur of the Salt Range. Beyond this it forks, north-west for Kābul and south-west for Sind. Kāmrān asserted his intention to enter the defile first, perhaps with the object of closing the Kābul road. Humāyūn insisted on his right to take precedence, and blows threatened between their followers. Mediation was made by Abū'l-baqā, the man who had led Bābar to offer himself for his son in 1530. He directed Humāyūn's attention to the superior force of Kāmrān, and he told Kāmrān that it was the right of Humāyūn to take precedence. In the end Humāyūn marched first and took the southern road. At the fork of the ways each commander and many a man must have made or confirmed his choice between the brothers. And so the mighty caravan split itself, and followed Kāmrān and ʿAskarī or Humāyūn.

With the Kābul section many women went to the safer asylum. They had no choice to make where the roads parted, but those of them who saw their litters turn southwards and themselves carried by a strange road, of which they knew that it took them from the old home in Kābul, must have had some bitter feelings about their destiny. I believe Gul-badan went with Kāmrān. She does not say so, but it comes out with tolerable clearness incidentally. Her mother, Dil-dār, had gone with Hindāl to Multān, and with her was Ḥamīda-bānū, Akbar's mother to be. Khānzāda seems to have gone with Humāyūn, for her niece mentions her later as an ambassador from him in Sind to Qandahār. No other writer speaks of this embassy, I think; but most tell of her other, made later from Kābul to Qandahār in the service of peace between Kāmrān and Humāyūn, after the latter had returned from his Persian exile (1545).

Khiẓr is not mentioned as with Humāyūn in the desert wanderings, but he was in Qandahār with ʿAskari in 1545. On the occasion of her reunion with Humāyūn in Kābul, in 1545, Gul-badan says that there had been a 'toil and moil of separation' lasting five years. The lustrum points to a farewell said at the Jhelam. One thing makes for her having gone with the royal party, and this is her lively account of what befell it; but she is equally lively about Persia; where she certainly did not go. She had excellent opportunity of hearing what went on in Sind because she met her mother again in 1543, after she had come to Kābul from Qandahār. She also met Ḥamida in 1545, and could hear from her not only about her wedding, concerning which she has such an excellent passage, but also about her visit to Persia. There was ample and easy opportunity for the two old companions to talk over the past and to refresh their memories when the book was being written in and after 1587 and when they were comfortably installed as the beloved and respected 'Beneficent Ladies' of Akbar. Moreover, Gul-badan has a note of acknowledgment to Khwāja Kīsīk for help derived from his writings, as to the early part of the royal wanderings. There is therefore nothing to contradict the probability that she continued under Kāmrān's protection from 1540, the date of her unwilling departure from Āgra, till 1545, when Humāyūn took Kābul.

During the lustrum in which she did not see Humāyūn, his adventures were too many and too remarkable for abbreviation in these pages. Mr. Erskine has told them with evident enjoyment, and Gul-badan supplements his narrative with some material he did not use; it may be interjected here that he had no knowledge of her book. For most of the period of the exile in Sind and Persia, Ḥamīda was a good authority, and more than once Gul-badan has prefaced a statement with 'Ḥamīda-bānū Begam says.' She was one in the cruel desert march to Umarkot; it will have been from her that the princess heard that Akbar's birthplace was a beautiful spot where food was very cheap; she was one of the little band which fled from Quetta; she shared the qualified hospitality of the Persian king, and, it should be said, reproduced only a sense of good treatment by him; and she came back to Qandahār with his auxiliary army.

In Kābul Gul-badan did not want for old friends and kinswomen. She had her own home occupations and her children to look after; of these, though she names one only, Saʿādat-yār, she may have had several; but there is no definite statement as to which of Khīẓr's children were also hers. She was not unkindly treated by Kāmrān, as were the other royal ladies whom he turned out of their usual homes and exploited in purse. Indeed, he wished to regard her as one of his own family and to distinguish between her and her mother; but of this she would not hear.

In 1543 she had again the society of Hindāl who, after losing Qandahār to Kāmrān, came as a prisoner upon parole to Kābul and his mother's house. The movements of Humāyūn were made known from Sind to Kābul with speed and completeness, and the news was acted on to Humāyūn's great detriment. There were domestic reasons why Shāh Ḥusain *Arghūn* should not be well disposed to Humāyūn, besides the substantial one of the latter's entry and long occupation of his country. Of the more intimate causes of ill-will one was inherited; Bābar had dispossessed the Arghūns from both Kābul and Qandahār, and not only so, but had given in marriage to his foster-brother Qasim an Arghūn girl, Māh-chūchak, daughter of Muqīm Mīrzā. This was a great offence, because it was a misalliance in Arghūn eyes and because it was enforced and the bride was spoil of battle. The story of her anger and of her rebellion at her fate is delightfully told by Mr. Erskine, and to his pages readers may be safely referred for the sequel of my brief allusion to it.

When Qasim *kūka* died, Māh-chūchak married her cousin, Shāh Ḥusain, and she was with him during Humāyūn's miserable stay in Sind.

Another cause of friction lay in the presence of a former wife of Ḥusain with Humāyūn's household. In 1524 Ḥusain had allied himself with Khalīfa's family by marrying his daughter Gul-barg. As the fact adds to the domestic complication, it may be mentioned that at the same time Ḥusain's stepdaughter, Nāhīd, the child of Qāsim and Māh-chūchak, married Khalīfa's son, Muḥibb'alī. Ḥusain and Gul-barg (Rose-leaf) did not get on well, and she left him after what Mīr Ma'sūm calls two years of wedded life. She then, says the same author, went to India with *Jannat-āshyānī* (Humāyūn) 'previous to the *fiṭrat.*' This last word is frequently used of the rout at Chausa in 1539, but the next nearest catastrophe to which it would apply after 1524 is the death of Bābar, because Gul-barg is named by Gul-badan in Humāyūn's household shortly after his accession. She was with him in Sind in 1541 onwards, and so, too, was Sulṭānam,[1] who was perhaps her mother, and both were unlikely to make the best of Shāh Ḥusain to Humāyūn.

---

[1] The presence of Sulṭānam here, and a royal permission allowed to her to go to Makka and take her daughter also, gives the impression that Khalīfa is dead.

In 1545 Kābul heard that Humāyūn was on his way back from Persia with the Shah's army behind him. A first result of this was to bring the little Akbar within reach of Khānzāda and to her charge. All the histories tell of his wintry journey from Qandahār taken with Bakhshī-bānū, the one being under three and the other about four. Their coming adds a touch of tenderness to the historic Khānzāda, who paces through the histories sad and wise and trusted. She kissed the baby feet and hands of Akbar, and declared they were the very hands and feet of Bābar, and that he was like him altogether. Her first marriage with Shaibāni had been made to save Bābar from captivity or death. She was divorced because suspected of leaning to his side when his interests conflicted with her husband's, and she had been restored to him (1511) when she was about thirty-three years old.[1] To the reader's fancy she wears a mourning garb; she is mentioned with deference, and is a dignified figure in the turmoil of her day. Her third marriage,—she was doubly widowed at Merv,—takes an impersonal colour, as an alliance which her age, story and loss of her only son make seem rather one contracted to confer honour and afford her a safe home, than on any ground of personal affection. She bore Mahdi no child; she adopted his sister Sulṭānam at the age of two, and reared her to become the wife of Hindāl.

By March 21st Humāyūn was besieging Qandahār, and he then sent an envoy to Kābul, who would be a welcome guest as teller of the events since Humāyūn had left Quetta in 1543. This was Bairām Khan *Bahārlū,* and with him went Bāyazid *bīyāt.* Bairām saw Akbar, and could take back to Ḥamīda news of his welfare; and also a number of princes who were kept in Kābul under Kāmrān's eye. These were Hindāl, Yādgār-nāṣir, some of the 'mīrzās,' Sulaimān, Ḥaram and Ibrāhīm.

Bairām spent six weeks waiting till Kāmrān should choose his

[1] The date of her return by Shāh Isma'īl to Bābar in 1511 falls in one of the long gaps (eleven years) of the Memoirs. This covers also, it is probable, Bābar's first association with Mahdī and the latter's marriage with Khanzāda.

course now that he knew his brother was the stronger; and when he left the city, he was accompanied by Khānzāda, charged to mollify Humāyūn and smooth the way for ʿAskarī when the latter should submit. She went into Qandahār, but her presence did not bring about the immediate surrender, and the weary siege carried on its burden of suffering. Many of the amīrs of the defence began to slip away; the two Khīẓrs, *Hazāra* and *Chaghatai,* dropped themselves over the wall. The first got away to the mountains with adventures which fit a Highland setting; the second sought Humāyūn and obtained forgiveness.

Qandahār was surrendered on September 3rd, and ʿAskarī and his amīrs came out with swords hung round their necks, and some having winding-sheets in their hands. He was forgiven, and a feast with wine and talk and music sped the night away. While ʿAskarī was gay with the rest, someone laid before him his own letters to the Biluchī chiefs of whom Gul-badan tells, urging them to capture Humāyūn when he was in flight from Quetta. This was Humāyūn's revenge.

Meantime Kāmrān was in singular isolation in Kābul. He heard of the fall of Qandahar, of the move of the royal army for Kābul, of the death of the travel-worn Khānzāda, and of the escape of some of his princely *détenus.* He was depressed and irritable. He sent troops out to meet Humūyān, but there was no fighting, and he fled by way of Ghaznī to Sind. Then came the end of the 'toil and moil' of separation, and Gul-badan met her brother again after five years, on November 15th, 1545. For awhile there was peace and festivity in Kābul. Ḥamīda followed the army in the spring; she had now a second child, a girl, born in Persia, and she took possession once more of her first-born. Humāyūn wished to see if Akbar, whom his mother had had to desert at Quetta when he was fourteen months old, would remember her now. He had him taken into a room in which a number of ladies had assembled and seated him on the *masnad.* The child recognized Ḥamīda, and made his way to her arms. Abū'l-faẓl, who tells the story, gives all the credit of the recognition to the boy; but to those not dazzled by the light in which Akbar lived for his historian, it seems extremely probable that the child had some help from the smile which he had known as one of the first happy things of life.

In the spring, too, Humāyūn set out on a campaign in Badakhshān. He sent word back to the governor of Kābul, Uncle Muḥmmad 'Ali, that he was to strangle Yādgārnāṣir, who had been tried and condemned to death for treachery. The khwāja declined the office. 'How should I kill the mīrzā, I who have never killed a sparrow?' This uncle (*ṭaghāī*) seems a mild man for his post. Another executioner was found, and the mīrzā 'was relieved of the pains of existence.'

Humāyūn took ʿAskarī with him as a precautionary measure. Of the ladies, Māh-chūchak went, and in attendance, Bībī Fāṭima, the chief armed woman of his *ḥaram* and mother of Zuhra, whom Ḥamīda's brother was to marry and murder. Near Khishm Humāyūn fell alarmingly ill and lay unconscious for four days. He had nurses at hand whose excellence is attested by the annals, and it adds life to the scene to know that the long watch over the unconscious man was broken by his opening his eyes just when Māh-chūchak was dropping pomegranate-juice into his mouth. He recovered, but it was a perilous time for him and his supremacy, and had a bad sequel.

News of the illness went to Sind, and Kāmrān, reinforced by his father-in-law, Ḥusain, hurried up and seized Kābul. Winter was at its depth on the passes, and the amīrs with the royal force were anxious to get back to protect their families. They had premonitions that he would take the city again, and many slipped away in small parties and went to Kābul, where they found all their anticipations and dread justified. It does not seem right to stigmatize their leaving Humāyūn as traitorous; they had their own people to save, and this might be done by slight show of submission to Kāmrān. No one can consider Humāyūn a man who had claim to fidelity when the lives and honour of wives and children were in the balance. Indeed, to have left Kābul under the charge of Muḥammad 'Alī was to court disaster, and to make reasonahle a good deal of independence of action in those whose unarmed people he could not protect.

Every fear of the amīrs was justified. On his northward march Kāmrān passed through Ghaznī, where Zahīd Beg was governor. He it was who when offered a Bengal appointment in 1538, had asked Humāyūn if he could not find another place to kill him in. He had not waited for a reply, but had left Bengal, and helped Hindāl to rebel in Āgra. Kāmrān now answered his question in Ghaznī, and after this murder hurried off towards Kābul. 'It was morning, and the Kābulīs were off their guard, and grasscutters and water-carriers were going in and out as usual. Mīrzā Kāmrān went in with all these common people.' So speaks the princess. The gentle-hearted governor was at the *ḥamām,* and was brought before Kāmrān, without time given to dress, and there and then sabred. The list of other ·cruelties and murders is too terrible reading for these pages, and the ensuing siege was full of barbarous acts. Humāyūn crossed the passes as soon as it was practicable, and sat down to take the city. When Kāmrān saw at length that he could not hold it, he escaped through a hole fashioned in the wall, got through the trenches and away to the mountains. Some say Hindāl let him pass the royal lines; others that Ḥājī Muḥammad Khān *kūka* overtook him later (so destitute that he was being carried by a man), and that Kāmrān appealed to their milk brotherhood and was allowed to go free. He then joined his hereditary foes, the Uzbegs.

In 1548 Humāyūn entered upon a campaign in Badakhshān which yielded interesting personal matters, such as this rivulet of the great stream of affairs can convey. He left Kābul on June 12th, and Ḥamīda bore him company with Akbar as far as Gul-bihār. As governor this time a soldier, and a man enraged against Kāmrān, was left in charge of Kābul. The campaign culminated in the capture of Tāliqān, which was made over on August 17th by Kāmrān, who was allowed to go to the refuge of all whose presence was undesired at home, Makka. Piety had no part in Kāmrān's intention to betake himself to the holy city, and when he had heard, with incredulous ears, that Humāyūn was meting out mercy without justice to the revolted amīrs he had captured, he took heart and himself asked forgiveness. It is almost incredible, and would be quite so if one did not know Humāyūn, that he was received with kettle-drums, trumpets, tears and pardon. Certainly Humāyūn never deprived himself of the luxury of tears and the loose rein on his feelings. So wonderful was the following scene that Mr. Erskine's words shall tell it: 'When Kāmrān approached the Emperor, who was sitting in state in the pavilion of public audience, he took a whip from the girdle of Muʿnim Khān, who stood by, and passing it round his neck, presented himself as a criminal. "Alas, alas!" exclaimed the Emperor, "there is no need of this; throw it away." The mīrzā made three obeisances, according to the usual etiquette of the Court, after which the Emperor gave him the formal embrace and commanded him to be seated. Kāmrān began to make excuses for his past conduct and to express his regret. "What is past is past," said the Emperor. "Thus far we have conformed to ceremony; let us now meet as brothers." They then rose and clasped each other to their breasts in the most affectionate manner, and both burst into tears, sobbing aloud, so as to affect all present. Humāyūn, on resuming his seat, desired his brother to sit next to him on the left, the place of honour, adding kindly in Tūrkī, the language of the family, "Sit close to me." A cup of sherbet was brought, of which the Emperor, having drunk one half, handed it to his brother, who drank the other. A grand entertainment followed, at which the four brothers (also Sulaimān), who now met for the first time after a long separation, sat on the same carpet and dined, or, to use the words of the historian, ate salt together. The festival was prolonged for two days in the midst of universal rejoicing. As Kāmrān, from the rapidity and hurried nature of his return, had left his tents behind him on the road, the Emperor ordered a set to be pitched close to his own, and, at his desire, consented to ʿAskarī's going to stay with him.'

For this historic feast Gul-badan has provided a *hors d'oeuvre* in shape of a story of improper conduct in Sulaimān which, if it expressed derision, as her vague wording does not forbid to be read, was fully justified by both what had been and what was to come. It is a very funny little tale, and readers are commended to it.

To tears and professions were added lands and freedom. Kāmrān received Kūlāb, where Ḥaram Begam's father had once ruled for Bābar and Humāyūn. He was now dead, and his son, Chakr ʿAlī, was left with Kāmrān there. The mīrza was not pleased with his fief. 'What!' he exclaimed to the bearer of the deed of grant, 'have I not been king of Kābul and Badakhshān? Kūlāb is a mere district of Badakhshān. How can I serve in it?' The bearer observed that he had heard Kāmrān was wise, and begged permission to remind him that the wonder was he had received anything at all. ʿAskarī, too, was given a fief, and then, leaving them neighbours and at large, Humāyūn went back to Kābul in October, 1548.

A campaign was planned for 1549 against the Uzbegs and Balkh. This was done despite marked instability in the royal following. Instability or, in a plainer word, desertion, was an accident to which Humāyūn was peculiarly liable. One cause of it is more interesting than the common one of personal gain, because it is rooted in theological bias. Humāyūn's coquetry with Shiism in Persia is one of the most entertaining of the episodes of his sojourn there, and it had consequences in arousing distrust of him, which cropped up from time to time. Bābar himself had lost ground because of his tolerance to variety of faith. But to this, both in the father and still more in the son, were added, as causes of desertion, the flux and reflux of weak government which forbid men to know who will keep the upper hand and have power to oppress.

To return to the Balkh campaign: spring was waited for and there was delay for men. Spring came, and the minds of the ladies turned to thoughts of excursions out of town. They remarked more than once to Humāyūn that the *riwāj* would be coming up in the hills. This is a plant of subacid flavour which some say is like sorrel and some like rhubarb. It was, at least, a plant that people made excursions to eat, much as others go blackberrying. To these hints

for change, the royal reply was that the army was going out; that it would pass by the Koh-idāman (which is renowned for its *riwāj);* and that the ladies should go too. Gul-badan must not be deprived of her story of the picnic, which illuminates the domestic ways of the court. The ladies went so far as to see the waterfall at Farza, and perhaps even to Istālif, twenty miles north of Kābul, and then returned.

There had been bad omens for the start and there followed plenty of bad news from the front to fix attention on them. Kāmrān broke his promise to come to Humāyūn's help. Gul-chihra's second husband, an Uzbeg prince, ran away when he came to know that the army was directed against his people. There was an extraordinary retreat without an enemy, and of which the cause seems to have been fear that, as Kāmrān was not there, he was oppressing Kābul. Humāyūn was left almost alone, and the Uzbegs attacked and killed many fugitives. His horse was wounded and the whole affair was a fiasco. After all, too, when Kābul was reached, there had been no sign of Kāmrān.

It was the expected that Kāmrān should not keep his word, but perhaps the unexpected was behind his conduct on the occasion of the Balkh campaign. Sulaimān and Ibrāhīm were with Humāyūn, and their presence might well have kept him away, for Gul-badan tells of an incident in which the three men had part and which did not make them good company for one another. It is a bit of scandal to which Ḥaram adds salt and vitality. It is repeated here because some little points do not quite stand clear in the begam's wording. While Kāmrān was in Kūlāb—*i.e.*, his last holding,—someone, who from her name of Tarkhān Begam must have been a woman of good birth, advised him to make love to Ḥaram Begam. Good, she said, would come of it. So Kāmrān sent a go-between with a letter and a kerchief to Ḥaram, who, furiously angry, at once summoned husband and son from wherever they were away from home, and told them of the advances made to her. She railed at Sulaimān, saying that it was clear he was thought a coward, and further observed that

Kāmrān feared neither *her* nor her son. Much was packed in the pronoun here; there was ground to fear the energetic and resolute woman who had the army of Badakhshān at her disposal. She was a forceful person and had the go-between torn to pieces. Kāmrān was audacious, and his advances look the more so that Ḥaram's sister was his wife; but they may have been made rather to the charms of her army than to those of its command ante.

The events of 1550 sum up in Jauhar's words: 'Mīrzā Kāmrān wandered about the country with bad intentions.' In his course he surprised Humāyūn in the Qibchāq defile, and an engagement took place which was attended by great loss of life. It was witnessed by Kāmrān's wives and daughters from a commanding height. Bāyazīd mentions that the ladies wore turbans *(dastār-bastī),* a detail which may have been suggested by the great heat of the weather. Why the women were on the scene is perhaps explained by a similar record in the Memoirs which concerns a wife of Sulṭān Ḥusain *Bāyqrā.* Shahr-bānū, a daughter of Sulṭān Abū-saʿīd Mīrzā, was, with Ḥusain's other wives, present at a battle between her husband and her brother, Maḥmūd Mīrzā. She did not, as the other ladies did, leave her litter and mount a horse, so as to be ready for flight if necessary, but trusting to her brother, in the case of her husband's defeat, remained comfortably in her litter while the fight went on. This dispassionate composure so much offended Ḥusain that he divorced her. Perhaps Kāmrān's family, too, had prepared for whatever was to be their fate by protecting themselves against the sun and by being ready to mount.

In this encounter Humāyūn was badly wounded. Gul-badan was able to hear the details of the misadventure, because Khiẓr Khwāja was with her brother and, it may be said, fighting against his own, Yasīn-daulat. Khiẓr and Mīr Sayyid Bīrka *Tīrmīzī* helped to hold the wounded man up on an ambling pony when he could not sit his horse, and so they led him out of the fray, sustaining his courage as they went by tales of other princes who had come through plights as bad. The wound was on the head, and was like one of Bābar's in that it was given through a covering turban and this was uninjured. The pain was great and caused faintness. Humāyūn took off his quilted coat and gave it to a servant. The man finding its weight an encumbrance, left it lying; it was taken to Kāmrān, who posted off with it to Kābul, showed it as evidence of death, and once more took possession of the unfortunate city.

Jauhar has quaint stories of the destitution in which Humāyūn now was, with his camp equipage lost and deprived of all necessaries. He was helped along through the night, cold and weakened, and in the morning was placed in safety by the arrival of a body of reliable troopers under Ḥaji Muḥammad *kūka.* He warmed himself in the sun, washed his wound, said his prayer kneeling on a scarlet stool, and borrowed a coat from a servant to replace his own, which was blood-stained. Then came an old woman of the place and offered him a pair of silk trousers, that he might discard his blood-stained ones. He accepted, while saying they were not fit for a man's wear, and remitted her taxes for life. This was drawing well in anticipation of the time when his account in those regions would stand to his credit.

It is said that while he sat with his face still to the *qibla* one of his followers, Sulṭān Muḥammad *qarāwāl,* performed again for him the rite his father had observed, and expressed his willingness to die for him. Humāyūn spoke reassuring words and comforted his faithful sacrifice.

For nearly three months Kābul believed Humāyūn dead. These words cover much feeling, sad and joyful; but there is no one to tell the truth and say whether it was thought by some to offer better hope of peace that Humāyūn should be dead. There was always a large following of powerful officers ready to join Kāmrān, and one cannot suppose their changes in allegiance mere folly and fickleness. But no courtly author has told Kāmrān's side of the whole matter, nor his view of his own position.

With Kābul Akbar came again into his uncle's hands.

He was kept safe through all the vicissitudes of his father's career, and was well cared for both by Kāmrān and by 'Askari. It has been said that on one occasion Kāmrān exposed him on the battlements of Kābul to his father's guns, and this charge finds support from our princess. She however, it may be observed, makes no mention of the act attributed by some writers to Māham *anaga,* of interposing her own body to shield the child; indeed, she never once mentions this latterly influential woman. But this incident notwithstanding, it must be admitted that the boy was well treated. 'Askarī's wife, who took charge of him after his capture at Quetta, is said to have been most kind to him. He was entrusted by Ḳāmrān to Khānzāda, itself an act of surety and kindness. Again and again he fell into his uncle's hands when Kāmrān was exasperated by foiled attempts to keep Kābul, and yet he survived. Kāmrān had a son; it would have surprised no one to learn that, as complement to his effort to oust Humāyūn from his higher place, he had killed Akbar to give his own son more chance. In this there is what fixes attention in the same way that it is fixed by Gul-badan's record of Kāmrān's anxiety to obtain from the elder ladies of his house sanction to have the *khuṭba* read in his name. It was in his power to have himself proclaimed ruler in Kābul, but he discussed his wish to be so proclaimed with the other members of the royal family before he did it, and the discussion was prolonged, and referred from Dil-dār to the greatest of the ladies, Khānzāda. In both these points there is something which, if better known, might mitigate the sweeping judgment usually passed upon Kāmrān as altogether wrong in all his doings.

Humāyūn spent some time in Ander-āb while his wound was healing and his army gathering, and here Ḥaram comes again upon the scene. Where Sulaimān and Ibrāhīm were, is not quite clear, but it was to Ḥaram a message went asking her for the army of Badakhshān. It was to come as quickly as possible, and fully equipped. It took the energetic woman only a few clays to put some thousands of men in the field. It was she, says our princess, who did it all, took thought, and overlooked everything. Then she led the men to 'the pass,'—amongst so many possible, one cannot fix on which,—and having done her work, went home. It seems probable that Sulaimān and Ibrāhīm were already with Humāyūn, and that Ḥaram despatched a supplementary force. The battle in which it was to engage was that important fight at Ushtur-grām which Humāyūn tried hard to prevent by previous mediation, and which was forced on by Kāmrān's chief officer, Qarācha Khān.

There was much previous discussion as to terms of peace, but Kāmrān and Qarācha would have nothing less than Kābul. A second embassy offered alliance of the 'unique pearl of the *khilāfat,'* Akbar, with the mīrzā's 'dear daughter' (who may be 'Āyisha), and that Kābul should be theirs; and suggested that Humāyūn and Kāmrān should join forces and again attack Hindūstān. All came to nothing, because Qarācha cried, and enforced his cry, 'Our heads or Kābul.' The battle that followed was a complete success for the royal arms, and to add to its good results, Akbar, of whose safety there had been doubt, was brought to Humāyūn's camp. His father vowed charitable gifts for his restoration, and also that he would never part from him again.

A pleasant chance befell Humāyūn on the stricken field, for when he had claimed, as his share of booty, two driverless camels, he found in their loads his own books which he had lost at the Qibchāq defile. Many would be MSS. of the Persian poets; Bābar knew these well and of ten quotes the Gulistān; and Humāyūn was too much of a dilettante and verse-lover not to have made himself familiar with their round.

Happily the tale of the doings of Kāmrān is drawing to a close. He made a night attack, by which Hindāl lost his life, on the royal forces on November 20th, 1551; sued for help in vain from Sālim Shāh, the Emperor of Hindūstān; from Adam Ghakkar, and was surrendered by him to Humāyūn; was blinded by the insistence of the amīrs on August 17, 1553, and allowed to go to Makka. He was accompanied, as all the writers tell, by his Arghūn wife Māh-chūchak, and by her equal in compassion, a servant of Humāyūn, Chilma Beg. He made the *ḥaj* four times and he died on October

5th, 1557. Māh-chūchak survived him seven months. She only of his wives is commemorated as accompanying him to Makka, but I see no reason why others may not also be accepted as equally faithful. Her father opposed her going, and she roundly upheld her view of her duty and has been taken into the texture of history, but her co-wives may have gone unopposed and unpraised. How interesting Kāmrān might have made a book of Memoirs in which he set down his life from his own point of view, his motives, ambitions, opinions of right and wrong, and above all, if he had spoken his inner mind about the religious duties he was enabled to perform before death, through his defeat and mutilation! We do not know all the truth about him; certain crimes, of murder and of treachery after promise given, could never be palliated, but in the matter of possession of Kābul there may be much brought forward which would place him rather in the position of the defender of rights than their assailant. He had no courtly chronicler, and has borne the blame of much that could plausibly be traced back to Humāyūn's own defects and their outcome of opportunity.

To end the story of the faithful brothers;—ʿAskarī too received leave to go to Makka from Badakshān in 1551; he died between that city and Damascus in 1558. Both he and Kāmrān thus lived long enough to see their house triumph again in India and their weary thwartings of its elder branch set at naught by the firmer hands of Akbar's chiefs. Of ʿAskarī one clear characteristic only comes out: he was true to the blood-tie with his mother's son and own senior, Kāmrān.

A little return must now be made, in order to bring up the tale of home events to the date of those military. In 1551 the first marriage of the younger generation was arranged by the betrothal of Bakhshi-bānū to Ibrāhīm, son of Ḥaram. The Badakhshī trio had certainly deserved well of Humāyūn and, while doing the best they could to strengthen their own position, had given him efficient help. It is good to tell all that is known of Ḥaram. She seems to have had several daughters who played a part in public events as seals of alliance. When Humāyūn had passed a short time of repose in Kābul after his victory of Ushtur-grām, he sent to Ḥaram to ask Shāhzāda Khānam, one of these girls, in marriage for himself. His envoys were two persons whom Ḥaram did not consider worthy of their office. They were members of the royal household, and trusted members too, for one was Khwāja Jalālu-d-dīn Maḥmūd, *mīr sārnān,*[1] who, on Akbar's accession, was made commander of 2,500; and the other was Bībī Fāṯima, whom we know as having helped to nurse Humāyūn in his illness of 1546.

Ḥaram, the dominant partner in the command of Badakhshān, mother of a girl in whose veins was reputed to flow the blood of Alexander and of Tīmūr, daughter of a tribal chief, and conscious of intrinsic claim to deference, inquired of the two lowly messengers why no begam or lady (*āghācha*) had come to prefer the royal request. She must have known that Humāyūn could not mean to affront her; he had just given his daughter to her son and had testified gratitude for help in substantial ways to Sulaiman at the same time. She allowed herself to be mollified on condition that he himself should come to fetch his bride. The wedding does not seem to have taken place and the alliance was handed on to the next generation, in which, besides Ibrāhīm's, there was a betrothal of Muḥammad Hakīm to a daughter of Ḥaram.

While speaking of Ḥaram and the alliances of her family with the royal house, there may be named a high-handed act about another quasi-royal marriage. One of Kāmrān's wives was Muhtarīma Khānam *Chaghatāi,* and on his death Sulaimān wished to marry her. Of her as co-wife, Ḥaram would not hear, and contrived to make her a daughter-in-law by marrying her to Ibrāhīm.

The death of Hindāl in the nigh t attack of Kāmrān, on November 20th, 1551, was a heavy blow to Gul-badan. She writes of it with

[1] This title is sometimes rendered 'butler,' but this is misleading, and a word not linked in English with intoxicants would be better. Jalālu-d-dīn it was who led Humāyūn to give up the use of drugs, unfortunately late in life, by a gentle and forcible reproach.

feeling, and casts light on the question of rank in the affections of a Musalmān wife. She asks why her son or her husband was not killed rather than her brother. Perhaps she spoke out of feeling born of the fact that no dead father's son can be replaced, and from the deeps of family affection. Dutiful and admirable as were many of the wives of this time, the tie between the husband and a wife can never be so close as it is where the husband's affection is never a divisible factor in the household. Gul-badan shows that Musalmāni affection centred on those of the same blood.

The royal ladies must have felt it hard when, after having mourned Humāyūn through Kāmrān for nearly three months, Hindāl was killed. This happened near Khiẓr Khwāja's fief of Jui-shāhī, which explains why the body was sent there for burial and entrusted to the khwāja. It was removed later to Kābul and laid at Bābar's feet. Hindāl was thirty-two years old, and left one daughter, Ruqaiya, who became the first wife of Akbar and survived him, a childless woman, to the age of eighty-four.

Unfortunately for her readers, our begam's book ends abruptly (just after she has mentioned the blinding of Kāmrān,) in the only MS. of which we have knowledge, *i.e.,* that belonging to the British Museum. The missing pages are a real loss. The narrative breaks off some three years before Akbar's accession, and for the future the best authority on our topics is silent. There is no occurrence of her own name in the histories until she goes to India in the first year of Akbar. Much of supreme importance happened to the royal family in the interval, and this makes regret the keener for the defective MS.

Set free from the burden of his brothers, Humāyūn determined, in 1554, to try his fortune again in Hindūstān.

He left Kābul on November 15th,—a date so near that of Bābar's start in 1525 that it looks as if both obeyed the same omen of the heavens,—and with Akbar dropped comfortably down the river from Jalālābād to Peshāwar. The course of his advance beyond the Indus can be followed in Mr. Erskine's pages, and need not be repeated here. He was proclaimed Emperor in Dihlī on July 23rd, 1555.

A little-known episode of the time is the visit to India and the court of Sīdī ʿAlī *Reis,* a Turkish admiral of Sulaimān the Great, who by the exigencies of war and weather found himself obliged to travel with a few officers and fifty sailors from Sūrat to Lāhōr and thence across all the wide intervening lands to Turkey.[1] He was welcomed by Musalmāns for his master's sake, and he was offered appointments in India, all of which he refused. He was received with great honour by Shāh Ḥusain *Arghūn,* of whom he says that he had then reigned forty years, and had become so invalided during the last five that he could not sit his horse and used only boats for travel. Elsewhere it is said of Shāh Ḥusain that he was subject to fever of such kind that he could live only on the river, and that he used to spend his time in going up and down from one extremity to the other of his territory in search of ease and health. Probably this is a detail of the admiral's remark. He heard of Māh-chūchak (wife of Ḥusain), whom he calls Ḥaji Begam, as prisoner of ʿĪsā *Tarkhān,* and of her return to Ḥusain. He heard, too, something which is not supported by other writers, namely, that she poisoned Ḥusain, and that he died in consequence ten days after she rejoined him. The improbability of this story is shown by the fact that later on she conveyed Ḥusain's body to Makka for interment, an act which would be incredible if the accusation of murder were true. Much that is interesting is told of the journey to the first place where Sīdī ʿAlī's route brought him into contact with Humāyūn's people, *i.e.,* Lāhōr. He arrived early in August, shortly after the Restoration (July 23rd), and there awaited royal orders, because the governor would not let him go on until the Emperor had seen him. When one tries to picture one's self without telegrams or newspapers, one judges that a kindly-disposed amir would endeavour to forward everyone who could tell a tale for the entertainment of the court. Humāyūn sent

[1] 'Travels and Adventures of Sīdī ʿAlī Reis'; Vambery; Luzac and Co., 1899.

for the admiral, and had him received, in the first half of October,[1] outside Dihlī by Bairām *Khān-i-khānān,* other great amirs, 1,000 men, and 400 elephants. He dined with the *Khān-i-khānān,* and was then introduced to the presence.

As was natural, the Emperor wished to keep his guest at court permanently, if possible, and if not this, then long enough to 'calculate solar and lunar eclipses, their degree of latitude and exact date, and to help the court astrologers to study the sun's course and the points of the equator.' What fastened interest on the Ottoman was that he learned to write verses in Chaghatāi Tūrkī so well that Humāyūn called him a second ʿAlī Shīr *Nawaī.* He had a turn for chronograms, too, and at his first audience presented one of the taking of Dihlī, and made others subsequently which were admired. He was a clever man, and his literary aptitudes suited his royal host and the tone of the entourage. But he had other acquirements than those which ring well the change of words and obtained him his sobriquet of 'book-man,' and these others he used to bring about an agreement between the Emperor and his own former host, Sulṭān Maḥmūd *Bhakkarī.* An official paper was drawn up, to which Humāyūn, literally, set his fist, for he dipped his clenched hand in saffron and laid it on the deed. Maḥmūd was much pleased, and both he and his vizier wrote their thanks to the mediator. This incident, and others too, gave occasion for other Tūrkī ghazels and higher praise. Sīdī ʿAlī was constantly in the royal circle, and there were contests in verse-making and dilettante amusements which reveal the true and newly-risen Huma once more at ease in untranquillized

[1] M. Vambery makes the Emperor urge, as a reason for keeping the admiral, that they were 'now close upon' the rains. But it was October, and, moreover, Humāyūn pointed out that the rivers were in flood and roads impassable. Perhaps this is a mistake of the admiral's, but still he saw the rivers, to his cost, in going to Dihlī. Those who may read the interesting little book, for which thanks are due to M. Vambéry, need to accept it in other places also with some caution—*e.g.,* p. 38, Sulṭān Maḥmūd *Bhakkrī* is called Ḥusain *Arghūn's* adopted brother, and, p. 40, his father. He was a *kūka.* Some of the mistakes may well be due to the difficulty of getting hold of a fact, and this especially on a journey. But *Cf.* p. 43 *n.*

India. The traveller had not much to coax court favour with in the way of gifts, and this plumed his poetic flights; when he was wearied by his detention, he carried two ghazels to the royal seal-bearer and let them plead for his departure. They were heard, and he got 'leave to go,' with gifts and passport.

His affairs were all in order for his start when there happened the fatal accident which ended Humāyūn's life. That Humāyūn should die violently was in keeping with the violent changes of his career; and that he met his death in a building of Shīr Shāh was a singular chance. His last hours of activity were filled by pleasant occupations; old friends had been seen who had just come back from Makka and would bring him news of both pilgrim brothers; letters had been read from home in Kābul; he had gone up to the roof of the Shīr Mandal, which he used as his library, and had shown himself to the crowd assembled below; then he had interested himself in the rising of Venus, with the object of fixing a propitious hour for a reception,—perhaps to include the farewell of the Turkish guest.

The Shīr Mandal is a two-storied building with flat roof in the middle of which rises a small cupola which looks like a shade from the sun. The roof is reached by two discontinuous, steep, and narrow flights of high and shallow granite steps, which are enclosed in walls and the upper one of which emerges through the roof. The Emperor on that Friday evening of January 24th, 1556, had started down the upper flight and was on its second step, when the *mu'azzin* raised the cry for prayer from the neighbouring mosque. Sīdī 'Alī says, as though it were some individual habit of Humāyūn, that the latter had the custom of kneeling whenever he heard the cry; other writers say that he tried to seat himself. His foot became entangled, some say in his mantle (*postīn*), his staff slid along the smooth step, and he fell to the bottom of the flight with severe injuries to head and arm. It is professed that a letter went after the fall from him to Akbar, but this may be a part of the well-meaning deception in which the dangerous nature of the injuries was shrouded; it would seem more probable from the admiral's account of the episode, which is silent as to any recovery of consciousness, that the injuries to the head were too severe to allow of restoration to sense. Three days later Humāyūn died, on January 27th, and in the forty-eighth year of his age.

'We come from God, and to Him we return,' and 'There is no guard against fate,' are the quoted comments of the Turkish admiral. He counselled that the death should be concealed until Akbar's return to Dihlī, and brought forward experience drawn from his own country's similar circumstances. This was done and various fictions were composed. A man personated the dead Emperor in public audience, and there were rejoicings over his recovery from the fall. Sīdī ʿAlī took leave of the grandees, and conveyed the false news of Humāyūn's restoration to health in a friendly way along his route. By the time he reached Lāhōr he found that Akbar had been proclaimed, and his name read in the Friday prayers. Here, as before, the traveller had to wait for royal orders, because the governor had, or invented, useful orders for the crisis, that no one should pass to Kābul. Then he was sent to the presence in Kilānūr, where Akbar honoured his father's passport and let the harassed and home-sick man continue his journey, with money for expenses and a strong escort to Kābul.

Before bidding him good-bye on his still lengthy journey, it may be said that he and his four escorting begs and his sailors marched to Peshāwar through the night to escape that Adam Ghakkar who had made over Kāmrān to Humāyūn; that they saw two rhinoceroses, an event which makes one wonder whether there still remained a part of the ancient lake of the plain of Peshawar to serve as habitat for the huge and now vanished beasts; and that they crossed the many-memoried Khaibar.

In Kābul the admiral saw Humāyūn's two sons, Muḥammad Hakīm and Farrukh-fāl, who were born in the same month of 1553, one being the child of Māhchūchak and the other of Khānish *āghā Khwārizmī.* This statement is a surprise, because Bāyazīd says that Farrukh died within a few days of birth. The admiral's information suggests an error in Bāyazīd's MS.

Sīdī ʿAlī found Kābul beautiful and speaks of its snowy girdle, its gardens and its running water. He traced pleasure and merriment and feasting everywhere, and even instituted comparison between it and Paradise to the disadvantage of the latter. But he had no time for 'frivolities,' and thought only of hurrying home. He saw Muʿnim Khān in the city, and being told by him that he could not cross the passes, observed that men had overcome mountains, and under the care of a local guide whose home was on the road, accomplished the feat with labour and safely. He took the road to Tāliqān and there saw our well-known friends, Sulaimān and Ibrāhīm, but he is silent as to Ḥaram. Here, too, he wrote and offered his ghazel, and was both welcomed and speeded. In Tāliqān we must leave him who has been a welcome new figure amongst familiar actors.

SECTION III—UNDER AKBAR

Protected by the capable men who upheld Akbar, the royal ladies had not again to flee before foes or to suffer violent change of fortune. Humāyūn had planned their journey from Kābul to India. Akbar more than once in his first year of rule had to cancel the orders be had given to effect it. Three military affairs disturbed the plan,—the suppression of the revolt of Abū'l-maʿālī, the operations against Sikandar *Afghān,* and the encounter with Hīmū at Pānīpat. At length amīrs were named to escort the ladies from Kābul. The officers set out, but on their march received orders to act first against Sulaimān Mīrzā, who, on hearing of Humāyūn's death, had come over from Badakhshān to besiege Kābul. This was the first of a series of his attempts on the city, to which he laid fanciful claim as head of the house of Tīmūr after Humāyūn. The approach of the imperial troops broke up his siege, and his claim having been accommodated by reading his name once in the *khuṭba* at Kābul, he went home and left the ladies free to start.

They made their journey in time to arrive during the first quarter of 1557 near where lay the royal camp, at Mānkot, in the western

Sewāliks. The Emperor came a stage from it to meet them, and was 'much comforted by the reunion.' With Ḥamīda-bānū Begam, to whom, as Empress-mother, the chief place must be assigned, were Gul-badan, Gul-chihra, Ḥājī, and Salīma Begams. There was also a large company of officers' wives.

Perhaps the ladies remained near the camp until it broke up and went to Lāhōr. It left that city on its march for Dihlī on December 7th, 1557; at Jalindhar it halted, and here, with pomp and amidst general interest, Bairām *Khān-i-khānān* married Salīma Sulṭān Begam, a granddaughter of Bābar. She was a half-niece of Humāyūn, and she had with Akbar cousinship of the 'four-anna' degree. Bābar was their common ancestor, and their differing grandmothers diluted the cousinly relation.

This alliance had been arranged by Humāyūn, and the use of *sipurdan* by Abū'l-faẓl when writing of it, shows that what was now celebrated was a marriage, and not a betrothal. This point is mentioned here because some writers fix Salīma's age at this time as five, an estimate which is not supported by known facts of her life. The bride was probably a reward for the surpassing services done by Bairam for Humāyūn, the newest being those of the Restoration. Bairam was a man to whom seems due the largesse of the hand of a king's daughter; he out-topped his contemporaries by his full stature in capacity, culture, faithfulness, and character. Salīma,[1] though much his junior, was in other respects a fit wife for him. She was an educated woman; ranks amongst verse-makers so completely as to have a pen-name (*takhallas*), and stands out gently, by birth, character, and attainments.

Khīẓr Khwāja Khān had gone to Hindūstān with Humāyūn in 1554, and early in 1556 had been appointed by Akbar to the government of Lāhōr. He was left to carry on operations against Sikandar *Afghān* when Akbar was called away by Hīmū's

[1] The histories have a definite statement about her descent which yet presents difficulties when looked into. Its points are considered in the Appendix, *s.n.* Salima.

movements, and he was defeated. The few words said about him give the impression that he was not a good soldier, and he is never again named in responsible command. The slight things recorded of him point to subsequent comfortable existence at court as the 'husband of the Emperor's aunt, Gul-badan Begam.' Once he made a gift of horses to Akbar; in 1563 he helped to nurse Akbar when the latter was wounded in Dihlī; and there is no record of his death. He was raised to high military rank, and at some time was *ainīru-l-umara'*, but the *Āin-i-akbarī* does not place him in its list of *manṣabdārs.* He stands twelfth in the general list of the *Ṭabaqāt,* and amongst the chiefs of 5,000.

From her coming to India in 1557 to the time of her pilgrimage in 1574, our princess is not mentioned by the historians. The interval held much of deep interest to her and to others of her generation whose lives were slipping away under the safeguarding of Akbar. Some survivors of an older day, witnesses of Bairām's fidelity to Humāyūn, must have felt his downfall keenly. Ḥamīda can hardly have been ignorant of the intrigue which brought this about, because she was related to the chief actors in it,—Māham *anaga,* Adham Khān, and Shihābu-d-dīn Aḥmad *Nishāpūrī.* The last was governor of Dihlī, where she lived, and part of the scheme to separate Akbar from Bairām took him to Dihlī to see her, and thus under the eye of Shihāb. Ḥamida must have had clear in memory the truly valid services done for her husband by Bairām during the Persian exile. The plot had its nucleus in a sayyid circle and in families religious by inheritance, and it was carried out at the point of the tongue. Muḥammad Bāqī Khān *kūka,* the *anaga's* elder son, does not appear as taking part in it. He served the Emperor till 1584, rose to be a chief of 3,000, and of his character nothing is known. His younger brother, Adham, although put to death in 1562, had become chief of 5,000. All that is said of him is bad, and he, like his mother, was fluent in detraction and did all in his power to poison the mind of Akbar against the worthiest of his amīrs.

Many comments have been made upon Māham *anaga,* both by

the Persian writers and by their European commentators. Abū'l-faẓl calls her a cupola of chastity, and it is now possible to wipe from her reputation the stain suggested by Professor Blochmann when writing of the parentage of Adham. She was wife of Nadīm Khān *kūka,* a faithful servant of Humāyūm. This fragment of useful information was brought to light by Mr. Beveridge, who found it in a MS. of Colonel Hanna, which may yield other valuable matter on quasi-domestic points. Māham *anaga* may be granted the praise she deserves as a nurse who earned the affection of Akbar to the end of her life; she is entitled to such praise as belongs to a mother who screens a son's every fault and pushes his fortunes with all her influence. She must take the dispraise of not pushing her elder son's as she did Adham's. Bāyazīd *bīyāt* speaks of her as kind to him, and tells little stories which show her the centre of small affairs. I have not discerned in her any sign of talent. Whatever influence Akbar's affection gave her would be strengthened by her connection with his mother, and perhaps, too, with other women who were de scended from Aḥmad *Jāmī.* Amongst these was Ḥājī Begam, Humāyūm's widow and a person much regarded by the Emperor.

In the year following Bairām's death, Adham Khān, who, says the *Ṭabaqāt,* held a place higher than the other courtiers because he was his mother's son, was on duty in Mālwa against Bāz Bahādur *Sūr.* Incidents resulted which emphasize regret that for such as the actors in them Bairam had had to make way. Māham *anaga* was *de facto* prime minister; Mū'nim Khān had been made *Khān-i-Khānān,* and it was looked for by his friend the *anaga* that he should become prime minister *de jure.* Bāz Bahādur was defeated and fled from Sārangpūr. Aping the Hindūs, he had ordered his servants to kill the women of his household in the event of his defeat. Several had been so killed, many had been wounded, when the sacrifice was interrupted by the imperialists under Adham. Badāyunī says that there followed slaughter by Adham and his colleague, Pīr Muḥammad Khān, of terrible extent, and his own eyes saw that these two regarded God's creation in mankind as leeks, cucumbers, and radishes,—a quaint turn of words which covers awful butchery. When remonstrated with in the name of the law, the murderers asked what was to be done with so many prisoners.

If the order for the death of the women of Bāz Bahādur's household had issued from a Rājpūt heart, there would have been no need for executioners while he was in flight. The victims were, however, not Rājpūtnīs, and they suffered only to gratify the vanity of a Moslim. Amongst those wounded was Rūp-matī, a dancing-girl renowned throughout Hindūstān for beauty, singing, and poetic gifts. Her name seems that of a Hindu. Her wounds, inflicted by Bāz Bahādur's order, were severe and she wished to die. Adham let her know that, if she would care for herself, he would send her to her master when she could travel. She took his promise as true, had her wounds dressed and recovered. When she claimed fulfilment of Adham's word, she was told to consider herself as his slave. He entered her room, raised her veil, and saw her dead by her own act.

Perhaps the point of deepest social degradation in this story is that Rūp-matī was, by men's decree, born to sin without blame, and yet she died because she loved one man. Her heart was single, and yet she was only the most charming, clever and beautiful of a crowd of dancing girls, purchased slaves, to whom no man's loyalty and no mercy were thought due.

Adham Khān took much booty from Bāz Bahādur, and he disregarded the rule which required the choicest part to be sent to the Emperor; be also comported himself more like an independent ruler than a king's lieutenant. This angered Akbar, and he hurried off to Sārangpūr, outdistanced a messenger of Māham *anaga* whom she had sent with warnings, and took Adham by surprise. She herself came in next day and counselled surrender of the spoil. This and other matters having been adjusted, the Emperor started for his capital. No sooner was he gone than Adham, with his mother's connivance, regained possession of two of the most coveted of the captive women. News of this went after Akbar, who ordered them to be returned to the royal camp. When they came again within her power, the *anaga* had them murdered, so that they might not tell the tale of their abduction.

Having spent so many years under the influence of Māham *anaga,* it is to the credit of Akbar's humanity and mental force that there are not more than the recorded blots on his scutcheon; at nineteen he rebelled against his nurse, when she had set his feet on the primrose path to ruin of person and empire. He did not punish the murder of the captive girls, but he soon manifested his intention to depose his nurse and her son from power. Instead of appointing their friend Muʿnim prime minister, he summoned his foster-father, Shamsu-d-dīn Aḥmad *Ghaznavī* and gave him the post. Shamsu-d-dīn was an unlettered man, but he was staunch and had sons who were true to Jī-Jī *anaga's* nursling.

The next episode in which Māham *anaga* and her son appear, was one to shake the home fabric to its foundations, for Adham murdered Shamsu-d-dīn, bursting in upon him as he sat in business audience and unsuspicious. It was done on the night of May 16th, 1562. The incident is well known, how the murderer rushed to the *ḥaram* door and on the appearance of Akbar began to palliate his crime, but was struck down by a blow of the royal fist and then killed by royal order.[1]

It was the Emperor who told Māham *anaga* of her son's death: 'Māmā! we have killed Adham,' are the words put into his mouth by Bāyazīd. She fell ill from anger and grief; this blow shattered her heart's idol and her ambition for him and herself. Badāyunī says that she died after having presented the food of the fortieth day of mourning, and this points to her belief that the souls of the dead take

---

[1] Some writers put into Akbar's mouth, when he addressed Adham, an epithet which would imply baseness in his birth and opprobrium of his mother; but am advised that from various considerations weight need not be given to the inference of the word, which, moreover, is not used by all the sources. The point is mentioned here because of the contradiction involved in the epithet with the statement of marria.ge with Nadīm *kūka,* and with the terms of respect employed towards the *anaga* by the Persian writer who uses the degrading epithet.

final departure from earth on that day and after partaking of the food of their choice which the care of relations sets for them. Mother and son were buried in one spot, and Akbar placed his shoulder under his nurse's bier in sign of his sentiment to her.

Quite stirring news for discussion through some years, amongst the elder ladies of the royal family, would be the conduct of Māh-chūchak Begam in Kābul. She was the last recorded wife of Humāyūn, and was married in 1546, after the coming of Ḥamīda from Qandahār to Kābul. She was not a woman of birth,—one gathers a general impression that few royal wives married late in life were so,—and her title of begam was probably owed to her having borne a son, Muḥammad Hakīm. In 1554 Humāyūn had left her three-year-old boy as nominal governor of Kābul under charge of Muʿnim Khān, and in 1556 Akbar had confirmed the appointment. When Muʿnim went to court in 1561, his son Ghanī became his *locum tenens,* but Ghanī had neither 'suavity nor sense,' and the begam shut him out of Kābul, one morning when he had gone to walk in the melon gardens. He went to India, and she took up the guidance of her boy's affairs. She chose three men to help her; two soon came by their deaths at her dictation, and the third became supreme. Akbar, and no doubt the ladies also, heard of these doings, and despatched Muʿnim Khān with men to put things straight. Māh-chūchak met Muʿnim at Jalālābad, utterly defeated him, and he fled to court. She then killed the last adviser of her trio and took another, whom she may have married, named Ḥaidar Qāsim *Kohbur.* These proceedings surprise one in Māh-chūchak, and bring her story down to the first half of 1564, when Abū'l-maʿālī appears upon her stage.

We cannot enter here into the previous history of Abū'l-maʿālī,—his rebellions, murders, imprisonment, pilgrimage, and reinvigorated return to wickedness. He now came to Kābul fresh from two assassinations in Hindūstān, a fugitive, and indited a letter to the ruling begam, with profession of affection and devotion to the memory of Humāyūn. She welcomed him, gave him her little daughter Fakhru-n-nisāʿ in marriage, and let him take the lead.

Before long he stabbed Māh-chūchak with his own hand, murdered Ḥaidar Qāsim, and stirred revolt against himself which led to woeful slaughter within the walls of Kābul. Word of all this went from Muḥammad Hakīm to Sulaimān and Ḥaram, with a prayer for help. Ḥaram approving and accompanying, the army of Badakhshān marched over the passes, met Abū'l-maʿālī in the Ghurband valley, captured him, and sent him bound to the prince, who had him strangled. Both he and Adham Khān had justified Bairām's distrust, which had prompted him to wish their death early in Akbar's reign.

A little story of Ḥaram may be inserted here, somewhat after date. She had not been always on perfect terms with Sulaimān. Not only, a little earlier, had there been the discussion between them of his wish to take Muhtarīma to wife, which Ḥaram had frustrated by marrying the khanām to Sulaimān's son instead of to himself, but she had been angered extremely by the murder of one of her brothers by her husband and her son. She took the resolution of deserting Sulaiman and went over to Kābul, where then Muʿnim Khān was governor, and she had meant to carry on her complaints to Akbar. Muʿnim, however, who had been begged to mediate by Sulaimān, gave her good advice and pacified her, so that at last she consented to return to Badakhshān. He rode out to bid her farewell; she bade her camel kneel and dismounted; he got off his horse, and there was exchange of friendly greeting. She told him she regarded him as a brother and that for his sake she would never bring the army of Badakhshān against Kābul. It came several times later and with her approval, but Ḥaram could swear and break even 'awful oaths.' Bāyazīd *bīyat* accompanied her to the Ghurband and was charmed by her suavity and agreeableness.

On the death of Abūʿl-maʿālī, Sulaimān sent home for a daughter and married her to Muḥammad Hakīm, partitioned out some of the lands of Kābul to his own people, and went home to Qilaʿ-i-ẓafar. Irritation against the interlopers led to their expulsion by the Kābulīs, and this brought the Badakhshī forces again to Kābul, in 1564. Muḥammad Hakīm hurried to the Indus and complained to his big brother and Sulaimān was made to retreat.

In 1566 he and Ḥaram and their girls were again before the coveted Kābul, and on this occasion Ḥaram tried to supplement their failing military action by treachery. She got Sulaimān to lay an ambush for Muḥammad Hakīm, whom, with 'awful oaths' of amity, she had persuaded to have a meeting with her under profession of desire to adopt him now that her son Ibrāhīm was dead. 'The end of this affair was, in net result to the Badakhshīs, nothing; Ḥaram went home and Sulaimān followed. With them went the unfailing daughters, of whom Ḥaram seems to have had many, or who were betrothed and not 'entrusted,' so many recorded times. They had been near capture by the Kābulīs in the Four-walled Garden, but the commandant of the city recalled his men and let the girls go free, because he did not think it seemly to capture women.

This is not the place to follow Sulaimān's interesting fortunes to their close, under Akbar's protection, by death in Lāhōr in 1589. For our purpose, it is enough to say that he held Badakhshān so long as Ḥaram's watchful eye was on him, and lost it at her death. It was Muhtarīma's son, Shāh-rukh, his own grandson, who turned him out of his beloved Badakhshān, and in this, too, there may be Ḥaram's hand. Muhtarīma would not be likely to teach her boy dutiful conduct to Ḥaram or to Ḥaram's husband, for the two women were foes, and Ḥaram had tried to separate Muhtarīma from her son, and to expel her from Badakhshān to her parental home in Kāshgbar. If Ḥaram had lived, her pride would have found content in two alliances of her grandson with daughters of the royal blood,—one a child of Muḥammad Hakīm, and the other of Akbar himself.

The ill-behaviour of Ḥamīda-bānū's brother, Khwāja Muʿaẓẓam, must have been a frequent annoyance to the inner circle of the elder ladies at court. From boyhood he had been fantastic and mischievous, and perhaps carried always the germ of the madness which overtook his last years. Bairām, the sensible, had exiled him, then had given him some countenance; on Bairām's fall he had received a fief, and, so far, had been favoured. But Akbar did not like him, and the murders he had committed were sufficient to warrant dislike. He was a true *parvenu,* assertive and relying on his sister to excuse his faults. Ḥamida had been conscious before her marriage that her lowly birth was a point against her wedding with Humāyūn. The disparity in her case, as in other misalliances of the time, had raised unworthy people to power. Now, in 1564, Bībī Fāṭima lamented to Akbar that Khwāja Muʿaẕẕam had threatened to kill his wife Zuhra, who was her daughter. The Emperor consequently sent the khwāja word that he was coming to his house, and followed the message closely. As he entered, the khwāja stabbed Zuhra and then flung his knife, like a challenge, amongst the royal followers. Abu'l-faẓl says that for punishment the murderer was flung into the river, but 'would not drown.' The more sensible Niẕāmu-d-dīn Aḥmad says he was beaten and then soused in the river. He died insane, in prison, at Guālīār. All the shortcomings and crimes of the man notwithstanding, Ḥamida must have cherished some warmth of feeling for the tricksy boy who had lifted suspicion from her in the matter of the stolen rubies of the Persian episode.

In 1571 another old acquaintance comes to the front in the person of Nāhīd Begam, in whom our princess must have maintained interest for the sake of her father Qāsim, Bābar's foster-brother. Nāhīd, as has been said earlier, was the daughter of Qāsim and of Māh-chūchak *Arghūn,* who must not be confounded with Kāmrān's wife of the same name, one common amongst the Arghūn women of the time. She had married Muḥibb-ʿalī, son of Niẕāmu-d-dīn ʿAlī *Khalīfa Barlās,* and who had risen to high military rank but now lived remote from soldiering and in reposeful retirement. Nahid's mother was now in her (third) widowhood for ʿĪsā *Tarkhān Arghūn,* and she was not well regarded by her last husband's son, Muḥammad Bāqlī *Tarkhān Arghūn,* the ruler of Tatta. Nāhīd, in 1571, went to see her mother, and perhaps conveyed to Bāqī the impression that her visit was something more than filial. He put Māh-chūchak in prison, and so behaved to Nāhīd that she hurried off to court and made bitter complaint of her own wrongs and of the rudeness shown to the royal attendants who had been with her in Sind. She told Akbar, too, that she had talked with Sulṭān Maḥmud *Bhakkarī,* that old retainer of Shāh Ḥusain who had kept the island-fort against Humāyūn in the forties, and for whom Sīdī ʽAlī *Reis* had negotiated terms in 1555. Maḥmūd had suggested an attack on Tatta, and, supported by him, Nāhīd pleaded for help from Akbar to act against Bāqī. She was very keen about her plan and persuaded the Emperor to give men and money.

Muḥibb-ʽ alī was disturbed from his repose, and put at the head of the force. With him went Nāhīd and also a wife named Sāmīa and her son, Mujāhīd. For Nāhīd's ends the long war that followed was infructuous. An amusing episode of it was that Samia, when things did not go as she wished, went into rebellion against Akbar, and actually held an entrenchment against the royal amīrs a day and a night. In the end, Muḥibb-ʽalī obtained a comfortable town appointment and nothing more is heard of the ladies. Probably they too accommodated themselves to the tolerant and forgiving atmosphere of Akbar's court.

Niẓāmu-d-dīn Aḥmad is somewhat more sober of diction than his fellow-penmen and so, when he says that the Gujrāt campaign of 1572 caused the royal ladies joy enough to last their lives, whole-hearted delight is pictured. This was the campaign which made beautiful Sīkrī the City of Victory (Fatḥ-pūr). Round one incident of the war womanly interest,—and surely compassion also,—will have centred. The veil of historic silence lifts for a brief moment, and shows Gul-rukh, Kāmrān's daughter, in flight with her son.

Gul-badan's long span of unchronicled life was probably spent in the peaceful occupation of a wife and mother, with variety from books, verse-making, festivities, and outside news. She must have found much to exercise her lively mind in Hindūstān. That she went about with the royal camp is shown by the record of the place assigned to her tent in the encampments. It was pitched next to Ḥamīda's, well within the great enclosure, and not far from the Emperor's own. Since she was a woman, she must have found food for observation in the doings and position of her sex under the conditions of their life in Hindūstān. How did *sati* look to her? What did she think of the *jūhar?* Both these Hindū customs were far different from those of her traditions in similar crises. She came of a tribe which boasts of the fidelity of its wives to the marriage tie. All the women of her house must have heard of the defiant act of Aīs-daulat, Bābar's grandmother, who had ordered her maids to stab a man to whom her captor had given her, and who then, for sole excuse, had observed that she was the wife of Yūnas Khān. Gul-badan had also in her own family history plenty of examples of the fate of captured girls, for many of her kinswomen had married foes of their tribe; and many too had become contented wives, well treated, and remaining in their foreign homes apparently without constraint.[1]

What Tīmūrid women saw amongst the Hindūs reveals another type of virtue and another standard of wedded life. Our princess must have heard something on the topic through her father's experience when she was a child. Wifehood and motherhood now gave her better insight into the problems which underlie social relations. She would hear that Rājpūtnīs died joyfully rather than be captured; that outmatched Rājpūts killed wives and children and went to certain death themselves,—a holocaust to honour. The early years of Akbar furnished plenty of such records.

How, one would like to know, did the Musalmānī regard the willing death by fire of the Hindū widow, in that exaltation which lifts thought above pain and terror and is admirable, whether in the martyr for faith or for wifely duty? Unfortunately, the barriers

---

[1] I think, and the impression is gathered from the Memoirs, that although women and children were often murdered by victorious soldiers, wives were often returned to their husbands or families, and that enforced marriage was usually with the defeated leader's daughters. Perhaps the Muḥammadan law of divorce helped the wives. Injustice might easily he done under the rough-and-ready expectation that family ties would be set at naught by conquerors who were Muḥammadans. There was certainly diversity of action and of degree of mercy and chivalry.

of language and habit must have kept Akbar's Rājpūt wives from charming the Musalmānī ladies by recital of the legends of their race. These Hindus can never have been welcome inmates of the palace to any of the Moslims; but, pagan as they were thought, their conduct as wives must have insinuated the thin edge of conviction that to no one form of faith is committed the nurture of the sense of duty.

One common thought Gul-badan and the rest could have shared with the Hindū ladies,—that of the duty of pilgrimage and of respect for holy places. When next history concerns itself with our begam, it is to tell of her setting out, in 1575, for Makka. The Emperor had been unwilling to part with her, and it may be, even, had delayed with the thought of accompanying her. His heart was now much set upon making the *ḥaj,* but he did no more than walk a short distance with a caravan from Āgra, dressed in the seamless wrapper of the Arabian ceremonies. Though debarred from leaving Hindūstān himself, he helped many others to fulfil this primary duty of their faith, and opened wide his purse for their expenses. Each year he named a leader of the caravan, and provided him with gifts and ample funds. Sulṭān Khwāja, Gul-badan's cicerone, took, amongst other presents, 12,000 dresses of honour. He did not bring her home again; this duty fell to Khwāja Yaḥyā (John). What circumstance extorted royal consent to Gul-badan's absence is not recorded; her advancing age,—she was past fifty,—and her dislike of the laxity in opinion and practice in matters of the Faith would add warmth to her request for leave to go.

Abū'l-faẓl has preserved the names of the chief ladies of the pilgrim party, but many others went with Gul-badan Begam, and for all the royal purse bore the cost. She was the lady of highest birth, and was probably a widow; next came Salīma Sulṭān Begam, widow of Bairām and wife of Akbar. It was not usual for a wife to make the pilgrimage, but Muḥmmadan law stipulates that permission shall be granted to such wives as strongly desire to do so, and Salīma's seems a case in point. Next comes a woman whose presence reveals pleasant things. She was Sulṭānam, widow of Akbar's uncle, 'Askarī, and of her it is recorded in Akbar's babyhood that she cared for him when captured, with tender affection. It is probable that she had spent many years under the care and at the cost of the Emperor. Then come two step-nieces of Gul-badan, daughters of Kāmrān,—Ḥājī and Gul-'izār Begams. I do not know which child of his is veiled under the title of Ḥajī. She seems to be making her second *ḥaj,* and may well have gone on her first when her father was in Arabia. To these two the pilgrimage would have humanly pious significance, as a visitation to their father's tomb and to that of Māh-chūchak *Arghūn,* whom all his children must have held in reverence. Next comes a granddaughter of Gul-badan herself, named Um-kūlsūm (Mother of Plumpness), presumably after the daughter of her Prophet. Whether she was the child of Sa'ādat-yār is not said, nor whether the last name on the list, Salīma Khānam, is that of a child of Gul-badan, as well as of Khīrẓ Khwāja Khān. Here some of the inconveniences of polygamy show themselves to the seeker after family facts.

An old associate of our princess accompanied her in the person of Gul-nār *āghācha,* who had been of Bābar's household and was, I think, one of the two Circassians sent as a present to him by Shāh Ṭahmāsp in 1526. She was now well on her way through life and considerably older than Gul-badan Begam. Another of the party had also been of Bābar's household, Bībī Sarū-qad, or Sarū-i-sahī (Straight Cypress). She had been, too, in Humāyūn's service and later had married, with full *nisbat,* Mu'nim *Khān-i-khānān.* She was a widow, had been a singer and reciter, and was a 'reliable woman.' Like her in accomplishments were Bībī Safīya and Shāham *āghā,* both formerly of Humāyūn's household. Of the first and of Bībī Sarū-qad we have the happy little record that they sang in the moonlight on the road to Laghman in 1549.

Fatḥpūr-sīkrī seems to have been the rallying-point of the caravan and October 15th, 1575, the day of departure from it. It started earlier than was usual, perhaps because the ladies could not travel fast. Caravans generally left Āgra in the tenth month—this left in the seventh—of the Muḥammadan year. Akbar's second boy, Murād, was told off to escort the ladies to the coast. Sālim met them one stage out to give last greetings. At Gul-badan's request, Murād was excused from his long task of escort to Sūrat, and he went back to Āgra. One smiles to find that the princes were five and four years old. The real charge of the caravan was with several amīrs, one being Muḥammad Bāqī Khān *kūka,* and another Rūmī Khān of Aleppo, who may have been Bābar's artillery officer.

It is a real loss that there is no record of the journey from our begam's pen. It was to be adventurous; even perilous; and it was of great interest whether as sight seeing travel or pious duty. Sūrat was the port of embarkation, but there are no details of the road taken to reach it. Father Rudolf Acquaviva passed between the same two terminal points in 1580, but the military movements of the interval may well have allowed him to travel where the ladies could not go. When they were first in Sūrat, it had been a royal possession for two years only, and even when the Father took the fairly direct route from it to Fatḥpūr-sīkrī, the Rajput peasantry was in arms against their new lord. The ladies were probably handed on from one garrisoned place to another as the immediate circumstances of conquest dictated. The main body of their *ḥaj* joined them by a tedious and weary route, first escorted through Goganda by the army which was on active service, and then passing on to Aḥmadābād, and, perhaps by water, to Sūrat.

The governor of the port, who was to have a good deal of trouble with this caravan, was Qulij Khān *Andijānī,* a sobriquet of pleasant sound in our begam's ears. He had inherited Tīmūrid service from many generations, and his father had been a grandee of Sulṭān Ḥusain *Bāyqrā.*

'There was peace with the isles of the Franks,' but it took the ladies a year to get to sea. The *Akbar-nāma* attributes some part of the delay to a foolish panic about the Firingīs which, after the ladies had embarked in their hired Turkish transport, the *Salīmī,* seized the other pilgrims who were to sail in the royal ship, the *Ilāhī.* The real ground appears to have been want of a pass. The Portuguese were then masters of the Indian waters, and no ship might dare to put to sea without toll paid and pass obtained. Alarm about the Portuguese was natural, for there were stories that the very pass was sometimes a letter of Bellerophon enjoining capture and death. Abū'l faẓl says that, although the ladies embarked, they were unwilling to put out and desert their fellow-pilgrims. This may be mere broidery, or the one ship may have had a pass and the other not. Perhaps, too, as theirs was a hired transport, it was also one privileged to sail free. However this may be, Badāyunī makes the difficulty clear by saying that Khwāja Sulṭān's ships lay idle from want of the pass. He also, it may be added, quotes a legal opinion that at this time it was not lawful to make the *ḥaj* from India because, of the two practicable routes, one lay through the Shiah country of 'Irāq, and the other obliged a pass which bore the idolatrous stamp of the heads of the Virgin Mary and of Jesus Christ ('on whom be peace').

The *mīr ḥaj* sent word to the Emperor of his plight, who at once despatched orders to Qulij Khān, in Īdar, to go to Sūrat and arrange the difficulty. Qulij took with him a Cambayan, who was presumably a man versed in seafaring business,—hurried to Sūrat and overcame the difficulty.

It took the ladies a year to get to sea; they sailed on October 17th, 1576. Their port of debarkation is not mentioned; some pilgrims sailed by the Arabian, some by the Persian Gulf. They spent three and a half years in Arabia, and were able to make the *ḥaj* four times.

Some day perhaps a pious and enlightened Musalmān will set down the inner meaning he attaches to the rites of the pilgrimage. How interesting it would have been if our princess had told us what it was in her heart that carried her through the laborious duties of piety she accomplished during her long stay in her holy land! She might have given us an essential principle by which to interpret the religious meaning which devout women attach to the rites commanded on the pilgrimage.

The visitation duties are set down in Hughes' 'Dictionary of Islam,' where even their brief recital is attractive and adds to the wish of gauging the sentiment of believers in their efficacy. The acts prescribed are exhausting, not only to the body but also, one thinks, to the mind, because the very conception of the pilgrimage as a Divine ordinance keeps brain and heart tense, as all obedience does which sets the human will parallel to the Divine.

The mere recapitulation of the prescribed ceremonies is impressive: The halt six miles from the city to put on the seamless wrapper (*iḥrām*); the chanting of the pilgrim song; the prayer of intention and of supplication for grace to make the visitation duly; the contemplation, touch, and salutation of the mystic black stone; the sevenfold encompassment of the *ka'ba,* towards which from distant homes has been directed the prayer of the bygone years; the ascent of the Mount of Purity (*Ṣafā*), and prayer and confession of faith upon it; the race seven times repeated from its summit to that of the Mount of Marwa; the common worship in the Great Mosque, and the sermon preached to the assemblage of common believers; the various pilgrimages and prayers of the eighth and ninth days; and on the tenth the extraordinary pelting of devils, which is symbolized by the patriarchal rite of the stoning of the pillars of Mina. Later in the same day occurs the final act of the *ḥaj,* an animal sacrifice. Whether the ladies could pay a substitute to perform this is not said.

During these ten busy days the seamless wrapper is worn; after the sacrifice it is laid aside, and attention may be paid to the neglected toilette. The pilgrim stays three days longer in Makka—days of the 'drying of the blood of sacrifice,' 'three well-earned days of rest after the peripatetic performance of the last four.' Still, all is not finished; there should be more circuits of the *ka'ba,* another stoning at Mina, and a draught drunk from the sacred well. Our princess would certainly do everything which was due, and probably would go to Medina, and she would also make visitation to the tombs of many pious persons buried in the desirable soil of Arabia.

In 1579 Khwāja Yaḥiyā was *mīr ḥaj,* a friend of Badāyunī,

and the charitable man to whom Ḥusain the Patcher (*tukriya*) was indebted for decent burial. He was commissioned to escort the ladies home, and also to bring back curiosities and Arab servants,[1] who may perhaps have been wanted for the Arab *sarai,* established near the mausoleum of Humāyūn, outside Dihlī.

The return journey was both adventurous and perilous. They were shipwrecked off Aden, and had to stay, some say seven, others twelve, months in that desolate spot, far less habitable then than now, with condensed water, a tide from the Suez Canal, occasional rain, and the British *rāj.* The governor did not behave well, and quitted the path of good manners, misconduct for which he was punished by his master, Sulṭān Murād of Turkey. One pleasant incident broke the gloom of the long delay. On a day of April, 1580, the rock-bound travellers saw a ship coming up from the south with the wind, and, wishing to know whose it was, sent a boat out to make inquiry. By a pleasant chance Bāyazīd[2] *bīyāt* with his wife and children were on board, and he shortened sail, though the wind was favourable, and gave and took news. Bāyazīd says that the persons who sent out the boat to him were Gul-badan Begam, Gul-ʿiẕār Begam, and Khwāja Yaḥyā. Perhaps he was instrumental in getting them ships for return to India.

I do not know when the ladies succeeded in leaving den, nor when they landed in Sūrat. Here they again waited long, and this

---

[1] The passage in the *Akbar-nama* about these servants is in its author's later and difficult style. This led to mistake in my article of the *Calcutta Review,* April, 1898. I referred a difficulty the khwāja experienced to the ladies, whereas it was the servants who were unwilling to leave their Arabian domicile. Several other errors of that article are corrected in this book.

[2] His wife and a child died in Arabia; he wished to end his days on the sacred soil, and so sent home his other children. His wish also was to be laid beside his wife, and he tried her grave for several hours to see that it was neither too narrow nor too short. Happily for his readers, he did not stay in Arabia. His children were captured by the Portuguese, and he had to go back to their rescue. He sailed in 1582, but had long to wait in Mocha harbour for a wind, and this, with other delays, kept him eight months on board.

delay is attributed partly to the rains and partly to the royal absence in Kābul. It was March, 1582, when they reached Fatḥpūr-sīkrī.

On the northward journey they visited the shrines of the Chishtī saints in Ajmīr, and there met Prince Sālim. Day after day there came an amīr with greetings from the Emperor, until he met the caravan at Khānwa. The night of reunion was kept awake by 'questions and entrancing stories; gifts were shown, and happiness brimmed over.' One item of home news would cloud the meeting: Bega Begam had died just too soon to welcome her old friends.

Arrived in Fatḥtpūr-sīkrī, Gul-badan Begam would find much to ruffle her orthodoxy; for Father Rodolf Acquaviva was installed there and was giving Prince Murād lessons in the Christian faith. She would hear of the reverence shown by her nephew for the sacred things of an alien faith, and of his liking for the society of the pious and learned guest. Hamida-banu is named by the Father as protesting, with other ladies of the *ḥaram,* against the royal countenance of Christianity, and assuredly Gul-badan would swell the chorus of complaint, in which, too, Hindū wives would join the Moslim lamentation.[1] When the Father was leaving Fatḥpūr-sīkrī, he accepted only so much money as would pay his expenses back to Goa, but he asked a favour from Ḥamīda-bānū Begam. She had amongst her household slaves a Russian of Moscow and his Polish wife, with their two children. These four the Father begged to take with him to Goa. 'The begam, who was no friend to the Firingīs, was most unwilling to give up the slaves; but the Emperor would ref use nothing to the Father,' and the family was carried off to freedom.

The next thing known of our princess is that she wrote her *Humāyūn-nāma.* The book is its sole witness, for no one speaks of it. It is not literature, but a simple setting down of what she knew or had heard, for the help of the *Akbar-nāma.* This was not her only

---

[1] The whole account of Father Acquaviva's stay at the court is extremely interesting, and much of it may be read in Father Goldie's 'First Christian Mission to the Great Mughal' (Dublin: Gill and Co., 1897).

composition, for she followed the fashion of her day and wrote verses. Mīr Mahdī Shīrāzī has preserved in his *Taẕkiratu-l-khwātīn* two lines of hers, in which her thought seems to be, 'No love, no fruit of life.'

"Har parī ki au bā 'ashaq khud yār nīst,
Tū yaqīn mīdān ki hech az 'umr bar-khur-dār nīst."

Nine copies were made of Bāyazīd's *Humāyūn-nāma,* which was written in obedience to the royal command obeyed by Gul-badan Begam and also by Jauhar the Ewer-bearer. Of these two went to the Emperor's library; three to the princes Sālim, Murād, and Danyal; one to our begam; two to Abū'l-faẕl; and one perhaps was kept by the author. This allotment brings out the little point that Gul-badan collected books. Badāyunī has a curious passage about himself which also discloses something 'bookish' of Salima: 'On account of the book *Khirad-afza,* which had disappeared from the library, and concerning Salīma Sulṯān Begam's study of which the Emperor reminded me, an order was issued that my allowance should be stopped, and that they should demand the book of me. 'He adds that Abū'l-faẕl did not lay his refutation before the Emperor, and he does not clear up the awkward doubt as to what he had done with Salīma's desired book.

The remaining records of Gul-badan Begam's life are few and scanty. When she was seventy, her name is mentioned with that of Muḥammad-yār, a son of her daughter, who left the court in disgrace; again, she and Salīma join in intercession to Akbar for Prince Salīm; again, with Ḥamīda, she receives royal gifts of money and jewels. Her charities were large, and it is said of her that she added day unto day in the endeavour to please God, and this by succouring the poor and needy. When she was eighty years old, and in February, 1603, her departure was heralded by a few days of fever. Ḥamīda was with her to the end, and it may be that Ruqaiya, Hindāl's daughter, would also watch her last hours. As she lay with closed eyes, Ḥamīda-bānū spoke to her by the long-used name of affection, *'Jiu!'* (elder sister). There was no response. Then, 'Gul-badan!' The dying woman unclosed her eyes, quoted the verse, 'I die,—may you live!' and passed away.

Akbar helped to carry her bier some distance, and for her soul's repose made lavish gifts and did good works. He will have joined in the silent prayer for her soul before committal of her body to the earth, and if no son were there, he, as a near kinsman, may have answered the Imam's injunction to resignation: 'It is the will of God.'

So ends the long life of a good and clever woman, affectionate and dutiful in her home life, and brought so near us by her sincerity of speech and by her truth of feeling that she becomes a friend even across the bars of time and creed and death.

PART II

GUL-BADAN BEGAM'S BOOK, THE 'HUMĀYŪN-NĀMA.'

It is not generally known to English students of the (so-called) Mughal period of Indian history that Gul-badan Begam wrote a book. It was not known to Mr. Erskine, or he would have given fuller and more accurate accounts of the families of Bābar and Humāyūn. It escaped even Professor Blochmann's wider opportunities of acquaintance with Persian MSS. Until the begam's *Humāyūn-nāma* was catalogued by Dr. Rieu, it was a literary *parda-nīshīn,* and since that time has been little better. Abū'l-faẓl, for whose information it was written, does not mention it, but the *Akbar-nāma* is not without indication of its use.[1]

---

[1] A passage about Bābar (*Bīb. Ind.,* edit. I. 87) closely resembles the begam's on the same topic; and a divergence, noted by Mr. Erskine (Mems., 218 n.) as made from

Bāyazīd's *Tārīkh-i-humāyūn* was reproduced several times on its completion. Gul-badan Begam's *Humāyūn-nāma* was written under the same royal order and for the same end. It would have been natural to reproduce it also, but no second example of it can be discovered by us in any of the accessible book-catalogues of Europe or India, and prolonged search, made by advertisement, private inquiry, and in person by my husband in India, has failed to disclose knowledge of its existence which may not conjecturally be traced to my own work upon it. Once hope arose that a second MS. was to reward the search, because a correspondent intimated that he possessed for sale a MS. which was inscribed as being the begam's. On examination this was found to be so, but the MS. was a copy of the *Kānūn-i-humāyūn* of Khwānd-amīr. It is now in the British Museum.

Hope was again aroused by a mention of Gul-badan's book in a recent work, the *Darbār-i-akbarī* of Shamsu-l-ulamā' 'Muḥammad Ḥusain *āzād*. Mr. Beveridge paid two visits to the author in Bombay, but could learn nothing from him. He appeared mentally alienated, denied all knowledge of the work, and that he had ever written of it. His reference may conjecturally be traced to my article in the *Galcutta Review* upon Gul-badan Begam's writings, and does not, unfortunately, appear to indicate access to a second MS.

The MS. from which I have translated belongs to the Hamilton Collection in the British Museum, and was bought in 1868 from the widow of Colonel George William Hamilton. It is classed by Dr. Rieu amongst the most remarkable of the 352 MSS. which were selected for purchase out of the 1,000 gathered in by Colonel Hamilton from Lucknow and Dihlī. It does not bear the vermilion stamp of the King of Oude, so the surmise is allowed that it came from Dihlī. It has been rebound (not recently, I believe), plainly, in red leather; and it is unadorned by frontispiece, margin, or rubric. Whether there has ever been a colophon cannot be said; the latter

---

Bābar's narrative by Abū'l-faẓl, is made also by the begam.

pages of the work are lost. The folio which now stands last is out of place, an error apparently made in the rebinding. Catchwords are frequently absent, and there are none on the last folio. There are blank fly-leaves, prefixed and suffixed, of paper unlike that of the MS.

The absence of a second MS., and, still more, the absence of mention of the work, seem to indicate that few copies ever existed.

Dr. Rieu's tentative estimate of the date of the British Museum MS. (seventeenth century) does not, I am counselled, preclude the possibility of transcription so late in the sixteenth century as 1587 (995 H.) onwards. It may be the first and even sole example.

Gul-badan Begam, as is natural, uses many Tūrkī words, and at least one Tūrkī phrase. Her scribe (who may be herself) does not always write these with accuracy; some run naturally from the pen as well-known words do; some are laboured in the writing, as though care had to be taken in the copying or original orthography.

Tūrkī was Gul-badan's native language; it was also her husband's; it would be the home speech of her married life. Persian was an accomplishment. These considerations awaken speculation: Did she compose in Persian? or in Tūrkī? That she read Tūrkī is clear from her upbringing and her references to her father's book. She has one almost verbal reproduction of a passage from it retained in Tūrkī.

The disadvantage of working from a single MS. is felt at every point, and nowhere more than when the MS. itself is under consideration.

TRANSLATION OF THE HUMĀYŪN-NĀMA OF GUL-BADAN BEGAM

NOTE ON THE PERSIAN TITLES.

Of these there are two:

1. '*Humāyūn-nāma.* Written by Gul-badan Begam, daughter of Bābar Pādshāh.' This is on the first fly-leaf, which is of paper differing in colour and texture from that of the body of the MS., and identical with that of four blank sheets which are bound up at the end of the MS., perhaps to allow of writing in the missing portion of the work.
2. 'Accounts of Humāyūn Pādshāh. Put together by Gul-badan Begam, a daughter of Bābar Pādshāh and a paternal aunt of Akbar Pādshāh.' This stands on the first folio of the MS., which by the original paging is folio 10, and by the British Museum marking folio 2 (a).

(2*b* of the Persian text.)

In the name of God, the Merciful, the Compassionate!

There had been an order [1] issued, 'Write down whatever you know of the doings of *Firdaus-makānī* and *Jannatāshyānī.'*[2]

At the time when his Majesty *Firdaus-makānī* passed from this perishable world to the everlasting home, I, this lowly one, was eight[3] years old, so it may well be that I do not remember much. However, in obedience to the royal command, I set down whatever there is that I have heard and remember.

First of all, by way of invoking a blessing (on my work), and in pious commemoration, a chapter (*juzū*) is written about my royal father's deeds, although these are told in his memoirs.[4]

From his Majesty *Sahīb-qirānī*[5] down to my royal father there was not one of the bygone princes who laboured as he did. He

---

[1] Probably that mentioned by Abū'l-faẓl, as issued for the gathering-in of material for the *Akbar-nāma.* (H. Beveridge, I. 29.) If so, the begam's book dates from about 1587 (995H.). There are indications of its use by Abū'l-faẓl.

[2] Bābar's and Humāyūn's posthumous names, 'Dwelling' and 'Nesting in Paradise.' Several women, and notably Akbar's mother, have been named after death *Maryam-makānī,* 'Dwelling with Mary.' Bābar's half-sister, Shahr-bānū, is styled by A.F. *Bilqīs-makānī,*—Bilqīs being the Queen of Sheba. Many other examples might be quoted of the custom which, amongst some savage tribes, takes the extreme form of total suppression at death of the name borne in life, and towards which affection and reverence incline the most civilized peoples.

[3] Lunar years. Bābar died December 26th, 1530. The begam's dates and numerical statements must always be taken lightly.

[4] From this treasury Gul-badan's meagre historical sketch can be filled in. The *Tūzūk-i-bābarī* (Leyden and Erskine: Longman, Rees, etc., 1826.) will be referred to in these notes as the 'Memoirs' or 'Mems.'. Mr. W. Erskine's 'History of India under Bābar and Humāyūn' will be indicated by 'B.&H.'.

[5] *Lord of the fortunate conjunction, i.e.,* of Jupiter and Venus, a posthumous title of Tīmūr (1336-1405), from whom Bābar was fifth in descent.

became king in his twelfth[1] year, and the *khuṭba*[2] was read in his name on June 10th, 1494,[3] in Andijān, the capital of Farghana. (3*a*)

For eleven full years his wars and struggles against the Chaghatāi and Tīmūrid and Uzbeg princes[4] in Māwarā'un-nahr (Transoxiana) were such that the tongue of the pen is too feeble and weak to recount them.

The toils and perils which in the ruling of kingdoms befell our prince, have been measured out to few, and of few have been recorded the manliness, courage and endurance which he showed in battle-fields and dangers. Twice he took Samarqand by force of the sword. The first time my royal father was twelve years old, the second nineteen, the third time he was nearly twenty-two.[5] For six months he was besieged[6] (in Samarqand), and neither Sulṭān Ḥusain Mīrzā *Bāyqrā,* his paternal uncle,[7] who (ruled) in Khurāsān, nor Sulṭān Maḥmūd Khān, his maternal uncle,[8] who ruled in

---

[1] Bābar was born February 14th, 1483 (Muḥarram 6th, 888H.). He therefore became king of Farghāna (Khokand) when ll 1/3 years old.

[2] The prayer and oration in which it is ordained that the name of the reigning sovereign should be recited. *Cf.* Dict. of Islām, Hughes, *s.v.*. The histories show that it was formerly so recited in India. The term 'Ruler of the Age' filled Victoria's place.

[3] Ramẓān 5th, 899H. [Text, 909H.].

[4] The first and second of this triad of foes were near and elder kinsmen; the third was the Shaibānī of the histories.

[5] Bābar occupied Samarqand three times. Twice he captured it, and the third time entered without a blow struck and amidst a popular welcome. The dates are respectively 1497, 1500, and 1511, and his age fifteen, seventeen, and twenty-nine.

[6] By Shaibānī, after the second occupation.

[7] *'ammū.* Ḥusain was of the fourth, and Bābar of the fifth degree of descent from their common ancestor, Tīmūr. Bābar's father was *(anglice)* Ḥusain's fourth cousin. As Ḥusain was of an elder generation, Bābar calls him 'uncle.' If *'ammū* were ever used to denote an uncle by marriage, it would have triple application here, since Ḥusain married in succession three paternal aunts of Bābar—Shahr-bānū, Latīf and Payanda. Ḥusain is the well-known Mæcenas of Herāt (1438-1506).

[8] *ṭaghāi* Sulṭān Maḥmūd Khān was full-brother of Qutluq-nigār, Bābar's mother, so that here *ṭaghāi* is exactly equivalent to our 'maternal uncle.' Maḥmūd is 'the Khān' and the 'elder Khān' of the Memoirs, and also *Jānakī* or *Khānakī* and *Jāngī.* He was murdered by Shaibānī in 1508.

AMĪR TĪMŪR (*ṢĀḤIB-QIRĀN*).

[*To face p.* 84.

Kāshghar, sent him help. When none came from any quarter, he grew desperate.[1]

At this difficult time, Shāhī Beg Khān[2] sent to say: 'If you would marry your sister Khānzāda Begam [3] to me, (3*b*) there might be peace and a lasting alliance between us.' At length it had to be done; he gave the begam to the khān, and came out himself (from Samarqand).[4] With 200 followers on foot, wearing long frocks on their shoulders and peasants' brogues on their feet, and carrying clubs in their hands,—in this plight, unarmed, and relying on God, he went towards the lands of Badakhshān (Badakhshānāt) and Kābul.[5]

Khusrau Shāh's[6] people and army were in Kunduz and the Badakhshānāt. He came and paid his respects to his Majesty,[7] my father, who, being as he was manly and kind and generous, did not in any way touch the question of retaliation, although Khusrau Shāh had committed such crimes as the martyrdom of Bayasanghar Mīrzā and the blinding of Sulṭān Masʿūd Mīrzā, both of whom were sons of my royal father's paternal uncle. In addition to this, when in the early days of the forays,[8] his Majesty chanced to cross his country, he was watched and rudely driven out. Now he was pleased to command that Khusrau Shāh should take whatever his heart desired of his (own) jewels and golden vessels, and so he got leave to go

[1] He was eighteen.

[2] Abū'l-fatḥ Muḥammad Shāhbakht Khān *Uzbeg* (Shāhī Beg Khān and Shaibānī).

[3] For details of her life and that of all other women named in this book and some other contemporary works, see Appendix.

[4] Early in 907H. (July, 1501).

[5] Muḥarram, 910H. (June, 1504).

[6] A Qipchāq Tūrk, chief beg of Sulṭān Maḥmiūd Mīrzā, the father of Bayasanghar and Masʿūd. He was put to death by Shaibānī's Uzbegs in 910H. (1505).

[7] Brevet rank. Bābar was an exile from his own kingdom of Farghāna, and not yet master of Kābul.

[8] Tūrkī, *qazzāqī,* from *qazzāq* (Cossack), the name of the nomads whom the Russians term Kīrghiz. I think Gul-badan uses it to describe the time of her father's military incursions, made when he was trying to carve out a ruler's seat.

to Khurasan in kindness and safety, and took with him five or six strings of camels and five or six of baggage mules.[1] (4*a*)

His Majesty now set out for Kābul, which was occupied by Muḥammad Muqīm, a son of Ẕū'l-nūn *Arghūn,* and grandfather of Nāhīd Begam.[2] He had captured it after Ulugh Beg Mīrzā's[3] death from Mīrzā 'Abdu-r-razzāq, son of his Majesty's paternal uncle (Ulugh Beg).

His Majesty reached Kābul in safety. Muḥammad Muqīm kept command for a few days, and then by pact and agreement made over charge to the royal servants, and went off with goods and chattels to his father in Qandahār. This was in the last ten days of Rabi II., 910H.[4] Being now master of Kābul, his Majesty went to Bangash, took it at a blow, and returned to Kābul.

Her Highness, the khānam,[5] his Majesty's mother, had fever for six days, and then departed from this fleeting world to the eternal home. They laid her in the New Year's Garden. His Majesty paid 1,000 coined *misqāl* to his kinsmen, the owners of the garden, and laid her there.

At this time urgent letters arrived from Sulṭān Ḥusain Mīrzā, saying: (4*b*) 'I am planning a war against the Uzbegs. It would be excellent if you came too.' My royal father sought counsel of God. At length he set out to join the mīrzā. On the way news came that the mīrzā was dead. His Majesty's amīrs represented that, this being

---

1 The begam's brevity makes Bābar's capacity and forbearance seem alike remarkable. He had gathered a force, and safety was the condition of Khusrau's surrender (1504). Mr. Erskine writes (B. & H., I. 208.): 'Bābar, whose abhorrence of Khusrau was as deep as it was just, ordered his treasurer to send back the treasure, horses, and whatever had been presented to him, just as they were; although, says our author (Mīrzā Ḥaidar), the King had only one horse suitable for a person of his rank, and that was used by his mother.'

2 Through his daughter Māh Chūchak.

3 A son of Abū-sa'īd, known as *Kābulī.* He died 1502.

4 October, 1504. Bābar was now twenty-three, and had acquired more territory than his lost Farghāna.

5 Qutluq-nigār. She died June, 1505.

so, it was advisable to return to Kābul, but he replied: 'As we have come so far, we will carry our condolences to the princes.' In the end he went on towards Khurāsān.[1]

When the princes[2] heard of the royal visit, they one and all set out to give him honourable meeting, except Bādīʿuz-zamān Mīrzā, who did not go because Barandūq Beg and Ẕū'l-nūn Beg—amīrs of Sulṭān Ḥusain Mīrzā—said, in effect, that as his Majesty was fifteen years younger than Bādīʿuz-zamān Mīrzā, it was right that he should be the first to bow, and that they should then embrace one another. Qasim Beg[3] rejoined: 'Younger he is by years, but by the *tūra,*[4] he has precedence because he has more than once taken Samarqand by force of the sword.' (5*a*) At length they agreed that his Majesty should bow on coming in, and that Bādīʿuz-zamān should then advance to show him honour, and they should embrace.

The Mīrzā was not attending when his Majesty came in at the door; Qasim Beg clutched my royal father's girdle and pulled it, and said to Barandūq Beg and Ẕū'l-nūn Beg: 'The agreement was that the Mīrzā should come forward and that then they should embrace one another. The prince then advanced in great agitation and they embraced.

As long as his Majesty was in Khurāsān, each one of the princes showed him hospitality, and feasts were arranged, and excursions to all the gardens and places of interest. They set forth to him the inconvenience of winter, and said: 'Wait till it is over, and we will fight the Uzbegs.' But they could not in any way settle about the

---

[1] Bābar set out in June, 1506 (Muḥarram, 912H.). Ḥusain had died in May (Ẕū'l-ḥijja, 911H.), on his way northwards from Herāt, and at Bābā Ilāhī. Word reached Bābar when he had already made a great journey and had crossed the Saighan and Dandān-shikan passes to Kahmard. Af ter receiving the news he marched some 800 miles to the mīrzās' camp on the Murgh-āb.

[2] Badīʿu-z-zamān and Muḥammad Muẕaffar Ḥusain, sons of Sulṭān Ḥusain Mīrzā. The meeting was on November 6th, 1506 (Jumāda II. 8th, 912H.).

[3] Bābar's Prime Minister and (I believe) relation. He was of the Qūchīn tribe to which Bābar's grandmother, Aīs-daulat, belonged.

[4] The Rules of Chingīz Khān. These are referred to again on points of etiquette.

war. Eighty years[1] long had Sulṭān Ḥusain Mīrzā kept Khurāsān safe and sound, but the mīrzās could not fill their father's place for six months. When his Majesty saw that they were careless[2] about his expenses and revenue, he went to Kābul on the pretext of seeing the places he had assigned to himself. (5*b*) Much snow had fallen that year. They took the wrong road. His Majesty and Qāsim Beg chose one[3] because of its shortness, but the amīrs had given other advice, and when this was not taken, they all left him without a thought for him. He and Qāsim Beg and his sons made a road in two or three days by removing the snow, and the people of the army followed. So they reached Ghūrband. Some Hazāra rebels having met his Majesty here, there was fighting; and cattle and sheep and goods without number belonging to the Hazāra fell into the hands of his people. Then they started for Kābul with their enormous booty.

At the skirts of Mīnār Hill they heard that Mīrzā Khān[4] and Mīrzā Muḥammad Ḥusain *Gūrkān*[5] had rebelled and were holding Kābul. His Majesty sent a comforting and cheering letter (to his friends in the fort), and said: 'Be of good heart! I too am here. (6*a*) I will light a fire on the Hill of the Moon-faced Lady; do you light one

---

[1] A well-rounded number. Sulṭān Ḥusain was born 842H. (1438), and died 911H. (1506). Bābar calls the joint-kingship of his sons a strange arrangement and one never heard of, and quotes Sa'dī's well known couplet as applicable—'Ten darvishes can sleep on one rug, but one climate cannot hold two kings.'

[2] While on the Murgh-āb, Bābar agreed to winter in Khurāsān, and he went with the joint-kings to Herāt in order to see the 'sights' of that renowned city. He certainly worked hard, for he names some fifty-two which he saw in twenty days. The invitation to winter was repeated, but neither quarters nor suitable conveniences (? revenues) were allotted. Bābar delicately says he could not explain his real motive for not remaining, and left under pressure of necessity on December 24th, 1506, after snow had fallen along a route which was a month's ordinary journey.

It was during this absence from Kābul that he married Māham, Humāyūn's mother.

[3] Through the Aimāq and Hazāra country, and south of his route to Herāt.

[4] Sulṭān Wais, a son of Bābar's paternal uncle, Maḥmūd, and his maternal aunt *(i.e.,* his mother's half-sister), Sulṭān Nigār Khānam.

[5] Father of Ḥaidar Mīrzā *Dughlāt,* author *of* the *Tārīkh-i-rashīdī.* He married Khūb-nigār, full-sister of Bābar's mother.

on the Treasury, so that I may be sure you know of our coming. In the morning we will fall on the enemy, you from that side and we from this.' But he had fought and won before the people of the fort came out.

Mīrzā Khān hid himself in his mother's house; she was his Majesty's maternal aunt. Mīrzā Muḥammad Ḥusain was in his wife's house. She was his Majesty's younger maternal aunt. He flung himself down on a carpet, and in fear of his life cried to a servant, 'Fasten it up!' His Majesty's people heard of this. They took him out of the carpet and brought him to the presence. In the end, his Majesty forgave the mīrzās their offences, for the sake of his aunts. He used to go, in his old fashion, in and out of his aunts' houses,[1] and showed them more and more affection, so that no mist of trouble might dim their hearts. He assigned them places and holdings in the plain-country. (6*b*)

God the most High, having freed Kābul from the power of Mīrzā Khān, committed it to my royal father's care. He was then twenty-three years old[2] and had no child and greatly desired one. In his seventeenth year a girl[3] had been born to him by ʿĀyisha Sulṯān Begam, a daughter of Sulṯān Aḥmad Mīrzā, but she had died in a month. The most high God blessed the taking of Kābul, for after it eighteen children were born. (1.) Of my Lady (*Akām*[4]) who was Māham Begam there were born his Majesty the Emperor Humāyūn, and Bārbūl Mīrzā, and Mihr-jān (jahān) Begam, and Ishān-daulat

[1] Text, *khāna khālī khālahā'ī.* This I do not understand, as there were certainly no mothers' brothers present in Kābul now.

[2] He was twenty-three when he took Kābul from Muḥammad Muqīm *Arghūn* in 1504. Mīrza Khān's rebellion took place two years later.

[3] Fakhru-n-nisāʿ, the Glory of Women. 'She was my first child, and I was just nineteen. In a month, or forty days, she went to the mercy of God.' (Mems. 90.)

[4] Written sometimes *Akām,* and sometimes *Akam.* The Tūrkī *Akā* is used as a title of respect from a junior to a senior. It has also the sense 'elder brother,' which makes application to a woman doubtful. (*Cf.* Vambéry's 'Cagataische Sprach-studien.') Bābar uses the word (Mems. 208.), and Mr. Erskine suggests to read 'My Lady.'

Begam, and Fārūq Mīrzā.[1]

(2.) Maʿṣūma Sulṭān Begam, daughter of Sulṭān Aḥmad Mīrzā, died in childbed. The mother's name they gave to the daughter.

(3.) Of Gul-rukh Begam were born Kāmrān Mīrzā, and ʿAskari Mīrzā, and Shāh-rukh Mīrzā, and Sulṭān Aḥmad Mīrzā, and Gul-ʿiẓār Begam.

(4.) Of Dil-dār Begam were born Gui-rang Begam, and Gul-chihra Begam, and Hindāl Mīrzā, and Gul-badan Begam, and Alwar Mīrzā.[2]

In short, in taking Kābul he got a good omen. All his children were born there except two begams who were born in Khost, viz., Mihr-jān Begam, a daughter of Māham Begam, and Gui-rang, a daughter of Dil-dār Begam. (7*a*)

The blessed birth of the Emperor Humāyūn, the first-born son of his Majesty *Firdaus-makānī,* occurred in the night of Tuesday, Ẓū'l-qaʿda 4th, 913H. (March 6th, 1508), in the citadel of Kābul, and when the sun was in the sign Pisces.

That same year his Majesty was pleased to order the amīrs and the rest of the world to style him emperor (*bādshāh*). For before the birth of the Emperor Humāyūn he had been named and styled Mīrzā Bābar. All kings' sons were called mīrzās. In the year of his Majesty Humāyūn's birth he styled himself *bādshāh.*

They found[3] the date of the birth in *Sulṭān Humāyūn Khān,* and also in *Shāh-(i)-fīroz-qadr.*[4]

After children had been born to him, news came that Shah Ismāʿīl had killed Shāhi Beg Khān.[5]

---

[1] Born 1525; died 1527. His father never saw him.

[2] Gul-badan or her copyist does not balance accounts. She says eighteen, and names sixteen children. This may be a clerical error only.

[3] *i.e.,* by *abjad. Cf.* Steingass' Persian Dictionary, *s.v. abjad.*

[4] 'The king, victorious in might.'

5 At Merv, December 2nd, 1510. *Cf.* B. & H., I. 302. On the removal of this formidable foe, Bābar again tried to regain his ancestral lands, but was still outmatched by the Uzbegs. Defeat by them led him to take a road of less resistance through Bajaur to

His Majesty at this time entrusted Kābul to Nāṣir[1] Mīrzā, and set out[2] for Samarqand, taking with him his people and wives and children, who were Humāyūn Mīrzā, and Mihrjahān Begam, and Bārbūl Mīrzā, and Maʿṣūma Begam, and Kāmrān Mīrzā. (7*b*)

With help from Shāh Ismāʿīl, he took Samarqand (October, 1511), and for eight (lunar) months the whole of Māwarā'u-n-nahr (Transoxiana) was in his power. Owing to want of co-operation in his brothers and to the opposition of the Mughals,[3] he was defeated at Kūl Malik by ʿUbaidu-l-lāh Khān. As he could not remain in those parts, he set out for Badakhshān and Kābul, and put out of his head further thought of Māwarā'u-n-nahr.

He had become master of Kābul in 910H. (1504). He had always desired to go into Hindūstān, and had not carried out his wish because of the feeble counsels of his amīrs and the non-agreement of his brothers. When at length these were gone,[4] and there remained no amīr such as could argue against it, he accomplished his desire.

Bajaur[5] he took in two or three hours and ordered a general massacre.

On the same day the father of Afghānī *āghācha,*[6] Malik Manṣūr Yūsufzai, came in and paid his respects. (8*a*) His Majesty took

---

Hindūstān.

[1] Bābar's half-brother, son of Umīd, an Andijānī.

[2] January, 1511 (Shawwāl, 916H.).

[3] For a more interesting cause of defeat, *Cf.* B. & H., I.321, *et seq.* ʿUbaidu-l-lāh was Shaibānī's nephew. Kūl (Lake) Malik is in Bokhārā. Bābar was again defeated by the Uzbegs in this same year (1511).

[4] *i.e.,* dead. Jahāngīr died in 1507 and Nāṣir in 1515, both from drinking. This passage resembles Bābar's own words. (Mems. 309.)

[5] Gul-badan is confusingly brief. Bajaur was attacked 925H. (1519) on the way to India, and its people put to the sword because they were 'rebels to followers of Islam' and addicted to infidel customs. (Mems. 246 *et seq.)*

[6] The Afghān Lady. It is thus that Gul-badan always speaks of Bībī (Lady) Mubārika, the Yūsufzai wife of Bābar. Pavet de Courteille defines *āghācha* thus: 'Se dit des femmes par opposition à begam et khānam; dame.' I do not in Gul-badan's work trace any disrespect attaching to *'āghācha,'* such as is indicated by '*concubine',* as which it is sometimes translated.

his daughter in marriage and then gave him leave to depart. He bestowed on him a horse and a suit of honour befitting a ruler, and said to him: 'Go and bring men and labourers, etc., to your native land and cultivate it.'

Qāsim Beg,[1] who was in Kābul, sent a letter saying: 'Another prince has been born. I have ventured to write as an omen of the conquest of Hind and of taking its throne. As for the rest, the Emperor is master, whatever is his pleasure'[2] (let it be done). In an auspicious hour his Majesty named him Mīrzā Hindāl.

Having subdued Bajaur, his Majesty went towards the Bhīra country, and on his arrival made peace without plundering. He took four *laks* of *shāhrukhīs*[3] and gave to his army, dividing them according to the number of his followers. He then set out for Kābul.[4]

Just now came a letter from Badakhshān saying: 'Mīrzā Khān is dead;[5] Mīrzā Sulaimān is young; the Uzbegs are near; take thought for this kingdom lest (which God forbid) Badakhshān should be lost.' (8*b*) Until there should be thought taken, Mīrzā Sulaimān's mother[6] had brought him (to the Emperor). Agreeably to this petition and their wish, the Emperor assigned to Mīrzā Sulaimān the lands and inheritance which had been his father's, and he gave Badakhshān to Mīrzā Humāyūn.

The mīrzā set out for his province. His Majesty and my Lady *(Akām)* followed and also went to Badakhshān, and there spent

---

1 Qāsim Beg *Qūchīn,* an ancient Beg of Andijān, and one of Bābar's best followers.

2 Qy., as to the child's name. His true name was Muḥ. Nāṣir, but he is only known as Hindāl. He was Gul-badan's full brother, and was given, before birth, to Māham Begam, who had lost all her children younger than Humāyūn. *Cf.* 24*a* n.

3 Estimated by Mr. Erskine at about £20,000 sterling.

4 End of February, 1519. In his winning fashion Bābar relates that he forbade the news of his return to be taken to Kābul, and that there was therefore no time to put his boys, Humāyūn and Kāmrān, on horseback, and that they were carried out in the arms of the nearest servants to offer their duty on his return, to a place between the fort gates and the citadel.

5 *Cir.* 926H. (1520) . *Cf.* Mems. 286 n., and *Tār. Rash.,* Ney Elias and Ross, 378 n.

6 Sulṭān Nigār Khānam.

several days together. The mīrzā remained and my royal father and my Lady came back to Kābul[1] (926H.—1520).

After a time his Majesty set out for Qilāt and Qandahar.[2] He was victorious at once in Qilāt, and went on to Qandahār and kept its garrison shut up for a year and a half. Then, by the Divine favour and after great fighting and skirmishing, he captured it. Much gold fell into his hands, and he gave moneys and camels to his soldiers and the people of the army. Qandahār he bestowed on Mīrzā Kāmrān, and himself set off for Kābul.

His advance camp having been set up,[3] he crossed the bill of Yak Langa, and gloriously alighted in the valley of Dīh-i-yaʿqūb on Friday, Ṣafar 1st, 932H. (November 17th, 1525), when the sun was in Sagittarius. (9*a*) He spent the following day there, and on the next set forth, march by march, for Hindūstān. In the seven or eight years since 925H. (1519)[4] the royal army had several times renewed the attempt on Hindūstān. Each time it used to conquer lands and districts, such as Bhīra, Bajaur, Sīalkūt, Dīpālpūr, Lāhōr, etc., up to the fifth time, when on Ṣafar 1st, 932H., his Majesty went, march by march, from his glorious encamping in Dīh-i-yaʿqūb towards Hindūstān. He conquered Lāhōr and Sirhind, and every country that lay on his path.

On Friday, Rajab 8th, 932H. (April 20th, 1526), he arrayed battle

---

[1] Humayūn was now thirteen years old. He was young to be sent so far as Badakhshān. That his parents went with him is one of Gul-badan's life-giving touches. *Akam* may now well have shown her boy to her father and her kinsfolk in Khost. (Memoirs of Bāyāzīd, I.O. MS., 26*a*.)

[2] Held now by Shāh Beg *Arghūn,* father of Shāh Ḥusain, Humāyūn's later enemy in Sind. Firishta gives three years as the duration of the siege, Khāfī Khan four years, and Mīrzā Ḥaidar five years. The occurrence unfortunately coincides with one of the gaps in the Memoirs. This was Bābar's culminating attempt on Qandahār; his first being in 1505,—this one seems to have ended in 1522 (928H.).

[3] Gul-badan, by a sudden transition, passes over some three years, and, as it seems, using her father's Memoirs, enters on the account of his last and successful expedition to Hindūstān. Yak Langa, is a hill between Kābul and Butkhāk, and on the road to Jalālābād.

[4] Text, 935H.; clearly a slip.

at Panipat[1] against Sulṯān Ibrāhīm, son of Sulṯān Sikandar, son of Bahlūl *Lodī.* By God's grace he was victorious, and Sulṯān Ibrāhīm was killed in the fight. His victory was won purely by the Divine grace, for Sulṯān Ibrāhīm had a *lak* and 80,000 horse, and as many as 1,500 head of fierce elephants; (9*b*) while his Majesty's army with the traders and good and all (*badr* (?) *bad,* bad) was 12,000 persons and he had, at the outside, 6,000 or 7,000 serviceable men.

The treasures of five kings fell into his hands. He gave everything away. The amīrs of Hind represented that in Hindūstān it was thought disgraceful to expend the treasure of bygone kings, and that people rather added and added to it, while his Majesty, on the contrary, had given all away.[2]

Khwāja[3] Kilān[4] Beg asked leave several times to go to Kābul. He said: 'My constitution is not fitted for the climate of Hindūstān. If leave were given, I should tarry awhile in Kābul.' His Majesty was not at all, at all willing for him to go, but at last gave permission because he saw him so very urgent. He said: 'When you go, I shall send some of the valuable presents and curiosities of Hind which fell

---

1 A far-reaching, almost illimitable level tract, broken only by insignificant undulations. Here and there, where the shallow soil is moistened from some niggardly watercourse, grow sparse grasses and stunted thorn-bushes. But, for the most part, the eye falls only on the uniform yellowish-gray waste of sterile earth. Everywhere empty silence reigns, and it would almost seem as if this desert had been designed for the battlefield of nations.' (Emperor Akbar, F. v. Noer., trs. A.S.B. I. 74.)

Thrice in modern times a decisive battle has been fought out here: (1) by Bābar against Ibrāhīm and the Lodīs, 1526; (2) by Akbar against the Indian Afghāns in 1556; and (3) by Aḥmad Shāh Durrānī against the Marathas in 1761.

2 Bābar distributed the treasure on the 11th or 12th of May, 1526, and left himself so little that he was dubbed *qalandar.*

3 M. Garçin de Tassy says, in his 'Mémoire sur la Religion Musalmane' (46 n.) that khwāja, like sayyid, is a title for a descendant of Muḥammad. Shaw's Tūrkī Dictionary states that khwāja is applied to the offspring of a sayyid by a woman of another family, also to their descendants. I find many instances where both titles are applied to the same man.

4 One of Bābar's most admirable followers and friends, and perhaps a relation. He was one of seven brothers, sons of Maulānā Muḥammad *Ṣadru-d-dīn,* who spent their lives in Bābar's service.

into our hands through the victory over Sulṭān Ibrāhīm, to my elder relations[1] and sisters and each person of the *ḥaram.* You take them. I shall write a list, and you will distribute them according to it. (10*a*) You will order a tent with a screen to be set up in the Garden of the Audience Hall for each begam, [2] and when a pleasant meeting-place has been arranged, the begams are to make the prostration of thanks for the complete victory which has been brought about.

'To each begam is to be delivered as follows: one special dancing-girl of the dancing-girls of Sulṭān Ibrāhīm, with one gold plate full of jewels—ruby and pearl, cornelian and diamond, emerald and turquoise, topaz and cat's-eye—and two small mother-o'-pearl trays full of *ashrafīs,* and on two other trays *shāhrukhīs,*[3] and all sorts of stuffs by nines—that is, four trays and one plate. Take a dancing-girl and another plate of jewels, and one each of *ashrafīs* and *shāhrukhīs,* and present, in accordance with my directions, to my elder relations the very plate of jewels and the self same dancing-girl which I have given for them. I have made other gifts;[4] convey these afterwards. (10*b*) Let them divide and present jewels and *ashrafīs* and *shah-rukhīs* and stuffs to my sisters and children and the *ḥarams*[5] and kinsmen, and to the begams and āghās[6] and

---

[1] *walīyu-n-ni'matān,* lords of beneficence. Gul-badan's application of it is to 'benevolent ladies,' *i.e.,* the numerous aunts. It is a title of respect for seniors.

[2] I think each begam was to encamp with her own establishment and within her own enclosure (*sarāparda*), and not in hasty camp fashion of community of quarters. This would exalt the assembly.

The *sarapārda* or enclosing canvas wall, run at optional distance round tents, was, it is stated in the *Ma'āsir-i-raḥīmī,* invented by Bairam *Khān-i-khānān,* and if this is true, it must at this date have been a quite modern convenience.

[3] It is waste of time to try to estimate the amount of these money gifts, made as they were in coins of uncertain value and recorded, probably on hearsay, more than fifty years after bestowal. Mr. Erskine puts the *shāhrukhī* at from l0d. to ls., Steingass, *s.v.ashrafī,* gives for its value about 16 *rupīs,* presumably of undegenerated rank.

[4] Qy., for the elder relations.

[5] Presumably of his kinsmen and of officers whose families were with Bābar's own in Kābul.

[6] This word seems to describe women who were heads of household departments and

nurses and foster-brethren and ladies, and to all who pray for me.' The gifts were made according to the list.

Three happy days they remained together in the Audience Hall Garden. They were uplifted by pride, and recited the *fātiḥa*[1] for the benediction and prosperity of his Majesty, and joyfully made the prostration of thanks.[2]

The Emperor sent by Khwāja Kilān a large *ashrafī;*[3] which weighed three imperial *sīr,* that is, fifteen *sīr* of Hind, for . . . 'Asas.[4] He said to the Khwāja: 'If 'Asas asks you, "What has the Emperor sent for me?" say, "One *ashrafī,*"' as there really was only one. 'Asas was amazed, and fretted about it for three days. His Majesty had ordered that a hole should be bored in the *ashrafī,* and that 'Asas should be blindfolded and the *ashrafī* hung round his neck, and that then he was to be sent into the *ḥaram.* The hole was bored and the *ashrafī* hung round his neck. He was quite helpless with surprise at its weight, and delighted and very, very happy. He took it in both hands, and wondered over it and said, 'No one shall get my *ashrafī.*' Each begam, too, gave (? him) ten or twelve *ashrafī,* so he had seventy or eighty. (11*a*)

---

not merely the guardians of *ḥarams.*

1 The first chapter of the Qurān.

2 In this prostration the forehead touches the ground.

3 Perhaps from the Lodi treasury. (*Cf* J.A.S.B. Proceedings, 1883; Thomas, 423; Richardson's Ar. & Per. Dict., *s.v. sikka;* Memoirs of the Mughal Empire, Jonathan Scott, 3 and 3 n.)

4 Lit. a night-guard. The words preceding 'Asas offer much difficulty. They may be read *ba 'ammū,—to* the paternal uncle of 'Asas. But the story is of 'Asas, the night-guard and not of his uncle. Perhaps *'ammū* is a clerical error for *'amah,* bewilderment, misleading, and this would suit the story well. Mr. Beveridge has suggested to me to read *'Umarī, i.e.,* an old servant of 'Umar Shaikh. This, too, would be appropriate, for the victim of the hoax is clearly an old man.

The title 'Asas is applied several times by Bābar. One 'Asas was a boon companion and partook of Bābar's vow before the battle of Khānwa. (Mems. 283 and 354; Firishta, Pers. Text, Briggs I.449.) Gul-badan names one (20*b*) as entrusted with the care of Bābar's tomb,—Muḥ 'Alī *'Asas.* I think he was brother to Māham Begam, and the governor of Kābul whom Kāmrān murdered in 1547.

After Khwāja Kilān Beg had started for Kābul, the Emperor made gifts in Agra to his Majesty Humāyūn and to all the Mīrzās and Sulṯāns and amīrs. He sent letters in all directions, urgently saying, 'We shall take into full favour all who enter our service, and especially such as served our father and grandfather and ancestors. If such will come to us, they will receive fitting benefits. Whoever there may be of the families of *Ṣāḥib-qirān* and Chingīz Khān, let them turn towards our court. The most High has given us sovereignty in Hindūstān; let them come that we may see prosperity together.'

Seven[1] daughters of Sulṯān Abū-sa'īd came (to Hindūstān): Gūhar-shād Begam, and Fakhr-jahān Begam, and Khadīja Sulṯān Begam, and Badī'u-l-jamāl Begam, and Āq Begam, and Sulṯān Bakht Begam.

(Also) Zainab Sulṯān Kḥānam, daughter of his Majesty's maternal uncle, Sulṯān Maḥmūd Khān, and Muḥibb Sulṯān Kḥānam,[2] daughter of *Ilācha* Khān (Aḥmad), his Majesty's younger maternal uncle.

In short, all the begams and khānams went, ninety-six persons in all, and all received houses and lands and gifts to their heart's desire. (11*b*)

All through the four years that (my father) was in Āgra he used to go on Fridays to see his paternal aunts. One day it was extremely hot, and her Highness my lady *(Akām)* said, 'The wind is very hot, indeed; how would it be if you did not go this one Friday? The begams would not be vexed.' His Majesty said, 'Māham! it is astonishing that you should say such things! The daughters of Abū-sa'īd Sulṯān Mīrzā, who have been deprived of father and brothers! If I do not cheer them, how will it be done?'

To the architect, Khwāja Qāsim, his Majesty gave the following order: 'We command a piece of good service from you. It is this: whatever work, even if it be on a great scale, our paternal aunts may

---

[1] Six only named.

[2] Wife of Mīrzā Ḥaidar *Dughlāt,* the historian.

order done in their palace, give it precedence, and carry it out with might and main.'

He commanded buildings to be put up in Āgra on the other side of the river,[1] and a stone palace to be built for himself between the *ḥaram* and the garden. He also had one built in the audience court, with a reservoir in the middle and four chambers in the four towers. On the river's bank he had a *chaukandī*[2] built. (12*a*)

He ordered a tank made in Dholpūr, ten by ten,[3] out of a single mass of rock, and used to say, 'When it is finished, I will fill it with wine.' But as he had given up wine before the fight with Rānā Sangā, he filled it with lemonade.

A year after Sulṭān Ibrāhīm's death, the rānā[4] appeared from the Mandū (or Hindu) side with a countless host. Amīrs and rājas and rānās, every one of those who had come earlier and paid duty to his Majesty, now became an enemy and went and joined the rānā, until Kūl-jalālī and Sambhal and Rāprī—every *pargana,*—and rāis and rajas and Afghāns became hostile. Nearly two *laks* of cavalry assembled.

At this time, Muḥammad Sharīf, the astrologer, said to the royal soldiers, 'It would be best for the Emperor not to fight, for the constellation *Sakkiz Yildoz* (Eight Stars) is opposite.' Amazing perturbation fell upon the royal army. They became exceedingly anxious and troubled,[5] and showed signs of cowardice. (12*b*) When

---

[1] *i.e.,* opposite the fort.

[2] 'A building on the roof which has a door on each of the four sides.' Vullers, 602. Badāonī uses *ghurfa,* upper room, as an equivalent. *Cf.* Elliot's History of India, V. 347 and 503.

[3] About 20 feet by 20 feet. (Mems. 398 n..)

[4] This decisive battle was fought on March 16th, 1527, on the skirts of the hill of Sīkrī, at Khānwa. Akbar's *prænomen* of Fatḥipūr—the City of Victory—was given to Sikri in 1573 to commemorate the Gujrat campaign.

[5] When the fight had been won, Bābar soundly rated Muḥammad Sharīf, gave him money, and dismissed him to the place from which he had emerged, apparently only to cause trouble. He had come to India with a royal kinsman from Kābul, and to Kābul in 1519 from Khost (Māham's home).

his Majesty saw his army in this state, he thought over the whole position. As the enemy was close at hand, this device occurred to his blessed mind; he ordered the remnant of what remained over and above deserters and enemies, to gather together. One and all came—amīrs and khāns and Sulṯāns; plebeian and noble, low and high. Then he addressed them, and said: 'Do you not know that there lies a journey of some months between us and the land of our birth and our familiar city? If our side is defeated, (God preserve us from that day! God forbid it!) where are we? where is our birthplace? where our city? We have to do with strangers and foreigners. It is in every way best for each man to set resolutely before himself the two alternatives: if we win, we are avengers of the cause of God; if we lose, we die martyrs. In either fate is our salvation; each is a step and upward stage in greatness.'

To this they all agreed. They swore by the divorce of their wives and on the Holy Book; they recited the *fātiḥa,* and said, 'O King! God willing, we will not spare ourselves in sacrifice and devotion, so long as there are breath and life in our bodies.'[1] (13*a*)

Two days before the battle his Majesty renounced wine, and, indeed, he forswore all forbidden things. Following his example, 400 young men of name, who had given proof of manliness and one-mindedness and friendship, also renounced these things when he did. His Majesty broke up all forbidden utensils,—vessels of gold and of silver, goblets and flasks, etc.; and he gave them to the poor and needy.

He also sent abroad *firmāns* with the announcement: 'We exempt (you) from all dues and octroi and tithe on corn, and from all illegal imposts, so that no one, trader or other, may be hampered in his comings and goings, but all may move unmolested and free from

[1] Mr. Erskine thus gives Bābar's words: 'Every man dies. God only survives unchangeable. He who comes to life's feast must drink the parting cup of death. How much better to die with honour than to live with infamy!'

Perhaps, as Gul-badan says, Bābar touched also the thought of home, and this would be recorded by the woman.

interference.'

In the night[1] before the battle word was brought that Qāsim Ḥusain Sulṭān,—a grandson of Sulṭān Ḥusain Mīrzā through a daughter, 'Āyisha Sulṭān Begam,—had come to within ten *kōs* (of the royal camp) on his way from Khurāsān. (13*b*)

This news delighted his Majesty greatly. He asked, 'How many men are with him?' When he heard 'thirty or forty,' he at once sent off 1,000 troopers, all armed and equipped, at midnight, so that they might march in again with Qāsim Ḥusain Sulṭān, and in this way the enemy and outsiders be let know that reinforcements had come in good time. Everyone who heard the plan thought it a good one. Next morning, which was March 16th, 1527 (Jumāda II [13th], 933H.), his Majesty arrayed battle against Rānā Sangā on the skirts of the hill of Sīkrī, where now Fatḥpur has been built[2] and peopled By the Divine grace he was victorious and became an avenger of the cause of God.[3]

A year later my lady (*akām*), who was Māham Begam, came from Kābul to Hindūstān. I, this insignificant one, came with her in advance of my sisters, and paid my duty to my royal father. When my lady reached Kūl(-jalālī—*i.e.*, 'Alighar), his Majesty had sent two litters with three horsemen. (14*a*) She went on post-haste from Kūl to Āgra. His Majesty had intended to go as far as Kūl-jalālī to meet her. At evening-prayer time someone came and said to him: 'I have just passed her Highness on the road, four miles out.' My royal father did not wait for a horse to be saddled but set out on

---

[1] Bābar says that Qāsim had come earlier and with 500 men. Muḥ. Sharīf, the 'rascally fellow' and 'evil-minded wretch,' was with him. (Mems., 352.)

[2] How beautifully built may, in small part, be seen by visiting the Oriental section of the South Kensington Museum and there examining the architectural reproductions, the drawings of Mr. W. B. Carpenter, the photographs, etc. The South Kensington Museum and the British Museum furnish numerous illustrations for Gul-badan Begam's MS., and add to it the charm of life and reality.

[3] *Ghāzī.* Bābar now assumed this title, because he had vanquished non-Muḥammadans.

foot. He met her near the house of Māham's *nanacha.*[1] She wished to alight, but he would not wait, and fell into her train and walked to his own house.[2]

At the time of her meeting his Majesty, she desired me to come on by daylight and pay my respects to him.

. . . [3]nine troopers, with two sets of nine horses and the two extra litters which the Emperor had sent, and one litter which had been brought from Kābul, and about a hundred of my lady's Mughal servants, mounted on fine (*tipūchāq*) horses,[4] all elegance and beauty.[5]

My royal father's Khalīfa[6] with his wife Sulṯanam[7] came as far as Naugrām[8] to meet (us). My *māmās*[9] had made me alight at the Little Garden, and having spread a small carpet, seated me on it. They

---

1 *dar pesh khāna nanacha Māham.* This might read 'in the advance camp.'Māham's *nanacha* appears thrice in the MS: here and at 18*b* and *26a.* She is clearly of the innermost circle. The word may be rendered 'dear little mother,' and is one of close affection.

2 *Cf.* Mems., 423.

3 *tūqūz.* The Tūrks made kings' gifts by nines and attached superstitious reverence to the number.

4 *A tipūchāq* horse, according to Shaw, is long-necked like a Tūrkmān horse, and it seems also to be one with speed, beauty, and specially-trained paces. Vambéry says, 'ein fettes, gutes Pferd.'

5 The above passage is inserted without break in the text and suggests transcription from an imperfect MS. It may be an enumeration of the items of the cortége which followed Māham with Gul-badan.

6 Sayyid or Khwāja Nizāmu-d-dīn 'Alī *Barlās* and Bābar's *vazīr.* His brother, Junaid *Barlās,* married Shahr-bānū, a half-sister of Bābar.

7 Clearly an intimate. There were close relations, as has been said, between this *Barlās* family and Bābar. *Cf.* Biographical Appendix, *s.n.* Sulṯanam.

8 Some four miles from Agra and on the east of the Jamna. The royal palace was not yet built on the western bank. *Cf.* Rājpūtāna Gazetteer, III. 274.

9 Steingass translates 'mother,' 'matron,' and 'old women.' One *māmā* is named later, 'Fakhru-n-nisā', my māmā.' (26*a*) She was the mother of Nadīm Khwāja *kūka.* She is several times mentioned, and it appears from a MS. belonging to Colonel Hanna which Mr. Beveridge has examined, that she was mother-in-law of the celebrated Māham *anaga* who was Nadīm's wife.

instructed me to rise when Khalīfa came in, and to embrace him. When he came, I rose and embraced him. Then his wife Sulṭanam came in too. (14*b*) I, not knowing, wished to get up, but Khalīfa raised objections, and said: 'She is your old serving-woman. There is no need to rise for her. Your father has exalted this old servant (? himself) by giving such an order[1] about him. So be it! what power have slaves?'

From Khalīfa I accepted 6,000 *shāhrukhīs* and five horses, and Sulṭānam gave me 3,000 and three horses. Then she said: '*A* hasty meal *(mā hazarī)* is ready. If you will eat you will honour your servants.' I consented. There was a raised platform in a pleasant spot, and a pavilion of red cloth with lining of Gujrātī brocade, and six canopies of cloth and brocade, each of a (differing) colour, and a square enclosure[2] of cloth with painted poles.

I sat in Khalīfa's quarters. The meal drew out to almost fifty roast sheep,[3] and bread and sherbet and much fruit. Having at length eaten my breakfast, I got into my litter and went and paid my duty to my royal father. (15*a*)

I fell at his feet; he asked me many questions, and took me for a time in his arms, and then this insignificant person felt such happiness that greater could not be imagined.

When we had been in Agra three months, the Emperor went to Dholpūr. Her Highness Māham Begam and this lowly person also went. *A* tank had been made there, ten (*gaz*) by ten, out of one piece (of rock). From Dholpūr his Majesty went on to Sīkrī. He ordered a great platform made in the middle of the tank, and when it was

[1] (?) as that she should rise to greet him.

[2] Text, *chahār chiūqa-i-sarāparda. Cf. Notices et Extraits,* Quatre-mère, XIV. 498.

[3] The 'fifty' sheep will not reduce by any reading I can suggest. *Cf. anglice* 'heaps of,' 'hundreds of,' etc. Perhaps the flock is a product of childish weariness recalled half a century later. Possibly one should read *panj āhār,* five foods, *i.e.,* courses, dishes. Gul-badan is now between five and six. Her doubt as to the reception due to Sulṭānam rings true, and Khalīfa's words suggest a little play-acting to please the small traveller; he treated her like a grown-up, and she tried to act one.

ready, he used to go and sit on it, or to row about. This platform still exists.

They also made a *chaukandī* in the Sīkrī garden, and my royal father put up in it a *tūr-khāna,*[1] where he used to sit and write his book.[2]

I and Afghānī *āghācha* were sitting in the front of the lower storey when my lady went to prayers. I said to Afghānī *āghācha:* 'Pull my hand.' She pulled, and my hand came out. My strength went and I cried. (15*b*) Then they brought the bone-setter and when he had bound up my hand, the Emperor went to Āgra.

After his arrival, word was brought that the begams were on the way from Kābul. My royal father went as far as Naugrām to give honourable reception to my dearest lady (*aka-jānam*),[3] who was my oldest paternal aunt and my royal father's eldest sister. All the begams who had come with her, paid their duty to the Emperor in her quarters. They were very happy and made the prostration of thanks, and then set off for Āgra. The Emperor gave houses to all the begams.

A few days later he made an excursion to the Gold-scattering Garden (*Bāgh-i-zar-afshān*). There was a place in it for ablution before prayers. When he saw it, he said: 'My heart is bowed down by ruling and reigning; I will retire to this garden. As for attendance, Tāhir the ewer-bearer will amply suffice. I will make over the kingdom to Humāyūn.' On this my lady (*akām*) and all his children broke down, and said with tears: 'God keep you in His own peace upon the throne many, many years, and may all your children after you reach a good old age!' (16*a*)

A few days later Alwar Mīrzā fell ill. His illness led to an affection of the bowels, which grew worse and worse in spite of all

---

1 "Perhaps a space enclosed by a low railing." (Mems., 202 n..) Possibly and suitably, a mosquito-room (*taur*, net). *Cf.* Khwānd-amīr, B.M. Or. 1,762, and Add. 30,774, ff. 25-114.

2 The *Tūzūk-i-bābarī*.

3 Khānzāda Begam.

that the doctors could do, and at last he passed from this transitory world to the eternal home. His Majesty was very sad and sorry, and Alwar's mother, Dil-dār Bēgam, was wild with grief for the child, who was a rarity of the world and unique of the age. As her lamentation passed due bounds, his Majesty said to my lady and the begams: 'Come, let us make an excursion to Dholpūr.' He himself went comfortably and pleasantly by water, and the begams also begged to go by boat.

Just then there came a letter from Maulānā Muhammad Farghārī (Parghālī) in Dihlī, saying: 'Humāyūn Mīrzā is ill and in an extraordinary state. Her Highness the begam should come at once to Dihlī, for the mīrzā is much prostrated.'[1] (16*b*)

My lady was very much upset on hearing this news, and started for Dihlī, like one athirst who is far from the waters. They met in Mathura. To her experienced eye he seemed ten times weaker and more alarmingly ill than she had heard he was. From Mathura the two, mother and son, like Jesus and Mary, set out for Āgra. When they arrived, this insignificant one went with her own sisters to visit that royal angel of goodness.

He was then growing weaker and weaker. Every time he came to his senses, his pearl-dropping tongue asked for us, and said: 'Sisters, you are welcome! Come, and let us embrace one another. I have not embraced you.' It might be three times that he raised his head and that his jewel-dropping tongue let fall these uplifting words.

When his Majesty came and saw how it was, his light-revealing countenance at once became sad and pitiful, and he began more and more to show signs of dread. (*17a*) On this my lady said: 'Do not be troubled about my son. You are a king; what griefs have you? You have other sons. I sorrow because I have only this

---

[1] *Cf. Bābar-nāma*, Ilminsky, 502 *et seq.*, and P. de Courteille, II. 457 *et seq.*, where is one of the supplementary fragments included in Kehr's *Bābar-nāma* (Tūzūk) and possibly taken from the Bukhārā MS. (*Cf.* Notes on the Tūrkī texts of the *Bābar-nāma*, A. S. Beveridge. Journal of the Royal Asiatic Society, July, 1900.)

BĀBAR IN PRAYER, DEVOTING HIMSELF FOR HIS SON.

[*To face p.* 105.

one.'[1] His Majesty rejoined: 'Māham! although I have other sons, I love none as I love your Humāyūn. I crave that this cherished child may have his heart's desire and live long, and I desire the kingdom for him and not for the others, because he has not his equal in distinction.'

During Humāyūn's illness[2] his Majesty walked round him and turned his face (in intercession) to his Reverence, Murtaẓa 'Alī Karīmu-l-lāh. He kept up that going-round from the Wednesday and made intercession from the Tuesday, in anxiety and deep dejection. The weather was extremely hot and his heart and liver burned. While going round he prayed, saying in effect: 'O God! if a life may be exchanged for a life, I who am Bābar, I give my life and my being for Humāyūn.'[3]

That very day he fell ill, and Humāyūn poured water on his head, and came out and gave audience. (17*b*) Because of his illness, they carried my royal father within, and he kept his bed for two or three months.

As he grew worse, a messenger was sent to summon his Majesty Humāyūn, who had gone towards Kalinjar. He came post-haste, and on paying his duty to the Emperor, noticed that he was very feeble. Filled with compassion, he began to break down, and kept

---

[1] All Māham's other children died in childhood.

[2] The account of Bābar's self-surrender which follows is somewhat puzzling to translate, but the sense is clear and the important statements are in accordance with other sources.

[3] One of Kehr's (Ilminsky's) 'fragments' (which, if it be not Bābar's own, it is not improbable was added to the *Tūzūk* by Jahāngīr) tells this story in Bābar's person. After rejection of the suggestion to sacrifice for Humāyūn's life the great diamond (? the Koh-i-*nūr*), the narrative continues (P. de C., II. 460.): 'J'entrai dans la chambre où il se tenait, et je tournai trois fois autour de lui, en commençant par la tête et en disant, "J'assume sur moi tout ce que tu souffres." En même instant je me sentis tout alourdi, tandis que lui se trouvait léger et dispos. Il se leva en pleine santé, etmoi je m'affaissai, accablé de malaise.'

Faith in the rite of circumambulation still prevails in Persia. Bābar, it is clear, believed his devotion to have borne fruit. (*Cf.* Hughes, Dict. of Islām, s.v. Intercession. For Karīmu-l-lāh, see Badāyunī, *Bib. Ind.* Text, III. 191.).

saying to the attendants: 'How has he come to such a lamentable pass all at once?' He sent for the doctors, and said to them: 'I left him well. What has happened all at once?' They said this and that in reply.

The whole time my royal father kept repeating: 'Where is Hindāl? What is he doing?' Just at this time some-one came in and said: 'Mīr Bardī Beg, the son of Mīr Khurd Beg,[1] conveys his obeisance.' My royal father, full of agitation, sent for him at once and asked: 'Where is Hindāl? When will he come? What trouble waiting gives!' (18*a*) Mīr Bardī said: 'The fortunate prince has reached Dihlī; he will wait on you to-day or to-morrow.' On this my royal father said to Mīr Bardī Beg: 'Ill-fated little fellow! I have heard that they married your sister in Kābul, and you in Lāhōr.[2] It is because of the wedding festivities that you have (not)[3] sooner brought my son, and so my weary waiting has been very long.' He asked: 'How tall has Hindāl Mīrzā grown?' and 'What is he like?' As Mīr Bardī was wearing one of the mīrzā's dresses, he showed it and said: 'This is a robe of the prince which he bestowed on his servant.' His Majesty called him nearer and said: 'Let me see how tall and how big Hindāl has grown.'[4] He kept repeating, 'Alas! a thousand times alas! that I do not see Hindāl,' and asking evervone who came in: 'When will Hindāl come?'

During his illness, he laid a command on my lady, and said: 'Marriages ought to be arranged for Gul-rang Begam and Gul-chihra Begam. (18*b*) When the royal aunt, my elder sister,[5] honours me with

---

[1] Hindāl's guardian from birth (1519-1530). He had previously been Bābar's bakāwal (house-steward). One of his sons, Khwāja Tāhir Muhammad, served under Humāyūn and Akbar, and was mīr farāghaṭ (master of comfort). He may be the Mīr Bardī (qy. a child's sobriquet, Master Full-of-fun) of this episode. Tāhir's son, Bāqī, was a sewer, *i.e.*, table-decker (*sufra*-chī).

[2] Hindāl, with whom doubtless Mīr Bardī and his father were travelling, was on his way from Badakhshān to the court.

[3] The text has no negative.

[4] Hindāl was now about eleven years old, so Mīr Bardī must also have been a boy.

[5] Khānzāda Begam—*aka-jānam*—dearest lady.

a visit, tell her that I say it has occurred to me to give Gul-rang to Isān-tīmūr Sulṭān and Gul-chihra to Tūkhta-būghā Sulṭān.'[1]

Dearest lady, the smiling one,[2] came, and they said to her: 'The Emperor spoke in this manner, and it has occurred to him in such a way. It now remains to know your pleasure. Let it be as you wish.' She said the same and, 'God grant blessing and peace! His idea is very good.' My *chīcha*[3] herself and Badī'u-l-jamāl Begam and Āq Begam, both of whom were paternal aunts of his Majesty, were conducted into the hall. Having raised an estrade[4] and spread carpets and chosen a propitious hour, Māham's *nanacha* made

---

[1] Isān (Ishān, or Yussun) was the ninth, and Tūkhta-būghā the tenth, son of Aḥmad Khān, Bābar's maternal imcle. They were uncles of Gul-badan's own husband, Khiẓr Khwāja.

[2] *tabassum kunān*.

[3] This Tūrkī word presents great difficulty.

Vambéry has jīcha, Kirghiz, mother, and *chīcha*, aunt (inferentially maternal); Shaw, *chīchā*, Qāzzāq, mother. P. de Courteille, Dict., *chīcha*, an elder sister. The word has in Samarqand the meaning 'maternal aunt.'

It occurs again in the text (23*a*), and is used for Gul-badan's sisters, the brides of this page (19*a*) ; so that it may be right (spite of the singular number) to read 'my elder sisters themselves'—*i.e.*, the brides. But it might be 'my mother.'

The word occurs at least once in the Memoirs. (Ilm., 446 ; Ers., 387.) It is preceded by one which Ilminsky writes *yanka*, and Erskine *Bikeh* (Bega). The letters of both words might be identical and the points only decisive. Shaw says yangā is an elder brother's wife ; Vambéry, *belle-sœur*, *Schwagerin*; and Erskine (208 n. .), bridesmaid, by which, I believe, is meant one who leads the bride to the bridegroom—an exactly appropriate use here, since Habība *yangā* brings her daughter Ma'sūma to marry Bābar. (N.B.—Shaw writes *yangā* and *chīchā*, where Vambéry and others have a final 'round *hā*.')

But if the *chīcha* of Mems., 387, is to be read 'elder sister,' Bābar can apply it only to Khānzāda Begam (elsewhere called by him *aulugh īgāchī* (Ilm., 116.); and this would, I believe, make the reading of *Bikeh* (*Bega*) difficult, since Khānzāda could not be called anything less than Khānam. The same objection would applv to the reading of *chīcha* as mother or as maternal aunt. This inclines one to read *yanka*, and not *bikeh*, at Mems., 387 ; and the Zainab of the sentence may be granddaughter (*nabīra*), through the female line, of the *belle-sœur*, or bridesmaid, of Khānzāda Begam. But nothing is clear as to the relationship.

[4] Text, *ṣufā dāda*. Perhaps, content was given to all, but *ṣuffa*, estrade, fits better with the following basāṭ.

both *sulṭāns* bow the knee[1] in order to exalt them to the rank of sons-in-law.

Meantime his Majesty's disorder of the bowels increased. The Emperor Humāyūn broke down again when he saw his father's condition worsen, and called the doctors, and said to them: 'Think it well over and find some remedy.' (19*a*) Having consulted together, they said: 'Small is our luck, for our remedies are of no avail. We hope that God, the most Holy, will soon give one from His invisible treasures.'

When they felt his Majesty's pulse, they came to the opinion that there were symptoms of the same poison as that given him by Sulṭān Ibrāhīm's mother. It was in this way: that ill-fated demon (the mother) gave a *tāla* of poison to one of her maids, and said: 'Take this and give it to Aḥmad the taster and tell him to put it in some way or other into the special dishes prepared for the Emperor.' And she promised him large rewards. The ill-fated demon did this although his Majesty used to call her "mother," and had assigned her place and lands with every favour, and had been kindly pleased to say: 'Consider me as in the place of Sulṭān Ibrāhīm.'[2] But as ignorance prevails amongst those people, she did not regard his kindnesses. The (fitting) hemistich is well known:

'Evervthing reverts to its original type,
(*Whether pure gold, or silver, or tin*).'[3]

To cut short the story: the cook (Heaven having made him blind and deaf,) spread the poison which had been brought and given to him, on the Emperor's bread only, and so little was eaten. But the symptoms of this illness were like that one's, seeing that day by day he lost strength and became more and more emaciated. (19*b*) Every

---

[1] *Zānū zanā'īnda*, literally, 'striking the knee.' Mems., 204 n..

[2] Her son, who died fighting Bābar at Pānīpat.

[3] Pers. and Hind. Proverbs, T. Roebuck, Calcutta, 1824, p. 124, and Mems., 13.

day the disorder increased and his blessed countenance changed.

Next day[1] he called his chiefs together and spoke after this wise: 'For years it has been in my heart to make over my throne to Humāyūn Mīrzā and to retire to the Gold-scattering Garden. By the Divine grace I have obtained all things but the fulfilment of this wish in health of body. Now, when illness has laid me low, I charge you all to acknowledge Humāyūn in my stead. Fail not in loyalty to him. Be of one heart and one mind with him. I hope to God that Humāyūn also will bear himself well towards men.

'Moreover, Humāyūn, I commit to God's keeping you and your brothers and all my kinsfolk and your people and my people; and all of these I confide to you.'

At these words hearers and onlookers wept and lamented. His own blessed eyes also filled with tears.

When his family and the people within the *ḥaram* heard of these occurrences, they were stupefied and overwhelmed, and cried and lamented.

Three days later he passed from this transitory world to the eternal home. The death took place on Monday, December 26th, 1530 (Jumāda I. 5th, 987H.). (20*a*)

They brought out our paternal aunt[2] and our mothers[3] on the pretence that the doctors were coming to look. All rose. They took all the begams and my mothers to the Great House.[4]

Black fell the day for children and kinsfolk and all. They bewailed and lamented; voices were uplifted in weeping; there was utter dejection. Each passed that ill-fated day in a hidden corner.

The death was kept concealed. After a time Araish Khān,—he was an amīr of Hind,—said: 'It is not well to keep the death secret, because when such misfortunes befall kings in Hindūstān, it is

[1] (?) after Humāyūn's arrival.

[2] Khānzāda Begam.

[3] Bābar's wives.

[4] Perhaps 'palace,' and the sense may be that they did not go to their separate residences but remained nearer to the dead.

the custom of the *bāzār* people to rob and steal; God forbid that the Mughals not knowing, they should come and loot the houses and dwelling-places. It would be best to dress someone in red, and to set him on an elephant, and to let him proclaim that the Emperor Bābar has become a dervish and has given his throne to the Emperor Humāyūn.' This his Majesty Humāyūn ordered to be done. People were at once re-assured by the proclamation, and all offered prayers for his welfare. On Friday, December 29th, 1530 (Jumāda I. 9th, 937H.), the Emperor Humāyūn mounted the throne, and everyone said: 'May all the world be blessed under his rule.' (20*b*)

After that he came to visit his mothers and sisters and his own people, and he made inquiry after their health and offered sympathy, and spoke with kindness and commiseration. He was pleased to order: 'Let each keep the office, and service, and lands, and residence which he has had, and let him serve in the old way.'

On the same day Hindāl Mīrzā, having come from Kābul, paid his homage to the Emperor, who received him with kindness, and was very happy, and bestowed on him many things from the treasures left by their father.

After my royal father's death, there were the good works and consecrated days of the first assembly[1] at his tomb.[2] His Majesty

---

[1] *ma'rka*. Raverty (Afghān Dict..) gives as the first meaning of this word 'a party of ambassadors, or persons sent to make peace between two tribes'; and, secondly, as 'the business of making peace, or an arrangernent between two tribes.' Lane and other writers render it 'battle-field' and 'battle,' etc. Steingass adds 'hubbub, turmoil' (modern colloquial). Gul-badan uses it for the common social assemblies she names, and here for the gathering of relations at a tomb.

[2] Bābar's body was laid first in the Rām or Arām Bāgh (Garden of Rest), on the opposite side of the river from the present *Tāj-mahāll*. Later it was taken to Kābul. Mr. Erskine (B. & M., I. 517 *et seq*..) quotes a charming passage from Burns' 'Travels in Bokhārā' (II. 121 *et seq*.), which deseribes Bābar's self-chosen resting-place. He follows this by an eloquent estimate of Bābar's character which makes clear his regret in bidding farewell to the great and vivid personality he has so admirably set before his readers.

named Muhammad 'Alī *'asas*[1] its guardian, and ordered the appointment of sixty good reciters of the whole Qurān and readers with good voices, so that the congregational prayers might be said five times daily and the whole Qurān recited, and prayer offered for the soul of the royal dweller in Paradise (*Firdaus-makānī*). (21*a*) The whole of Sīkrī—now known as Fathpūr—together with five *laks* charged on Bayāna, was given as an endowment to the tomb, for the support of the men of learning (*'ulamā*) and the reciters who were attached to it.

My lady made an allowance of food twice daily: in the morning an ox and two sheep and five goats, and at afternoon prayer-time five goats. She gave this from her own estate during the two and a half years that she remained in the prison of this world.

During my lady's life I used to see his Majesty in her residence. When she fell into bad health, she said to me: 'It will be very hard that when I am gone, the Emperor Bābar's daughters should see their brother in Bībī Gulbarg's[2] house.' Just as though her words were in the royal heart and mind, his Majesty used always, so long as he was in Hindūstān, to come to our house. He used to visit us and showed us kindness and affection and favour without stint. He used to come to the house of this insignificant one, and there would come Ma'ṣūma Sulṭān Begam, and Gul-rang Begam, and Gul-chihra Begam,[3] etc.—all the married ladies—and pay their duty to him. (21*b*)

In short, after the death of my royal father and my lady, his Majesty, in the fulness of his affection, showed this broken one such favour, and spoke with such boundless compassion to this helpless one, that she did not know she was orphaned and headless.[4]

---

1 *i.e.*, of the night-guard. I believe he was the brother of Māham Begam.

2 *Cf.* post. 29*b*, and 'Biographical Appendix,' s.n..

3 These three were her half and full sisters respectively.

4 Gul-badan was about eight at her father's death. At three she had been adopted by Māham Begam.

During the ten[1] years after the death of his Majesty *Firdaus-makānī* that his Majesty *Jannat-āshyānī* was in Hind, the people dwelt in repose and safety, and obedience and loyalty.[2]

Six months after the death of his Majesty *Firdaus-makānī,* Biban[3] and Bāyazīd advanced from the direction of Gaur. On the news of this, his Majesty at once left Āgra and moved to meet them. He defeated them, and then went to Chanāda (Chunār),[4] took it, and thence returned to Āgra.

My lady, who was Māham Begam, had a great longing and desire to see a son of Humāyūn. Wherever there was a good-looking and nice girl, she used to bring her into his service. Maywa-jān, a daughter of Khadang (? Khazang), the chamberlain (*yasāwal*),[5] was in my employ. One day (after) the death of his Majesty *Firdaus-makānī,*[6] my lady said: 'Humāyūn, Maywa-jān is not bad. Why do you not take her into your service?' So, at her word, Humāyūn married and took her that very night. (22*a*)

Three days later Bega Begam[7] came from Kābul. She became in

---

[1] Really about nine.

[2] This rose-coloured picture accords neither with the facts nor with the narrative of Gul-badan. It may be that some limiting word has slipped out ; e.g., 'in Āgra,' or 'the people of the country,' in opposition to the dispossessed Afghāns, conquerors of earlier date, or Bābar's people, *i.e.*, household.

[3] Text, Bibban. Biban and Bāyazīd were two distinguished Afghān chiefs and supporters of the fallen Lodī dynasty. The defeat named here occurred at Daura, on the Gumtī, 1531 (937H.).

All who love the story of an adventurous life, chequered through character of individuals in a marked degree, should fill out Gul-badan's brief narrative from Mr. Erskine's life of Humāyūn.

[4] 1532 (938H.). Taken from Shīr Shāh late in 1532 (939H.).

[5] An attendant on a man of rank, who carries a gold or silver staff (Johnson, Pers. Dict., *s.v.*.) ; chamberlain in the service of Khāns of Tūrkistān (Zenker, *s.v.*.) Gul-badan's use of the word (815) would allow a more extended sense.

[6] Text has also *dar hayāt khud*. This is not the only instance of a similar redundant expression.

[7] Bega had had one son, Al-amān. She is known in the later histories as Ḥājī Begam, but she made her pilgrimage in 972H.. She was captured at Chausa in 1539 (946H.) by Shīr Shāh; and most writers give her at this date the brevet title of Hājī. It is probable

the family way. In due time[1] she had a daughter, whom they named 'Aqīqa. Maywa-jān said to Lady (*Aka*) Māham Begam, 'I am in the family way, too.' Then my lady got ready two sets of weapons, and said: 'Whichever of you bears a son, I will give him good arms.' Then she packed up the arms, and got ready gold and silver walnuts. She procured also the (special) arms of a Mughal commander, and was very happy, and kept saying: 'Perhaps one of them will have a son.' She kept watch till Bega Begam's 'Aqīqa was born. Then she kept an eye on Maywa-jān. Ten months went by. The eleventh also passed. Maywa-jān said: 'My maternal aunt was in Mīrzā Ulugh Beg's[2] *ḥaram.* She had a son in the twelfth month; perhaps I am like her.' So they sewed tents and filled pillows.[3] But in the end everyone knew she was a fraud.

His Majesty who had gone towards Chanāda (Chunār), returned safe and sound.

My lady who was Māham Begam, gave a great feast. (22*b*) They lit up the bāzārs.[4] Before that time people used to illuminate the bāzārs (only). Then she gave orders to the better class and to the soldiers also to decorate their places and make their quarters beautiful, and after this illumination became general in India.

. . . a jewelled throne,[5] ascended by four steps, and above it gold-embroidered hangings, and laid on it a cushion and pillows embroidered in gold.

---

that Bega was not her personal name. It is the title of a lady of rank, and answers to beg.

[1] Text, *b'ad az yak sāl*, which, read literally, spoils the story.

[2] This will be Bābar's paternal uncle, known as *Kābulī*.

[3] *i.e.*, made all preparations. Perhaps khirgāhā dokhta is not 'sewed tents,' but 'pitched tents.' *Cf. zamīn-doz*.

[4] I am very doubtful as to the meaning of the following paragraph. It can hardly be true that India waited for Māham to instruct it in the art of illumination or decoration. I have conjecturally read that, whereas formerly only bāzārs were made to look festive, she had other houses adorned.

[5] Here follows a list of arrangements, plenishing and gifts for the feast. There are here and at p. 123 *ff.* many difficult words in it.

The covering of the pavilions and of the large audience tent was, inside, European brocade, and outside, Portuguese cloth. The tent-poles were gilded; that was very ornamental.

(My lady) had prepared a tent-lining and a *kannat*[1] and *sar-i-kannat* of Gujrātī cloth-of-gold, and a ewer for rose-water, and candlesticks, and drinking-vessels, and rose-water sprinklers,—all of jewelled gold.

With all her stores of plenishing, she made an excellent and splendid feast.

. . . twelve strings of camels, and twelve of mules, and seventy *tipūchāq* horses, and one hundred baggage horses. She gave special robes of honour to 7,000 persons. The festivities lasted several days.[2]

At this time came news that Muḥammad-zamān Mīrzā[3] had killed the father of Ḥājī Muḥammad Khān *kūkī,*[4] and was meditating

---

[1] Ar., a pent over a doorway, a veil, an umbrella. Perhaps *qanāt*, a screen, an enclosure for tents, the tent walls.

[2] The feast here credited to Māham Begam may be that of the first anniversary of Humāyūn's accession. Of this Gul-badan gives an account, minus such details as are set down here, at 24*a et seq*..

At the 'accession feast,' held December 19th, 1531, and thus not quite a year after the accession, it is said by Nizāmu-d-dīn Aḥmad that 12,000 robes were bestowed, 2,000 of these being 'special.' For details as to *khil'at*, *Cf.* Memoirs, 274 n..

Lists are dull reading, unless each item calls up an image. It is easy to add splendour and beauty to Gul-badan's few poor words by looking at actual things of the kinds she names, as may be done in the Oriental Section of the South Kensington Museum. The links between Persia and India in her day and earlier and later were many and close. Many Persians born and bred in Persia or by descent formed part of the Mughal court. Persian art and manufacture were at their highest development, experts say, in the fourteenth and fifteenth centuries. The uncritical eye doubts if the products of those centuries, as exhibited in the examples England possesses, can be excelled for splendour and satisfying charm. With such things the personages of our begam's book surrounded themselves.

[3] Son of Badī'u-z-zamān Mīrzā, and grandson of Sulṭān Ḥusain Mīrzā *Bāyqrā*, and husband of Ma'sūma, a daughter of Bābar. He was drowned in the Ganges at the rout of Chausa.

4 *Cf.* B. & H., II., *s.n.*.

rebellion. (23*a*) His Majesty sent to summon them[1] to the presence, and having laid hands on them, imprisoned them in Bayāna, in charge of Uncle Yādgār. Uncle Yādgār's men sided with Muḥammad-zamān Mīrzā, and let him escape (1533—940H.). At this time it was ordered that Sulṭān Muḥammad Mīrzā[2] and Nai[3] (Walī) Khūb Sulṭān Mīrzā should both be blinded. Nai Khūb Sulṭān lost his sight, but the man who had the blinding of Muḥammad Sulṭān did not injure his eyes.[4] Muḥammad-zamān Mīrzā and Muḥammad Sulṭān Mīrzā, with his sons, Ulugh Mīrzā and Shāh Mīrzā, made their escape a few days later.

There was perpetual disturbance from these people during the years we were in Hind.

When his Majesty returned from the campaign against Biban and Bāyazīd, he was in Āgra[5] for about a year. He said to my lady: 'I am sad at heart in these days. If you approved, I would go with you to Gualīār.'[6] Her Highness my lady, and my mother (*ājam*),[7] and my sisters Ma'sūma[8] Sulṭān Begam, whom we used to call Elder sister[9] Moon, and Gul-rang Begam, whom we used to call Elder

---

1 *Sic*; apparently the names of his fellow-rebels are omitted. They occur below.

2 Grandson, through a daughter, of Sulṭān Ḥusain Mīrzā *Bāyqrā*, and thus, a cousin of Muḥammad-zamān.

3 Called both Nai and Walī in the histories.

4 See Mr. Erskine's interesting note on blinding. (B. & H.. II. 14 n.).

5 'Occupied in dreamy speculations of false sciences'—*i.e.*, astrology. (B. & H., II. 14.) The date is 1534 (941H.).

6 The histories tell us that the Gualīār expedition was a military demonstration against Bahādur Shāh of Gujrāt. Khwānd-amīr fixes its date as Sha'bān 939H. (February, 1533).

7 Taken as it is written, this name might be charmingly translated as 'Ma desirée,' but considered with other words in this text after which the enclitic am (my) is incorrectly written, it seems that prosaic 'my mother,' Tūrkī, achām, is safer. In favour, however, of reading ājam, desire, is the wording on 25*b* (No. 48 of the guest-list), *ājam wālida-i-mā*, our mother. *Ājam* occurs also at 29*b*.

8 Her husband, Muliammad-zamān, is the rebel of this name just spoken of.

9 *Chīcha*; which I have rendered 'elder sister' to suit the actual relationship between Gul-badan and her two sisters. *Cf.* 18*b* n..

sister Bose,—we all were in Gualīār in attendance on the beneficent ladies.[1]

As Gul-chihra Begam was in Oude, and her husband, Tūkhtā-būghā Sulṭān, went to the mercy of God, her attendants wrote to his Majesty from Oude and said: 'Tūkhtā-būghā Sulṭān is dead. (23*b*) What is the order about the begam?' His Majesty said to Mīr Zāycha:[2] 'Go and bring the begam to Āgra. We also are going there.'

At this time her Highness my lady said: 'If you approve, I will send for Bega Begam and 'Aqīqa, so that they also may see Gualīār.' She despatched Naukār[3] and Khwāja Kabīr, who brought them from Āgra.

They let two months slip by in one another's company in Gualīār, and then set out for Āgra, which they reached in February, 1534 (Sha'bān, 940 H.).[4]

In April (Shawwāl) my lady was attacked by a disorder of the bowels. On the 27th of the same month (13th Shawwāl) she passed from this transitory life to the eternal home.

The stamp of orphanhood was set anew on my royal father's children, and especially on me, for whom she herself had cared. I felt lonely and helpless and in great affliction. Day and night I wept and mourned and grieved. His Majesty came several times to comfort me, and showed me sympathy and kindness. I was two years old when her Highness my lady took me into her own house and cared for me, and I was ten when she departed from this life.

---

[1] The aunts, presumably.

[2] The Chief Astrologer.

[3] Bābar names this man as being sent from India in charge of gifts to Kābul (Mems., 337.), and Gul-badan names him again (67*b*) as guardian of the begams' doorway in the citadel of Kābul.

[4] This date cannot be right. The following are approximately correct for this time: Visit to Gualiār undertaken, Sha'bān, 939H. (February, 1533). Return to Āgra and Māham's illness, Shawwāl (April). Death of Māham, 13th Shawwāl (May 8, 1533). Forty days of mourning carries on the time to late in Zū'l-qa'da (June). Start for Dihlī, begin-ning of Zū'l-hijja,—after June 24. The building of Dīnpanā was begun Muḥarram, 940H. (July, 1533).

(24*a*) I remained one year more in her house.[1] When I was eleven,

---

[1] Māham had also adopted Hindāl. Bābar details the circumstances, but the abbreviation, as it seems, of the Persian text, has led to an error. (Mems., 250.) Those children of Bābar who died young, were not born in 'this year' (925FL), as will be seen in the fuller rendering of Ilminsky, 281, and of P. de C, II. 44: 'Apres Humāyūn (b. 913H.) j'eus encore plusieurs enfants, nes de la meme mere que lui, mais qui ne vecurent pas.'

We know from Gul-badan that these were Bārbūl, Mihr-jahān, and Ishān-daulat.

'Hindāl n'etait pas encore venu dans le monde. Comme j'etais dans ces parages [Kehrāj, in Mandesh, and on his way to India], il m'arriva une lettre de Māham, dans laquelle elle me disait, "Sera-ce un fils ou une fille? Prononcez vous-meme sur la part que me reserve la fortune ; ā moi de mettre l'enfant dans le monde [Erskine, 'I will regard the child as mine'] et de l'elever." Le vendredi, 26 du mois, toujours ā ce meme campement, j'adjugeai Hindāl ā Māham [before birth], et je lui écrivis à ce sujet une lettre qui lui fut portee ā Kābul par Yūsuf 'Alī rikūb-dār [courier] quoique Hindāl ne fut pas encore ne.'

A passage now follows which, as is noted by P. de C., is neither in the Persian version of the Memoirs nor in the English translation:

'Pour bien comprendre tout ce qui à été dit plus haut. il faut savoir que jusqu'à cette époque, de tout les enfants nes de la même mère que Humāyūn, soit un fils [*i.e.*, Bārbūl], cadet par rapport à lui, l'ainé par rapport à mes autres enfants et trois filles, dont l'une etait Mihr-jān, il n'y en avait pas un qui ne fiit mort en bas age. Je souhaitais vivement de lui voir naitre un frere ou une sceur. [*i.e.*, a child of Māham. There were other children of other wives.]

'Précisément à cette epoque Dil-dār āghācha se trouvait enceinte. Je ne cessais de répéter, "Plût à Dieu que l'enfant qui va naitre, sortit du même sein que Humāyūn !" A quoi ma mere [*sic*. Tūrkī text, Ilminsky, 271, hazrat wālida] me répondait, "Si Dil-dār āghācha met au monde un fils, ne pourrais-je pas le prendre et m'en charger ?" "Rien de mieux," faisais-je à mon tour.

'D'ordinaire les femmes ont la maniere suivante de consulter le sort, quand elles veulent savoir si elles auront un fils ou une fille. Elles prennent deux morceaux de papier; sur l'un elles écrivent, Alī ou Ilasan, sur l'autre Fāṭima; puis elles les placent dans deux boules de limon qu'elles mettent dans une coupe d'eau. Celles des deux qui s'ouvre la premiere, leur sert à prognostiquer l'avenir ; si elle renferme le nom d'un garcon, il y aura un garcon ; si c'est celui d'une fille, il y aura une fille, disent-elles. On employa cette methode; ce fut un enfant mêle qui en sortit. En recevant cette bonne nouvelle, j'écrivis aussitôt pour en faire part à ma mere [*sic*]. Quelques jours plus tard, effectivement Dieu me donna un garcon. Trois jours apres sa naissance et avant de l'annoncer, on enleva l'enfant, bon gre, mal gré, à sa mere et on l'apporta chez moi ou on le garda. Lorsque j'en donnai avis à ma mere [*sic*], celle-ci apprenant qu'elle avait obtenu l'objet de ses vceux, donna au jeune prince le nom de Hindāl, qui etait pour nous de bon augure. Par cet arrangement cet enfant fut pour moi [? nous]

and his Majesty went to Dholpūr, I accompanied my mother.[1] This will have been before he went to Guālīār and began to build.[2]

At the end of the mourning for my lady, his Majesty went to Dihlī[3] and began to build the fort of Dīn-panā.[4] He then returned to Āgra.

Dearest lady[5] (Khānzāda Begam) said to his Majesty: 'When will you make Mīrzā Hindāl's marriage feast?' His Majesty replied: '*B'ismu-l-lāh.* 'When Mīrzā Hindāl was married, my lady (Māham) was living, but there was delay in arranging the feast. (Khānzāda Begam) said: 'The things for the Mystic Feast are also ready. Let us first celebrate this, and afterwards Mīrzā Hindāl's.' His Majesty said: 'Let whatever my royal aunt wishes be done.' She replied: 'May God bless it and make it good.'

à la fois un frere cadet (for Humāyūn) et un fils (for Māham aṇd himself).

The words *hazrat wālida* cannot mean the mother of Bābar She had been dead some fourteen years. They may be equivaleni to Sultān-wālida—*i.e.*, the mother of the heir-apparent. Certainly it was Māham who adopted Hindāl. This initial misconception as to the identity of Hazrat wālida runs through the whole translation of this most interesting passage. According to Gul-badan, Fārūq (born in 932H.) was Māham's son. Bābar names the birth. (Mems., 343.)

1 *i.e.*, returned to her own mother's charge *i.e.*, Dil-dār's.

2 An obscure passage. Humāyūn was building about this time. (Elliot, V. 126.)

3 Beginning of Zū'l-ḥijja, 939H. (June—July, 1533).

4 Humāyūn-nāma, Khwānd-amīr. (Elliot, V. 125.)

5 *Cf.* 156 n.,

DESCRIPTION OF THE HOUSE OF FEASTING WHICH WAS SET UP ON THE BIVER'S BANK, AND WHICH WAS CALLED THE MYSTIC[1] HOUSE:

First there was a large octagonal room with an octagonal tank in the centre, and again, in the middle of the reservoir, an octagonal platform on which were spread Persian (*wilāyatī*) carpets. (24*b*) Young men and pretty girls and elegant women and musicians and sweet-voiced reciters were ordered to sit in the tank.[2]

The jewelled throne which my lady had given for the feast was placed in the fore-court of the house, and a gold-embroidered divan[3] was laid in front of it, (on which) his Majesty and dearest lady sat together.

On her right sat her paternal aunts, the daughters of Sulṭān Abū-sa'īd Mīrzā:

1. [4]Fakhr-jahān Begam.
2. Badī'u-l-jamāl Begam.
3. Āq[5] Begam.
4. Sulṭān Bakht Begam.
5. Gūhar-shād Begam.
6. Khadīja Sulṭān Begam.

Upon another cushion sat our paternal aunts, the sisters of his Majesty, *Firdaus-makānī:*

---

[1] *Ṭilism*; Greek, τέλεσμα, talisman. Perhaps an epithet drifted from astrological phraseology. This feast commemorated the accession of Humāyūn. *Cf. Humāyūn-nāma*, trs. Sada-sukh La'l (B.M. Add. 30,774, p. 76.) : 'talismanic palace,' which may be the building named by Gul-badan. *Cf.* 'samite, mystic,' of Tennyson. Khwānd-amīr speaks at length of this feast in his *Humāyūn-nāma*, and calls the building in which it was held *'imārat-i-ṭilism.*

[2] The sequel to this order follows later.

[3] *tūshak*, (?) anglice, squab.

[4] Translator's numbering. For details as to each woman *cf.* Appendix *s.n.*.

[5] This epithet,—the Fair,—is given to several persons, not all women; and in some instances the true name is also known—e.g., Yasīn-daulat Sulṭān, Kāmrān's son-in-law, and Salīqa, daughter of Sulṭān Aḥmad Mīrzā.

7. Shahr-bānū Begam.
8. Yādgār Sulṭān Begam.
(N.B.—Other guests of the right follow).
9. 'Āyisha Sulṭān Begam, daughter of Sulṭān Ḥusain Mīrzā.
10. Ulugh Begam, daughter of Zainab Sulṭān Begam, a paternal aunt of his Majesty.
11. 'Āyisha Sulṭān Begam.
12. Sulṭānī Begam, daughter of Sulṭān Aḥmad Mīrzā, paternal (great-) uncle of his Majesty[1] and mother of Kilān Khān Begam. (25*a*)
13. Bega Sulṭān Begam, daughter of Sulṭān Khalīl Mīrzā, paternal (grand-)uncle of his Majesty.
14. Māham Begam.[2]
15. Begī Begam, daughter of Ulugh Beg Mīrzā *Kābulī,* paternal (grand-)uncle of his Majesty.
16. Khānzāda Begam, daughter of Sulṭān Mas'ūd Mīrzā; on her mother's side, granddaughter of Pavanda Muḥammad Sulṭān Begam, paternal (grand-)aunt of his Majesty.
17. Shāh Khānam, daughter of Badī'u-l-jamāl Begam (No. 2.).
18. Khānam Begam, daughter of Aq Begam (No. 3.).
19. Zainab Sulṭān Khānam, daughter of Sulṭān Mahmūd Khān, eldest maternal (grand-)uncle of his Majesty.
20. Muhibb Sulṭān Khānam, daughter of Sulṭān Aḥmad Khān,—known as Ilācha Khān, the younger maternal uncle of the elder[3] Emperor (Bābar).

---

[1] The words used of Sulṭāni do not grammatically apply to 'Āyisha, but I believe she is also a daughter of Sulṭān Aḥmad Mīrzā and is Bābar's first wife, who left him under the influence of an elder sister, perhaps Salīqa Sulṭān (Āq Begam). Salīqa married a son of Sulṭān Mahmūd Mīrzā, and may have acted under the evil impulses of the family quarrels which did so much to embitter, if also to stimulate, Bābar's early ambitions.

[2] This is not 'my lady,' whose death has been already recorded.

[3] *kilān*; perhaps, great.

21. Khānish, sister of Mīrzā Ḥaidar and daughter of (a) maternal (great-)aunt of his Majesty.
22. Bega Kilān Begam.[1]
23. Kīchak Begam.
24. Shāh Begam, mother of Dil-shād Begam, and daughter of Fakhr-jahān Begam (No. 1.), paternal (great-) aunt of his Majesty.
25. Kīchakna Begam.
26. Apāq (Āfāq) Begam, daughter of Sulṭān Bakht Begam (No. 4.).
27. Mihr-līq (? Mihr-bānū) Begam, paternal aunt of his Majesty.
28. Shād Begam, granddaughter of Sulṭān Husain Mīrzā, and daughter of a paternal aunt of his Majesty (? No. 22.).
29. Mihr-angez Begam, daughter of Muẓaffar (Husain) Mīrzā, and grandchild of Sulṭān Husain Mīrzā. (25*b*) They had great friendship for one another (? Shād and Mihr-angez), and they used to wear men's clothes and were adorned by varied accomplishments, such as the making of thumb-rings[2] and

---

[1] Probably the daughter of Sulṭān Mahmūd Mīrzā and mother of Shād Begam (No. 28.) by a son, Ḥaidar, of Sulṭān Husain Mīrzā.

[2] Text *zih-gīrī tarāshī*, which might be experimentally rendered carving thumb-rings, a gentle art of the day. But if *wa* be inserted, each word would represent a separate accomplishment of the well-bred in knightly arts. These would be congenial to a lady who played polo (*chaugān*). *Cf.* Bābar's account of Ḥaidar's accomplishments (Ilminsky, 14, Mems., 13, P. de C., 22.), and Ḥaidar's own recital in his prologue to the *Tārīkh-i-rashīdī*.

I suggest to take *tārashī* (a word not used by Bābar or Ḥaidar) as equivalent to the fletchery (*auq*), or the 'making arrow-heads' (*paikān*), of Bābar.

Another possible reading has been suggested to me by Mr. Beveridge—*(a)z hikīrī tarāshī*, 'by cutting arrows.' Hikrī is a Hindī name for cultivated reeds grown on low marshy grounds. (Wilson's Glossary, *s.v.*, and Platt's Hindustānī Dict..) There is nothing improbable in Gul-badan's use of a Hindī word. Arrows were fashioned from these reeds and men-at-arms practised the art. Gujrāt reeds were exported for arrows to Persia. The omission of the *alif* of *az* is not infrequent in the MS..

A few words on the *zih-gīr* find fit insertion here. It is a thumb-ring worn on the right hand as a protection against the fret of the bow-string both in drawing and release. Persians, like the Japanese and Mongols and Chinese, drew with the thumb. The *zih-gīr* is of eccentric thickness and unequal width, elongating on one side into a tongue. This elongation lies along the inner side of the thumb, and points towards the thumb-tip. In drawing, the thumb crooks round the string which pulls against the

arrows, playing polo, and shooting with the bow and arrow. They also played many musical instruments.

30. Gul Begam.
31. Fauq Begam.
32. Khān (? Jān) Begam.
33. Āfroz-bānū Begam.
34. Āgha Begam.
35. Fīroza Begam.
36. Barlās Begam.

There were other begams, very many, adding up altogether to ninety-six stipendiaries. There were also some others.

After the Mystic Feast (938 H.) came Mīrzā Hindāl's wedding-feast (Jauhar, 944 H.). Some of the begams already named went away,[1] and (of those) some had sat at the right hand in that assembly (*i.e.,* the Mystic Feast).[2]

Of our begams:

37. Āgha *(Aghā,—passim, āgha),* Sulṭān *āghācha,* mother of Yādgār Sulṭān Begam.
38. *Atūn māmā.*
39. Salīma.

---

zih-gīr. The arrow is released by straightening the thumb, and the string then flies over the hard surface of the ring. The *zih-gīr* is of jade, crystal, ivory, brass, gold, etc. Some are chased and carved, and some are jewelled. In December, 1898, a remarkable one was offered for sale at an auction in Edinburgh of Lord Dalhousie's collections and the jewels of his daughter, Lady S. G. Brown (Connemara). It is cut from a single emerald, and inscribed: *'Jihat zihgīr shāh-i-shāhān Nādir sāhib-qirān bar tashhīr-i-hind az jawāhar-khāna intikhāb shud'* ('Selected for a thumb-ring for the king of kings and lord of happy conjunction Nādir, from the jewel-room on the conquest of Hind').

An interesting account of Persian archery is included in the 'Book of Archery,' G. Agar Hansard (Lond., 1840.). It, however, calls the *zih-gīr*, *safn*. *Safn* is the rough skin of a fish or lizard which is used to smooth the arrow-shafts. (*Cf.* Lane's Ar. Dict..)

[1] *Ba wilāyatī*. (?) to Kabul and other outside places.

[2] Perhaps this is an explanation of the paucity of right-hand wedding-guests.

40. Sakīna.
41. Bībī Habība.
42. Hanīfa Bega.

And the others who had sat[1] at the Emperor's left on embroidered divans.

43. Ma'sūma Sulṭān Begam.
44. Gul-rang Begam.
45. Gul-chihra Begam.
46. This insignificant one, the broken Gul-badan.
47. 'Aqīqa Sulṭān Begam.
48. Ājam, our mother, who was Dil-dār Begam.[2]
49. Gul-barg Begam.
50. Bega Begam. (26*a*)
51. Māham's *nanacha.*
52. Sulṭānam, the wife of Amīr (Nizāmu-d-dīn) *Khalīfa.*
53. Alūsh Begam.
54. Nāhīd Begam.
55. Khurshīd *kūka,* and the children of my royal father's foster-brothers.
56. Afghānī *āghācha.*
57. Gul-nār *āghācha.*[3]
58. Nāz-gul *āghācha.*
59. Makhdūma *āgha,* the wife of Hindū Beg.
60. Fatīma Sulṭān *anaga,* the mother of Raushan *kūka.*

---

[1] (?) At the Mystic Feast. Its left-hand guests have not been specified. There are no repetitions of names, although the list seems to give the guests at both feasts. Perhaps down to and including No. 36 the names are of begams who were at the first feast, and then went away. Then come 'our begams' of the right, whose home was near Humāyūn, and who were at both feasts.

[2] *Cf.* 23*b* n..

[3] Nos. 57 and 58 are, perhaps, the two Circassians whom Shah Tahmāsp sent as a gift to Bābar (Mems., 347.). Gul-nār is named in Ābū 'l-fazl's list of pilgrims who went with Gul-badan to Makka in 983H., and as being of Bābar's household. They (Nos. 57 and 58) are named also by Firishta.

61. Fakhru-n-nisā'*anaga,* the mother of Nadīm *kūka.*
62. The wife of Muḥammadī *kūka.*
63. The wife of Mu'yid Beg.
64. The *kūkas* of his Majesty: Khurshīd *kūka.*
65. Sharīfu-n-nisā'*kūka.*
66. Fath *kūka.*
67. Babī'a Sulṭān *kūka.*
68. Māh-liqā *kūka,*
69. Our nurses (*anaga*).
70. Our *kūkas.*
71. The begams' people and the wives of the amīrs.

Those who were on the right.
73.Salīma Bega.
74. Bībī Neka.
75. Khānam *āgha,* daughter of Khwāja 'Abdu-l-lāh *Marwārīd.*
76. Nigār *āgha,* mother of Mughal Beg.
77. Nār Sulṭān *āgha.*
78. Āgha *kūka,* wife of Mu'nim Khān.
79. Daughter of Mīr Shāh Ḥusain, (illegible) Bega.
80. Kīsak Māham.
81. Kābulī Māham.
82. Begī *āgha.*
83. Khānam *āgha.*
84. Sa'ādat Sulṭān *āgha.*
85. Bībī Daulat-bakht.
86. Nasīb *āgha.*
87. (Illegible) Kābulī.

Other begas and āghas, the wives of the amīrs, sat on this hand, and all were present at the marriage feast. (26*b*)

This was the fashion of the Mystic House: (there was) a large octagonal room in which they gave the feast, over against this a small room, also octagonal. In both every sort of profusion and splendour appeared. In the large octagonal hall was set the jewelled throne, and above and below it were spread out hangings (*adsaqahāī*) embroidered with gold, and wonderful strings of pearls (*shadhīhā*) hung, each 1½ yards (*gaz*) in length. At the end of each string (*larī*) were two glass globes. There had been made and hung some thirty or forty strings.

In the small room, in an alcove, were set a gilded bedstead and *pān*-dishes,[1] and water-vessels and jewelled drinking-vessels, and utensils of pure gold and silver.

Facing west (was) the audience hall; facing east, the garden; on the third side and facing south, the large octagon; and on the side facing north, the small one. In these three houses were three upper rooms. One they named the House of Dominion,[2] and in it were nine military appurtenances, such as a jewelled scimitar and gilded armour, a broad dagger and a curved dagger, and a quiver, all gilt, and a gold-embroidered overmantle.[3] (27*a*)

In the second room, called the House of Good Fortune, an oratory had been arranged, and books placed, and gilded pen-cases,[4] and splendid portfolios,[5] and entertaining picture-books written in beautiful character.[6]

In the third room, which they called the House of Pleasure, were set out a gilded bedstead and a coffer of sandal-wood, and

---

1 This word excites curiosity as to the time when Gul-badan's people learned to eat *pān*.

2 As to this threefold classification, Elliot and Dowson, V., 119, may be consulted.

3 Six articles only are separately named, but the *qūr* (translated armour) may be taken in the sense given to it in the *Āīn* (Bloch-mann, 109.), and include four weapons, which makes the total the mystic nine. *Cf. Āīn, l.c*, and plates. (N.B.—The numbering of the weapons [*l.c.* p. 110.] does not agree with that of the plates. Plate X. should be consulted.)

4 *qalam-dān*. Several such are to be seen at the S. K. M. They are boxes damascened or painted with pictures, about 10 inches by 3 inches, and contain writing implements. 'Gilded' does not seem an appropriate epithet. Perhaps the dictionaries definē imperfectly.

5 *juz-dān*. Perhaps the beautiful book-covers of the day. Those having flaps might be called portfolios.

6 *muraqqa'*.

all imaginable pillows. Then in front were spread specially choice coverlets,[1] and before these table-cloths, all of gold brocade. Various fruits and beverages had been got ready, and everything for merriment and comfort and pleasure.

On the feast-day of the Mystic House, his Majesty ordered all the mīrzās and begams to bring gifts,[2] and everyone did so. He said: 'Divide the gifts into three heaps.' They made three trays of *ashrafīs* and six of *shāhrukhīs.* One of *ashrafīs* and two of *shāhrukhīs* he gave to Hindu Beg and said: 'This is the share of Dominion; give it to the mīrzās and chiefs and vazīrs and soldiers.' (21*b*)

He gave in the same way to Mullā Muḥammad Farghārī (Parghālī) and said: 'This is the share of Good Fortune. Give it to those who are eminent and respectable, and to theologians and religious men, to ascetics and graybeards, and dervishes and devotees, and the poor and the needy.'

Concerning one tray of *ashrafīs* and two of *shāhrukhīs* he said: 'This is the portion of Pleasure. This is mine. Bring it forward.' They did so. He said: 'What need is there to count?' First he himself vouchsafed his blessed hand and said: 'Let them take to the begams on one small tray *ashrafīs* and on another *shāhrukhīs.* Let each person take her hands full.' What was left, that is two trays of *shāhrukhīs,*—which may have been 10,000,—and all the *ashrafīs,* —about 2,000—he gave in largesse, and scattered[3] first before the *walī 'u-n-ni'matān* (beneficent seniors), and then to those present at the entertainment. No one received less than 100 or 150, and those in the tank especially received very much. (28*a*) His Majesty was pleased to say: 'Dearest lady! if you approved, they might put water in the tank.' She replied: 'Very good,' and went herself and sat at the top of the steps. People were taking no notice, when all at once

[1] *nihālcha.* Placed, I presume, over carpets.

[2] *sāchaq.* This word appears to have a special meaning of wedding-gifts, but Gul-badan uses it elsewhere more widely.

[3] *nisār.* Again a word which, like *sāchaq*, would seem to rit the marriage feast better than the accession.

(?) the tap was turned and water came. (28*a*) The young people got very much excited. His Majesty said: 'There is no harm; each of you will eat a pellet of anise[1] and a bit of comfit[2] and come out of there.' Upon this, everyone who would eat the comfit came out quickly. The water was as high as their ankles. To end the story, everyone ate the comfit and all came out.

Then the viands of the feast were set forth, and robes of honour were put on,[3] and gifts bestowed, and head-to-foot dresses given to the comfit-eaters and others.

On the margin of the tank was a room (*tālār*)[4] fitted with talc windows, and young people sat in the room and players made music. Also a woman's bāzār[5] had been arranged, and boats had been decorated. In one boat was made (?) the semblance of six people (*kāsī*) and six alcoves (*kanj*); in (another) an upper room, and below it a garden with amaranthus and cockscombs and larkspurs[6] and tulips. In one place there were eight boats, so that there were eight pieces.[7]

---

1 *shīt*. The text has no points and would yield seb, apple ; but anise is the better remedy against cold.

2 *ma'jūn*, any medical confection, but commonly an intoxicant. Here it may be some preventive of chill.

3 It was now that 12,000 khil'ats are said to have been distributed. In this passage Gul-badan twice uses the expression *sar u-pāī*. Perhaps one might say that the 'young people' were given new clothes from head to foot, and so shake off the fetters of the rigid *khi'lat*, *sar-u-pāī*, and 'honorary dresses.'

4 The dictionaries I have seen, explain *tālār* as a saloon built of wood and supported on four columns, and this is appropriate here. Le Strange and Haggard (Vazīr of Lonkurān) say, 'Alcove or chamber in which a ruler sits to give public audience and hear suitors.' It is raised above the level of the (e.g.) courtyard, so that petitioners are below the hākim. Approaching this meaning is the 'throne' of the dictionaries.

5 *Cf. Āīn*, Blochmann, 276; *Khushroz*, or Day of Fancy Bazārs.

6 *nā-firmān*, stubborn, (?) because they will break and not bend. Balfour (Cyclopaedia) and Forbes (Hind. Dict.) give larkspur; Fallon, poppy. An account of the boats, etc, may be read in B.M. MS. Add. 30,774, where is a translation by Sir H. Elliott's *munshī* from Khwānd-amīr.

7 *parcha*. Perhaps flower-gardens; perhaps Fr. *pièce*. *Cf. Un appatrtement de deux, trois pièces*.

In short, everyone was astonished and amazed who beheld what gift of contrivance the great God had bestowed on the blessed mind of his Majesty. (28*b*)

THE DESCRIPTION OF MĪRZĀ HINDĀL'S (MARRIAGE) FEAST IS AS FOLLOWS:[1]

Sulṭānam Begam (*i.e.,* the bride) was a sister of Mahdī Khwāja.[2] My father's brother-in law (*yazna*) had no child except Ja'far Khwāja, and there was no child (?) of Khānzāda Begam).[3] Dearest lady had taken care of Sulṭānam as though she were her child. Sulṭānam was two years old when Khānzāda Begam took charge of her. She (Khānzāda) loved her very much, and thought of her as a brother's child of her own. She made a most entertaining and splendid feast.

A kūslika[4] and hangings (*adṣaqa*)[5] and five divans and five pillows for the head (*yīstūq*), and one large pillow and two round ones (*galūla*)*;* and girdles (*qūshqa*) and veils (*naqāb*)*,* together with a tent[6] .... with three gold-embroidered cushions and head-to-foot dresses for a prince, with collar and bordering of gold embroidery, and bath-wrappers (*fauṭa*) and napkins (*rūpāk*) and embroidered towels (*rūmāl*) and an embroidered mantle (*qūrposh*) to be worn over the armour.

---

1 Jauhar's date for this is 944H. (1537).

2 Many difficulties gather round this name. *Cf.* Appendix *s.n.* Mahdī Khwāja.

3 The copyist has perhaps omitted one *āka-janām*.

4 M. Quatremère uses this word twice with perhaps two meanings. (Noticēs et Extraits, XIV. 324, 325 and 406-8.) At p. 408 he translates it kiosques, and it seems to be a building. At pp. 324 and 406 he leaves it untranslated. (Here it may have the sense given by Gul-badan.) It is named amongst items prepared for ambassadors at a post-house. These are: 'kat, trône; *bastar*, estrade; . . . *kushka*; *jinlik*; *sandali*, siége,' etc. Gul-badan might intend to name a canopy or screen for a sleeping-place in a large room or a movable kiosk with sleeping comforts.

5 *Cf.* 226.

6 A word follows *tent* which I cannot make out. It resembles *j-(h,ch)-l-gh* (no vowels).

For Sulṭānam Begam: nine jackets (*nīm-tana*)[1] with garniture of jewelled balls,[2] one of ruby, one of cornelian, one of emerald, one of turquoise, one of topaz, and one of cat's-eye.

Again: of necklaces, nine; and one embroidered collar and bordering, and four short jackets[3] with ball-trimming (*hukma-dār*), and one pair of ruby earrings and another of pearls, three fans,[4] and one royal umbrella.

One *dirakht*[5] and two *khuṭb*[3] and other furniture and effects, and household goods and chattels and workshops[6] of all sorts. (29*a*) Khānzāda Begam gave evervthing she had collected, and she

---

1 *nīm-tana*, *i.e.*, demi-corps. Like many of Gul-badan's words, this is marked by Steingass as 'modern colloquial.' Apropos of this, Dr. Fritz Rosen says in the preface of his Modern Persian Colloquial Grammar, that the Persian of Irān differs 'in every respect' from the Persian of India. The Persian of Gul-badan allows one to feel at home with the vazīr of Lonkurān, and with Dr. Rosen's own book. Perhaps the difference he indicates is between the literary and colloquial. Gul-badan's Persian, however, is presumably that of contemporary Irān, and her teachers were probably Persian born. Dr. Rosen's remark appears to require some restriction.

2 *tukma* (dār), usually translated *buttons*; but the button is so associated with the button-hole as to suggest a fastening. A dressmaker might say 'ball-trimming.' Globular buttons were and are placed round the neck and hem of a boddice. The vazīr of Lonkurān ordered a jacket with garniture of twenty-four gold buttons, smaller than a hen's and larger than a pigeon's. Vests trimmed with 'buttons' (Mems.) are repeatedly named by Bābar as gifts.

3 *chār qartījī*; a suggested rendering only. Johnson gives karti (qartī) as a short boddice reaching to the hips, and the qar recurs in other words, having the sense of a body garment; e.g., qartaq, a short-sleeved jacket; qarza, a woman's vest.

4 *pankha*.

5 I find no help as to these words in the dictionaries. My only suggestion as to their possible meaning is too slightly based to be of value. It is this : In the South Kensington Museum, Oriental Section, I have seen tall lamp-stands so shaped that they recall the Quṭb pillar outside Dihlī. That such stands would be a part of good household furnishing the South Kensington Museum allows us to suppose. We have our 'tall lamps,' our 'pillar lamps,' and also our 'branched candle-sticks,' which may be a term parallel to *dirakht*, a tree.

6 *kār-khānahā*. These may be the kitchen and its plenishing; the goldsmith's, with his tools, furnaces, and appliances; the perfumer's, etc. *Cf. Āīn*, Blochmann, and Tār. Basli., E. & R., 470.

arranged a feast such as had not been made for any other child of my royal father. She planned it all and carried it all out.

. . . nine *tipūchāq* horses, with jewelled and gold-embroidered saddles and bridles; and gold and silver vessels and slaves,[1] Tūrkī and Circassian and Arūs (?Būs) and Abyssinian,—of each (race) a royal gift of nine.

What my royal father's brother-in-law[2] (Mahdī Khwāja) gave to the mīrzā was a set of nine *tipūchāq* horses, with jewelled and gold-embroidered saddles and bridles; and gold and silver vessels, and two other sets of nine horses, baggage aninials, with velvet saddles and bridles; and brocade and Portuguese cloth, and Tūrkī and Habshī and Hindi slaves,—in all, three sets of nine; and three head of elephants.

In his Majesty's leisure after the feast came news that the vazīr of Sulṭān Bahādur, Khurāsān Khān by name, had attacked Bayāna. His Majesty despatched Mīrzā 'Askarī, with several amīrs, Mīr Faqr-'ali Beg and Mīr Tardī Beg, etc.. These went to Bayāna and fought and defeated Khurāsān Khān.[3] *(29b)* The Emperor set out for Gujrāt shortly afterwards, in prosperity and safety. It was on the 15th of the revered Rajab 941H.[4] that he quite decided to go himself to Gujrāt. He set up his advance camp in the Gold-scattering Garden, and there spent a month while the forces were gathering in.

---

[1] *ghulāmān*, which I have rendered slaves, because they were a gift. But I know no warrant for such servitude as is thus implied.

[2] *yazna*, which is explained by Vambéry and Steingass as 'husband of the king's sister.' Nizāmu-d-dīn Aḥmad styles Mahdī Khwāja damād, which Meninsky and Steingass explain as 'husband of the king's sister' and 'son-in-law.' I do not find *yazna* rendered son-in-law by any of the dictionaries. To read yazna 'brother-in-law of the king' agrees with the detailed statement of Mahdī's relation to Bābar made by Bāyazīd *bīyāt*. *Cf.* Appendix, *s.n.* Khānzāda.

[3] *Mīrzā Muqīm*, Khurāsān Khān.

[4] January 29th, 1535. Abū'l-fazl gives Jumāda I., 941H. (November, 1534) as the time for collecting the troops. Perhaps the begam's date is that of departure, a day liable to postponement when Humāyūn was in pleasant quarters.

On court days, which were Sundays and Tuesdays, he used to go to the other side of the river. During his stay in the garden, *ājam* (Dil-dār Begam) and my sisters and the ladies (*ḥaramān*) were often in his company. Of all the tents, Masūma Sulṭān Begam's was at the top of the row. Next came Gul-rang Begam's, and *ājam's* was in the same place. Then the tent of my mother,[1] Gul-barg Begam and of Bega Begam[2] and the others.

They set up the offices (*kār-khānahā*) and got them into order. When they had put up the pavilions (*khaima*) and tents (*khar-gāh*) and the audience tent (*bār-gāh*), the Emperor came to see the camp and the splendid set-out, and visited the begams and his sisters. As he had dismounted some-what near Ma'sūma Sulṭān Begam's (tent), he honoured her with a visit. All of us, the begams and my sisters, were in his society. (30*a*) When he went to any begam's or sister's quarters, all the begams and all his sisters used to go with him. Next day he came to the tent[3] of this lowly person, and the entertainment lasted till the third watch[4] of the night. Many begams were there, and his sisters, and ladies of rank (*begahā*) and of position (*āghāhā*), and other ladies (*āghāchahā*), and musicians and reciters. After the third watch his Majesty was pleased to command repose. His sisters and the begams made resting-places (*takīa*) in his presence.[5]

---

[1] It may be that the copyist has transferred the words 'my mother' from a quite usual place,—preceding or following the ājam of the previous sentence. They are inappropriate to Gul-barg Begam; at least, I have never seen them used to describe a brother's wife, and such I believe this Gul-barg to be. We know of a 'Bībī Gul-barg,' mentioned somewhat condescendingly (21*a*) by Māham Begam ; I incline to take Gul-barg there and here as Khalīfa's daughter, and the former wife of Mīr Shāh Husain Arghūn. *Cf.* Appendix, *s.n.* Gul-barg.

[2] This is, I think, Humāyūn's wife and the mother of 'Aqīqa. The object of Gul-badan's enumeration of the tents seems to be desire to show that Bābar's daughters and widow had places of honour higher than Humāyūn's family.

[3] *khāna*, lit., house.

[4] *pahr*. Gul-badan names the Hindūstānī division of time into watches on which her father had commented as being a novelty to himself. (Mems., 331.)

[5] It seems, as again later on, that they fell asleep where they were seated, on mattresses and provided with pillows

Bega Begam woke (us) up, and said: 'It is time for prayers.'[1] His Majesty ordered water for ablution[2] made ready where he was, and so the begam knew that he was awake. She began a complaint, and said to him: 'For several days now you have been paving visits in this garden, and on no one day have you been to our[3] house. Thorns have not been planted in the way to it. We hope you will deign to visit our quarters also, and to have a party and a sociable gathering there, too. How long will you think it right to show all these disfavours to us help-less ones? We too have hearts. Three times you have honoured other places by visits, and you have run day and night into one in amusement and conversation.' (30*b*)

When she had finished, his Majesty said nothing, and went to pravers. At the first watch of the day he came out and sent for his sisters and the begams, and for Dil-dār Begam, and Afghānī *āghācha,* and Gul-nār *āghācha,* and Meywa-jān and Āghā-jān, and the nurses (*anagahā*). We all went, and he said not a word, so everyone knew he was angry. Then after a little he began: 'Bībī, what ill-treatment at my hands did you complain of this morning?' and: 'That was not the place to make a complaint. You all (*shvmā*) know that I have been to the quarters of the elder relations (*walī'u-n-nī'matān*) of you all (*shumāyān*). It is a necessity laid on me to make them happy. Nevertheless, I am ashamed before them because I see them so rarely. It has long been in my mind to ask from you all a signed declaration (*sijlī*), and it is as well that you have brought me to the speaking-point. I am an opium-eater. If there should be delay in my comings and goings, do not be angry with me. Rather, write me a letter, and say: "Whether it please you to come or whether it please you not to come, we are content and are thankful to you."'

[1] The early morning prayers, about which the opinion is expressed that prayer is better than sleep.

[2] wazū', ablution before prayers. *Cf.* Hughes, Dict. of Islām.

[3] From what follows, Gul-barg would seem to be the fellow-sufferer.

Gul-barg Begam wrote to this effect at once, and he settled it with her.[1] Bega Begam insisted a little, saying: 'The excuse looked worse than the fault.[2] (31*a*) We complained in order that your Majesty might lift up our heads by your favour. Your Majesty has carried the matter to this point! What remedy have we? You are Emperor.' She wrote a letter and gave it to him, and he made it up[3] with her also.

On February 18th, 1534 (Sha'bān 14th, 941 H.), he set out from the Gold-scattering Garden and marched for Gujrāt, to fall upon Sulṭān Bahādur. They confronted one another at Manhasūr (Mandsūr); a battle was fought, and Sulṭān Bahādur, on his defeat, fled to Champānīr. Then his Majesty resolved to pursue him. Sulṭān Bahādur left Champānīr and went towards Aḥmadābād.[4] His Majesty took the country of Aḥmadābād also, and portioned out the whole of Gujrāt to his men. Aḥmadābād he bestowed on Mīrzā 'Askarī,[5] Bahrūch on Qāsim Husain Sulṭān,[6] and Patan on Yādgār-nāṣir Mīrzā.[7]

He himself, with a small following, went from Champānīr to visit Kanbāyat[8] (Cambay). *A* few days later there came a woman with news, and said: 'Why are you sitting here? The men of Kanbāyat

---

1 *ba Gul-barg Begam daryāftand.*

2 A familiar proverb. *Cf.* Steingass, 840, *s.v.* *'azr*.

3 *daryāftand*. Gul-badan frequently uses this word as meaning to embrace and to greet, a sense not mentioned by Johnson or Steingass. The *ba* of the earlier instance (note 1.) induced me to give it the notion of coming to an understanding. *Cf.* 16*b*.

4 Taking his treasure with him, Sulṭān Bahādur fled before Humāyūn to Champānīr, Aḥmadābād, Cambay and Diu.

5 Humāyūn's half-brother.

6 Grandson, through a daughter, of Sulṭān Husain Mīrzā *Bāyqrā*; on his father's side an Uzbeg.

7 Humāyūn's first cousin, the son of Bābar's half-brother Nāsir. He was a posthumous child. Mr. Beveridge has drawn my attention to the fact,—of which there are other examples,—that he is called Yādgār, a souvenir, of Nāsir, his father.

8 This excursion preceded the allotment of fiefs. Gul-badan's way of putting the pursuit of Bahādur is borne out by some other writers. This was Humāyūn's first sight of the sea, and the spectacle seems to have been more in her mind than was Bahādur. Akbar's first sight of the sea is also commemorated in the histories.

have gathered, and will fall upon you unless your Majesty rides off.' The royal amīrs attacked the rabble,[1] and got them into their hands and cut them in pieces. (31*b*)

His Majesty then went to Baroda, and from there towards Champānīr.[2] We had settled down, when there was a tumult, and Mīrzā 'Askarī's people left Aḥmadābād and came to the Emperor. They represented to him that Mīrzā'Askarī[3] and Yādgār-nāsir Mīrzā had conspired, and wished to go to Āgra. On hearing this, he himself was forced to go; he left the important affairs of Gujrāt [(?) its pacification], and turned away and went to Āgra. Here he spent as much as a year.[4]

---

1 Abū'l-fazl calls them Bhils and Gawārs. (H.B. I. 309.) They were rude tribesmen acting in Bahādur's interests. Maternal affection saved the small royal camp. The 'woman' had a son a slave in it, and she purchased his freedom by revealing the designs of her fellow-tribesmen. Although Cambay had not furnished the assailants, it paid in fire and pillage for the attack. It lay near, was an enemy's town, and such an incident as the onslaught of the Bhils would not allow of fine distinction of race and person.

2 Behind this dull statement is a stirring episode. Humāyūn took Champānīr after a four months' blockade, by night escalade of a rock so nearly perpendicular that seventy or eighty iron spikes had to be driven in to allow ascent. Thirty-nine men climbed up. Bairām Khān was the fortieth, Humāyūn the forty-first of the three hundred who mounted. Such a Bābar-like episode makes regret the keener that Humāyūn's life was ruined and stained by his slavery to a drug. The loot of Champānīr was enormous; it had been regarded as impregnable, and was full of treasure. It was taken in 1536 (943 H.). Humāyūn now relapsed into an evil mood of feasting and indolence. He remained near Champānīr, and affairs entered on a recurrent phase. There was complete relaxation of disciplinē.

Gul-badan's 'we had settled down' (*nishista budīm*) allows the inference that she and other lādies had joined the camp. A later instance will be found of the inopportune presence of women and children with the army. But it may mean merely 'we were comfortably awaiting events' in Agra.

3 He was thinking of having the khuṭba read in his own name in Āgra. Such an aspiration in Humāyūn's brothers was encouraged by his own abdications of sovereignty.

4 A fatal year which allowed Shīr Khān to gather force. Gul-badan's recital of the historical events of this time has no value.

SHĪR SHĀH *AFGHĀN*.

[*To face p.* 133.

He then went to Chanāda (Chunār), and took it,[1] and also Benares. Shīr Khān was in Charkanda,[2] and made an offer of service, saying: 'I am your old servant. Give me a place with a fixed boundary in which I may establish myself.'

His Majesty was considering this, when the king of Gaur Bangāla[3] came wounded and a fugitive. For this reason he gave no attention (to Shīr Khān), but marched towards Gaur Bangāla. Shīr Khān knew that his Majesty had gone there, and went himself also with a large detachment of horse, and joined his son (Jilāl Khān), who was in Gaur with his servant Khawāṣ Khān. Shīr Khān sent them out, and said: 'Go and fortify Garhī.'[4] (32*a*)

Both came and occupied Garhī. His Majesty had written to Jahāngīr Beg: 'Advance a stage, and go up to Garhī.' There was fighting, and Jahāngīr Beg was wounded and many men were slain.

When the Emperor had spent three or four days in Kohlganū (Colgong), it became advisable for him to march on and halt near Garhī. He marched forward, and when he came near Garhī, Shīr Khān and Khawās Khān fled by night, and he entered Garhī next day. Thence he went to Gaur Bangāla, and took it.

He was nine months in the far-away country of Gaur, and named it Jannatābād.[5]

He was comfortably and safely in Gaur, when news came that

---

[1] Shīr Khān.

[2] Jhārkand.

[3] Sayyid Maḥmūd Shāh. He had been defeated by Shīr Khān. (*Cf.* Erskine's notes on Stewart's Jauhar, B. M. Add. 26,608, p. 12.)

[4] 'The gate of Bengal,' a pass between it and Bihār, and which has a hill on one hand and the Ganges on the other. It is the Teria garhī or Tilia gulley of our maps.

[5] City of Paradise. The demoralizing effects of life in Gaur were felt under Akbar. Humāyūn, with his empire crumbling around him, was now (as Jauhar testifies) 'so much devoted to pleasure and sensual enjoyment that, after the first month, he was never seen, as he was always shut up in a private apartment of the palace.' Naturally, Gulbadan's next item of narrative is of rebellion,—this time by her own brother, Hindāl.

some of the amīrs had deserted and joined Mīrzā Hindāl.[1]

Khusrau Beg[2] (*kūkaltāsh*) and Zahīd Beg[3] and Sayyīd Amīr[4] paid their respects to the mīrzā, and said: 'The Emperor has gone comfortably far away, and the mīrzās, Muḥammad Sulṭān Mīrzā and his sons, Ulugh Mīrzā and Shāh Mīrzā, have again raised their heads,[5] and continually keep showing themselves in company.' (32*b*)

Just at this time the asylum of shaikhs, the servitor (*bandagī*) Shaikh Bahlūl, hid[6] armour and horse-accoutrements and military stores in an underground place, and would have loaded them on carts and sent them to Shīr Khān and the mīrzās.[7] Mīrzā Hindāl would not believe it, so Mīrzā Nūru-d-dīn Muḥammad was sent to inquire into the matter. He found the armour and accoutrements, and had *Bandagī* Shaikh Bahlūl killed.[8] The Emperor, on hearing news of it, set out for Āgra.

He was coming by that side of the Ganges (*i.e.,* the left bank) opposite Mungīr, when his amīrs represented: 'You are a great king! Beturn by the way you came, lest Shīr Khān should say: "Forsaking his road of advance, he took another of retreat."'[9] The Emperor

---

1 He was only nineteen, and the crown may well have seemed at anyone's service. The date is 1538 (945H.). Humāyūn in Gaur was cut off from his capital by Shīr Khān.

2 Bābar first names him in 1507-8 as coming from Harāt. There are two men named Khusrau kūkaltāsh by Bābar, but they were not contemporaries. One died in 1502-3, before the other came upon the scene.

3 Husband of the sister of Bega Begam, Humāyūn's wife. He was put to death by Mīrzā Kāmrān at Ghaznī in 1547.

4 Sayyid Nūru-d-dīn Mīrzā, the father of Salīma Sulṭān Begam, and the husband of a daughter of Bābar. *Cf.* App. *s.n.* Gul-rang.

5 Hindāl had recently defeated them. (Erskine, II. 89 *et seq..*) For causes of Hindāl's rebellion, and for Bega Begam's part in it, see Erskine's Jauhar, l.c., p. 13.

6 Some words seem to be omitted, e.g., 'was accused of.' Gul-badan cannot have believed the accusation. Perhaps, however, her long friendship with Nūru-d-dīn's daughter Salīma would make her pen discreet in blaming his murder of the shaikh.

7 The rebels mentioned on p. 23*b*.

8 For the probable facts, *Cf.* B. & H., II. 162 *et seq..*

9 It was Mu'yid Beg Duladai Barlās who urged this foolish point of honour, and

returned to Mungīr, and brought many of his people and his family by boat up the river as far as Hajīpūr-Patna.

When he went (to Bengal) he had left Qāsim (Husain Sulṭān Uzbeg) there. Now came news of Shīr Khān's approach. Whenever there was fighting, the royal troops won.

Just now Bābā Beg (*Jalāīr*) came from Jaunpūr and Mīrak Beg from Chanāda (Chunār), and Mughal Beg from Oude. (33*a*) As these three amīrs joined the Emperor, corn became dear.

Then,—such was God's will,—they had halted without precaution, when Shīr Khān came and fell upon them. The army was defeated, and many kinsmen and followers remained in captivity. His Majesty's own blessed hand was wounded. Three days he remained in Chunār, and then came to Araīl.[1]

When his Majesty reached the river's bank, he stopped, bewildered as to the crossing, and said: 'How to cross without boats!' Then came the rāja (Bīrbahān) with five or six horsemen and led him through a ford. For four or five days his people were without food or drink. At last the rāja started a bāzār, so that the people of the army lived some days in comfort and repose. The horses also were rested. Many men who were on foot bought fresh mounts. In short, the rāja rendered fitting and dutiful services. Later on his Majesty gave him leave to go, and at the hour of mid-day prayer came himself, safely and comfortably, to the bank of the Jamna. The army crossed at a ford they had found. A few days later they came to Karra, where corn and grass were plentiful, because it was his Majesty's own country. (33*b*)

---

who thus led to the disaster at Chausa. He was a cruel man as well as one ignorant in military matters. He was a favourite of Humāyūn, but the Emperor's followers rejoiced when he died.

[1] Gul-badan's brevity (natural enough even if she were more historic in method) is somewhat misleading. Mr. Erskine allows one to follow the misadventures which culminated in the defeat. This—the rout at Chausa—occurred near to where the Sōn fails into the Ganges and at Chūpat Ghat, on June 27th, 1539 (Safar 9th, 946H.). The statement of Humāyūn's visit to Chunār, I do not find elsewhere. Chunār was then held by royalists. The Araīl named is presuniably that near Allāhābād.

When his people were rested, he went on to Kalpī, and then marched on to Āgra.

Before his arrival in Āgra, he heard news that Shīr Khān was coming (from) the direction of Chausa. Great anxiety fell upon his people.

Of many who were in that rout (at Chausa) there was never heard, in any way soever, news or sign. Amongst them were 'Āyisha Sulṭān Begam, daughter of Sulṭān Husain Mīrzā[1] (*Bāyqrā*); and Bachaka, who was a *khalīfa* of my royal father;[2] and Bega-jān *kūka;* and 'Aqīqa Begam;[3] and Chānd Bībī, who was seven months with child, and Shād Bībī, all three[4] (*sic*) of whom were of his Majesty's *ḥaram.* Of these several people, he never heard even a word, as to whether they were drowned or what became of them. In spite of all possible inquiry and search, what had become of them was never found out.

His own illness[5] dragged on for forty days, and he then grew better.

At this time, when Khusrau Beg (*kūkultāsh*), and Diwāna Beg, and Zahīd Beg, and Sayyid Amīr, had come on in advance of his Majesty, news again arrived that the mīrzās, Muḥammad Sulṭān Mīrzā and his sons, had come to Kanauj. (34*a*)

After Shaikh Bahlūl's murder, Mīrzā Hindāl went to Dihlī. He took with him Mīr Faqr-'alī and other well-wishers to frustrate and

---

[1] Wife of Qāsim Husain Sulṭān Uzbeg, whose timely arrival gave Bābar so much satisfaction. (13*a*) Qāsim had been Governor of Patna (32*b*), but, from the circumstance of his wife's being at Chausa, would seem to have left it with Humāyūn.

[2] A Bachaka, who was a khalīfa of Bābar's household, escaped with him from Samarqand in 1501 (907H.), some thirty-eight years before the Chausa episode. *Khalīfa*, as applied to a woman, denotes a servant or slave who exercises surveillance over other women-servants, and has charge of rooms,—an upper maid-servant.

[3] Bega Begam's daughter, who will have been about eight years old.

[4] Perhaps the copyist has omitted a name; perhaps, as a child of Humāyūn, Aqīqa is 'of the *ḥaram*.'

[5] From his wound or from distress of mind. The 'forty days' suggest the ceremonial term of mourning.

disperse the mīrzās. The mīrzās fled, and came into the Kanauj quarter. Mīr Faqr-'alī brought Mīrzā Yādgār-nāṣir to Dihlī. As there was neither friendliness nor confidence between Mīrzā Hindāl and Mīrzā Yādgār-nāṣir, Mīrzā Hindāl, when Mīr Faqr-'alī made this mistake, sat down out of sheer annoyance and besieged Dihlī.[1]

When Mīrzā Kāmrān heard these things, there arose in him also a desire of sovereignty. With 12,000 fully equipped horsemen he went to Dihlī. Mīr Faqr-'alī and Mīrzā Yādgār-nāsir closed the city gates on his approach. Two or three days later, Mīr Faqr-'alī, having made an agreement, went and saw Mīzrā Kāmrān. He represented: 'The news heard of his Majesty and Shīr Khān may be so and so.[2] Mīrzā Yādgār-nāsir, from thought of his own interest, does not wait on you. The advisable course at this crisis is, that you should lay hands on Mīrzā Hindāl, go to Āgra, and not think of establishing yourself in Dihlī.' (34*b*)

Mīrzā Kāmrān gave heed to Mīr Faqr-'alī's words, and bestowed on him a head-to-foot dress. He then seized Mīrzā Hindāl and came to Āgra. He visited the tomb of *Firdaus-makānī,*[3] saw his mother and sisters, and halted in the Rose-scattering[4] Garden.

At this time Nūr Beg brought word of his Majesty's coming.[5] As Mīrzā Hindāl was excluded from the presence because of the murder of Shaikh Bahlūl, he went to Alwar.[6]

A few days after his Majesty's arrival, Mīrzā Kāmrān came from the Rose-scattering Garden and paid his respects to him. We paid our respects on the evening of the day he came. He took notice

---

[1] The whole of the above paragraph it would be safest to hide with Hindāl under his sister's charitable cloak. For a historical account of the time, see B. & H., II., Book IV., Cap. IV.

[2] Clearly the ill news of the rout at Chausa.

[3] Bābar's remains then had not been conveyed to Kābul in 1539.

[4] (?) Gold-scattering. Mr. Erskine calls it so, and it is likely to be that already mentioned by Gul-badan more than once.

[5] Retreating from Chausa.

[6] His own *jāgīr*.

of this insignificant one, and was kindly pleased to say: 'I did not know you at first, because when I led the army (whose footprints are victorious[1]) to Gaur Bangāla, you wore the high cap (*tāq*), and now when I saw the muslin coif[2] I did not recognise you. And oh, my Gul-badan, I used very often to think of you, and was sometimes sorry, and said: "I do wish I had brought her!" But at the time of the disaster (*jitrāt*) I was thankful I had not, and I said: (35*a*) "Thank God I did not bring Gulbadan!" For although 'Aqīqa[3] was young, I have been consumed by a hundred thousand regrets and cares, and have said: "Why did I take her with the army?"'

A few days later he came to see my mother. He had with him the Holy Book. He commanded the attendants to retire[4] for awhile, and they rose and there was privacy. Then he said to *ājam* (Dil-dār Begam) and this insignificant one, and to Afghānī *aghācha,* and Gul-nār *āghācha,* and Nār-gul *āghācha,* and my nurse *(anaga):* 'Hindāl is my strength[5] and my spear;[6] the desirable light of my eyes, the might of my arm, the desired, the beloved. May what I do be right! What shall I say to Mīrzā Muḥammad Hindāl about the affair of my[7] Shaikh Bahlūl? What was to be has been! Now there

---

1 ẓafr-aẓar. This, after Chausa, can only be a precative of Gulbadan's.

2 This change appears to indicate that Gul-badan, who is about eighteen or nineteen years old, has been married. The Persian has *lachaq qaṣāba*, without conjunction. Steingass and Johnson describe the *lachaq* as a square mantle worn by women, doubled into a triangle, but here the description given in the Burliān-i-qātī' is more àpropos, *i.e.*, a square of stuff folded cornerwise and put upon the head so that the corners tie under the chin. It is often (l.c.) elaborately embroidered in gold. Qaṣāba appears to have the same meaning as larliaq.

3 *Cf.* p. 33*b*.

4 *kināra kardand*. This metaphor recalls the arrangement of carpets in Persian rooms, with the carpet proper in the centre, an upper end (*sar-andāz*) and borders (kināra). 'Go aside' might be a good rendering.

5 *qūl*, Mongolian,—main body of an army.

6 Ar. *qanāt*.

7 Here and in the apostrophe to Gul-badan I have allowed the man to indicate the affection Humāyūn had for his half-sister and for the revered shaikh. It might be, however (as at 'Now there is no anger,' *Cf.* text), the simple first person.

is no anger in my heart against Hindāl. If you do not believe it' . . . He had lifted up the Holy Book when her Highness my mother, Dildār Begam, and this poor thing snatched it from his hand. All cried, 'May what you do be right! Why do you say such things?'

Then again he spoke: 'How would it be, Gul-badan, if you went yourself and fetched your brother, Muḥammad Hindāl Mīrzā?' (35*b*) Her Highness, my mother, said: 'This girlie *(dukhtarak)* is young. She has never made a journey (alone). If you approved, I would go.' His Majesty said: 'If I give you this trouble, it is because it is clearly incumbent on fathers and mothers to feel for their children. If you would honour him with a visit, it would be a healing-balm applied for us all.'

Then he sent Mīr Abū'l-baqā[1] with her Highness my mother, to fetch Mīrzā Hindāl. At once on hearing this news: 'She has come to see me!' Muḥammad Hindāl Mīrzā made his mother happy by giving her honourable meeting. He came with her from Alwar, and paid his duty to his Majesty.[2] About Shaikh Bahlūl he said: 'He used to send arms and military appurtenances to Shīr Khān. When this was ascertained, I killed the shaikh on account of it.'

To put it briefly: in a short time came news that Shīr Khān had come near Lakhnau.

In those days his Majesty had a certain servant, a water-carrier. (36*a*) As he had been parted from his horse in the river at Chausa and this servant betook himself to his help and got him safe and sound out of the current, his Majesty now seated him on the throne. The name of that menial person we did not hear, some said Nizām, some said Sambal. But to cut the story short, his Majesty made the water-carrier servant sit on the throne, and ordered all the amīrs to

---

1 B. & H., II., *s.n.*.

2 Hindāl was received in the presence of Kāmrān and other kinsmen. Humayūn said to Kāmrān : 'You know who is to blame! Why did Hindāl rebel ?' Kāmrān passed on the question to Hindāl himself, who, with profound shame, pleaded that being young he had listened to bad advice, and begged forgiveness. (Erskine's notes on Stewart's Jauhar, B. M. Add. 26,608.)

make obeisance to him. The servant gave everyone what he wished, and made appointments. For as much as two days the Emperor gave royal power to that menial. Mīrzā Hindāl was not present at his court;[1] he had taken leave, and had again gone to Ahvar with the intention of getting arms ready. Neither did Mīrzā Kāmrān appear. He was ill, and sent to say to his Majesty: 'Gifts and favours of some other kind ought to be the servant's reward. What propriety is there in setting him on the throne? At a time when Shīr Khān is near, what kind of affair is this to engage your Majesty?'

In those days Mīrzā Kāmrān's illness increased amazingly. He became weak and so thin that his face was not in the least his own, and there was no hope of his life. (36*b*)

By the Divine mercy he grew better. He suspected that the Emperor's mothers,[2] by his Majesty's advice, had given him poison. His Majesty came to hear of this, and instantly went to see the mīrzā and swore that he had never had such a thought, nor given such an order to any one. Nevertheless, Mīrzā Kāmrān's heart was not purged. Afterwards he got worse, day after day, and he lost power of speech.

When news came that Shīr Khān had left Lakhnau, the Emperor marched towards Kanauj, and left Mīrzā Kāmrān in Āgra to act for him. In a few days the mīrzā heard that he had made a bridge of boats and crossed the Ganges. On this, he himself marched out of Āgra towards Lāhōr.[3]

We had settled down[4] when he sent[5] a *farmān* like a king's, and said: 'You[6] are commanded to go with me to Lāhōr.' He must have said[7] to his Majesty about me something of this sort: 'I am very ill

[1] Lit., in that assembly.

[2] *i.e.*, Bābar's widows.

[3] A treacherous defection.

[4] The royal family, after the Emperor's and the mīrzā's departure.

[5] Perhaps from his first halting-place outside the city.

[6] Clearly Gul-badan.

[7] Before either brother left Āgra.

and very miserable and lonely, and I have no one[1] to sympathize with me. (37*a*) If you will order Gul-badan Begam to go with me to Lāhōr, it will be a real favour and kindness.' For his sake his Majesty will have said: 'She shall go.' Two or three days after the Emperor had gone towards Lakhnau, the mīrzā sent a *farmān,*[2] in royal style, to the effect: 'Most assuredly you will come with me.' Then my mother must have said: 'She has never travelled apart from us.' He replied:[3] 'If she has not travelled alone, do you also go with her.' He sent as many as 500 troopers and trusty grooms, and both his foster-father and his foster-brother, and said (to my mother): 'If she may not go with me (to Lāhōr), come all of you one stage.' When one stage was reached, he began to declare, on his oath: 'I will not let you go.' Then he took me by main force, with a hundred weepings and complaints and laments, away from my mothers, and my own mother and my sisters, and my father's people, and my brothers, and parted us who had all grown up together from infancy.[4]

I saw that the Emperor's command also was in the affair. I was helpless. (37*b*) I wrote a suppliant letter, saying: 'I never expected your Majesty to cut off this insignificant one from your service, and to give her to Mīrzā Kāmrān.' To this humble note he sent a compassionate answer (*salām-nāma*), to this effect: 'I had no heart to part with you, but the mīrzā persisted, and was miserable, and begged very hard, and I was obliged to trust you to him. For just now there is important work[5] on hand. God willing, I will send for you when it is settled.'

---

[1] *i.e.*, of his kinsfolk, and especially of his women kinsfolk.

[2] This, I think, is the one already named.

[3] *īshān farmudand*. This seems to mean Humāyūn, and to refer the following speech back to the earliest discussion of the project of Gul-badan's journey at the time Humāyūn was still in Āgra. The whole episode is confused in narrative.

[4] It must be remembered that Gul-badan's husband, Khiẓr Khwāja, was a brother of Āq Sulṭān (Yasīn-daulat), Kāmrān's son-in-law, and Kāmrān may have had other motives than affection for desiring her presence, e.g., the attraction of her husband's contingent.

[5] The opposition of Shīr Khān, soon to be closed at Kanauj. Gulbadan's enforced departure with Kāmrān saved her a painful and hazardous flight.

When the mīrzā was starting, many people, amīrs and traders and so on, made preparation with the intention of letting their wives and families march under his escort to Lāhōr. When we reached (the city) news came of a battle on the Ganges, and that defeat had befallen the royal army.[1]

At least there was this limit to misfortune,—his Majesty and his brothers came safely through the peril.[2] Our other relations[3] came from Āgra by way of Alwar to Lāhōr. (38*a*)

Just now the Emperor said to Mīrzā Hindāl: ''Aqīqa Begam disappeared in that first interregnum (*fiṯrat*[4]), and I repented extremely, and said: "Why did I not kill her in my own presence?" Now, again, it is difficult to convey women with us.' Mīrzā Hindāl answered: 'What it would be to your Majesty to kill a mother and a sister, speaks for itself! So long as there is life in me, I will fight in their service. I have hope in the most high God, that,—poor fellow as I am,—I may pour out my life's blood for my mother and my sisters.'

Then the Emperor set out for Fathipūr (Sīkrī) with Mīrzā 'Askarī and Yādgār-nāsir Mīrza and the amīrs who had come safely off the battlefield.[5]

Mīrzā Hindāl sent on before him[6] her Highness his mother, who

---

[1] May 17th, 1540 (Muharram 10th, 947H.). Mīrzā Ḥaidar gives an admirable account of it as 'the battle of the Ganges.' Gul-badan's full brother, Hindāl, led the van at Kanauj, and defeated Shīr Khān's son, Jalāl. Hindāl was a successful general. 'Askarī, Kāmrān's full brother, was defeated by Khawās Khān.

[2] As at Chausa, so at Kanauj, Humāyūn was nearly drowned. Here he was saved by Shamsu-d-dīn Muḥammad of Ghaznī, whose wife, under the sobriquet of Jī-jī *anaga*, became a nurse of Akbar.

[3] They were convoyed by Hindāl. See *infra*.

[4] *i.e.*, battle of Chausa. Fitna would read more easily here. Perhaps behind *fiṯrat* is the notion of relaxation in effort, or of an interval between two periods of good fortune.

[5] Amongst them was Ḥaidar Mīrzā, who describes the fugitives as 'broken and dispirited, and in a state heartrending to tell.' Sīkrī must have rubbed salt into their wounds, since it recalls Bābar's triumph. Their halting-place there was his garden, a token of his genius for living.

[6] The known enenry, Shīr Khān, was in the rear. With Hindāl's marriage-feast fresh in

was Dil-dār Begam, and his own sister, Gul-chihra Begam, and Afghānī *āghācha,* and Gul-nār *āghācha,* and Nār-gul *āghācha,* and the amīrs' wives and families, etc.. He was marching along when the Gawārs pursued him in great numbers. (38*b*) Some of his troopers charged and defeated them. An arrow struck his horse.[1] There was much fighting and confusion. Having saved the helpless women from the bond of the Gawārs, he sent on (to Lāhōr) his mother and sister, and many of the amīrs' people, etc, and went to Alwar. Here he got together tents and pavilions and numerous requisites, and then started for Lāhōr. He arrived in a few days, and brought what was wanted for the princes and the amīrs.

His Majesty alighted in Khwāja Ghāzī's garden near Bībī Hāj-tāj.[2] Every day there was news of Shīr Khān; and during the three months that the Emperor was in Lāhōr word was brought day after day: 'Shīr Khān has advanced four miles,' 'six miles,' till he was near Sirhind.

One of the amīrs was named Muẓaffar Beg. He was a Tūrkmān. The Emperor sent him with Qāzī 'Abdu-l-lāh to Shīr Khān to say: 'What justice is there in this? I have left you the whole of Hindūstān.

---

mind, one may give a thought to Sulṭānam. She was probably of this party, since her husband's contingent was with Humāyūn, and he was not on his *jāgīr* of Alwar.

1 *Asp i-mubārik*, (?) the horse which had the happiness to bear him. Perhaps asp is a mistake for some word to which 'blessed' would be a more fit adjective.

2 Abū'l-fazl says that Hindāl's quarters were in Khwāja Ghāzī's garden, and Humāyūn's in Khwāja Dost *munshīs*.

Bībī Ḥaj, Bībī Tāj, Bībī Nūr, Bībī Ḥūr, Bībī Gūhar, and Bībī Shābaz are said to have been daughters of 'Aqīl, brother of 'Alī (Muḥammad's son-in law). They were famous for piety and asceticism. After the murder of Imām Ḥusain at Kerbela, these ladies left Syria for India in obedience to a secret intimation. They alighted outside Lāhōr at the place named by Gul-badan and where their shrine now is. They converted many of the townspeople to their faith, and thus angered the, presumably Hindu, governor. He sent his son to command their departure, but the son fell under their influence, and remained near them. This still more angered his father, who went out against them and their followers with an armed force. The ladies prayed that their honour might be preserved, and they not be seen by strange men. Immediately the earth opened and swallowed them. (*Khazīna'u-l-asfiyā*, II. 407.)

Leave Lāhōr alone, and let Sirhind, where you are, be a boundary between you and me." (39*a*) But that unjust man, fearless of God, did not consent, and answered: 'I have left you Kābul. You should go there.'

Muẓaffar Beg marched at once, and sent on an express to say: 'A move must be made.' As soon as this message came, his Majesty set off. It was like the Day of Resurrection. People left their decorated places and furniture just as they were, but took with them whatever money they had. There was thankfulness to God, because mercifully a ford was found across the Lāhōr water (Rāvi) where everyone crossed. His Majesty halted a few days on the river's bank. Then an ambassador came from Shīr Khān. The Emperor had decided to see him next morning, when Mīrzā Kāmrān made a petition, saying: 'To-morrow there will be an entertainment, and Shīr Khān's envoy will be present. If I may sit on a corner of your Majesty's carpet, so that there may be distinction between me and my brothers, it will be a cause of my exaltation.'[1]

Ḥamīda-bānū Begam says it was his Majesty who wrote and sent the following verse to the mīrzā.[2] I had heard that he sent it to Shīr Khān by the envoy. This is the verse:

---

[1] For an account of Kāmrān's odious and fruitless treachery see B. & H., II. 200 *et seq*.. The meaning of his message to Humāyūn is not clear to me. Perhaps he wished to show the envoy that he was not on the level of Hindāl and Askarī, but able to claim recognition as a ruler and as Humāyūn's equal. Perhaps it was a hint to Humāyūn that he must recognize Kāmrān's equality in the lands in which the latter had been supreme while he himself ruled in Dihlī.

At this time Humāyūn was strongly advised to put Kāmrān to death. He refused, but later on and after a dreary waste of good nature, his filial piety had to yield to the common-sense of his victimized followers and allow the blinding.

[2] At the time when the verse was written Hamīda was not married. The discussion in 1587 (circa) of a 'point' between the ladies is a living touch to the old MS.. Which was likely to be right,—Hamīda who might later have heard the story from her husband, or Gul-badan who was in Lāhōr? Gul-badan puts the difference of opinion gently but does not surrender, and leaves her readers to draw their own inferences.

'Although one's image be shown in the mirror,
It remains always apart from one's self.' (39*b*)
'It is wonderful to see one's self in another form:
This marvel will be the work of God.'

When Shīr Khān's ambassador arrived he paid his respects.

The Emperor's blessed heart was cast down. He fell asleep in a sad mood, and saw in a dream a venerable man, dressed in green from head to foot and carrying a staff, who said: 'Be of good cheer; do not grieve and gave his staff into the royal hand. 'The most high God will give you a son who shall be named Jalālu-d-dīn Muḥammad Akbar.' The Emperor asked: 'What is your honourable name?' He answered: 'The Terrible Elephant,[1] Aḥmad of Jām;' and added: 'Your son will be of my lineage.'[2]

In those days Bībī Gūnwar[3] was with child. Everyone said: 'A son will be born.' In that same garden of Dost *munshī* and in the month of Jumāda'u-l-awwal, a daughter was born whom they named Bakhshī-bānū.

At this time his Majesty appointed Mīrzā Ḥaidar to take Kashmīr. Meantime, news was brought that Shīr Khān was there. A wonderful confusion followed, and the Emperor decided to march off next morning. (40*a*)

While the brothers were in Lāhōr, they conferred and took

---

1 *Zinda-fīl.*

2 Humāyūn was of the lineage of Aḥmad of Jām through his mother Māham. (A. N., *Bib. Ind.*, ed. I. 121.) To give force to the prophecy, however, the coming child's mother had to be of the same descent, since Humāyūn's claim to rank as of the saint's lineage required no prophetic announcement. Indeed this story seems to cast doubt on that claim. Akbar's mother, Hamīda, was of the line of Aḥmad of Jām. So, too, was Bega (Hājī) Begam. Another of the same family was Bābū or Bānū *āghā*, wife of Shihābu-d-dīn Aḥmad of Nishāpūr.

3 To give value to Aḥmad's prophecy, Bībī Gūnwar ought also to have traced back to him. She does not seem to have been a woman of rank. The girl now born was at least the third child of Humāyūn, there having been Al-amān and 'Aqīqa, children of Bega Begam and now both dead.

counsel and asked advice, but they did not settle on any single thing. At last the news was: 'Shīr Khān is here.' Then, as there was no help for it, they marched off at the first watch of the day (9 a.m.).

The Emperor's wish was to go to Kashmīr, where he had sent Mīrzā Ḥaidar *Kāshgharī;* but news of the mīrzā's success had not yet come, and people counselled: 'If your Majesty were to go to Kashmīr, and the country was not conquered at once, it would—with Shīr Khān in Lāhōr—be a very difficult time.'

Khwāja Kilān Beg[1] was in Sīālkōt, and disposed to serve his Majesty. With him was Mū'yid Beg, who wrote: 'The khwāja greatly wishes to serve you and would come, but he has Mīrzā Kāmrān to consider. If your Majesty would come quickly, his help would be made easy in an excellent way.' The Emperor at once took arms and equipment, and set out to go to the khwāja, and joined company with him and brought him along.[2]

The Emperor was pleased to say: 'With my brothers' concurrence, I shall go to Badakhshān. (40*b*) Let Kābul remain the fief of Mīrzā Kāmrān.' But Mīrzā Kāmrān would not consent to (his Majesty's) going to Kābul,[3] and said: 'In his lifetime the Emperor *Firdaus-makānī* gave Kābul to my mother (Gulrukh Begam). It is not right (for you) to go to Kābul.'

Then said his Majesty: 'As for Kābul, his Majesty *Firdaus-makānī* often used to say, "My Kābul I will give to no one; far from it! Let none of my sons covet it. There God gave me all my children, and many victories followed its capture." Moreover, this expression of opinion is recorded many times in his *Wāqi a-nāma.* What was the good of my showing kindness to the mīrzā from civility and brotherliness, if he now keep on talking in this way!'

Let his Majesty talk as he would, pacifying and conciliating, the mīrzā resisted more and more. When he saw that there was a

---

1 The well-known old servant of Bābar and now one of Kāmrān's chief amīrs.

2 The begam's story here does not agree with that of Mr. Erskine's authorities. Mū'yid Beg is the ill-adviser of the march from Bengal to Chausa.

3 Kāmrān may well have feared that Humāyūn would get no further than Kābul on his way to Badakhshān.

large following with Mīrzā Kāmrān, and that the mīrzā was in no way willing for him to go to Kābul, he had no resource but to move towards Bhakkar and Multān. Having arrived in Multān, he halted one day. (41*a*) *A* small quantity of corn was obtained in the fort and having divided that little amongst his men, he marched on till he came to the bank of a river which was seven rivers in one.[1] He stood distracted. There were no boats, and he had a large camp with him. Then there came word that Khawās Khān,[2] with several amīrs, was coming up behind.

There was a Balūchī named Bakhshū (*sic*) who had forts and many men. His Majesty sent him a banner and kettledrums, and a horse, and a head-to-foot suit, and asked for boats and also for corn. After a time Bakhshū *Balūchī* got together and sent about a hundred boats, full of corn too, for the royal service,—a proper attention which pleased the Emperor very much. He divided the corn amongst his people, and crossed the water[3] safe and sound. May mercy be shown to Bakhshū for his dutiful service!

After a weary journey, they reached Bhakkar at last. The fort is in the middle of the river and very strong. The governor, Sulṭān Maḥmūd (*Bhakkarī*),[4] had fortified himself in it. (41*b*) The Emperor alighted safe and well over against the fort, near which was a garden[5] made by Mīrzā Shāh Husain *Samandar*.[6]

---

1 *i.e.*, the Indus. The begam's 'seven' is interesting. *Cf.* 'Sketch of the Hindūstānī Language,' C. J. Lyall, p.1 n.. '*Hindo* represents an earlier *Hindau*, being the modern Persian for the ancient Hendava, *i.e.*, a dweller in the country of the sapta *hindū* (Sk. *sapta sindhu*), or "seven rivers," now called, with the omission of two (probably the Saraswati and Drishadwati or Ghaggar) the Panj-āb.'

2 A follower of Shīr Khān.

3 The Gāra, near Uch.

4 Foster-brother of Shāh Husain Arghūn, and the man for whom Sīdī 'Alī Reis negotiated terms with Humāyūn in 1555.

5 A delightful garden, the Chār-bāgh of Rūhrī (Lūhrī), on the left bank of the Indus. Shāh Husain felt no anxiety as to military operations after hearing that Humāyūn had camped here. Chār-bāgh seems to denote a royal and private garden.

6 'A place in Hindūstān from which aloes are brought.' (Steingass, *s.v.*.) *Cf. Samandūrī*, aloe-wood, of the Āīn. (Blochmann 80.) Samandar seems an equivalent for Sind.

At length his Majesty sent Mīr Samandar to Shāh Husain Mīrzā with this message: 'We have come into your territory under compulsion. May your country be blessed to you! We shall not take possession of it. Would to Heaven you would yourself come and pay us your respects, and do us the service which is our due! We intend to go to Gujrāt, and should leave you your own country.' By tricks and wiles, Shāh Husain kept his Majesty as much as five months in Samandar; then he sent a person to wait on him, and to say: 'I am arranging my daughter's wedding-feast, and I send (someone) to wait on you. I shall come (later).' His Majesty believed him, and waited still three months. Sometimes there was corn to be had, sometimes not. The soldiers killed and ate their horses and camels. Then his Majesty sent again, by Shaikh 'Abdu-l-ghafūr,[1] to ask: 'How much longer will you be? What prevents you from coming? (42*a*) Things have come to such a pass that there is inconvenience, and many of my men are deserting.' The reply was: 'My daughter[2] is promised to Mīrzā Kāmrān, and a meeting with me is impossible. I could not wait on you.'

As at this time Mīrzā Muḥammad Hindāl crossed the river, some said he might be going to Qandahār.[3] On hearing this his Majesty sent several people after him to make inquiry and to say: 'It is reported that you plan going to Qandahār.' When questioned, the mīrzā said: 'People have given a wrong impression.' On this

---

[1] Humāyūn's treasurer (mīr-i-mūl) whose official functions must now have been of the least pressing.

[2] The admirable Māh-chūchak who insisted upon accompanying the blinded Kāmrān to Makka. As her peer in compassion may be commemorated Chilma Beg *kūka*. (B. & H., II., 418.)

[3] He encamped at Pāt (text, Patr), about twenty miles west of the Indus and about forty miles north of Sehwān. Pāt is in the sarkār of Sīwīstān, a little to the east of the highroad to Hyderābād, and not far north of Meānī, the scene of Napier's victory of 1848. I am indebted to Major-General Malcolm K. Haig for the information that Pāt is 'now a ruin, having been destroyed in the latter part of the eighteenth century when two Kalhora chiefs of Sind called in the Afghāns to quell domestic troubles.'

the Emperor came[1] to see her Highness my mother.

The mīrzā's *ḥaram* and all his people paid their respects to his Majesty at this meeting, Concerning Hamīda-bānū Begam, his Majesty asked: 'Who is this?' They said: 'The daughter of Mīr Bābā Dost.' Khwāja Mu'aẓẓam[2] was standing opposite his Majesty, who said: 'This boy will be one of my kinsmen (too?).'[3] Of Hamīda-bānū he said: 'She, too, is related to me.' (42*b*)

In those days Hamīda-bānū Begam was often in the mīrzā's residence (*maḥalī*). Another day when his Majesty came to see her Highness my mother, he remarked: 'Mīr Bābā Dost is related to us. It is fitting that you should give me his daughter in marriage.' Mīrzā Hindāl kept on making objections, and said: 'I look on this girl as a sister and child of my own. Your Majesty is a king. Heaven forbid there should not be a proper alimony, and that so a cause of annoyance should arise.'[4]

His Majesty got angry, and rose and went away. Then my mother wrote and sent a letter, saying: 'The girl's mother has

---

1 Leaving his troops to prosecute the siege of Bhakkar, and passing through Dārbila where was his cousin, Yādgār-nāsir. From the wording it might be supposed that Gul-badan was with her mother in Pāt, but I believe she was in Kābul at this time.

2 *Cf.* Appendix, s.n. Hamīda-bānū.

3 (?) interrogative, but the preceding verb is guftand, and not pursīdand.

4 This looks like a side-glance at the wasted fortunes of royalty. No kingdom! No revenues! Whence then the dowry? It is clear from the sequel that the important point was being pressed.

Jauhar says that Hamīda had been already asked in marriage, but not betrothed or perhaps promised. Her objections to marry Humāyūn seem personal, and may indicate preference for another and dislike for him. She is said to have been fourteen years old and Humāyūn was thirty-three, an opium-eater, and much married already. Her objections, whatever their true basis, must have been strong or they could hardly have survived, for Gul-badan to record, through the many years of prosperity and proud motherhood which her husband's renewed sovereignty in India and her son's distinction secured to her.

Behind Gul-badan's story of the wooing of Hamīda there were doubtless many talks over 'old times' when the royal authoress was freshening her memory for her literary task, begun (it seems probable) when she was about sixty-five and Hamīda some few years younger.

even before this been using persuasion.[1] It is astonishing that you should go away in anger over a few words.' He wrote in reply: 'Your story is very welcome to me. Whatever persuasion you may use, by my head and eyes, I will agree to it. As for what they have written about alimony, please Heaven, what they ask will be done. My waiting eye is on the road.' My mother fetched his Majesty, and on that day she gave a party. When it was over, he went to his own quarters. (43*a*) On another day he came to my mother, and said: 'Send someone to call Hamīdā-bānū Begam here.' When she sent, the begam did not come, but said: 'If it is to pay my respects, I was exalted by paying my respects the other day. Why should I come again?' Another time his Majesty sent Subhān Qulī, and said: 'Go to Mīrzā Hindāl, and tell him to send the begam.' The mīrzā said: 'Whatever I may say, she will not go. Go yourself and tell her.' When Subhān Qulī went and spoke, the begam replied: 'To see kings once is lawful; a second time it is forbidden. I shall not come.' On this Subhān Qulī went and represented what she had said. His Majesty remarked: 'If she is not a consort *(nā maḥram),* we will make her a consort *(maḥram).*'

To cut the story short: For forty days the begam resisted and discussed and disagreed. At last her highness my mother, Dil-dār Begam, advised her, saving: 'After all you will marry someone. Better than a king, who is there?' The begam said: 'Oh yes, I shall marry someone; but he shall be a man whose collar my hand can touch, and not one whose skirt it does not reach.' Then my mother again gave her much advice. (43*b*)

At last, after forty days (discussion), at mid-day on Monday (fault) Jumīdu-l-awwal (*sic*) 948H. (September, 1541), and in Pātr (*sic*), his Majesty took the astrolabe into his own blessed hand and, having chosen a propitious hour, summoned Mīr Abū'l-baqā and ordered him to make fast the marriage bond. He gave the mīr two

[1] *Mādar-i-dukhtar az īn kam peshtar nāz mīkanad.* Perhaps, 'caressed the idea.'

laks of ready money for the dower[1] (*nikāḥāna*), and having stayed three days after the wedding in Pātr, he set out and went by boat to Bhakkar.

He spent a month at Bhakkar and he sent Mīr Abu l-baqā to Sulṭān *Bhakkarī.* The mīr fell ill while away, and went to the mercy of God.[2]

His Majesty then gave Mīrzā Hindāl leave to go to (Jandahār, and he dismissed Mīrzā Yādgār-nāsir to his own place, Lār. He himself went towards Seāwān[3] (Sehwān), which is six or seven days' journey from Tatta.[4] Sehwān has a strong fort, in which was Mīr 'Alīka, a servant of his Majesty the Emperor.[5] There were several cannon, so no one could possibly go near. Some of the royal soldiers made trenches, and got near and gave him ('Alīka) advice, and said: (44*a*) 'Disloyalty is not well at such a time,' but Mīr 'Alīka did not agree with them. Then they made a mine and cast down a tower, but they could not take the fort. Corn became dear and many men deserted. The Emperor spent six or seven months there.

Mīrzā Shāh Husain treacherously laid hands on the royal soldiers in all directions, and made them over to his people, and said: 'Take

[1] Perhaps the ladies romance a little here. Humāyūn was certainly at a loss for money now and later.

[2] This is not a historic account of the death. He was sent to Yādgār-nāsir and was shot while crossing the river on his return to Kūhrī by adherents of Shāh Husain. His death caused great grief to Humāyūn. (B. & H., II., 222.)

[3] At the end of September, 1541. Ḥindāl's leave is a sisterly gloss on his acceptance of an invitation to Qandahār given by its governor, Qarācha Khān.

[4] Semblance of relevance can be given to this statement only by reference to other writers. Humāyūn had intended to go to Tatta at this time, and was diverted from the journey by a slight success of arms. He then besieged Sehwān.

[5] Certainly not so, for 'Alīka was an Arghūn and follower of Shāh Husain. Perhaps Gul-badan wrote or intended to convey that 'Alīka had served Bābar as once all the Arghūns had done. Perhaps she has confused the import of the story that Mīr 'Alīka when sent by Shāh Husain to take command of Sehwān, actually passed through Humāyūn's lines and the bāzār without recognition as an enemy.

them and throw them into the salt sea.' Three[1] or four hundred would be gathered into one place and flung into boats and thrown into the sea, till as many as 10,000 were cast forth.

[2]As after this there were few men even with the Emperor, (? Shāh Husain) filled several boats with cannon and muskets, and came from Tatta against him. Sehwān is near the river. (? Mīr 'Alīka) hindered the coming of the royal boats and provisions, and sent to say: '(?) I am maintaining my loyalty. March off quickly.' Having no remedy, the Emperor turned to Bhakkar.

When he came near and before he could reach it, Mīr (Shāh) Husain *Samandar* had sent word to Mīrzā Yādgārnāsir: (44*b*) 'If the Emperor, when he is retreating, should come near Bhakkar,[3] do not let him in. Bhakkar may remain your holding. I am with you; I will give you my own daughter.' The mīrzā believed him and did not allow the Emperor to enter the fort, but wished to make him go on, either by force or fraud.

His Majesty sent a messenger to say: 'Bābā,[4] you are as a son to me. I left you in my stead, so that you might help me in case of need. What you are doing is done by the evil counsel of your servants. Those faithless servants will be faithless to you also.' Whatever his Majesty urged had no effect.[5] Then he said: 'Very well! I shall go to Rāja Māldeo.[6] I have bestowed this country on you, but Shāh Husain will not let you keep it. You will remember my words.' Having said this to the mīrzā, the Emperor marched away by way

[1] Text, thirty—*sīsad*. No wonder Humāyūn's force vanished! He is said to have left Hindūstān, *i.e.*, Lāhor, with a following of 200,000. This presumably included Kāmrān's party, and was made up of soldiers and women, children, traders, servants, etc.. At this time Humāyūn had lost both Hindāl's and Yādgār-nāsir's troops.

[2] The narrative becomes much confused here.

[3] The mīrzā was at Eūhrī and had not possession of the fort. *Cf.* B. & H., II., 226, for a good account of his treachery and credulity.

[4] (?) 'My dear boy'—the Persian word of endearment. The relative position and ages of Hurnāyīin and Yādgār-nāsir make 'father' in-appropriate.

[5] In this extremity Humāyūn turned his thoughts towards Makka.

[6] Rāja of Jūdpūr (Mārwār), who had proffered help.

of Jīsalmīr, towards Māldeo. He reached Fort Dilāwar (Dirāwal), on the rāja's frontier, a few days later. (45*a*) He stayed there two days. Neither corn nor grass was to be had. He then went to Jīsalmīr, and on his approach the rāja sent out troops to occupy the road, and there was fighting. The Emperor and some others went aside off the road. Several men were wounded: Alūsh[1] Beg, brother of Shāham *Jalāīr* and Pīr Muhammad the equerry, and Raushang the wardrobe-keeper, and some others.[2] At length the royal troops won and the infidels fled into the fort. That day the Emperor travelled 60 *kos* (*civ.* 120 miles), and then halted on the bank of a reservoir.

Next he came into Sītalmīr, where he was harassed all day till he reached Pahlūdī, a *pargana* of Māldeo. The rāja was in Jodhpūr, and sent armour and a camel's-load of *ashrafīs,* and greatly comforted his Majesty by saying: 'You are welcome! I give you Bīkanīr.' The Emperor halted with an easy mind, and despatched *Atka* Khān (Shamsu-d-dīn *Ghaznavī*) to Māldeo, and said: 'What will his answer be?'[3]

In the downfall and desolation in Hind, Mullā Surkh, the librarian, had gone to Māldeo, and had entered his service. (45*b*) He now wrote: 'Beware, a thousand times beware of advancing. March at once from wherever you are, for Māldeo intends to make you prisoner. Put no trust in his words. There came here an envoy from Shīr Khān who brought a letter to say: "By whatever means you know and can use, capture that king. If you will do this, I will give you Nagōr and Alwar and whatever place you ask for." '*Atka* Khān also said when he came: 'This is no time for standing.' So at afternoon prayer-time the Emperor marched off. When he was mounting, they captured two spies and brought them bound before him. He was questioning them when suddenly they got their hands

---

[1] Var., Lūsh and Tarsh,—all three names of such disagreeable import as to suggest that they are either nicknames or were bestowed to ward off evil influences. Perhaps ūlūs should be read. *Cf.* App. *s.n.*.

[2] Muqīm Harāwī, father of Nizāmu-d-dīn Aḥmad, took part in this engagement.

[3] Presumably to Atka Khān's message from Humāyūn.

free, and one snatched a sword from the belt of Muhammad *Girdbāz*[1] and struck him with it, and then wounded Bāqī *Guālīārī*. The other at once unsheathed[2] a dagger and faced the bystanders, wounded several and killed the Emperor's riding-horse. They did much mischief before they were killed. (46*a*) Just then there was a cry, 'Māldeo is here!' The Emperor had no horse fit for Hamīda-bānū Begam. He may have asked for one for her from Tardī Beg,[3] who apparently did not give it. He then said: 'Let the camel of Jauhar, the ewer-bearer, be got ready for me. I will ride it, and the begam may have my horse.' It would seem that Nadīm[4] Beg heard that his Majesty was giving his horse to the begam and thinking of riding a camel, for he mounted his own mother on a camel and gave her horse to the Emperor.

His Majesty took a guide from this place, and mounted and rode for 'Umrkōt. It was extremely hot; horses and (other) quadrupeds[5] kept sinking to the knees in the sand, and Māldeo was behind. On they went, thirsty and hungry. Many, women and men, were on foot. (46*b*)

On the approach of Māldeo's troops, the Emperor said to Īshān(Īsān)-tīmur Sultān and to Mu'nim Khān[6] and a number of others: 'You all come slowly, and watch the enemy till we have gone on a few miles.' They waited; it grew night, and they missed their way.

All through that night the Emperor went on, and at dawn a watering-place was found. For three days the horses had not drunk.

---

[1] (?) gird-bāzū, strong-limbed.

[2] Doubtful translation; *az mayān yak hashīda*.

[3] This excellent officer is frequently a scapegoat. Our bēgam, how-ever, imputes her blamē tentatively. For estimate of his character see B. & H., I. and II., *s.n.*. Jauhar brings Raushan Beg into a similar story of this terrible journey.

[4] The husband of Māham *anaga*, Akbar's celebrated nurse. (R.A.S.J., January, 1899, art. Māham *anaga*, H. Beveridge.) His mother was Fakhru-n-nisā'. *Cf.* Gul-badan, 26*a* and 71*a*.

[5] Perhaps ponies only. Text, *chārwā*.

[6] Gul-chihra's husband.

He had dismounted when a man ran in, shouting: 'The Hindus are coming up in numbers, mounted on horses and camels.' Then the Emperor dismissed Shaikh 'Alī Beg (*Jalāīr*), and Raushan *kūka* and Nadīm *kūka,* and Mīr Payanda Muhammad, brother of Muhammad Walī, and many others.

They recited the *fātiha,* and his Majesty said: 'Go, fight the infidels!' He thought: 'Īshān-tīmūr Sultān, and Mu nīm Khān,[1] and Mīrzā Yādgār,[2] and the rest whom we left behind, have been killed or captured by these people who have now come to attack us.' He mounted and left the camp with a few followers.

Of the band which his Majesty had sent out to fight after reciting the *fātiha,* Shaikh 'Alī Beg struck the Rājpūt captain with an arrow, and cast him from his horse. (47*a*)

Several more (of the royal troop) hit others with arrows; the infidels turned to flee, and the fight was won. They brought in several prisoners alive. Then the camp went slowly, slowly on; but his Majesty was far ahead. Those who had recited the *fātiha* came up with the camp.

There was a mace-bearer named Bihbūd. They sent him galloping after the Emperor, to say: 'Let your Majesty go slowly. By Heaven's grace, a victory has been vouchsafed, and the infidels have fled.' Bihbūd himself was taken to the presence, and conveyed the good news.[3]

His Majesty dismounted, and a little water even (*ham*)[4] was found, but he was anxious about the amīrs, and said: 'What has happened to them?' Then horsemen appeared in the distance, and again there was a cry: 'God forbid ! Māldeo !'[5] His Majesty sent a

---

[1] The well-known Khān-i-khānām of Akbar's reign.

[2] Perhaps 'Uncle Yādgār' (ḷaghāī), the father of Bega Bēgam. Yādgār-nāsir was not here, but still in Sind.

[3] And also, tied to his girths, two heads of foes which he flung at Humāyūn's feet.

[4] to brim of the cup of joy.

[5] These cries remind one that even now Humāyūn must have had with him a huge contingent of helpless beings, women and children and non-combatants.

man for information, who came running back and said: 'Īshān-tīmūr Sultān, and Mīrzā Yādgār, and Munim Khān are all coming, safe and sound.' They had missed their way. Their return rejoiced the Emperor, who rendered thanks to God.

Next morning they marched on. For three days they found no water. (47*b*) On the fourth, they came to some very deep wells, the water of which was extraordinarily red. The Emperor halted and alighted near one of the wells; Tardī Beg Khān was at another; at a third, Mīrzā Yādgār, and Mu'nim Khān, and Nadīm *kūka;* and at the fourth, Īshān-tīmūr Sultān, and Khwāja Ghāzī, and Raushan *kūka.*

As each bucket came out of the wells into reach, people flung themselves on it; the ropes broke, and five or six persons fell into the wells with the buckets. Many perished from thirst. When the Emperor saw men flinging themselves into the wells from thirst, he let anyone drink from his own water-bottle. When evervone had drunk his fill, they marched on again at afternoon prayer-time.

After a day and a night they reached a large tank. The horses and camels went into the water and drank so much that many died. There had not been many horses, but there were mules and camels. (48*a*) Beyond this place water was found at every stage on the way to 'Umrkūt,[1] which is a beautiful place with many tanks.

The rānā[2] gave the Emperor an honourable reception, and took him into the fort, and assigned him excellent quarters. He gave places outside to the amīrs' people. Many things were very cheap indeed; four goats could be had for one *rupī.* The rānā made many gifts of kids and so on, and paid such fitting service that what tongue could set it forth?

Several days were spent in peace and comfort.

The treasury was empty. Tardī Beg Khān had a great deal of

---

[1] The little desert town must indeed have seemed a haven after the terrible journev, and not least so to the young wife who some two months later became the mother of Akbar. Humāyūn reached 'Umrkōt on August 22nd, 1542 (Jumāda I. 10th, 949H.).

[2] Text, *passim, ra'nā*. The 'Umrkōt rānā's name was Parsād.

money, and the Emperor having asked him for a considerable loan, he lent 80,000 *ashrafis* at the rate of two in ten.[1] His Majesty portioned out this money to the army. He bestowed sword-belts and *cap-a-pie* dresses on the rānā and his sons. Many people bought fresh horses here.

Mīr Shāh Husain had killed the rānā's father. For this, amongst other reasons, the rānā collected 2,000 or 3,000 good soldiers and set out with the Emperor for Bhakkar.[2] (486)

In 'Umrkot he left many people, and his family and relations, and also Khwāja Mu'azzam to have charge of the *haram.* Hamīda-bānū Begam was with child. Three days after his Majesty's departure, and in the early morning of Sunday, the fourth day of the revered Rajab, 949H.,[3] there was born his imperial Majesty, the world's refuge and conqueror, Jalālu-d-dīn Muhammad Akbar *Ghāzī.* The moon was in Leo. It was of very good omen that the birth was in a fixed Sign, and the astrologers said a child so born would be fortunate and long-lived. The Emperor was some thirty miles away when Tardī Muhammad Khān took the news to him. He was highly delighted, and by way of reward and largesse (*nisār*) for the tidings he forgave all soever of Tardī Muhammad Khān's past offences. He gave the child the name he had heard in his dream at Lāhōr, the Emperor Jalālu-d-dīn Muhammad Akbar.

On leaving this place, the Emperor went towards Bhakkar with as many as 10,000 men who had gathered round him, people of the rānā and of the outlying tribes and Sūdmas (Sodhas) and Samīchas. (49*a*) They reached the district of Jūn, where there was one of Shāh Husain's servants with some troopers. He fled.[4] Here there was the Mirror Garden, a very pleasant and enjoyable place where the Emperor alighted. He assigned its villages (? of Jūn) in *jāgīṛ* to his followers.

---

1 (?) 20 per cent. *Cf.* Mems., 138.

2 After a stay of seven weeks in 'Umrkōt.

3 October 15th, 1542.

4 *Cf.* B. & H., II., 256, for stories of the taking of Jūn.

It is a six days' journey from Jūn to Tatta. The Emperor was as much as six[1] months in Jūn, and brought his family and people and the whole 'Umrkōt party there.[2] The Emperor Jalālu-d-dīn Muhammad Akbar was six months old when they took him to Jūn. The party which had come from various places with the royal family and the *haram* now broke up. As for the rānā, he marched off at midnight for his own country, on account of a coolness[3] caused by some talk between him and Tardī Muhammad Khān.[4] All the Sūdmas and Samīchas went off by agreement with him, and the Emperor was left alone, as before, with his own people.

He sent brave Shaikh'Alī Beg (*Jalāīr*) and Muzaffar Beg *Turhnān,* towards the large district of Jājkā (Hāj-kān). (49*b*) Mīrzā Shāh Husain sent a force to attack him, and there was a famous fight. At last Muzaffar Beg was routed and fled, and Shaikh 'Alī Beg (*Jalāīr*) was killed and perished with all his men.[5]

A squabble arose between Khālid Beg[6] and Tarsh Beg, a brother of Shāham Khān *Jalāīr* and his Majesty turned all his favour to Tarsh Beg. So Khālid Beg deserted and went with all his men to Mīr Shāh Husain. Then the Emperor ordered Khālid Beg's mother, Sulṯanam, to prison and this made Gul-barg[7] Begam angry. Then he forgave Sulṯanam and gave her leave to go to the blessed Makka with Gul-barg Begam. Soon after this Tarsh Beg also deserted. The

---

1 Other writers say nine.

2 Hamīda and her baby were good travellers. They left 'Umrkōt when the child was under five weeks old (November 20th), and joined Humāyūn early in December (1542).

3 *shukr rangi.* I do not find this word in dictionaries, and translate tentatively on the analogy of *shukr-āb*, a tiff.

4 Other writers give Khwāja Ghāzī as the second in the quarrel.

5 A stubbom fight, and fateful for Humāyūn. It occurred in November, 1543.

6 Son of Nizāmu-d-dīn 'Alī Khalīfa Barlās and of Sulṯanam who appears to be Gul-badan's former hostess (14*a*)

7 Daughter of Khalīfa, and as such sister or half-sister of Khālid, and daughter or stepdaughter of Sulṯanam. She is, I believe, the Gul-barg of earlier episodes and a wife of Humāyūn.

INCIDENTS FOLLOWING THE BIRTH OF AKBAR.

At the top, on the right, are Hamīda-bānū and the child ; on the left, the news is announced with sound of castanets and tambourines.

In the middle, the hour of birth is being communicated to the astrologers.

At the foot, the news is being given to Humāyūn by Tardī Beg, and is welcomed by music and dancing.

[*To face p.* 158.

Emperor cursed him, and said: 'For his sake, I dealt harshly with Khālid Beg, who on this account left the circle of the faithful for the circle of the disloyal. Tarsh Beg will die young.' So it was ! Fifteen days later, a servant killed him with a knife as he lay sleeping in a boat. When the Emperor heard of it he grew sad and thoughtful. (50*a*) Shāh Husain Mīrzā brought boats up the river to near Jūn, and his men and the Emperor's often fought on board, and many were killed on both sides. Day by day there were desertions to Shāh Husain. In one of these fights was killed Mullā Tāju-d-dīn whom his Majesty held in the greatest favour as a pearl of knowledge.

There was a squabble between Tardī Muhammad Khān and Mu'nīm Khān. Mu'nīm Khān consequently deserted.

Very few amīrs remained; amongst them were Tardī Muhammad Khān and Mīrzā Yādgār and Mīrzā Pavanda Muhammad and Muhammad Walī and Nadīm *kūka* and Kaushan *kūka* and Khadang[1] the chamberlain. Then there was word brought: 'Bairām Khān has reached Jājkā (Hāj-kān) on his way from Gujrāt.' The Emperor was delighted, and ordered Khadang and others to give him honourable meeting.

Meantime Shāh Husain Mīrzā had heard of Bairām Khān's coming and sent to capture him. Bairām Khān rashly went into a hollow, and there they fell upon him. (50*b*) Khadang the chamberlain was killed. Bairām Khān and the rest escaped, and the khān came and paid his respects to the Emperor.

At this time letters arrived (addressed to) Mīrzā Hindāl for his Majesty from Qarācha Khān, saying: 'You have been long near Bhakkar, and during the whole time Shāh Husain Mīrzā has given no sign of good-will but the reverse. By Heaven's grace, an easy way is open, and it is best for the Emperor to come here (to Qandahār). This is really advisable. If he will not come, come you yourself without fail.' As his Majesty's coming was delayed, Qarācha Khān

---

[1] Probably the father of Maywa-jan. Bairam arrived April 12th, 1543 (Muharram 7th, 950H.).

NAUTCH IN CELEBRATION OF AKBAR'S BIRTH.

[*To page p.* 160.

went out and met Mīrzā Hindāl, and made over the town to him (in the autumn of 1541).

Mīrzā 'Askarī was in Ghaznīn, and to him Mīrzā Kāmrān wrote: 'Qarācha Khān has given over Qandahār to Mīrzā Hindāl. Qandahār must be considered.' His idea was to take it from Mīrzā Hindāl.

On hearing of these things, his Majesty came to his aunt Khānzāda Begam,[1] and said with great urgency: 'Pray do me the honour of going to Qandahār and advising Mīrzā Hindāl and Mīrzā Kāmrān. (51*a*) Tell them that the Uzbegs and the Turkmāns are near them, and that the best plan is to be friends amongst themselves. If Mīrzā Kāmrān will agree to carry out what I have written to him, I will do what his heart desires.'

Mīrzā Kāmrān came to Qandahār four days after the begam's arrival.[2] Day after day he urged: 'Read the *khuṭba* in my name '; and again and again Mīrzā Hindāl said: 'In his life-time his Majesty *Firdaus-makānī* gave his throne to the Emperor Humāyūn and named him his successor. We all agreed to this, and up till now have read the *khuṭba* in his name. There is no way of changing the *khuṭba*.'[3] Mīrzā Kāmrān wrote to her Highness, Dil-dār Begam:[4] 'I have come from Kābul with you in mind. It is strange that you should not once have come to see me. (51*b*) Be a mother to me as you are to Mīrzā Hindāl.' At last Dil-dār Begam went to see him, and

[1] From this it would seem that Khānzāda was in Sind with Humāyūn. No other writer, I believe, mentions this or the embassy on which she is now sent. The Uzbegs and Turkmāns do not appear āpropos here. If, as Gul-badan says,—and her authority is good,— Khānzāda now went to Qandahār, she will have gone on to Kābul, possibly with Hindāl after he surrendered the town to Kāmrān. Of Mahdī Khwāja, Khānzāda's husband, I find no mention made by any historian after Bābar's death,—a singular fact and matched by the similar disappearance of the great Khalīfa. Abū'l-fazl names his tomb. *Cf.* App. *s.n.* Khānzāda.

[2] She had a weary journey from Jūn to Qandahār, and Kāmrān had another, but less toilsome, from Kābul. Kāmrān kept Hindāl besieged, but there seems to have been a good deal of communication between besiegers and beleaguered.

[3] Our memory is better than the begam's, and we remember that Hindāl found no dimculty in changing the *khuṭba* to his own name in Dihlī.

[4] She would be probably with her son Hindāl in the fort.

HYMN OF PRAISE FOR AKBAR'S BIRTH.

Of especial interest are the faces of the open-mouthed singers. Hamīda-bānū is probably the featureless person on the estrade.

[*To face p.* 162.

he said: 'Now I shall not let you go till you send for Mīrzā Hindāl.' Dil-dār Begam said: 'Khānzāda Begam is your elder kinswoman, and oldest and highest of you all. Ask her the truth about the *khuṭba.*' So then he spoke to *Aka.* Her Highness Khānzāda Begam answered: 'If you ask me! well! as his Majesty *Firdaus-makānī* decided it and gave his throne to the Emperor Humāyūn, and as you, all of you, have read the *khuṭba* in his name till now, so now regard him as your superior and remain in obedience to him.'

To cut the matter short, Mīrzā Kāmrān besieged Qandahār and kept on insisting about the *khuṭba* for four months. At last he settled it in this way: 'Very well! the Emperor is now far away. Read the *khuṭba* in my name and when he comes back, read it in his.' As the siege had drawn out to great length, and people had gradually come to cruel straits, there was no help for it; the *khuṭba* was read. (52*a*) He gave Qandahār to Mīrzā 'Askarī and promised Ghaznīn to Mīrzā Hindāl. When they reached Ghaznīn, he assigned the Lamghānāt and the mountain passes (Tangayhā)[1] to the mīrzā, and all those promises were false.[2]

Mīrzā Hindāl went off to Badakhshān, and settled down in Khost and Andar-āb. Mīrzā Kāmrān said to Dil-dār Begam: 'Go and fetch him.' When she arrived, the mīrzā said: 'I have withdrawn myself from the turmoil of soldiering, and even[3] Khost is a hermitage. I have quite settled down.' The begam answered: 'If you intend to lead the darvish-life, even[3] Kābul is a hermitage. Live where your family and kinsfolk are. That is the better plan.' Then she made him come, and for awhile he lived as a darvish in Kābul.

About this time, Mīr Shāh Husain sent to the Emperor to say: 'The course favouring fortune is for you to march for Qandahār. That is the better plan.' His Majesty was willing, and replied:

---

1 (?) The *Tangī* of Rudyard Kipling.

2 The Tārikli-i-badāyunī states that Ghaznīn was given to Hindāl and then taken away, and Mr. Erskine comments on this as probably untrue. (B. & H., II. 265 n..) Gul-badan here supports 'Abdu-l-qadīr.

3 'as good as any other place 'is perhaps the import of the ham.

'Horses and camels are scarce in my camp; give me some to travel with to Qandahār.' (526) Shāh Husain Mīrza agreed, and said: 'There are a thousand camels on the other side of the river, which I will send to you as soon as you have crossed.'

[If words by Khwāja Kasak (? Kīsīk), kinsman of Khwāja Ghāzī, are recorded about the journey from Bhakkar and Sind, they are copied from the writings of the said Khwāja Kasak.[1]]

At length the Emperor went on board boats, with kinsfolk and family, army and the rest, and travelled for three days on the great river. At the frontier of Shāh Husain Mīrzā's territory is a village called Nuāsī.[2] Here they halted, and his Majesty sent Sultān Qulī, the head-camel-driver, to fetch the camels. Sultān Qulī brought a thousand, all of which his Majesty gave to his amīrs, and soldiers, and others, ordering them to be apportioned.

The camels were such that one might say they had not known city, or load, or man for seven, or rather seventy, generations. As horses were few, many people took camels to ride on, and what were left were assigned for the baggage. Every camel which was mounted, at once flung its rider to the ground, and took its way to the jungle. (53*a*) Every pack-camel, when it heard the sound of horses' feet, jumped and bounded and tossed off its load, and went off and away to the jungle. If a load was fixed so fast that, jump as it would, it could not get it off, it carried it away and ran with it into the jungle. This was the way the Emperor started for Qandahār. Some 200 camels must have gone off like this.

Shāh Husain Mīrzā's head-camel-driver Mahmūd was in Sīwī (Sībī), and when the Emperor came near, he strengthened the citadel and retired into it. His Majesty came prosperously to within twelve miles' distance. Then word was brought that Mīr Allāh-dost and

---

[1] We surmise that this is a gloss of Gul-badan. who has copied from a diary or writings of Khwāja Kasak. This name may be the Turki *kīsīk*, a guard, a sentinel. No Persian word seems appropriate.

[2] Bunāī, B. & H., II. 262. The text is clear.

Bābā Jūjūk'[1] had arrived in Sīwī from Kābul two days earlier, and were going on to (visit) Shāh Husain Mīrzā. By them Mīrzā Kāmrān had sent a dress of honour, and *tipūchāq* horses, and much fruit, and they were to ask for Mīrzā Shāh Husain's daughter.[2]

The Emperor said to Khwāja Ghāzī: 'As there is the tie of father and son[3] between you and Allāh-dost, write and ask him in what way Mīrzā Kāmrān stands towards me, and what he will do if I go into his neighbourhood.' (53*b*) He also gave this order to Khwāja Kasak: 'Go to Sīwī, and ask Mīr Allāh-dost whether he thinks it advisable for me to come to Kābul.' The khwāja set out, and the Emperor said: 'We will not march till you have returned.' When the khwāja came near Sīwī, Mahmūd, the head-camel-driver, caught him, and asked: 'Why are you here. 'To buy horses and camels,' he answered. Mahmūd ordered: 'Feel under his arm and search his cap. Heaven forbid that he should have brought a letter to win over Allāh-dost and Bābā Jūjūk.' They searched, and brought out the letter from under his arm. He had no chance to twist it into a fold.[4] Mahmūd took it and read it, and, not letting the khwāja go, forthwith conveyed Allāh-dost and Bābā Jūjūk into the fort, and with various roughnesses made them swear: 'We had no knowledge of his coming here.' (54*a*) (?) He has taken the initiative;[5] and 'Khwāja Ghāzī is related to us and he was with Mīrzā Kāmrān,[6] and this is why he has written.' Mahmūd decided to send all three to Shāh Husain, and Mīr Allāh-dost and Bābā Jūjūk spent the whole

---

1 Both these names may be sobriquets. Abu'l-fazl names Shaikh 'Abdu-l-wahab as Allāh-dost's companion. (A. N., *Bib. Ind.* ed. I. 189 *et seq.*.)

Jūjūk is perhaps the Tūrkī 'sweet-savoured,' and an epithet of'Abdu-l-wahab, a lawyer with persuasive tongue.

2 The daughter has already been named as promised.

3 Probably a spiritual relationship; that of religious teacher and disciple.

4 (?) to toss it secretly into a corner.

5 sabq khwānda ast. Perhaps Kasak as a pupil 'has said his lessons to us,' *i.e.*, to Allāh-dost.

6 He had been Kāmrān's dīwān up to the time when the royal family left Lāhōr, and he joined Humāyūn when the brothers parted for Sind and for Kābul.

night smoothing him down and entreating him, and in the end they were set free.

Mīr Allāh-dost sent 3,000[1] pomegranates and 100 quinces for his Majesty's use, and wrote no letter, because he was afraid it might fall into the wrong hands. By word of mouth he sent to say: 'If a letter should come from Mīrzā Askarī or the amīrs, it would not be bad to go to Kābul; but if not, it will be clear to your Majesty that nothing is to be gained by going. You have few followers. What, then, will happen?'

Kasak came and reported this. The Emperor was stupefied and bewildered, and said: 'What is to be done? Where am I to go?' They all consulted together. (54*b*) Tardī Muhammad Khān and Bairām Khān gave it as their opinion that it was impossible to decide to go anywhere but to the north and Shal-mastān,[2] the frontier of Qandahār. 'There are many Afghans in those parts,' they said, 'whom we shall draw over to our side. Mīrzā 'Askarī's people, too, will join us.'

Having settled it in this way, they recited the *fātiha* and went, march by march, for Qandahār. Near Shalmastān they halted in a village named Ranī (? Ralī), but as it had snowed and rained, and was extremely cold, they determined to go on to Shal-mastān. At afternoon prayer-time an Uzbeg youth, mounted on a sorry and tired-out pony, came in, and cried out: 'Mount, your Majesty! I will explain on the way; time presses. There is no time to talk.'[3] The Emperor mounted the very hour the alarm was given, and went off.

He went two arrows' flight, and then sent Khwāja Mu'aẓẓam and Bairām Khān to fetch Hamīda-bānū Begam, (55*a*) They went and mounted her, but there was not a chink of time in which to take the Emperor Jalālu-d-dīn Muhammad Akbar. Just when the begam

---

[1] Text, *sīsad*, but perhaps only 300 should be read.

[2] Approximately Quetta. The route seems to have been over the Bolan.

[3] The youth was Chupī Bahādūr, a former servant of Humāyūn. Gul-badan's story differs in some details from that told by other writers.

left the camp to join his Majesty, Mīrzā 'Askarī came up with 2,000 troopers. There was an outcry, and when he heard it, he entered the camp[1] and asked: 'Where is the Emperor?' People said: 'He went hunting long ago.' So the mīrzā knew that his Majesty had gone away just as he himself came in. Then he took possession of the Emperor Jalālud-dīn Muhammad Akbar, and gave him in charge to his wife Sulṭanam,[2] who showed him much kindness and affection. He made all the royal followers march, saying: 'Go to Qandahār.'

His Majesty, when he left, took the road to the mountains. He went eight miles, and then travelled as fast as possible.[3] (55*b*) He had with him Bairām Khān, Khwāja Mu'aẓẓam, Khwāja Nīāzī, Nadīm *kūka*[4] and Raushan *kūka,* and Hājī Muhammad Khān, and Bābā-dost the paymaster, and Mīrzā Qulī Beg *chūlī,*[5] and Ḥaidar Muhammad the master of the horse, and Shaikh Yūsuf *chūlī,* and Ibrāhīm the chamberlain, and Hasan 'Alī, the chamberlain, and Yaqūb the keeper of the armoury, and 'Ambar the superintendent and the royal aġent (*mulk-mukhtār*), and Sambal captain of a thousand, and Khwāja Kasak.[6]

Khwāja Ghāzī says: 'I also was in attendance.' This company went with the Emperor, and Hamīda-bānū Begam says,[7] 'There were as many as thirty people,' and that of women there was, besides herself, the wife of Hasan 'Alī, the chamberlain.

The prayer before sleep had passed before they reached the foot of the mountains. The snow lay deep, so there was no road to go

---

1 Late in 950H. (1543). The little Akbar reached Qandahār on December 15th, 1543.

2 I believe she was in Qandahār, and that she received the child on his arrival there.

3 Perhaps he rode four kos, and then, having waited for Hamīda, hurried on.

4 His wife, Māham *anaga*, remained behind with Akbar. With Akbar was also Aika Khān (Shamsu-d-dīn Muhammad) and his wife, Jī-jī *anaga*.

5 Humāyun's sobriquet for those who went to Persia with him; from chūl, a desert. Others in this list might claim it.

6 Nizāmu-d-dīn Aḥmad puts the number of the party at twenty-two.

7 The tense used suggests conference and talking over. Jauhar says that Khwāja Ghāzī joined Humāyūn in Persia from Makka. This looks like a contradiction of Jauhar.

up by. Their minds were full of anxiety lest that unjust creature, Mīrzā ‘Askarī, should follow them. At last they found a way up, and climbed it in some sort of fashion. They were all night in the snow, and (at first) there was neither wood for fire nor food to eat.

They grew very hungry and feeble. (56*a*) The Emperor gave orders to kill a horse. There was no cooking-pot, so they boiled some of the flesh in a helmet, and some they roasted. They made fires on all four sides, and with his own blessed hand the Emperor roasted some meat which he ate. He used to say: ‘My very head was frozen by the intense cold.’

Morning came at last, and he pointed to another mountain, and said: ‘There are people on that; there will be many Biluchīs there; and there we must go.’ On they went, and reached the place in two days. They saw a few houses near them, and a few savage Biluchīs whose speech is the tongue of the ghouls of the waste.

The Emperor halted on the skirt of the mountain. There were about thirty people with him. The Biluchīs saw him, and collected and came near. He had settled comfortably in his tent, so they knew from far off that he was halting. They said to one another: ‘If we seize these people and take them to Mīrzā ‘Askarī, he will certainly give us their arms, and many gifts besides.’ (56*b*)

Hasan ‘Alī, the chamberlain, had a Bilūchī wife who understood what the ghouls of the waste were saying, and who made it known that they meant mischief. Early in the morning the Emperor thought of marching on, but they said: ‘Our chief is not here. When he comes, you shall go.’ Besides this, the time had become unsuitable, and so the whole night was spent there in strict watchfulness.

Part of the night had gone when the chief arrived. He waited on the Emperor, and said: ‘A *farmān* has come from Mīrzā Kāmrān and Mīrzā ‘Askarī, in which it is written: “It is reported that the Emperor may visit your dwellings. If he does, beware!—a thousand times beware!— of letting him go. Seize him and bring him to us. You can keep his goods and horses. Take him to Qandahār.’ As I had not seen your Majesty, I at first had this evil thought, but now I will sacrifice my life and the lives of my family, I have five or six sons, for your Majesty's head, or rather for one hair of it. (57*a*) Go where you wish. God protect you! Mīrzā 'Askarī may do what he likes.' The Emperor gave him a ruby and a pearl and some other things.

At dawn he marched to honour Fort Bābā Hājī[1] by a visit. He reached it in two days. It belongs to the Garmsīr,[2] and lies on the river (Halmand). There are many sayyids there, and they waited on the Emperor and showed him hospitality.

Next morning Khwāja 'Alāwalu-d-dīn (Jalālu-d-dīn) Mahnmd,[3] having left Mīrzā 'Askarī, came with an offering of a string of mules, and one of horses and tents, etc, whatever he had. Once more the royal heart was at ease. Hājī Muhammad Khān *kūkī*[4] brought thirty or forty troopers and offered a string of mules.

Being helpless because of the disunion of his brothers[5] and the desertion of his amīrs, it now seemed best to the Emperor,—with reliance on the Causer of causes,—to decide upon going to Khurāsān.[6] (57*b*)

After many stages and a journey of many days, he came to parts adjacent to Khurāsān. When Shāh Tahmās (*sic*) heard that he had reached the Halmand. he remained sunk in wonder and thought, and said: 'The Emperor Humāyun has come to our frontier by the perfidious revolution of the firmament,—the firmament unpropitious and crooked of gait! The Lord, whose existence is necessary, has led him here!'

---

1 Fort of the Pilgrim Father.

2 *i.e.*, a warm climate, a winter habitation in low ground, and cultivated fields.

3 He was a revenue-collector of the mīrzā.

4 Son of Bābā Qūshka, an intimate of Bābar.

5 Kāmrān was master of Kābul and Ghaznī, Qandahār, Khutlān and Badakhshān. 'Askarī was attached to his full-brother's fortunes, and Hindāl was a prisoner in Kābul. Shīr Shāh ruled Bābar's Indian Empire, and Shāh Husain was in Sind. Certainly there seemed no 'crack' to hold Humāyūn. The date is December, 1543.

6 *i.e.*, on his way to Persia proper. Humāyūn's messenger to the Shāh was Chupī Bahādur. (55*a* and n..)

He sent all sorts of people to give honourable reception, nobles and grandees, low and high, great and small. All came to the Halmand to meet the Emperor.[1]

The Shāh sent all his brothers to meet his Majesty,— Bahrām Mīrzā, and Alqās Mīrzā, and Sām Mīrzā. All came and embraced him, and escorted him with full honour and respect. As they drew near (the Shāh) his brothers sent him word, and he also came riding to meet the Emperor. They embraced. (58*a*) The friendship and concord of those two high-placed pāshas was as close as two nut-kernels in one shell.[2] Great unanimity and good feeling ensued, so that during his Majesty's stay in that country, the Shāh often went to his quarters, and on days when he did not, the Emperor went to his.

In Khurāsān[3] his Majesty visited all the gardens and the flower-gardens, and the splendid buildings put up by Sultān Husain Mīrzā, and the grand structures of olden days.

There was hunting eight times while he was in 'Irāq, and each time trouble was taken for him also. Hamīdabānū Begam used to enjoy the sight from a distance in either a camel or a horse litter. Shāhzāda Sulṭ̤anam,[4] the Shāh's sister, used to ride on horseback,

---

1 He had crossed the river without receiving invitation or permission, because of Kāmrān's threatened approach. The incidents of Humāyūn's visit to Persia are very entertaining. (B. & H., II. 275 *et seq*..)

2 A figure of speech too compact to leave room for the facts. The intercourse of the pāshas was dramatic with human passion and foible. Much of the story would be distasteful to Gul-badan's family pride and vexatious to her orthodoxy.

3 Not only in Khurāsān but on and off the route to Tahmāsp's summer quarters where the pāshas met, did Humāyūn visit note-worthy places. He saw Harāt as his father had done, and later his devious journey took him to Jām, where he saw the shrine of his own and of Hamīda's ancestor, the Terrible Elephant, Ahmad. He visited the tomb of the Founder of the Safī dynasty at Ardabīl, and the date of his visit (1544) makes it probable that he trod that 'Holy Carpet' of Ardabīl which had been woven in 1540 for the shrine and which now attracts our respectful admiration in the Oriental Section of the Victoria and Albert Museum (S. K. M.).

4 This lady afforded Humāyūn vital assistance in Persia, and even pleaded for his life when it was in the balance. She was highly esteemed by Tahmāsp, and had influence in state affairs.

and take her stand behind her brother. His Majesty said (to Hamīda-bānū): 'There was a woman riding behind the Shāh at the hunt. She stood with her reins held by a white-bearded man. People told me it was Shāhzāda Sulṯanam, the Shāh's sister.' (58*b*) In short, the Shāh showed the Emperor much hospitality and courtesy, and laid a charge (on his sister) to show motherly and sisterly hospitality and sympathy (to Hamīda-bānū Begam).[1]

One day, when Shāhzāda Sulṭanam had entertained the begam, the Shāh said to her: 'When (next) you offer hospitality, let it be arranged outside the city.' It was on a beautiful plain, rather more than four miles out, that they pitched tents (*khaima*) and folding-tents (*khirga*) and an audience-tent (*bargā*), and also set up *chatr*[2] and *ṭāq*.[3]

In Khurāsān and those parts they use enclosing screens (*sarāparda*), but they do not put them at the back. The Emperor set up an all-round screen after the Hindu fashion (*hindūāna*). Having pitched the tents, the Shāh's people put coloured chicks (*cheghhā*) all round. His kinswomen and his paternal aunt were there, and his sisters and the lādies of his *ḥaram,* and the wives of the khāns and sultāns and amīrs, about 1,000 women in all splendour and adornment.

That day Shāhzāda Sulṭanam asked Hamīda-bānū Begam: (59*a*) 'Are such *chatr* and *ṭāq* met with in Hindūstan?' The begam answered: 'They say two *dāng*[4] with respect to Khurāsān, and four *dāng* with respect to Hindustān.

---

1 An obscure passage in the text, and conjectural only in translation. The Persian words I have rendered 'motherly and sisterly' are *mādarāna iva khwāharāna*. On this saine page occurs *hindūāna*; at 435, nikāhāna, and at 62*a*, *pādshāhāna*.

2 (?) umbrella-shaped tents.

3 round-topped tents or balconies, or arched erections.

4 or *dānak*. Hazarding a guess, the meaning 'quarter of the world' seems fittest to select from the several of *dāng* or *dānak*. Others conceivably applicable are 'a small grain' (anglice, peppercorn in this connection), and the sixth of anything (anglice, the colloquial 'fraction'). Doubtless my difficulty is none to those experienced in colloquial Persian.

Hamīda's ready use of a colloquial phrase to express that the reputedly greater contains the less is neat and diplomatic.

When a thing is found in two *dāng,* it is clear it will be found better in four.'

Shāh Sulṭanam said also, in reply to her own paternal aunt, and in confirmation of the begam's words: 'Aunt, it is strange that you ask, "Where are two *dāng?* where are four *dāng*?" It is clear anything would be found better and more wonderful (in four than in two).'

They passed the whole day very well in sociable festivity. At the time of eating, all the amīrs' wives stood and served, and the Shāh's lādies placed[1] food before Shāhzāda Sulṭanam.

Moreover, they were hospitable[2] with all sorts of stuffs, embroidered and others, to Hamīda-bānū Begam, as was incumbent and fitting. The Shāh went on in advance[3] and was in his Majesty's quarters till the prayer before sleep. (59*b*) When he heard that Hamīda-bānū Begam had arrived, he rose from the presence and went home. To such a height of pleasantness and kindness was he amiable!

Raushan *kūka,* spite of his former fidelity and services, was now faithless, in that foreign and perilous country, about some valuable rubies. These used to be kept in the Emperor's amulet-case (*ṭumar*[4]), and of this he and the begam knew and no one else. If he went away anywhere, he used to give the amulet-case into her charge. One day she was going to wash her head, so she bundled the case up in a handkerchief, and put it on the Emperor's bed. Raushan *kūka* thought this a good chance to steal five rubies. Then he agreed with Khwāja Ghāzī, and trusted them to him, meaning by-and-by to barter them away.

When the begam came back from washing her head, the Emperor gave her the amulet-case, and she at once knew from its lightness in her hand that it had lost weight, and said so. (60*a*) The Emperor

---

1 *māndand*, used transitively; also at 4*a*.

2 *mihmānī kardand*. (?) In the way of gifts, or perhaps by lavish decoration.

3 *i.e.*, from the place of entertainment to the town.

4 Also ṭūmār, an amulet-case of gold or silver suspended on the neck.

asked: 'How is this? Except you and me, no one knows about them. What can have happened? Who has taken them?' He was astonished.

The begam said to her brother, Khwāja Mu'aẓẓam: 'So and so has happened. If at this pinch you will act the brother to me and will make inquiry in some way quietly, you will save me from what one may call disgrace. Otherwise, as long as I live, I shall be ashamed in the royal presence.'

Khwāja Mu'aẓẓam said: 'One thing occurs to me ! I, who am so closely connected with his Majesty, have not the means to buy even a poor pony,[1] but Khwāja Ghāzī and Raushan *kūka*[2] have each bought themselves a *tipūchāq* horse. They have not paid the money for them yet. This purchase is not without a ray of hope.'

The begam answered: 'O brother! now is the time for brotherliness! That transaction must certainly be looked into.' Khwāja Mu'aẓẓam answered: 'O elder moon-sister ![3] tell no one about it. Heaven willing, I have hope that the right will be righted.' (60*b*)

He went out, and inquired at the house of the horse-dealers: 'For what price did you sell those horses? When is the money promised? What security has been given for the pavment?' The dealers answered: 'Both men promised us rubies, and took the horses.'

From them he went to the khwāja's servant, and said: 'Where is the khwāja's wallet, with his honorary dress and his clothes?[4] Where does he keep it?' The servant answered: 'My khwāja has no wallet and no clothes. He has one high cap which, when he goes to sleep, he puts under his head or his arm.' Khwāja Mu'aẓẓam saw the meaning of this, and made up his mind for certain that the rubies

---

[1] Text, *tātū*.

[2] Jauhar states that amongst other disaffected persons these two men, and a third, Sultān Muhammad, the spearman (*nazabāz*), had just returned from Makka, and were of Kāmrān's party. Gul-badan makes it seem probable that Jauhar's statements apply only to Sultān Muhammad (*Cf.* list of companions of Humāyūn on his journey, 55b.)

[3] *māh chīcham. Cf.* 18b n..

[4] *nārī wa parī.*

were with Khwāja Ghāzī, and were kept in his high cap. He came and represented to his Majesty: 'I have found trace of those rubies in Khwāja Ghāzī's high cap. In some way I will steal them from him. (61*a*) If he should come to your Majesty and seek redress against me, let your Majesty say nothing to me.' The Emperor listened, and smiled.

Khwāja Mu'aẓẓam then repeatedly played off tricks and little jokes and pleasantries on Khwāja Ghāzī, who came and set it forth to the Emperor. 'I am a lowly man,' said he, '(? but) I have a name and a position. What does the boy Khwāja Mu'aẓẓam mean by playing off these tricks and jokes, and making fun of me in this foreign land, and insulting me?' His Majesty said: 'On whom does he not? He is young. It often comes into his head to do terrifying and ill-bred things. Do not take it to heart. He is only a boy.'

Another day, when Khwāja Ghāzī was seated in the reception-room, Khwāja Mu'aẓẓam, pretending an aceident, filched his cap from his head. Then he took out the matchless rubies, and laid them before his Majesty and Hamīda-bānū Begam. His Majesty smiled, and the begam was delighted, and said, 'Bravo!' and 'Mercy be upon you.' (61*b*)

Khwāja Ghāzī and Raushan *kūka,* in shame at their deed, made secret communications to the Shāh, and carried their talk so far that his heart was troubled. His Majesty saw that the Shāh's intimacy and confidence were not what they had been, and at once sent some of whatever rubies and other jewels[1] he possessed as a gift to him, who then said: 'Khwāja Ghāzī and Kaushan *kūka* are in fault; they turned my heart from you, and truly I used to regard you as a brother.' Then the two sovereigns again became of one mind, and made clean heart to one another.

The two wrong-doers were excluded from the presence, and

[1] It was now that Humāyūn gave to the Shāh the 'diamond which had been obtained from Sultān Ibrāhīm's treasury,' *i.e.*,the Koli-i-nūr. (Asiatic *Quarterly Review*, April, 1899, art. 'Bābar's Diamond,' H. Beveridge.)

were made over to the Shāh, who, when opportunity occurred, got possession of those rubies,[1] and, as to the men, ordered: 'Let them be kept in custody.'[2]

His Majesty's time in 'Irāq was (now) spent happily. In various ways the Shāh showed good feeling, and every day sent presents of rare and strange things. (62*a*)

At length the Shāh despatched his own son and khāns and sultāns and amīrs with his Majesty to help him, together with good arms and tents, folding and audience tents; and *chatr* and *ṯāq* and *shamiāna,* excellently wrought, and all sorts of the things necessary and iit for a king, from the mattress-warehouse and the treasury and the workshops and kitchen and buttery. In a propitious hour those two mighty sovereigns bade one another farewell, and his Majesty left that country for Qandahār.[3]

At the time of his departure, he asked pardon from the Shāh for the offence of those two faithless ones (Khwāja Ghāzī and Raushan *kūka*), and, having himself forgiven them, took them with him to Qandahār.

When Mīrzā 'Askarī heard (1545) that he was on his way from Khurāsān and approaching Qandahār, he sent the Emperor Jalālu-d-dīn Muhammad Akbar to Mīrzā Kāmrān in Kābul, who gave him into the care of Dearest Lady, Khānzāda Begam, and our paternal aunt. (62*b*) He was two and a half years old when she received him into her charge. She was very fond of him, and used to kiss his hands and feet, and say: 'They are the very hands and feet of my brother the Emperor Bābar, and he is like him altogether.'[4]

---

1 (?) those already bartered away.

2 They were, it would seem, let down by tent-ropes into the celebrated underground prison of Sulaimān's *Diwān*. (Jauhar, Stewart, 72.)

3 Humāyūn again indulged his love of travel and sights, and delayed so long in Persian territory that the Shāh, coming unexpectedly upon him, angrily turned him off without ceremony.

4 The child was just over three. It was now that he and Bakhshī-bānū travelled together to Kābul in the snow.

When Mīrzā Kāmrān was sure that the Emperor was approaching Qandahār, he went to Dearest Lady and cried, and was very humble, and said with countless pains:[1] 'Go you (May your journey be safe!) to Qandahār to the Emperor and make peace between us.'

When she left (Kābul) she made over the Emperor Akbar to Mīrzā Kāmrān, who gave him into the care of (Muhtarīma) Khānam. Then she travelled as fast as possible to Qandahār. The Emperor besieged Mīrzā Kāmrān[2] and Mīrzā 'Askarī for forty days in the city, and he sent Bairām Khān on an embassy to Mīrzā Kāmrān.[3] (63*a*) Mīrzā 'Askarī grew dejected and humble, admitted his offences, and came out and paid his duty to the Emperor, who then took possession of Qandahār (September 4th, 1545). He bestowed it upon the son of the Shāh, who in a few days fell ill and died.[4] When Bairām Khān[5] arrived, it was given into his charge.

The Emperor left Hamīda-bānū Begam in Qandahār and set out after Mīrzā Kāmrān. Dearest Lady, Khānzāda Begam, went with him, and at Qabal-chak[6] she had three days of fever. The doctors' remedies were of no avail, and on the fourth day of her illness she passed to the mercy of God. At first she was buried at Qabal-chak, but three months later her body was brought to Kābul and laid in the burial-place of my royal father.[7]

During several years that Mīrzā Kāmrān was in Kābul, he had never made a hostile raid,[8] and now, all at once, when he heard of

---

1 of persuasion.

2 The context shows that this is wrong, and so do the histories.

3 Bairām saw Akbar in Kābul, and also Hindāl, Sulaimān, *Ḥaram*, Ibrāhīm and Yādgār-nāsir, all under surveillance. The embassy reached Kābul before Khānzāda left, and she travelled with Bairām on his return to Humāyūn.

4 He was an infant.

5 The begam's chronology is faulty here. Bairām had returned before the capitulation.

6 For location of this place *cf. Akbarnāma* H. B., I. 477 n.. It seems to have been in the mountain district of Tīri, between the basins of the Halmand and the Arghand-āb.

7 Khānzāda, Mahdī (her husband) and Abū'l-ma'ālī are buried in the same spot.

8 *tākhht raftan*. I do not know what the begam wishes to say. Kāmrān had made hostile raids to Badakhshān and against the Hazāras. One might read 'hunting expedition.'

his Majesty's approach, desire to break forth (? hunt) seized him, and he went into the Hazāra country.[1] (63*b*)

Mīrzā Hindāl, who had chosen the darvish's corner (in Kābul), now heard of the Emperor's return from 'Irāq and Khurāsān, and of his success in Qandahār. He saw his chance, aud sent for Mīrzā Yādgār-nāsir, and said: 'The Emperor has come to Qandahār, and has been victorious. Mīrzā Kāmrān sent Khānzāda Begam to sue for peace, but the Emperor did not agree to his sort of peace. The Emperor sent Bairām Khān as his envoy, and Mīrzā Kāmrān did not agree to what he proposed. Now the Emperor has given Qandahār to Bairām Khān and has set out for Kābul. Come now, let us, you and I, plan and agree together, and scheme how to betake ourselves to his Majesty.' Mīrzā Yādgār-nāsir agreed, and the two made their plan and compact. Mīrzā Hindāl said: 'You make up your mind to run away and when Mīrzā Kāmrān hears of it, he will certainly say to me: "Mīrzā Yādgār-nāsir has gone off; go and persuade him to come back with you." (64*a*) You go slowly, slowly on till I come. Then we will go as quickly as we can and pay our respects to the Emperor.'

Having so settled it, Mīrzā Yādgār-nāsir ran away. The news went to Mīrzā Kāmrān, who came back at once to Kābul and sent for Mīrzā Hindāl and said: 'Go and persuade Mīrzā Yādgār-nāsir to come back.' Mīrzā Hindāl mounted at once, and joined Mīrzā Yādgār-nāsir with all speed. Then they travelled post-haste for five or six days, when they were honoured by paying their duty to the Emperor.

They advised the Khimār[2] Pass as the best route. On Kamzān 9th, 951H. (the third week of October, 1545), his Majesty ordered a halt in that pass. News of this went to Mīrzā Kāmrān on the same day

---

[1] He had a Hazāra wife. Perhaps the passage about Kāmrān's hostile raid or hunting is merely an introduction to Hindāl's plan of scape. (*Cf.* B. & H., II. 314, 315, for this story.)

[2] (?) *himār*, the Ass's Pass.

and disturbed him greatly. He had his tents taken out very quickly and encamped in front of the Guzar-gāh.[1] (64*b*)

On the 11th of the same month, the Emperor ordered a halt in the valley of (?) Tīpa, and Mīrzā Kāmrān[2] also came and drew up opposite to fight. Then all his amīrs deserted and were exalted by kissing the royal feet. Even Bāpūs[3] who was one of his well-known officers, deserted him with all his following and was exalted by kissing the royal feet. The mīrzā was left solitary and alone. 'No one remains near me,' he thought, so he threw down and destroyed the door and the wall of the house of Bāpūs[4] which was near, and went softly, softly past the New Year's Garden and the tomb of Gul-rukh Begam,[5] dismissed his 12,000 troopers, and went off.

When it was dark, he went on in the same direction to Bābā Dashtī,[6] and halted near a piece of water, and sent back Dostī *kūka* and Jūkī *kūka* to fetch his eldest daughter Habība, and his son Ibrāhīm Sultān Mīrzā, and Hazāra Begam[7] who was the brother's child of Khiẓr Khān (Hazāra), and Māh Begam[8] who was sister of H aram (Khurram) Begam, and Māh-afroz, mother of Hājī Begam,[9] and Bāqī *kūka.*[10] (65*a*) This party went with the mīrzā, who planned to go to Tatta and Bhakkar. In Khiẓr Khān Hazāra's country, which lies on the way to Bhakkar, he married Habība Begam to Āq Sultān and entrusted her to him, while he himself went on.

---

1 (?) The Ferry Garden, or perhaps Bābar's burial-place.

2 Not in person, I believe. His troops were under Qāsim Barlās.

3 Governor (*ātalīq*) of Yasīn-daulat (Āq Sulṭān), the betrothed husband of Habība.

4 Mr. Erskine says that Kāmrān escaped by a breach opened in a wall. He went by way of Bīnī-ḥisār to Ghaznī, where 'Askarī still was.

5 (?) His mother.

6 The Desert Father; perhaps a shrine in a lonely spot. (*Cf.* Khwāja Khiẓr, *infra*, 706.)

7 A wife.

8 Probably a wife.

9 Brevet rank at this time. She made one pilgrimage in 983H. (1576). She may, however, have gone earlier with her blinded father, but not so early as 1545.

10 (?) The elder brother of Adham and son of Māham *anaga*. Mahām *anaga* would be in Kābul now.

The victorious Emperor dismounted in triumph in the Bālā-i-ḥisār when five hours of the night of Ramzān 12th had passed,—prosperously and with safety and good luck.[1] All those followers of Mīrzā Kāmrān whohad been promoted to the roval service, entered Kābul with drūms beating (November, 15-45).

On the 12th of the same month, her Highness my mother, Dil-dār Begam, and Gul-chihra Begam, and this lowly person paid our dutv to the Emperor. For five years we had been shut out and cut off from this pleasure, so now when we were freed from the moil and pain of separation, we were lifted up by our happiness in meeting this Lord of beneficence again. Merely to look at him eased the sorrow-stricken heart and purged the blear-eyed vision. (60*b*) Again and again we joyfully made the prostration of thanks. There were many festive gatherings, and people sat from evening to dawn, and plavers and singers made continuous musie. Many amusing games, full of fun, were played. Amongst them was this: Twelve players had each twenty cards and twenty *shāhrukhīs.* Whoever lost, lost those twenty *shuhrukhīs,* which would make five *misqals.* '[2] Each player gave the winner his twenty *shāhrukhīs* to add to his own.[3]

To widows and orphans, and kinsfolk of men who had been wounded and killed at Chausa and Kanauj, or Bhakkar, or who were in the roval service during those interrnissions,[4] he gave pension, and rations, and water, and land, and servants. In the days of his

---

1 The hour was probably fixed by astrological counsel. Abū'l-fazl, who may follow the begam's statement. savs that the entry took place on the 12th ; other writers name the 10th. The only reason for dwelling on the point is the agreement of Abū'l-fazl and Gul-badan.

2 One shāhrukhīs was about ten pence. Four shāhrukhls made one misqāl.

3 Mr. Erskine savs that the earliest mention of cards as made known to him by an Oriental writer is when Bābar sends some to Shāh Husain Arghūn who was 'very fond' of them. by Mīr 'Alī, the armour-bearer, in 933H. 11526-27). No doubt such an easy means of speeding the hours was known to the ladies of Bābar's family as early as to anyone else, and Gul-badan is perhaps merely describing a new game.

4 Text, *faṭrathā*. The begam writes this word sometimes with a *tā* and sometimes with a *to'e*.

Majesty's good fortune, great tranquillity and happiness befell soldiers and peasants. They lived without care, and put up many an ardent praver for his long life. (66*a*)

A few days later he sent persons to bring Hamīda-bānū Begam from Qandahār. When she arrived, thev celebrated the feast of the circumcision of the Emperor Jalālu-d-dīn Muhammad Akbar. Preparations were made, and after the New Year[1] they kept splendid festivity for seventeen days. People dressed in green,[2] and thirty or forty girls were ordered to wear green and come out to the hills. On the first day of the New Year they went out to the Hill of the Seven Brothers and there passed many days in ease and enjoyment and happiness. The Emperor Muhammad Akbar was five years old when they made the circumcision feast in Kābul. Thev gave it in that same large Audience Hall Garden.[3] They decorated all the bazārs. Mīrzā Hindāl and Mīrzā Yādgār-nāsir, and the sultāns and amīrs, decorated their quarters beautifully, and in Bega Begam's garden the begams and lādies made theirs quite wonderful in a new fashion.

All the sultāns and amīrs brought gifts to the Audience Hall Garden. (66*b*) There were many elegant festivities and grand entertainments, and costly *khi'lats* and head-to-foot[4] dresses were bestowed. Peasants and preachers, the pious, the poor and the

---

[1] *i.e.*, Persian era. Nizāmu-d-dīn Ahmad plaees the date of entry into Kābul by Humāvōn on Ramzān 10th, 953H., and says Akbar was then four years, two months and five days old. 'Some place the event in the year 952H., but God knows the truth.' It is strange that there should be doubt about a historical event occurring not more than fifty years before this resigned statement was made. Abū'l-fazl gives Ramzān 12th, 952H. (November 17th, 1545), as the date of entry, which would fix the feast for March. 1546, when Akbar was three years and five months old. (Bora October 15th. 1542.)

[2] Probably in honour of the spring season.

[3] This is the garden where the ladies rejoiced after the victory at Pānīpat. (10*b*) Hence, perhaps. the use of the word 'same.'

[4] Perhaps there is expressed here a difference of degree of honour in the *khi'lat* and *sar-u-pāī*.

needy, noble and plebeian, low and high,—everybody lived in peace and comfort, passing the days in amusement and the nights in talk.

Then the Emperor went to Fort Victory (Qila'-i-zafar).[1] In it was Mīrzā Sulaimān, who came out to fight but could not stand face to face with his Majesty and so decided to run away. The Emperor then entered the fort safe and sound. Then he went to Kishm, where, after a little while, an illness attacked his blessed frame and he slēpt day and night.[2] When he came to his senses, he sent Mun'im Khān's brother, Fazā'il Beg, to Kābul, and said: 'Go! comfort and reassure the people of Kābul. Set them at ease in various ways.[3] Let them not quarrel. Say: "It began ill, but has ended well."' (67*a*)

When Fazā'il Beg had gone, he (Humāyūn) went one day nearer Kābul.[4]

False news having been sent to Mīrzā Kāmrān in Bhakkar, he set out post-haste for Kābul. In Ghaznī he killed Zāhid Beg[5] and then came on. It was morning; the Kābulīs were off their guard; the gates had been opened in the old way, and water-carriers and grass-cuts were going in and out, and the mīrzā passed into the fort with all these common people. He at once killed Uncle Muhammad

---

1 Sulaimān had not made submission to Humāyūn,—hence this expedition to Badakhshān.

2 He is said to have been insensible for four days. He was nursed by Māh-chūchak and Bībī Fāṭima, an armed woman (*ordū-begi*) of the haram. She was, it would seem, mother of Zuhra *āghā*, the wife of Khwāja Mu'azzam, and to save whose life Akbar nearly lost his own. (Elliot, V. 292; B. & H., II. 330 *et seq.*.)

3 (?) As to his health, and their own safety from Kāmrān's return, and the continuance of the situation as he had left it. The illness and convalescence lasted at least two months. He fell ill in Shāhdān, between Kishm and Qila'-i-Ẕafar, and Qarācha Khān, his vazīr, behaved with decision and good sense, so that Humāyūn's authority was upheld.

4 Doubtful translation. Humāyūn is elsewhere said to have gone to Qila'-i-Ẕafar to recruit, and Fazā'il to have arrived in Kābul a few hours after the first news there of the illness. Perhaps one of these occurrences is behind this obscure statement.

5 Husband of Bega Begam's sister.

Alī[1] who was in the hot bath. He alighted at the college of Mullā 'Abdu-l-khāliq.

When the Emperor was starting for Qila-i-Ẓafar, he placed Naukār[2] at the door of the *haram.* Mīrzā Kāmrān must have asked: 'Who is in the Bālā-i-ḥisār?' and someone must have said: 'It is Naukār.' Naukār heard of this and at once put on a woman's dress and went out. The mīrzā's people laid hands on the doorkeeper of the fort, and took him to Mīrzā Kāmrān, who ordered him to be imprisoned. (61*b*) The mīrzā's people went into the Bālā-i- ḥisār, and plundered and destroyed innumerable things belonging to the *haram,* and they made settlement[3] for them in Mīrzā Kāmrān's court (*sarhār*). He put the great begams into Mīrzā 'Askarī's house and there he shut up a room with bricks and plaster and (?) dung-cakes, and they used to give the lādies water and foocl from over the four walls.[4]

In what was once Mīrzā Yādgār-nāsir's house he put Khwāja Mu'aẓẓam[5] and ordered his own wives and family to stay in the palace where the royal *haram* and the begams once lived. He behaved very ill indeed to the wives and families of the officers who had left him for the Emperor, ransacking and plundering all their houses and putting each family into somebody's custody.[6]

When the Emperor heard that Mīrzā Kāmrān had come from Bhakkar and was acting in this way, he returned from Qila'-i-Ẓafar and Andar-āb safe and sound to Kābul. Qila'-i-Ẓafar he gave to Mīrzā Sulaimān. (68*a*)

---

[1] Brother of Māham Begam.

[2] Probably the servant sent with gifts by Bābar from Agra to Kābul. The name looks like that of an Abyssinian. Is it 'new in work,' and a sobriquet given in youth and retained'?

[3] *zabt wa rabt*. Is this an indication of Gul-badan's opinion that Kāmrān profited by the robbery of his relations ? His cruelties at this time make theft look innocent. (B. & H., II. 336 *et seq*..)

[4] The translation of this passage is doubtful.

[5] An undue honour, perhaps prompted by the Khwāja's disgrace with Humāyūn.

[6] Probably for the exploitation so often named in the histories.

When the Emperor was starting for Qilaʿ-i-ẕafar, he placed Naukār[1] at the door of the *ḥaram*. Mīrzā Kāmran must have asked: 'Who is in the Bālā-i-ḥiṣār?' and someone must have said: 'It is Naukār.' Naukār heard of this and at once put on a woman's dress and went out. The Mīrzā's people laid hands on the doorkeeper of the fort, and took him to Mīrzā Kāmrān, who ordered him to be imprisoned. (67*b*) The Mīrzā's people went into the Bālā-i-ḥiṣār, and plundered and destroyed innumerable things belonging to the *ḥaram*, and they made settlement[2] for them in Mīrzā Kāmrān's court (*sarkār*). He put the great begams into Mīrzā ʿAskarī's house and there he shut up a room with bricks and plaster and (?) dung-cakes, and they used to give the ladies water and food from over the four walls.[3]

In what was once Mīrzā Yādgār-nāsīr's house he put Khwāja Muʿaẕẕam[4] and ordered his own wives and family to stay in the palace where the royal *ḥaram* and the begams once lived. He behaved very ill indeed to the wives and families of the officers who had left him for the Emperor, ransacking and plundering all their houses and putting each family into somebody's custody.[5]

When the Emperor heard that Mīrzā Kāmrān had come from Bhakkar and was acting in this way, he returned from Qilaʿ-i-ẕafar and Andar-āb safe and sound to Kābul. Qilaʿ-i-ẕafar he gave to Mīrzā Sulaimān. (68*a*)

When he came near to Kābul, Mīrzā Kāmrān sent for her Highness my mother and for me from the house,[6] and gave my

---

1 Probably the servant sent with gifts by Bābar from Āgra to Kābul. The name looks like that of an Abyssinian. Is it 'new in work,' and a sobriquet given in youth and retained?

2 *zabṯ wa rabṯ*. Is this an indication of Gul-badan's opinion that Kāmrān profited by the robbery of his relations? His cruelties at this time make theft look innocent. (B. & H., II. 336 *et seq*..)

3 The translation of this passage is doubtful.

4 An undue honour, perhaps prompted by the khwāja's disgrace with Humāyūn.

5 Probably for the exploitation so often named in the histories.

6 Presumably the brick and mud quarters of the ladies.

mother orders to reside in the armourer's house. To me he said: 'This is your house as well as mine. You stay here.' 'Why,' I asked, 'should I stay here? I will stay with my mother.' He then went on: 'Moreover, write to Khiẓr Khwāja Khān and tell him to come and join me and to keep an easy mind, for just as Mīrzā ʿAskarī and Mīrzā Hindāl are my brothers, so is he. Now is the time to help.' I answered: 'Khiẓr Khwāja Khān has no way of recognizing a letter[1] from me. I have never written to him myself. He writes to me when he is away, by the tongue of his sons. Write yourself what is in your mind.' At last he sent Mahdī Sulṭān[2] and Shīr ʿAlī to fetch the khān. From the first I had said to the khān: 'Your brothers may be with Mīrzā Kāmrān, (but) God forbid that you should have the thought of going to him and joining them. (68*b*) Beware, a thousand times beware of thinking of separating yourself from the Emperor.' Praise be to God! The khān kept to what I said.

When the Emperor heard that Mīrzā Kāmrān had sent Mahdī Sulṭām and Shiīr ʿAlī to fetch Khiẓr Khwāja Khān, he himself despatched Qambar Beg, the son of Mīrzā Ḥājī, to the khan, who was then in his own *jāgīr*, and said: 'Beware, a thousand times beware! Let there be no joining Mīrzā Kāmrān. Come and wait on me.' The result of this auspicious message was that the khān set out at once for court, and came to the ʿUqabain (Hill of the two eagles) and paid his respects.

When the Emperor passed Minār Hill, Mīrzā Kāmrān sent forward all his well-ordered soldiers under Shīr Afkan,[3] the father of Shīroya, so that they might go out and fight. We saw from above[4] how he went out with his drums beating, out beyond Bābā Dashtī,

---

[1] *Suād na dārad ki khaṭ-i-marā shinasad.* I understand that he had not seen her handwriting, and would not know whether a letter purporting to be hers was a forgery. Gul-badan names one son only, Saʿādat-yār, as being her own. She is now about twenty-five.

[2] Brother of Khiẓr and of Yasīn-daulat (Āq Sulṭān).

[3] Son of Quch Beg, an amīr who lost his life in trying to protect Bega Begam at Chausa.

[4] From the citadel where the ladies were.

and we said, 'God forbid you should fight' and we wept. (69*a*) When he reached the Afghans' village (*Dih-i-Afghānān*), the two vanguards came face to face. The royal advance-guard at once drove off the Mīrzā's[1] and, having taken many prisoners, brought them to the Emperor. He ordered the Mughals to be cut to pieces.[2] Many of the Mīrzā's men who had gone out to fight were captured and some of them were killed and some were kept prisoners. Amongst them was Jūkī Khān, one of Mīrzā Kāmrān's amīrs.

In triumph and glory and to the sound of music, the Emperor entered the 'Uqabain, with Mīrzā Ḥindāl in attendance and a splendid cavalcade. He set up for himself tents and pavilions and an audience hall.[3] He gave Mīrzā Ḥindāl charge of the Mastān bridge,[4] and stationed the amirs one af ter another. For seven months he kept up the blockade.[5] (69*b*)

It happened one day that Mīrzā Kāmrān went from his own quarters to the roof (? of the citadel), and that some one fired a gun from the 'Uqābain. He ran and took himself off. Then he gave this order about the Emperor Akbar: 'Bring him and put him in front.'[6] Someone let his august Majesty (Humāyūn) know that Mīrzā Muḥammad Akbar was being kept on the front, so he forbade the guns to be fired and af ter that none were aimed at the Bālā-i-ḥiṣār. Mīrzā Kāmrān's men used to fire from the town upon the Emperor on the 'Uqābain. The royal soldiers put Mīrzā 'Askari to stand right in front and made fun of him.

---

1 The begam underrates Humāyūn's victory. The straggle was fierce, renewed and stubborn.

2 Doubtful translation.

3 I think she merely wishes to say that Humāyūn camped out on the 'Uqābain, and did not take up quarters under a roof.

4 Under it flows the stream which issues from the defile of Dihi-ya'qub. *Cf. Āīn,* Jarrett, I. 404.

5 Of the Bālā-i-ḥiṣār, the actual citadel.

6 Gul-badan's narrative does not support the story that Māham *anaga* exposed herself to save Akbar. This person,—who later on became so important,—is nowhere named by the begam as in charge of Akbar. Her husband, Nadim *kūka*, is so named.

Mīrzā Kārnrān's men also used to make sallies from the fort, and on both sides many were killed. The royal troops were often the victors and then the others had not courage to come out. For the sake of his wives and children and the begams and the household, etc., the Emperor did not have the cannon fired nor did he place the large houses in difficulty. (70*a*)

When the long siege was ended, they (*i.e.*, the ladies) sent Khwaja Dost Khāwand *madārchī*[1] to his Majesty to say: 'For God's sake, do whatever Mīrzā Kāmrān asks, and save the servants of God from molestation.'[2]

The Emperor sent for their use from outside nine sheep, seven flasks of rose-water, one of lemonade, and seven sets of nine dress-lengths[3] and some made-up jackets.[3] He wrote:[4] 'For their sakes, I could not use force against the citadel, lest I should give an advantage to their enemies.'[5]

During the siege Jahān Sulṭān Begam who was two years old, died. His Majesty wrote: 'Some time or other, if we had used force against the citadel, Mīrzā Muḥammad Akbar would have disappeared.'

To finish the story: There were always people in the Bālā-i-ḥiṣār from evening prayer till dawn, and there was a continuous uproar. The night Mīrzā Kāmrān went away,[6] prayer-time passed and indeed bedtime came, and there was no noise at all. (70*b*)

There was a steep stair by which people came up from below. When all the city was asleep, there suddenly sounded (on the stair)

---

[1] Follower of the Musalmān saint Madār.

[2] This message seems one from the imprisoned ladies. The khwāja to whom it was entrusted may now, as in the earlier siege of Kābul, have been Kāmrān's envoy to Humāyun.

[3] *pārcha* and *nīmcha dokhta*. There seems between these words an apposition which I render by the Englishwoman's colloquial terms.

[4] Presumably to some kinsman or official to whom the gifts were consigned.

[5] *i.e.*, by injuring the royal household.

[6] April 27th, 1547 (Rabīʿ I.7th, 954H.).

a clashing and clinking of armour, so that we said to one another: 'What a noise!' Perhaps a thousand people were standing in front (of the fort). We were afraid, but all at once, without warning, off they went. Qarācha Khān's son Bahādur brought us word that the Mīrzā had fled.[1]

Having thrown a rope, they (or he) brought up Khwāja Muʿaẕẕam by way of the wall.[2]

Our people and the begam's people and the rest who were outside, took away the door which had kept us fastened in. Bega Begam urged: 'Let us go to our own houses.' I said: 'Have a little patience. We should have to go by the lane and perhaps too someone will come from the Emperor.' At that moment ʿAmbar Nāẓir came and said: 'This is the royal order: "They are not to leave that place till I come."' 'In a little while the Emperor came and embraced Dil-dār Begam and me, and then Bega Begam and Ḥamīda-bānū Begam, and said: 'Come quickly out of this place. (71*a*) God preserve His friends from such a house, and let such be the portion of His foes.' He said to Nāẓir: 'Guard one side,' and to Tardī Beg Khān: 'Guard the other, and let the begams pass out.' All came out, and we spent the evening of that day with the Emperor in perfect content till night became morning. We embraced Māh-chūchak Begam and Khānīsh *āghā* and those of the *ḥaram* who had been with the Emperor on the campaign.

In Badakhshān Māh-chūchak had a daughter born. On the same night the Emperor had this dream: 'Fakhru-n-nisāʿ, my *māmā,*[3] and Daulat-bakht came in by the door, and brought something or other,

---

1 Niẕāmu-d-din Aḥmad says that Kāmrān escaped by a hole fashioned for the purpose in the wall 'on Khiẓr Khwāja's' side. This suggests that Gul-badan's husband connived at the evasion, unless one remembers that Khīr Khwāja is a place outside Kābul.

2 I do not understand this sentence. Either the followers of Kāmrān drew the khwāja up into the fort-precincts to take him with them, he having displeased Humāyūn and being nearly connected with him, or the ladies had him drawn up. He was, it seems, not a prisoner. (67*b*)

3 Fakhru-n-nisāʿ, the mother of Nadīm *kūka*, would seem from this to have been Humāyūn's own attendant in childhood.

and then left me alone.' Consider it as he might, he could only ask: 'What does this dream mean?' Then it occurred to him that, as a daughter had just been born, he would call her after the two, and taking *nisā'* from one, and *bakht* from the other, would run them together into *Bakht-nisā'*.

Māh-chūchak had four daughters[1] and two sons,—Bakht-nisā' Begam, and Sakīnā-bānū Begam, and Amīna-bānū Begam, and Muḥammad Hakīm Mīrzā, and Farrukh-fāl Mīrzā. (71*b*) She was with child when the Emperor went to Hindūstān (1554), and bore a son, in Kābul, whom they named Farrukh-fāl Mīrzā. A little later Khānish *āghā* had a son whom they named Ibrāhīm Sulṭān Mīrzā.

The Emperor spent a full year and a half in Kābul, prosperously and happily, and in comfort and sociability.[2]

After taking flight from Kābul, Mrrza Kāmrān went to Badakhshān, and there stayed in Tāliqān. One day the Emperor was in the Inner Garden,[3] and when he rose at dawn for prayers, news came that many of the amīrs who formerly were with the Mīrzā, had gone to him again. Amongst them were Qarācha Khān and Muṣāḥib Khān, and Mubāriz Khān and Bāpūs.[4] Many wretches fled by night and went to join the Mīrzā in Badakhshān.

In a propitious hour the Emperor also started for Badakhshān. He besieged the Mīrzā in Tāliqān, and after a time made him agree to submit and become obedient (72*a*) when he waited on the Emperor, who bestowed Kulāb on him, and gave Qila'-i-ẓafar to Mīrzā Sulaimān, Qandahār (*sic*; (?) Kunduz) to Mīrzā Hindāl, and

---

[1] Gul-badan does not name Fakhru-n-nisā' who became the wife of Shāh 'Abū'l-mā'alī and of Khwāja Ḥasan *Naqshbandī*. Perhaps she is Bakht-nisa'.

[2] From 1547; but a term of one and a half years does not quite fit the facts. Humāyūn started for the north on June 12th, 1548. (B & H., II. 352.)

[3] *ōrta- bāgh.*

[4] Perhaps it may be taken as an indication of the degradation of 'home life' that Qarācha and Bāpūs again joined Kāmrān, although the latter had exposed Qarācha's son and a wife of Bāpūs on the battlements, with the utmost dishonour, and had killed three of the latter's children and flung their bodies from the ramparts.

Tāliqan to Mīrzā ʿAskarī.

One day at Kishm[1] they had set up[2] the tents and there was an assembly of the brothers, his Majesty the Emperor Humāyūn, and Mīrzā Kāmrān, and Mīrzā ʿAskārʿ, and Mīrzā Hindāl, and Mīrzā Sulaimān.[3]

His Majesty enjoined certain regulations[4] which are fixed for interviews with kings, and said: 'Bring ewer and basin so that we may wash our hands and eat together.' He washed his hands and Mīrzā Kāmrān washed his. By years Mīrzā Sulaimān (b. 920H.) had precedence of Mīrzā ʿAskarī (b. 922H.) and Mīrzā Hindāl (b. 925H.). So, to show him respect, the two brothers set the ewer and basin first before him.

After washing his hands Mīrzā Sulaimān did something improper with his nose. Mīrzā ʿAskarī and Mīrzā Hindāl were much put out, and said: 'What rusticity is this? (72*b*) First of all, what right have we to wash our hands in his Majesty's presence? but when he bestows the favour and gives the order, we cannot change it. What sense is there in these nose-wagging performances?' Then the two mīrzās went and washed their hands outside and came Lack and sat down. Mīrzā Sulaimān was very much ashamed. They all ate at one tablecloth.

At this gathering his Majesty graciously remembered this lowly person, and said to his brothers: 'Gul-badan Begam used to say in Lābōr: "I wish I could see all my brothers together!" As we have been seated together since early morning, her words have occurred to my mind. If it be the will of the most high God, may our assembly

---

1 Abū'l-faẓl says the meeting was at Ishkārnish, and this seems to agree with the movements of Humāyūn better than Kishm.

2 *khirgā dokhta budand.* Certain tents are termed *dokhta,* sewed. They seem to have been large, and were laced together, whence, perhaps, dokhta.

For an interesting account of this historic family gathering see B. & H., II. 358 *et seq.*.

3 'Brother' by courtesy and custom; *anglice*, 'cousin.'

4 Tūtā, the Institutes of Chingīz Khān of which the begam makes other mention.

be kept in His own place! He knows without shadow that it lies not in my heart's depths to seek any Musalmān's ill; how then, should I seek the hurt of my brothers? May God grant to you all the same divine and beneficent guidance, so that our agreement and concord may endure!' (73*a*)

There was wonderful cheerfulness and happiness because many officers and their followers met their relations again, for they too had been sundered because of their masters' quarrels. Nay! one might rather say they had thirsted for one another's blood. Now they passed their time in complete happiness.

On his return from Badakhshān the Emperor spent a year and a half in Kābul and then resolved to go to Balkh. He took up his quarters in the Heart-expanding Garden,[1] and his own residence was over against the lower part of the garden, and the begams were in Qulī Beg's house because it was close by.

The begams said to the Emperor over and over again: 'Oh, how the *rīwāj*[2] will be coming up !' He replied: 'When I join the army,

[1] *i.e.*, moved out of the city as a preliminary to marching.

[2] The following account of this plant is taken from Conolly's Travels, I., 213 n.. It is translated by him from the *Makhāzinu-l adwiya* (Treasury of Medicines). '*Rībās, rīvās, rīwāj* or *jigarī* (so named from a person of Nishāpūr who first discovered it) is a shrub two or three feet high, in appearance like beet (*salq*). In the middle are one or two short stems of little thickness; the leaves, which separate lengthwise like those of a lettuce, are downy and green, but towards the root, of a violet or whitish colour. The heart is white, delicate, juicy, acidulous and slightly astringent. Altogether the stalk is the size of a man's arm and when the plant is large every leaf has the size of a man's hand. Ārd-shīr was named *Rāwand-dast* (rhubarb-hand) from the length of his hands. The root is called *rāwand* (rhubarb). The top is like the claw of a fowl. The flower is red, and the taste is subacid with a little sweetness. The seed is formed at the top of a long slender stalk which springs up annually in the centre of the plant. It grows where snow lies and in mountainous countries. The best grows in Persia. It is medicinally attenuating and astringent, gives tone to the stomach, and improves the appetite. A collyrium of the juice strengthens the eye and prevents opacity, and a poultice of it with barley-meal is a useful application to sores and boils. The juice of the *rīvās* is harsher than that of unripe grapes.' For mention of the name *rīwāj* see *Ṭabaqāt-i-akbarī*, Lucknow lith. ed., 215; *Tūzūk-i-jāhangirī*, 47. Vullers, *s.v.*, etc. . Mr. Erskine writes (Mems., 138 n ..): 'It is described as somewhat like beetroot, but

I shall travel by the Koh-dāman, so that you may come out and see the *rīwāj* growing.' It was at afternoon prayer-time that he rode out[1] (of Kābul) to the garden. Qulī: Beg's house where the begams were, was close by and overlooked it, and his Majesty pulled up as he passed, and all the begams saw him, and rose and made the *kōrnish.* (73*b*) Directly they had made this salutation, he beckoned with his own blessed hand, to say: 'Come.'[2]

Fakhru-n-nisā' *māmā* and Afghānī *āghācha* went on a little ahead. There was a stream in the lower part of the garden which Afghānī *āghācha* could not cross, and she fell off her horse. For this reason there was an hour's delay.[3] At last we set out with his Majesty. Māh-chūchak Begam not knowing, her horse went up a little.[4] His Majesty was very much annoyed about this. The garden was on a height and the walls were not yet made. Some vexation now showed itself in his blessed countenance and he was pleased to say: 'All of you go on, and I will follow when I have taken some opium and got over my annoyance.' He joined ns when we had, as he ordered, gone on a little. The look of vexation was entirely laid aside and he came with a happy and beautiful look in his face.

It was a moonlight night. (83*a*) We talked and told stories,[5] and Mīr (fault) and Khānish *āghācha* and Ẕarīf the reciter and Sarū-sahī and Shāham *āghā* sang softly, softly.

---

much larger, red and white in colour, with large leaves that rise little from the ground. It is a pleasant mixture of sweet and acid. It may be the rhubarb, *rāwand.*'

[1] Presumably from Kābul, and on the day of starting for Balkh *viâ* the Koh-dāman.

[2] The ladies seem to have been waiting for this signal to start.

[3] Probably to allow for the coming of a less unpropitious hour. This expedition to Balkh ended in a way calculated to attract notice to ill-omens such as the begam's misadventures would seem

[4] *andak buland raft*. Perhaps the horse reared, the begam not knowing how to manage it; but the later and otherwise irrelevant sentence about the unfinished wall suggests that the begam went too high up the hill. The party is now on its way to see the *rīwāj* growing, and Humāyūn's temper is tried by the various contretemps of the ladies' cavalcade.

[5] A folio of the MS. is, I believe, misplaced, and folio 83 should come in here. In the MS. volume this is the last folio.

Up to the time of our reaching Laghmān, neither the royal tents nor the pavilions of the *begams* had arrived, but the *mihr-amez*[1] tent had come. We all, his Majesty and all of us, and Ḥamīda-bānū Begam sat in that tent till three hours past midnight and then we went to sleep where we were, in company with that altar of truth (Humāyūn).

Early next morning he wished to go and see the *rīwāj* on the Kōh. The begams' horses were in the village, so the starting-time passed before they came up. The Emperor ordered that the horses of everyone who was outside should be brought. When they came he gave the order: 'Mount.'

Bega Begam and Māh-chūchāk Begam were still putting on their head-to-foot dresses, and I said to the Emperor: 'If you think well, I will go and fetch them.' 'Go,' he answered, 'and bring them quickly.' I said to the begams and to Māh-chūchāk Begam and the rest of the ladies: 'I have become the slave of his Majesty's wishes. What trouble waiting gives!' I was gathering them all together and bringing them when he came to meet me and said: 'Gul-badan! the proper hour for starting has gone by. (83*b*) It would be hot the whole way. God willing, we will go after offering the afternoon prayer.' He seated himself in a tent with Ḥamīda-bānū Begam.[2] After afternoon prayers, there was the interval between two prayers before the horses arrived. In this interval he went away.[3]

Everywhere in the Dāman-i-kōh the *rīwāj* had put up its leaves. We went to the skirts of the hills and when it was evening, we walked about. Tents and pavilions were pitched on the spot and there his Majesty came and stayed. Here too we passed the nights together in sociable talk, and were all in company of that altar of truth.

---

[1] Perhaps a tent of Humāyūn's invention, in the name of which *mīhr* means *sun*. *Cf.* 'another of his (Humāyūn's) inventions was a tent which had twelve divisions, corresponding to the signs of the Zodiac. Every sign had a lattice through which the lights of the stars of dominion shone.' (*Akbar-nāma*, H. Beveridge I. 361.)

[2] Perhaps, a tent of Hamīda having come, he seated himself in it.

[3] (?) the start was made to see the *rīwāj*.

In the morning at prayer-time, he went away to a distance *(bīrūn),* and from there wrote separate letters to Bega Begam and to Ḥamīda-bānū Begam and to Māh-chūchāk Begam and to me and to all the begams,[1] saying: 'Becoming spokeswoman of your own fault, write apologizing for the trouble you have given. God willing, I shall say farewell and go to join the army either at Farẓa or Istālīf, and if not we shall travel apart.' (74*a*)

Then everyone wrote to apologize for having given trouble, and sent the letter for his holy and elevating service.

In the end his Majesty and all the begams mounted and rode by Lamghān to Bihzādī. At night each one went to her own quarters, and in the morning they ate (? alone), and at mid-day prayer-time rode to Farẓa.

Ḥamīda-bānū Begam sent nine sheep to the quarters of each one of us. Bībī Daulat-bakht had come one day earlier to Farẓa and had got ready plenty of provisions and milk and curds and syrup and sherbet and so on. We spent that evening in amusement. In the early morning (we went) above Farza to where there is a beautiful water fall. Then his Majesty went to Istalif and passed three days, and then in 958H.[2] marched towards Balkh.

When he crossed the pass, he sent *farmāns* to summon Mīrzā Kāmrān and Mīrzā Sulaimān and Mīrzā ʿAskarī, and said: 'We are on the march to fight the Uzbegs; now is the time for union and brotherliness. You ought to come as quickly as possible.' Mīrzā Sulaimān and Mīrzā ʿAskari came and joined him. (74*b*) Then march by march they came to Balkh.

In Balkh was Pir Muḥammad Khān,[3] and on the first day his men

---

[1] Humāyūn's comprehensive displeasure looks like a fit of temper directed against every and anyone. It is possible, however, that a page which might describe other untoward matters besides unpunctuality, has been altogether lost. The sentence which now continues the story, places all the ladies, deprived of their evening of talk and amusement, in chastened solitude.

[2] B. & H., II 368, has 956H. (1549), and other differences of detail.

[3] Son of Jānī Beg, and uncle of the famous ʿAbdu-l-lāh Khān Uzbeg. He ruled till 974H. (1566-67).

sallied out and drew up in battle array. The royal army carried off the victory, and Pīr Muḥammad's men tasted defeat and returned to the city. By the next morning the khān had come to think: 'The Chaghatāī are strong; I cannot fight them. It would be better to get out and away.' Just then the royal officers joined in representing that the camp had become filthy, and that it would be well to move to a desert place *(dasht)*. His Majesty ordered them to do so.

No sooner were hands laid on the baggage and packsaddles, than others raised a clamour and some cried out: 'We are not strong enough.' Since such was the Divine will, the royal army took the road without cause from a foe, without reason or motive.[1] The news of their march reached the Uzbegs and amazed them. Try as the royal officers would, they produced not a scrap of effect. It could not be hindered: the royal army ran away. (75*a*)

The Emperor waited a little, and when he saw that no one was left, he too had to go. Mīrzā ʿĀskarī and Mīrzā Hindāl, not having heard of the confusion, rode up to the camp. They found no one and saw that the Uzbegs had gone in pursuit, so they too took the road and made for Kunduz. After riding a little way, his Majesty stopped and said: 'My brothers are not here yet: how can I go on?' He asked the officers and attendants whether anyone would bring him news of the princes. No one answered or went. Later on word came from the Mīrzā's people in Kunduz that they had heard of the disaster and did not know where the princes had gone. This letter upset the Emperor very much. Khiẓr Khwāja Khān said: 'If you approve, I will bring news.' 'God's mercy on you!' rejoined his Majesty. 'May they have gone to Kunduz!' (75*b*)

Two days afterwards the khwāja, to the Emperor's great delight, brought word that Mīrzā Hindāl had arrived at Kunduz safe and sound. His Majesty gave Mīrzā Sulaimān leave to go to his own

---

[1] From other sources we learn that the royalists were anxious on two grounds; (1) as to the threatened arrival of an overwhelming Uzbeg force from Bukhara, and (2) lest Kāmrān should again take Kābul and have their families at his mercy. The last was perhaps the dominant motive for the flight without a pursuer.

place, Qilaʿ-i-ẕafar, and came himself to Kābul (1550, 957H.).

While Mīrzā Kāmrān was in Kūlāb, a woman named Tarkhān[1] Bega, who was a thorough cheat, showed him the way by saying: 'Make a declaration of love to Ḥaram Begam.[2] Good will come of it.' Acting on these words of an ill-judging adviser, he actually sent a letter and a kerchief[3] to Ḥaram Begam by the hand of Begī *āghā.* This woman laid the letter and the kerchief before the begam and then set forth the Mīrzā's devotion and passion. *Ḥaram* Begam said: 'Keep that letter and that kerchief now and bring them again when the Mīrzā come home.' Begī *āghā* then wept, and moaned, and coaxed, and said: 'Mīrzā Kāmrān has sent you this letter and this kerchief; he has loved you a long time, and you have no pity for him.' (76*a*) Ḥaram Begam began to show her disgust and violent anger, and at once sent off for her husband, Mīrzā Sulaimān, and her son, Mīrzā Ibrāhīm. She said to them: 'Mīrzā Kāmrān must have come to think you are cowards, since he sends me a letter like this. Have I deserved to be written to in this way? He is as your elder brother, and I am to him as a younger brother's wife.[4] Send off a letter for me about it and rebuke him. As for this wretch of a woman, tear her piece by piece. Let her be a warning to others that no man may cast the evil eye of sinful thought upon another man's womanfolk. What does such a man deserve who, the son of a mother, yet does such monstrous things, and who fears neither me[5] nor my son?'

Instantly hands were laid on Begī *āghā* Bībī, condemned of fate

---

1 This title indicates rank. A 'Tarkhan Begam' was wife of Sulṯān Aḥmad Mīrzā. (Mems., 22..)

2 or Khurram. One of her sisters was a wife of Kāmrān.

3 What fascination may lurk in an embroidered kerchief can be guessed by inspecting the dainty examples in the South Kensington Oriental Section.

4 *kīlīn*. Both here and at 77*b* this word seems to have wider meaning than is given by the Turkī and Persian dictionaries.

5 The begam's martial character spices this story, since her husband did not dare even to make war without her consent. Perhaps Kāmrān's devotion extended to the armed force she disposed of. It was clearly in Tarkhan Bega's eye.

to die, and she was torn in pieces. In consequence of this affair, Mīrzā Sulaimān and Mīrzā Ibrāhīm were displeased with Mīrzā Kāmrān, or rather they became his enemies. (76*b*) They wrote to the Emperor that Mīrzā Kāmrān wished to thwart him and that this could not be better seen than in his failure to go to Balkh with him.

After this the Mīrzā, in Kūlāb,[1] could not find, in his terror-stricken thoughts, any better remedy than to become a darvish. He sent his son, Abu'l-qāsim (Ibrāhīm) to Mīrzā 'Askari, and betook himself to Tāliqān with his daughter 'Ayisha (Sulṭān Begam), and said to his wife (Muḥtarīma Khānam): 'Do you and your daughter follow me later. I will send for you to whatever place I settle on. Till then go and stay in Khost and Andar-āb.' The khānam was related to the Uzbeg khāns, and some of her kinsfolk let the Uzbegs[2] know: 'If you want booty, there are goods and men and women servants; take these, and let the lady go free, for if 'Āyisha Sulṭān Khānām's[3] nephew hears to-morrow (that she has been hurt), he will certainly be very angry with you.' By a hundred plans and wiles, and with a hundred anxieties, and without her goods, she got free from the Uzbeg bondage, and reached Khost and Andar-āb. Here she stayed.

When Mīrzā Kāmrān heard of the royal disaster in Balkh, he said: 'The Emperor is not so friendly to me as he was.' (77*a*) So he left Kūlāb, and went hither and thither. At this time (1550) his Majesty came out from Kābul.

When he reached the Qibchāq defile, he incautiously halted in a low-lying place, and Mīrzā Kāmrān, coming from higher ground, armed and equipped, poured down foes upon him.

Since such was the Divine will, a barbarian,—inwardly blind, an ill-fated oppressor and ill-omened tyrant,—inflicted a wound on the

---

1 In Kūlāb were the kinsfolk of his wife, Māh Begam, sister of Ḥaram Begam, daughter of Sulṭān Wais Qibchāq, and sister of Chakr 'Alī Khān.

2 *i.e.*, across whose country she had to travel.

3 (?) Mughal Khānam.

Emperor. The blow reached his blessed head, and all his forehead and his dear eyes were stained with blood.

It was just like it was in the Mughal war when the blessed head of his Majesty *Firdaus-makānī,* the Emperor Bābar, was wounded by a Mughal, and his high cap and the turban wrapped round it were not cut, but his blessed head was badly hurt. His Majesty Humāyūn used to say with surprise: 'I wondered at it, for cap and cloth were whole, and yet the head was cut.'[1] The very same thing happened now to his own head.

After the rout in the Qibchāq defile, his Majesty went to Badakhsbān, and Mīrzā Hindāl, and Mīrzā Sulaimān, and Mīrzā Ibrāhīm came and waited on him. (77*b*) He went[2] to Kābul and the Mīrzās were in attendance, friendly and united and at peace together, when Mīrzā Kāmrān approached. His Majesty sent a message to Ḥaram Begam: 'Ask my *kūlīn*[3] to send me the army of Badakhshān as quickly as possible and ready for service.' In a few days,—a very short time,—the begam had given horses and arms to some thousands of men. She herself superintended and took thought and she came with the troops as far as the pass. From here she sent them forward, and while she went back they went on and joined the Emperor.

---

[1] 'Tambol let fall a heavy sword-blow on my head. It is a singular fact that, though not a thread of my cap of mail was injured, yet my head was severely wounded.' (Mems., 266. Also 111.)

[2] Niẓāmu-d-dīn Aḥmad, 'after forty days.'

[3] *Cf.* 77*a* n.. This story bears out Ḥaram's military reputation. Kāmrān's power of attraction and Humāyūn's present risk can be gauged by the fact that even after the defeat at Chārīkārān some 1,500 horse were with the former, and many amīrs again went over to him.

It was now that the remarkable compact which effected Kāmrān's downfall was made between Humāyūn and his amīrs. (B. & H., II. 338.) These swore fidelity by whatever oath would bind them and then, at the instance of Ḥājī Muḥammad Khān kūka, Humāyūn bound himself to,—do as he was told. The compact was effective. 'The amīrs were the long-suffering victims of Humāyūn's folly and their present turning was, he admitted, justifiable.

Either at Chārīkārān or Qarā-bāgh there was fighting with Mīrzā Kāmrān and his Majesty's army was successful. The Mīrzā fled to the mountain passes *(tangayhā)* and Lamghānāt.[1]

Āq Sulṯān (Yasīn-daulat) who was the Mīrzā's son-in-law, said in effect to him *(gufta bāshad)*: 'You are continually thwarting the Emperor. What is the meaning of it? It is not what should be. (78*a*) Either make your submission and obeisance to the Emperor or give me leave to go, so that men may distinguish between us.' Mīrzā Kāmrān said fiercely: 'Have my affairs come to such a pass that *you* offer me advice?' Āq Sulṯān also spoke angrily, 'If I stay with you, my position will be unlawful,' and left him at once, and went with his wife (Ḥabība) to Bhakkar. The Mīrzā wrote to Mīrzā Shāh Ḥusain, and said: 'Āq Sulṯān has displeased me and has gone away. If he comes to Bhakkar, do not let his wife be with him. Part them and tell him to go where he likes.' Shāh Ḥusain Mīrzā at once, on receiving the letter, deprived Ḥabība Sulṯān Begam of the company of Āq Sulṯān and let him depart for the blessed Makka.[2]

In the fight at Chārīkārān, Qarācha Khān[3] and many of Mīrzā Kāmrān's well-known officers were killed.

'Āyisha Sulṯān Begam[4] and Daulat-bakht *āghācha* wern in flight for Qandahār, and were captured at the Khimār Pass, and brought in by the Emperor's people. Mīrzā Kāmrān went to the Afghāns,[5] and stayed amongst them. (78*b*)

From time to time his Majesty used to visit the orange gardens. That year also, according to his old habit, he went to the mountain passes (*tangayhā*) to see the oranges. Mīrzā Hindāl was in attendance, and of the ladies (*ḥaramān*), there went Bega Begam,

---

[1] Niẕāmu-d-dīn Aḥmad, 'mountains of Mandrūd.' B. & H., II. 393, 'by the Pass of Bādpaj towards the Afghān country.'

[2] Kāmrān was the son-in-law of Mīr Shāh Ḥusāin Arghūn, and was therefore able to secure this interference with Āq Sulṯān domestic affairs.

[3] *Cf.* Elliot, V. 233.

[4] Kāmrān's daughter.

[5] *i.e.*, Lamghān.

Ḥamīda-bānū Begam, Māh-chūchak Begam and many others. I could not go because my son, Saʿādat-yār, was ill at the time. One day his Majesty, attended by Mīrzā Hindāl, was hunting near the mountain passes. They had very good sport. The Emperor went towards where the mīrzā was hunting and had made a very good bag. Following the rules of Chingīz Khān, the mīrzā proffered his game to the Emperor, for it is a rule of Chingīz Khān that inferiors should so act towards their superiors. In short, he gave the Emperor all his game. Then it occurred to him: 'There is still my sisters' portion. (79*a*) They shall not complain again. I will hunt once more and get them a share.' Again be busied himself in hunting, and had taken one head of game, and was returning, when someone sent by Mīrzā Kāmrān blocked the road, and shot an arrow at the unwitting mīrzā which struck his blessed shoulder. Acting on the thought 'God forbid my sisters and womenfolk should be upset by news of this,' he wrote off at once to say: 'Ill begun has ended well![1] Do not be anxious, for I am getting better.' To finish the story: as it was hot, his Majesty went back to Kābul, and in the course of a year the arrow-wound got better.

A year later word was brought that Mīrzā Kāmrān had collected troops and was preparing for war. His Majesty also, taking military appurtenances, set out for the mountain passes (*tangayhā*) with Mīrzā Hindāl. He went safe and well, and made his honouring halt in the passes. Hour by hour, and all the time, spies kept bringing news: 'Mīrzā Kāmrān has decided that an attack must be made to-night.' (79*b*) Mīrzā Hindāl went to the Emperor and submitted his advice: 'Let your Majesty stay on this high ground, and let my brother (nephew) Jalālu-d-dīn Muḥammad Akbar *pādshāh* stay with you, so that careful watch may be kept on this height.' Then he called up his own men, and encouraged and cheered them one by one, and said: 'Put earlier services in one scale and the service of this night in the other. God willing! whatever claim you can make, you shall

[1] Repetition of a proverb already quoted.

be exalted to its degree.'[1] One by one he allotted their posts, and then called for his own cuirass and surtout, and high cap and helmet.

His wardrobe-keeper had lifted up the wallet when someone sneezed,[2] and he set it down for a while. Because of this delay, the Mīrzā sent to hurry him. Then the things were brought quickly, and he asked: 'Why were you so long?' The man replied: 'I had lifted the wallet when someone sneezed, and I therefore put it down. So there was a delay.' (80*a*)

The mīrzā replied: 'You were wrong. (You should have) said rather: "May there be a blessed martyrdom."' 'Then he went on: 'Friends all! be my witness that I abjure all forbidden things and all indecorous acts.' Those present recited the *fāṭhiha* and prayed: 'May there be benediction.' He said: 'Bring my vest and cuirass and surtout.' He put them on and went out to the trenches to encourage and solace his men. Just then his *ṯabaqchī,*[3] hearing his voice, cried: 'They are attacking me.' The mīrzā, hearing this, dismounted and said: 'Friends, it is far from brave to give no help when my servant is at the point of the sword.' He himself went down into the trench but not one of his followers dismounted. Twice he sallied from the trenches, and in this endeavour became a martyr.

I do not know what pitiless oppressor slew that harmless youth[4] with his tyrant sword! Would to Heaven that merciless sword had

---

[1] Perhaps the notion of this sentence is, 'To-night's service will equal or outweigh previous services, and the lower to-night's scale is forced, the greater will be my largesse.'

[2] It is hardly necessary to say that sneezing is by many nations regarded as an omen of other things than catarrh.

[3] Clerk of the scullery who has charge of plates and dishes, utensils which are often of value by material and by workmanship.

[4] Hindāl was killed on Ẕī'l-qa'dā 21st, 958H. (November 20th, 1551). He was born before March 4th, 1519 (Mems., 258.), and was therefore in his thirty-third year.

Gul-badan always speaks of her brother with affection, and her story shows that she mourned his loss many years. Her book lets us see a group of living and feeling men and women.

touched my heart and eyes, or Sa ādatyār, my son's, or Khiẓr Khwāja Khān's! Alas! a hundred regrets! Alas! a thousand times alas! (80*b*)

HEMISTICH.

O well-a-day! O well-a-day! O well-a-day!
My sun is sunk behind a cloud.

All may be said in a word: Mīrzā Hindāl gave his life freely for his sovereign.

Mīr Bābā Dost lifted him up and carried him to his quarters. He told no one, and fetched servants and placed them at the entrance and gave orders: 'Tell everyone who asks, that the mīrzā is badly wounded and that the Emperor forbids anyone to enter.'

Then he went and said to his Majesty: 'Mīrzā Hindāl is wounded.' The Emperor called for a horse; 'I will go and see him.' Mīr 'Abdu-l-ḥaī said: 'He is badly hurt. It is not desirable that you should go.' He understood, and however much he tried,[1] he could not help it, he broke down.

Jūī-shāhī[2] was Khiẓr Khwāja Khān's *jāgīr.* The Emperor sent for him and said: 'Take Mīrzā Hindāl to Jūī-shāhī and care for his burial.' The khān took the camel's bridle,[3] and when he was going away with weeping and lament and voice uplifted in grief, (81*a*) his Majesty heard of the mourning and sent him word: 'We must have patience! This sorrow touches my heart more closely than yours, but I do not give way because I think of our bloodthirsty, tyrannical foe. With him at hand, there is no help but patience.' Then the khān with a hundred regrets, miserable and stricken, conveyed the body to Jūī shāhī, and there laid and left it.

---

1 *ḥafẓ kardand.* Perhaps as a matter of etiquette which demands composure in public.

2 Text, Jūsāhī, the modern Jalālābād, on the road to Kābul.

3 *i.e.*, that of the camel which bore the corpse.

If that slayer of a brother, that stranger's friend, the monster, Mīrzā Kāmrān had not come that night, this calamity would not have descended from the heavens.

His Majesty sent letters to his sisters in Kābul, and the city at once became like one house of mourning. Doors and walls wept and bewailed the death of the happy, martyred mīrzā.

Gul-chihra Begam had gone to Qarā Khān's house. When she came back, it was like the day of resurrection.[1] Through weeping and sorrow she fell quite ill and went out of her mind.

It was by Mīrzā Kāmrān's evil fate that Mīrzā Hindāl became a martyr. From that time forth we never heard that his affairs prospered. On the contrary, they waned day by day and came to naught and perished. (81*b*) He set his face to evil in such fashion that fortune never befriended him again nor gave him happiness. It was as though Mīrzā Hindāl had been the life, or rather the lightgiving eye of Mīrzā Kāmrān, for after that same defeat he fled straight away to Salīm Shāh, the son of Shīr Khān. Salīm Shāh gave him a thousand *rupīs*.[2] Then the mīrzā told in what position he was, and asked help. Salīm Shāh said nothing openly in reply, but in private he remarked: 'How can a man be helped who killed his own brother, Mīrzā Hindāl? It is best to destroy him and bring him to naught.' Mīrzā Kāmrān heard of this opinion and one night, without even consulting his people, he resolved on flight and got away, and his own men had not even a word of it. They stayed behind and when news of the flight reached Salim Shah, he imprisoned many of them.

Mīrzā Kāmrān had gone as far as Bhīra and Khūsh-āb when Adam Ghakkar, by plot and stratagems, captured him and brought him to the Emperor. (82*a*)

To be brief, all the assembled khans and Sulṭāns, and high and low, and plebeian and noble, and soldiers and the rest who all bore the mark of Mīrzā Kamrān's hand, with one voice represented to

---

[1] Khwānd-amīr compares a hustle of people to the day of resurrection.

[2] A scornful measure of Kāmrān's fall. The date is the end both of 1552 and of 959H..

his Majesty: 'Brotherly custom has nothing to do with ruling and reigning. If you wish to act as a brother, abandon the throne. If you wish to be king, put aside brotherly sentiment. What kind of wound was it that befell your blessed head in the Qibchāq defile through this same Mīrzā Kāmrān? He it was whose traitorous and crafty conspiracy with the Afghāns killed Mīrzā Hindāl. Many a Chaghatāī has perished through him; women and children have been made captive and lost honour. It is impossible that our wives and children should suffer in the future the thrall and torture of captivity. (82*b*) With the fear of hell before our eyes[1] (we say that) our lives, our goods, our wives, our children are all a sacrifice for a single hair of your Majesty's head. This is no brother! This is your Majesty's foe!'

To make an end of words, one and all urgently set forth: 'It is well to lower the head of the breacher of a kingdom.' His Majesty answered: 'Though my head inclines to your words, my heart does not.' All cried out: 'What has been set before your Majesty is the really advisable course.' At last the Emperor said: 'If you all counsel this and agree to it, gather together and attest it in writing.' All the amirs both of the right and left assembled. They wrote down and gave in that same line (*mīṣrá*): 'It is well to lower the head of the breacher of the kingdom.' Even his Majesty was compelled to agree.

When he drew near to Rohtās, the Emperor gave an order to Sayyid Muḥammad: 'Blind Mīrzā Kāmrān in both eyes.' The sayyid went at once and did so.

After the blinding, his Majesty the Emperor[2] …

---

1 *bar jahannum*, which I take as an oath. *Cf. bar ḥaq*.

2 Here in the MS. volume follows folio 83, which I have conjectured should follow folio 73*b*, and have placed there.

APPENDIX A

BLOGRAPHICAL NOTICES OF THE WOMEN MENTIONED BY BĀBAR, GUL-BADAN, AND ḤAIDAR.[1]

I. Āfāq (Āpāq) Begam.

Princess of the Universe; Ar. *āfāq,* four quarters, universe, etc..

She is mentioned, without clue to her parentage, by Bābar, as a wife of Sulṭān Husain Mīrzā *Bāyqrā.* He mentions her again, with others of the mīrzā's widows, as seen in Harāt in 912H. (1506-7), and here his wording, both in the Turkī and the Persian texts, allows the inference that she is a daughter of Sulṭān Abū-saīd *Mīrān-shāhī.* Mr. Erskine translates the passage thus: 'Pāyanda Sulṭān Begam, my father's sister, Khadīja Begam and the other (Turkī, *yena;* Pers., *dīgar)* daughters of Sulṭān Abū-sa'īd Mīrzā.'

When greeting the ladies, Bābar gave Āfāq precedence over Khadīja, and notes the fact. Khadīja was not a woman of birth.

Husain *Bāyqrā* married three daughters of Abūsa'īd, Shahr-bānū, Pāyanda, and Āfāq. The last bore him no child, but she reared and educated nine children of his by her own foster-sister, Bābā *āghācha.*

Early in 932H. (1525) she went from Harāt to Kābul and was received by Bābar (before his depar-ture for India in November,

[1] This Appendix makes no pretence at completeness. It contains the gatherings in of work on Gul-badan Begam's *Humāyūn-nāma.*

1525) with all possible respect and kindness. He gives the impression that she was an affectionate and devoted woman, and says that her tender care of her husband in illness sur-passed that of all the other ladies of the *ḥaram.*

News of her death reached Bābar when he was besieging Chandīrī in 934H. (January, 1528).

Mems., 182, 183, 204.

II. Āfāq Begam. (No. 26.)[1]

She was a daughter of Sulṭān-bakht Begam; her father's name has not yet come to my knowledge; she was a granddaughter of Sulṭān Abū-sa'īd Mīrzā.

Bābar mentions the arrival of a daughter of Sulṭān-bakht Begam in Āgra in 935H. (October, 1528), and Gul-badan supplies the name Āfāq by naming an Āfāq of this parentage as at the Mystic Feast in 938H. (1531).

Gul-badan. Persian text, *25b.*

Mems., 387.

(*Afghānī āghācha,* the Afghān lady. See Mubārika Bībī.)

III. Afroz-bānū Begam. (No. 33.)

Pers. *afruz,* dazzling, illuminating, and *bānū,* (?) a form of *bān* (*vān*), which in composition means holding, possessing. Also a prince or chief.

Nothing is said to identify her. She was at the Mystic Feast (1531).

Gul-badan, 25*b.*

IV. Āghā Begam. (No. 34.)

Turkī, *āghā,* a title of honour, and Ar. *sulṭān,* sway, pre-eminence. Steingass classes the word *āgkā* as Persian. It may be *āka,* lady. The dictionaries do not apply it to women.

---

[1] Numbers so entered are those of Gul-badan's guest-list, 24*b et seq.*.

Mentioned as at the Mystic Feast in 1531. She may be *Bāyqrā* (*infra*).

Gul-badan, 25*b*.

V. Āghā Begam *Bāyqrā.*

She was a daughter of Sulṭān Husain Mīrzā *Bāyqrā* and of Pāyanda Sulṭān Begam *Mīrān-shāhī,* Her descent being so high through both parents, her name *Āghā* rises above its frequent application to wives of less degree. Here it may have the meaning of *chief* or *great.* She married her cousin Murād who was a son of Bābi'a-sulṭān Begam (Bedka). The *Ḥabību-s-siyār,* 327 *et seq*. (lith. ed.), states that she died before she reached maturity, but this does not agree with Bābar's statements. The *Ḥabīb* places her death earlier than 912H (1506).

Mems., 181.

Ḥabību-s-siyār, lith. ed., 327 *et seq*..

VI. Aghā *kūka.* (No. 78.)

Wife of Munim Khān; at Hindal's Feast (1537).

Gul-badan, 26*a*.

VII. Āghā-sultān *āghācha.* (No. 37.)

(?) The lady of chief honour.

She was a wife of 'Umar Shaikh Mīrzā (died 1494), and mother of Yādgār Sulṭān Begam (Bābar's half-sister). She was present at Hindāl's marriage feast (1537), and probably at the Mystic Feast, in 1531. She is classed amongst 'our begams.'

Gul-badan, 25*b*.

Mems., 10, 14.

VIII. Āghā-sulṭān Sulṭānam *Dugldāt.*

She was a daughter of Muḥammad Ḥaidar Mīrzā *Dughlāt,* and therefore aunt of the author of the *Tārīkh-i-rashīdī.* She married 'Abdu-l-qadūs Beg *Dughlāt* in Kāshghar, after 877H. (1472-73).

Her husband was alive in 900H. (1494-95), and was governor of Khost for Sulṭān Maḥmūd Mīrzā *Mīrān-shāhī.*

Mems., 27.

Tūr. Rash., E. and R., 95, 103.

IX. Āī Begam *Mīrān-shāhī.*

Turkī, *āī*, moon. Her name is not mentioned in the Memoirs, but is so by Ilminsky (Mems., 30; Ilminsky, 34, line 7 from foot).

She was the fourth daughter of Sulṭān Maḥmūd Mīrzā *Mīrānshāhī* and Khānzāda Termiẕī II.; and wife of Jahāngīr Mīrzā, half-brother of Bābar. She was betrothed in 901H. (1495-96), married in 910H. (1504-5), bore one daughter, and was widowed not later than 914H. (1508-9).

Mems., 30, 128.

Pavet de Courteille, I. 57, 262.

X. Āka Begam *Bāyqrā.*

Aka is clearly a title; her personal name I have not found. Her sister who is styled *Bedka,* appears to be named Kābi'a-sulṭān.

Daughter of Manṣūr Mīrzā *Bāyqrā* and Fīroza Begam *Mīrān-shāhī,* full and elder sister of Sulṭān Husain Mīrzā. Bābar states (Mems., 176, 177) that she married (his uncle) Sulṭān Aḥmad Mīrza, and had a son, Kīchak Mīrzā (the young or small prince). But he does not mention her, either as Āka or otherwise, amongst Aḥmad's wives (Mems., 22), and he says that Aḥmad had two sons who died young. Kīchak, however, lived to change his military occupations for literature.

It is singular that a marriage of the oldest *Mīrān-shāhī* of his generation with the oldest *Bāyqrā* girl should not have been entered in Aḥmad's biographical notice.

Mems., 22, 23, 176, 177.

(Ālūsh—Anūsh—Begam, 'Ūlūs, *q.v..)*

XI. Amīna Begam *Mīrān-shāhī.*

Ara., *amīn,* faithful.

Daughter of Humāyūn and Māh-chūchak.

Gul-badan, 7*1a.*

XII. *Āq* Begam *Bāyqrā.*

Turkī, *āq,* fair. The word is frequently a sobriquet and the bearer's personal name is occasionally known; *e.g.,* Yasīn-daulat, Āq Sulṭān; Salīqa Begam, Āq Begam. But frequently the personal name is not traceable.

Daughter of Sulṭān Husain Mīrzā *Bāyqrā* and Pāyanda Sulṭān Begam *Mīrān-shūhī;* first cousin of Bābar; wife of Muḥammad Qāsim *Ārlāt.*[1] She had one daughter, known as the Black-eyed *(qarā-gūz)* Begam.

Mems., 181.

XIII. Āq Begam *Mīrān-shāhī.* (No. 3.)

Āq Begam was a daughter of Abū-sa'īd *Mīrānshāhī* and Khadīja. She was one of the several paternal aunts of Bābar who went to India at his invitation. She reached Āgra in October, 1528 (Safar, 935H.), and was met by her nephew. She was present at the double wedding of Gul-rang and Gul-chihra in 1530 (937H.), and was probably at Bābar's death-bed. She was at the Mystic Feast on December 19th, 1531 (Jumāda I. 9th, 938H.).

Gul-badan, 11*a*, 18*b*, 20*a,* 24*b.*

Mems., 179, 182, 387.

XIV. Aq Begam *Mīrān-shāhī.*

Third daughter of Sulṭān Maḥmūd Mīrzā *Mīrān-shāhī* and Khānzāda Begam Termiẕī*;* and first cousin of Bābar. The Memoirs do not mention her marriage or (as usual alternative) early death. She was full sister of a wife of Bābar, Zainab.

---

[1] Muḥammad Qāsim was a Tītnūrid through his grandmother, Bega Begam, the sister of 'Abdu-l-qāsim Bābar qalandar, King of Khurāsān (died 1457).

Mems., 30.
(Aq Begam, Salīqa, *q.v.*)

XV. 'Aqīqa ('Afīfa) Begam *Mīrān-shāhī.* (No. 47.)

Her name may be 'Aqīqa, a cornelian, etc., or 'Afīfa, a chaste, modest woman. Our begam's MS. allows both readings. I have used the first but the second seems the more appropriate in sense.

She was a daughter of Humāyūn and Bega and second child of both parents. She was born in Āgra in 1531. It is only from her aunt Gul-badan that anything is known of her. She went to Guālīār with her mother in (?) 1534; she was at Hindāl's feast in 1537, and she was lost at Chausa on June 27th, 1539.

Gul-badan, 22*a*, 23*b*, 25, 33*b*, 34*b*.

XVI. *Ātūn māmā.* (No. 38.)

An *ātūn* is a teacher of reading, writing, and embroidery, etc. *Māmā* seems to be the title of old women-servants.

Bābar mentions an *ātūn* in 1501. He met her at Pashāghar whither she had come on foot from Samarqand and where she again joined her old mistress, Bābar's mother, Qutluq-nigār Khānam. She had been left behind in the city after Shaibānī's capture of it because there was no horse for her to ride.

Gul-badan mentions an *ātūn māmā* as at Hindāl's wedding feast, and as *māmā* seems to be used for old servants, it is possible that she is the woman mentioned by Bābar.

Gul-badan, 26*a*.
Mems., 99.

XVII. 'Āyisha-sulṭān Begam *Bāyqrā.* (No. 9.)

Ar. '*aish,* joy, and *sulṭān,* sway, pre-eminence. *Cf.* App. *s.n.* Daulat.

Daughter of Sulṭān Husain Mīrzā *Bāyqrā* and Zobaida *āghācha* of the Shaibān sulṭāns. 'Āyisha married, (1) Qāsim Sulṭān *Uzbeg,* a Shaibān sulṭān, and by him became the mother of Qāsim Husain Sulṭān *Uzbeg,* an amīr of Bābar and Humāyūn; (2) by *yanga-lik (Cf.*

App. *s.n.* Jāmal), Būran Sulṭān, a kinsman of Qāsim Sulṭān, and by whom she had 'Abdu-l-lāh Sulṭān *Uzbeg* who entered Bābar's service.

'Āyisha was at the Mystic Feast in 1531, and she was lost at Chausa in 1539 (946H.).

Khwānd-amīr gives 929H. (1522-23) as a date at which 'Āyisha was in Qāsim Sulṭān's *ḥaram,* but this does not agree with Bābar's narrative. His entry that 'Abdu-l-lāh was in his service and although young, acquitting himself respectably, cannot at latest have been made after 1530. From 1522 to 1530 is all too short for widowhood, remarriage, birth of 'Abdu-l-lāh, and his growth to respectable military service.

Gul-badan, 24*b*, 33*b*.

Mems., 182.

Ḥabību-s-siyār, lith. ed., 327 *et seq*..

XVIII. 'Āyisha-sulṭān Begam *Mīran-shāhī.* (? No. 11.)

Third daughter of Sulṭān Aḥmad Mīrzā *Mīrān-shāhī* and Qūtūq (Katak) Begam. She was a first cousin of Bābar, and his first wife. They were betrothed in Samarqand when he was five years old, 894H. (1488-89), and married in Sha'bān, 905H. (March, 1500), at Khojand during the 'troubles' *i.e.,* conflict with Khusrau Shāh and Aḥmad Tambol. Bābar says that at first he had no small affection for 'Āyisha and that it declined. She was the mother of his first child, Fakhru-n-nisā' (born 907H., 1501). She left Bābar before the overthrow *(wirānī)* of Tāshkand by Shaibānī in 909H. (1503), being influenced by the 'machinations' of her elder sister, probably Salīqa, who was married to one of those many kinsmen who tried to overthrow the boy-king of Farghāna.

Gul-badan mentions an 'Āyisha Sulṭān Begam (No. 11) as being at the Mystic Feast, without describing her. The following entry (No. 12) is that of Sulṭānī, a daughter of Sulṭān Aḥmad Mīrzā, and described as being such. It seems likely that Gul-badan meant this note as to parentage to apply to both begams (Nos. 11 and 12). *(Cf.*

App. *s.n.* Sulṭānam)

Gul-badan, 6*b*, 24*b*.

Mems., 22, 78, 90.

XIX. Āyisha-sulṭān Begam *Mīrān-shāhī.*

Daughter of Kāmrān Mīrzā.

Firishta (lith. ed., 241) and Khāfī Khān (I. 122) say that Kāmrān left one son and three daughters.

The son is called Ibrāhīm by Gul-badan, and in the early part of the *Akbar-nāma.* (*Bib. Ind.,* ed., I. 226.) Later the A. N. and other sources call him Abū'l-qāsim, which may be a hyonymic *(kunyat)*.

As to the three girls, Firishta, without naming them, gives the information that:

No. 1 married (*a*) Ibrāhīm Husain Mīrzā *(Bāyqrā)*.

No. 2 " (*b*) Mīrzā 'Abdu-r-rahman *Mughal.*

No. 3 " (*c*) Fakhru-d-dīn *Mashhadī* who died in 986H. or 987H. (No. 88 of Blochmann's list. *Āīn-iakbarī,* p. 406).

Khāfī Khān's information coincides with Firishta's verbally as to No. 3, and actually as to No. 1 and No. 2. For Ibrāhīm can be described as a son of a 'paternal uncle,' if these words are used in the wide sense given to them by contemporary writers. So, too, can 'Abdu-r-rahman, if he be No. 183 of Blochmann's list—a Dughlāt Mughal and cousin of Mīrzā Ḥaidar.

If we take the girls' names from other sources we can (conjecturally in part) fill up the table.

1. Gul-rukh is known in history as the wife of Ibrāhīm Husain Mīrzā *Bāyqrā.*
2. Kāmrān's eldest daughter, Hābība, was forcibly parted from her husband, Āq Sulṭān, in about 1551-52, and this would allow re-marriage to *(b)* or *(c)*. Āq Sulṭān went to Makka from Sind 1551-52 *(cir.),* and his name disappears thenceforth.
3. 'Āyisha may also have married *(b)* or (*c*).

In the list of the pilgrims of 983H. (A. N. *Bib. Ind.* ed., III. 145) are included 'Ḥājī and Gul-'izār, *farzandān* of Mīrzā Kāmrān.'[1] We have already the three names required by Firishta and Khāfī Khān, *i.e.*. Gul-rukh, Habība and 'Āyisha. Gul-'izār is 'superfluous.' Perhaps *farzandān* may be read 'offspring,' and she may be a granddaughter. Or Habība or 'Āyisha may have predeceased Kāmrān, and for this reason three girls only be specified by historians who wrote of the time of his death.

Which one of the daughters was the Hājī Begam of 983H. is not clear.[2] It would seem that this was her second pilgrimage, since she is enrolled as Hājī before starting. Kāmrān's daughters may have gone—one or all—to Makka after his blinding and during the four years of his life there. Of the three, Gul-rukh is the only one of whom it is on record that she was widowed in 983H., and therefore quite free to make the *Ḥaj*. Ibrāhīm Husain died in 981H. (1573).

Hājī Begam was visited by Akbar and she died in 991H. (1583).

Gul-badan, 77*a*, 78*a*.

Akbar-nāma, III. 145, 373, 375.

XX. 'Āyisha-sulṭān Khānam and Khātīm, Mughal Khānam, *Chaghatāī Mughal.*

Daughter of Sulṭān Maḥmūd Khān. In 909H. (1503) she, together with other ladies of her father's household, was captured by Shaibānī and was married by him. She bore him a son, Muhammād-rahīm Sulṭān. She wrote Turkī verses, and her name appears in the biography of poetesses by Fakhrī *amīrī.* Mīrzā Ḥaidar says that some of her children and of two other Mughal khānams (Daulat and Qūt-līq) who were forcibly married at the same time, were living and reigning in Transoxiana at the time of his writing the *Tārikh-*

---

[1] Mr. Beveridge tells me that a MS. *Akbar-nāma* belonging to the R.A.S. has *wa* (and) before *farzandān*, but it does not seem practicable to read this.

[2] Professor Blochmann (*Āīn*, p. 465, No. 187) has (by a slip of reference numbering) confused Hājī Begam, daughter of Kāmrān, with Ḥājī Begam, Bega Begam, widow of Humāyūn. The latter died in 989H. before Gul-badan's party returned. Bega Begam went to Makka in 972H..

i-rashīdī. She is, I think, the 'Āyisha named by Gul-badan on 76*b*.

Tār.Rash., 160, 192, 193.

Gul-badan, 76*b*.

Jawāhiru-l-'ajāib. Fakhrī *amīrī* (Bodleian MS.).

XXI. Bābū *āghā (Māmā āghā).*

Professor Blochmann writes the name *Bābū;* but *Bobā,* darling, or *Bānū,* lady, would seem more appropriate for a Persian woman.

She was the wife of Shihābu-d-dīn Aḥmad Khān *Nishāpūrī,* and was related to Ḥamīda-bānū Begam *Jāmī,* Akbar's mother. Abū'l-fazl calls her Māmā *āghā.* He says that she was a good woman, and that on her death Akbar went to her house and offered condolence because of her relationship to his mother.

Shihābu-d-dīn was *damād* of Māham *anaga,* and as *damād* is presumably used here in its more common sense of 'son-in-law,' Bābū *āghā* would seem to be a daughter of Māham *anaga.*

Akbar-nāma, Bib. Ind. ed., III. 716.

Aīn-i-akbarī, Blochmann, 333.

XXII. Bachaka *Khalīfa.*

Gul-badan, Bachaka; Mems., Bachaka; Ilminsky, Bīchkā. Vambéry *(Chaghatāische Sprachstudien)* has an appropriate word. *bechek,* Chok. (? Kokand), *zierrath; ornament.* The name is presumably Chaghatāī Turkī, as the bearer of it was an old family servant of a Farghāna household.

Bachaka was a head woman-servant *(khalīfa)* of Bābar's household, and was one of two women who escaped with his mother and him from Samarqand in 1501. There was a Bachaka whom Gul-badan calls a '*khalīfa* of my royal father,' lost at Chausa in 1539, and the two references may well be to the same woman.

Mems., 98.

Gul-badan, 33*b*.

Ilminsky, 116.

XXIII. Badī'u-l-jamāl Khānam *Chaghatāī Mughal.*

The khānam of rare beauty; Ar. *badī',* astonishing, rare; *jamāl,* beauty.

Daughter of Sa'īd Khān *Chaghatāī Mughal,* ruler of Kāshghar; and first cousin, once removed, of Bābar. She married Bāush Sulṭān of the Uzbeg Kazāks. On her father's death, her brother Rashīd insisted upon her divorce, and then gave her in marriage to Muhammadī *Barlās* whom Ḥaidar Mīrzā styles 'a peasant.'

Tār. Rash., E. & R., 453.

XXIV. Badī'u-l-jamāl Begam *Mīrān-shāhī.* (No. 2.)

She was a daughter of Sulṭān Abū-sa'īd Mīrzā *Mīrān-shāhī.* She went to India during Bābar's life; was at the double wedding of his daughters, and at the Mystic Feast in 1531.

Mems., 387.

Gul-badan, 11*a*, 18*b*, 24*b*.

XXV. Bairām (Maryam) Sulṭān.

Ilminsky calls her Bairam; Khwānd-amīr, Maryam.

The Mems. give her no name.

She was the elder daughter of Sulṭān Husain Mīrzā *Bāyqrā* and Mīnglī-bī *āghācha Uzbeg.* She married Sayyid 'Abdu-l-lāh Mīrzā of Andikhūd (a Tīmūrid through his mother). She bore a son, Sayyid Birka, who served Bābar.

Ilminsky, 209.

Mems., 181.

Ḥabību-s-siyār, 327 *et seq.*.

XXVI. Bakhshī-bānū Begam.

Princess Good-fortune. Pers. *bakhsh,* fortune, and *bānū (vān),* possessing.

She was a daughter of Humāyūn and of Gūnwar Bībī, and was born in Jumāda L, 947H. (September, 1540), the year of the Tīmūrid exodus from India. She fell into the hands of her uncle 'Askarī with her father's camp and the baby Akbar in 1543. In 1545 she was sent with Akbar in the depth of winter from Qandahār to Kābul. In 957H. (1550), and when ten years old, she was betrothed by her father to Ibrāhīm, son of Sulaimān and *Ḥaram*. Ibrāhīm (b. 1534) was six years older than Bakhshī-bānū, and he was killed in 1560, leaving her a widow of twenty. In the same year she was given in marriage by Akbar to Mīrzā Sharafud-dīn Husain *Ahrārī.*

Gul-badan, 39*b*.

Akbar-nāma, s.n..

XXVII. Bakhtu-n-nisa' Begam.

Felicity of womanhood; Pers. *bakht,* felicity, fortune, and *nisā',* woman.

She was a daughter of Humāyūn and Māh-chūchak, and was born in 957H. (1550). Gul-badan says that she received her name in accordance with Humāyūn's interpretation of a dream. There is, however, ground for thinking that she and Fakhru-n-nisā', both mentioned in the histories as daughters of Māh-chūchak, are one and the same person. Gul-badan enumerates three daughters of Māh-chūchak, and says that there were four. It is her habit to state, in such matters, one more than she names. She mentions Bakht, but not Fakhr.

Of Bakhtu-n-nisā' it is recorded in the histories that she came from Kābul to India with her son Diwālī, after the death of Mīrzā Muḥammad Hakīm, her brother (993H.—1584-85), and that she was concerned in a reconciliation effected by Salīma-sulṭān Begam between Akbar and Salīm.

Of Fakhru-n-nisā' it is recorded that she married Shāh Abū'l-ma'ālī Termiẕī and Khwāja Hasan *Naqsh-bandī.*

Gul-badan, 71*a*.

Khāfī Khān *(Bib. Ind.* ed.), I. 226.

Badāyunī, Lowe, 72.

Akbar-nāma, s.n..

Aīn-i-akbarī, Blochmann, 322.

XXVIII. Bakht-sulṭān Begam *Mīrān-shāhī.* (No. 4.)

Daughter of Sulṭān Abū-sa'īd Mīrzā *Mīrān-shāhī* and mother of Āfāq (No. 26). She went to India shortly after its conquest by Bābar, and was at the Mystic Feast.

Mems., 387.

Gul-badan, 11*a*, 24*b*, 25*b*.

XXIX. Barlās Begam. (No. 86.)

There is no clue given by which to identify this lady. Others who were, like herself, at the Mystic Feast might, by tribal descent, be styled *Barlās.*

Gul-badan, 25*b*.

(Bedka, Rabī'a, *q.v.*.)

XXX. Bega *āghā.*

Bega is perhaps not a personal name. It appears to be a feminine of *beg,* but its application is not always to the daughters of *begs,* as may be seen by the instances here given. For a confusion of *bega* and *ganga Cf.* App. *s.n.* Zainab.

A messenger of Mīrzā Kāmrān to *Ḥaram* Begam.

Gul-badan, 75*b*.

XXXI. Bega Begam *Bāyqrā.*

Daughter of Sulṭān Husain Mīrzā *Bāiyqrā* and Pāyanda-sulṭān Begam *Mīrān-shāhī;* full sister of Ḥaidar *Bāyqrā;* first cousin of Bābar; wife of Bābar Mīrzā of Hājī Tarkhān who was her first cousin and the son of Rabī'a-sulṭān (Bedka) *Bāyqrā.*

Khwānd-amīr says that she married 'Khwāja Māulānā.' This may be a second marriage or a confusion with Kīchak, her sister.

Mems., 177, 181.

Ḥabību-s-siyār, 327 *et seq.*.

XXXII. Bega Begam and Bībī.

The Emperor Jahāngīr, when in his Memoirs enumerating the gardens of Kābul, mentions one which belonged to Bega Begam, a widow of his father's grandfather, *i.e,* Bābar. Which of Bābar's wives is indicated by this title cannot be said with certainty.

Jauhar has a story of Kāmrān's want of consideration for 'Bega Begam,' in which the points useful here are that on the day in 1545 when Humāyūn took Kābul from Kāmrān, he asked for food from Bega Begam, and he said of her that she was the very person who had brought Bābar's bones and laid them in Kābul.

These two references of Jahāngīr and Jauhar are probably to the same lady. Of Bābar's wives, Bībī Mubārika *(Afghānī āghācha)* appears to me the most suitable to the time and task.

Bābar's body was still in its Āgra tomb in 1539. (Gul-badan, 34*b*.) Māham was then dead; Dil-dār's movements exclude her from consideration; Gul-rukh, if living, will have left Āgra with her son Kāmrān before the Tīmūrid exodus was enforced by defeat at Kanauj; Bībī Mubārika remains, the probable and appropriate agent for fulfilling Bābar's wish as to the final disposition of his body. She lived into Akbar's reign, and her character and respected position in the household add to the sum of probability that she would discharge this duty.

Bābar's body was not removed till after the *fiṭrat, i.e.,* the Tīmūrid downfall and exodus. Bega Begam, or, as we may call her with Jauhar for the sake of clearness, the Bībī, must therefore have remained behind the rest of the royal family. This may have occurred in one of two natural ways. She might have stayed in Āgra under the protection of one of the religious families and safeguarded by pious duty to Bābar's tomb, until Shīr Khān gave permission to remove the body and a safe escort for her journey to his frontier; or she may even have been in Bengal and at Chausa with Humāyūn, and, like Bega *(Ḥājī)* Begam, have been made captive. It would harmonize with Shīr Khān's known actions if he had allowed Bābar's widow to remove his bones, and if he had aided her pious task.

Tūzūk-i-jahāngīrī, lith. ed., 51.

Humāyūn-nāma, Jauhar, Pers. text, *s.a.* 951H. (November, 1545).

B. & H., II. 325 n..

XXXIII. Bega Begam *Mīrān-shāhī.* (No. 15.)

This Bega was a daughter of Mīrzā Ulugh Beg *Mīrān-shāhī* who was king of Kābul and known as *Kābulī.* She was Bābar's first cousin, and may be that daughter of her father who married Muḥammad Ma'sūm Mīrzā *Bāyqrā.* Gul-badan styles her *'ama,* paternal aunt, of Humāyūn; *anglice,* she and he were first cousins, once removed. She was at the Mystic Feast in December, 1531.

Gul-badan, 24*b*.

Mems., 180.

XXXIV. Bega Begam *Mīrān-shāhī.* (? No. 22. Bega Kilān Begam.)

Daughter of Sulṭān Maḥmūd Mīrzā and Khānzāda II. Termiẕī*;* wife of Ḥaidar Mīrzā *Bāyqrā* and mother of Shād Begam (No. 28).

In 901H. (1496) Sulṭān Husain *Bāyqrā* was besieging Ḥiṣār which was held for Bega's brother Mas'ūd, and in which she was. Husain became apprehensive about the spring rains and patched up a peace, the seal of which was Bega's marriage with his son Ḥaidar, her first cousin through his mother, Pāyandasulṭān. The betrothal took place outside the fort, with assistance of such music as could be procured, and later when the bride was taken to Harāt, the marriage was celebrated with the splendour loved by Husain and befitting a Tīmūrid alliance. Ḥaidar was a full Tīmūrid; Bega was one on her father's side, and probably as a Termiẕī sayyida's daughter, drew through her also a strain of the same blood.

Ḥaidar died before his father; *i.e.,* before 912H. (April, 1506).

Mems., 30, 38, 180.

Gul-badan, (?) 24*b*, No. 22.

XXXV. Bega *(Ḥājī)* Begam (?) *Begchik Mughal.* (? No. 50.) She was a daughter of Uncle (*ṭaghāī*) Yādgār Beg who was, I think, a brother of Sulṭān 'Alī Mīrzā, father of Kāmran's wife, Gul-rukh. Abū'l-fazl calls Bega Begam *dukhtar-i-ṭaghāī-i-wālida-i-Jannat-āshyānī.* Yādgār and 'Alī *Begchik* are both styled *Mīrzā,* but this elevation is due, it seems, to their alliances with the royal house. Ḥaidar calls their brothers *mirs.*

Bega married Humāyūn, her first cousin, and she was the wife of his youth. It is out of harmony with the custom of his house that his chief wife should be of less than royal descent. So far as I have been able to trace the matter, he never made an equal marriage. Gul-barg *Barlās,* 'Khalīfa's' daughter, whose second husband he was, had best claim to high birth.

The first son, perhaps first child, of Bega and Humāyūn was Al-amān, born 934H. or 935H. (1528) when his father was about twenty-one and was in Badakhshān. Bābar has commemorated his birth both by mentioning it and by preserving his own congratulatory letter to the young father. Al-amān died in infancy.

Bega came to India after Bābar's death (December, 1530), and her second and last-mentioned child, 'Afīfa ('Aqīqa) was born in 1531.

In 1534 (*circa*) Gul-badan's story (296, 306) shows Bega as resenting neglect by Humāyūn who accepts invitations to his sisters' quarters in camp in preference to hers and Gul-barg's. Some impressions of this story make one question whether the Bega it tells of is Humāyūn's wife or another. But the circum-stances that she is associated with a wife, Gul-barg; that Gul-badan does not speak of her as being other than the 'Bega Begam' of the home circle; Humāyūn's allusions to the elder kinswomen; and the absence of the deference customary to an elder woman, seem sufficient justification for identifying the complaining Bega with the wife. (Gul-badan, it may be observed, mentions one other Bega Begam—*i.e., Mīrān-shāhī,* daughter of Ulugh Beg *Kābulī.)*

Bega was with Humāyūn during the idleness of his decadence in

Bengal, and with her was her sister, the wife of Zahīd Beg. Zahīd offended Humāyūn, and Bega tried in vain to obtain his forgiveness.

She was captured at Chausa by Shīr Khān, and here she lost her little girl, 'Aqīqa. The historians all call her *Ḥājī* Begam in recording her capture; it is only Gul-badan who calls her Bega Begam. She was returned in safety to Humāyūn under the escort of Shīr Khān's best general, Khawās Khān, How soon she was returned I am not able to say. Support is to be found for the view that she was sent to Āgra directly after Humāyūn's arrival there, and also for the view that she was not returned to him until after a considerable time had elapsed. I do not know whether she went to Sind with the exiles or was sent later direct to Kābul. She was in Kābul with the royal family after 1545. She remained there with the other ladies when Humāyūn made his expedition to recover Hindūstān, and she came with Hamīda, Gulbadan, and the rest to join Akbar in 964H. (1557). After this she built her husband's tomb near Dihlī, and became its faithful attendant.

Akbar is said to have been much attached to her, and she was to him like a second mother. She went to Makka in 972H. (1564-65), and returned three years later. One thing raises the question whether this was her first pilgrimage, *viz.,* the fact that all the sources, except Gul-badan's, call her *Hājī* Begam. Why is she singled out to bear this title? It had been earned by many royal ladies before any one of the trio of great writers under Akbar had put pen to paper. The same unexplained distinction is conferred by the histories on a daughter of Kāmrān. In both these cases a renewed pilgrimage might serve as the explanation of the distinction.

Bega Begam died in 989H. (1581), shortly before Gul-badan's return from Makka. She had almost certainly passed her seventieth year, and was perhaps still older. Abū'l-fazl says that her affairs were settled by one Qāsim 'Alī Khān. He also records a visit of Akbar to her in her last illness, as well as an earlier visit of hers to him made from Dihlī in 981H..

Gul-badan, 22*a*, 23*b*, 29*b*, 30*b*, 78*b*, 83*a*.

Mems., 388, 390.

Akbar-nāma, Bib. Inā. ed., index, *s.n.*.

Aīn-i-akbarl, Blochmann, 465. (Confusion has been made here with Kāmrān's daughter.)

Badāyunī, Lowe, 308 n..

History of the Afghāns, Dorn, I. 103.

XXXVI. Bega *Kilān* Begam. (No. 22.)

She was at the Mystic Feast. No clue is given to her identification. The '*kilān*' of her title indicates a pre-eminence which would suit Bega *Mīrān-shāhī,* daughter of Sulṭān Maḥmūd Mīrzā. *(Cf. supra.)*

Gul-badan, 24*b*.

XXXVII. Bega Sulṭān Begam *Mavī.*

Daughter of Sanjar Mīrzā of Marv; first wife of Sulṭān Husain Mīrzā *Bāyqrā;* mother of Badī'u-z-zamān Mīrzā. 'She was extremely cross-tempered, and fretted the mīrzā beyond endurance, till, driven to extremities by her insufferable humour, he divorced her. What could he do? He was in the right:

A bad wife in a good man's house,
Even in this world, makes a hell on earth.

May the Almighty remove such a visitation from every good Moslim; and God grant that such a thing as an ill-tempered, cross-grained wife be not left in the world.'

There is no later record of her.

Mems., 181, 182.

XXXVIII. Bega Sulṭān Begam *Mīrān-shāhī.* (No. 13.)

Daughter of Sulṭān Khalīl Mīrzā *Mīrān-shāhī;* granddaughter of Sulṭān Abū-sa'īd; first cousin of Bābar.

Gul-badan, 24*b*.

XXXIX. Begam Sulṭān.

Daughter of Shaikh Kamāl. Died 945H. (1538).

Beale's 'Oriental Biography,' *s.n.*.

(Begam Sulṭān, Sa'ādat-bakht, *q.v.*.)

XL. Begī Sulṭān *āghācha.*

Inferior wife *(chāhar-shambihī)* of Sulṭān Husain Mīrzā *Bāyqrā.*

Mems., 183.

XLI. Buwā Begam.

Mother of Sulṭān Ibrāhīm *Lōdī Afghān.* She attempted to poison Bābar in December, 1526 (933H.) in the manner which is told in most of the histories. The *Iqbāl-nāma* adds the interesting detail that she was deported from India, and that on her enforced journey to Kābul she drowned herself in the Indus.

Mems., 347.

Gul-badan, *19a.*

XLII. Chūlī Begam *Azāk.*

The Desert Princess; Pers. *chūl,* desert. The Memoirs have *Jūlī,* but the meaning of *chūlī* (which looks like a sobriquet) suits the descent of the begam better than anything which can be extracted from *jūl.* Ilminsky writes *Jūlī,* but for this the Mems. are his possible warrant. B.M. Pers. Or. 16,623, f. 123, 1. 7., has a clearly-pointed *chūlī;* also on f. 124*b*.

Chūlī (Jūlī) Begam was a daughter of a beg of the Azāks, and married Sulṭān Husain *Bāyqrā* before he conquered Khurāsān in 878H. (1473). She was the mother of Sulṭānam, his eldest girl and her only child, and she died before 912H. (1506).

Mems., 181, 182.

Ḥabību-s-siyār, 327 *et seq.*.

XLIII. Daulat-bakht *āghācha.*

(?) The lady of happy horoscope (*bakld*).

She may be the mother of Kāmrān's daughter 'Āyisha, with whom she was in flight for Qandahār. *(Cf.* 'Āyisha.)

Gul-badan, 78*b*.

XLIV. Daulat-bakht Bībī. (No. 85.)

She was clearly an active and working member of Humāyūn's household. She appeared to him in a dream (*71a*), and her name formed a part of Bakhtu-n-nisā's. She went on before the main body of begams when they visited the waterfall at Farza, and saw to the commissariat. She is named as being at Hindāl's marriage feast.

She may be the Daulat-bakht *āghācha* of the preceding notice.

Gul-badan, 26*b*, 71*a*, 74*a*.

XLY. Daulat-kitta (?) *Arghūn.*

Kitta I find only as a Turkī word, meaning noble, powerful. With it the name would be a mongrel of Arabic and Turkī. Perhaps Daulat-gītī might be read.

She was a servant in Mīrzā Muḥammad Muqīm *Arghūn's* house, and was an intermediary in effecting the elopement of her master's daughter, Māhchūchak *Arghūn,* from Kābul. Mr. Erskine tells the story admirably.

B. & H., I. 348 *et seq.,* and the sources there referred to.

XLYI. Daulat-nigār Khānam *Chaghatāī Mughal.*

Good-fortune itself; the very image of felicity.

Ar. *daulat,* and Pers. *nigār,* effigy, image.

Daughter of Isān-būghā Khān *Chaghatāī;* wife of Muḥammad Ḥaidar Mīrzā *Dughlāt.*

Tār. Rash., E. & R., 88.

XLVII. Daulat-sulṭān Khānam *Chaghatāī Mughal.*

Ar. *daulat,* fortune, and *sulṭān,* sway. In many proper names, *sulṭān* does not appear to be a title, but rather to indicate the sway or dominance of the quality imputed by the first word of the name; *e.g., Latīf-sulṭān, Daulat-sulṭān.* In giving these names, one might suppose the prophetic notion to be that the first child should be a regnant delight and the second a prevailing felicity.

Youngest child of Yūnas Khān *Chaghatāī* and Shāh Begam

Badakhshī; half-sister of Bābar's mother; wife by chance of battle, of Tīmūr Sulṭān *Uzbeg;* mother by him of a daughter.

In 907H. (1501-2) she was in Tāshkand, and Qūt-līq-nigār Khānam went to visit her after thirteen or fourteen years of separation. Bābar, dejected and an exile, joined the family party in the next year. In 909H. (1503) Shaibānī sacked Tāshkand and forcibly married Daulat-sulṭān to his son Tīmūr. She bore him a daughter, and she remained in his *ḥaram* until Bābar took possession of Samarqand in 917H. (1511), and she joined him. She went south with him in 1513, and remained several years in Badakhshān with another nephew, Mīrzā (Wais) Khān who behaved to her like a son.

Another nephew, Sa'īd, her own brother Aḥmad's son, then invited her, with costly gifts, to visit him in Kāshghar. She made the long and dimcult journey; joined him in Yarkand; and with him she spent the rest of her life.

Bābar mentions that her foster-brother brought him news and letters from her in 925H. (September 8th, 1519). In the same year Mansūr, Sa'īd's eldest brother, went to Kāshghar to visit her, his 'beloved aunt.'

The Persian text of the *Tārīkh-i-rashīdī* says that Mansūr went so that by looking at her kind face his grief for the loss of his father might be mitigated. The Bible Society's Turkī version reads: 'Being prompted thereto by the extreme warmth of his affection for her.' Both statements illumine her character. The second seems the more appropriate, since the death of Sulṭān Aḥmad Khān took place in 909H. (1503) and Mansur's visit in 926H. (1520).

There is no mention of her remarriage, and her story is that of an affectionate and leisured aunt.

Mems., 14, 99, 105, 274.

Tār. Rash., E. & E., 108, 117, 156, 160, 351, 352, 356.

XLVIII. Daulat-sulṭān (?) *Sakanj* Begam.

Sakanj I cannot explain. B. M. Add. 24,090 (44*b*) has no points, and the word may be S-k-n-gh. B. M., Or. 137 (48*a*) has k-m-n-j or b-k-n-j. The Turkī (Bible Society's MS. translations) has Daulat.

Daughter of Amīr Shaikh Nūru-d-dīn *Qibchāq Mughal,* governor of Turkistān; wife of Wais Khān *Chaghatāī Mughal.*

Tār. Rash., E. & R., 64 and 64 n..

XLIX. Dil-dār Begam. (No. 48.)

The Heart-holding Princess; Pers. *dil,* heart, and *dār,* holding.

Neither her husband, Bābar nor her daughter, Gulbadan gives any clue to her parentage. Her marriage is not spoken of in the Memoirs; it, as well as Gul-rukh's, probably occurred in the missing decade of 1509-19. If Bābar held the view that four wives were a lawful number, Dil-dār, of whatever parentage, may be counted amongst them, since in 1509 Māham only remained of his earlier wives, 'Ayisha, Zainab, and Ma'sūma having disappeared from the household by death or divorce.

Dil-dār is mentioned once in the Turkī text of Kehr and Ilminsky, and then as *āghācha.* I am too ignorant of the import of this word in the domestic circle to venture to draw from its use an inference as to social status. It, however, as used by Bābar and by Gulbadan, supports Pavet de Courteille's definition of a 'lady' in contradistinction to a 'begam,' and does not convey reproach to the woman as its occasional English rendering (concubine) does.

The *Akbar-nāma (Bib. Ind.* ed., II. 62) makes use of the words 'Dil-dār *āghācha* Begam,' and adds *āghā* as a variant *(Cf.* App., *s.n. āghā).* Gul-badan always styles her mother begam, and sometimes *ḥazrat.* In enumerating her father's children and their mothers, she does not mention the parentage of any wife besides Ma'sūma *Mīrān-shāhī,* a Tīmūrid, but no deduction as to the lower birth of the others can be drawn safely from this, and there is some ground for supposing that Dil-dār was of *Mīrān-shāhī* birth. *(Cf. infra,* p. 277.)

Perhaps some indication of non-royal birth is given by Māham's forcible adoption of Dil-dār's son in 1519, but I am too ignorant of the *nuances* of Muḥammadan etiquette to venture on assertion or even on opinion in such a matter. That Māham did not take

Gul-rukh's[1] son tells nothing, since the chief factors in the adoption, *i.e.,* Māham's loss of her own children and wish to adopt, may have become operative only when they were put into practice in 1519.

Five children of Dil-dār are mentioned by Gulbadan: Gul-rang, born between 1511 and 1515; Gul-chihra; Abū-n-nāsir Muḥammad (Hindāl), born 1519; Gul-badan, born 1523; and Alwar, who died in India in 1529.

She is very frequently written of by her daughter; some other authors give of her a clear and pleasant impression; and she is always spoken of with respect and as a good and sensible woman.

Gul-badan, 6*b*, 16*a*, 23*a*, 25*b*, 29*b*, 30*a*, 35*a*, 35*b*, 38*a*, 42*a*, 50*b*, 51*b*, 65*a*, 70*b*.

Jauhar, Stewart, 30, 31.

Ilminsky, 281.

Akbar-nāma, Bib. Ind. ed., *s.n.*.

B. & H., II. 164, 220, 302.

L. Dil-shād Begam.

The Heart-rejoicing Princess; Pers. *dil,* heart, and *shād,* rejoicing.

Daughter of Shāh Begam and granddaughter of Fakhr-jahān Begam *Mīrān-shāhī.* Of her paternal descent nothing is recorded.

Gul-badan, 246.

LI. Dūdū Bībī.

Wife of Sulṭān Muḥammad Shāh *Lohānī,* Afghān King of Bihār; mother of Sulṭān Jalālu-d-dīn; regent for her son in his minority from 1529.

B. & H., *s.n.*.

LII. Fakhr-jahān Begam *Mīrān-shāhī.* (No. 1.)

The world's ornament. Ar. *fakhr,* ornament, and Pers. *jahān,* world.

She was a daughter of Sulṭān Abū-sa'īd Mīrzā; a paternal aunt of

[1] For erratum in my Introduction as to Gul-rukb, *Cf.* App. s.n..

Bābar; the wife of Mīr 'Alā'u-l-mulk Termizī; and mother of Shāh and Kīchak Begams.

She went to India in 1526, the first year of Bābar's occupation, with her sister Khadīja, and stayed there nearly two years. She took leave of Bābar before starting on her return journey to Kābul on September 20th, 1528 (Muharram 5th, 935H.). She was again in Āgra and at the Mystic Feast in 1531.

Gul-badan, 11*a*, 24*b*.

Mems., 374, 382.

P. de Courteille, II. 453. (This is a fragment, supplied by Kehr and Ilminsky, which has the appearance of memoranda and which concerns a period already and variously written of in the *Bābar-nāma* of Kehr and contained in the Memoirs of Mr. Erskine.)

Aīn-i-akbarī, Blochmann, 322.

LIII. Fakhru-n-nisā'.

The ornament of womanhood; Ar. *fakhr,* ornament, and *nisā',* woman.

She was a daughter of Bābar and 'Āyisha-sulṭān, and his first child, born when he was nineteen. She died when about a month old.

Mems., 90.

Gul-badan, 6*b*.

LIV. Fakhru-n-nisā' *anaga* and *māmā*.

Mother of Nadīm *kūka,* mother-in-law of his wife, Maham *anaga.*

She and Nadīm are several times mentioned by Gulbadan.

Gul-badan, 26*a,* 46*a,* 71*a,* 73*b*.

Journal of the Royal Asiatic Society, January, 1899, art. Māham *anaga,* H. Beveridge.

LV. Fakhru-n-nisa' Begam *Mīran-shahī.* (No. 61.)

Daughter of Humāyun and Māh-chuchak; sister of Muhammad Hakim; wife (1) of Shāh Abu'l-ma'āli and (2) of Khwāja Hasan *Naqshbandī;* (*Cf.* Bakhtun-nisā'.)

Akbar-nāma, Bib. Ind. ed., *s.n.*.
Aīn-i-akbarī, Blochmann, *s.n.*.
Badāyunī, Lowe, 72.

LVI. Fāṯima Sulṭan *āghā.*

Ar. *Fāṭima,* a name given presumably in honour of the Prophet's daughter. The meaning of *sulṭān* here is not apparent. It does not seem as, *e.g.,* in *Daulat-sulṭān,* safe to consider it as a part of a compound word, and to read Fatīma-sulṭān. Nor from the bearer's parentage does it suit to take it as a title, implying that she is of the sulṭāns of her tribe.

There are points in the use of the word *sulṭān* which require fuller discussion than is practicable here. One Fāṯima Sulṭān and her sister Bairām (Maryam) were the children of Husain *Bāyqrā* by an Uzbeg servant of one of his royal wives. They are not given any further title, but their brothers are *mīrzās.*

Daughter of the chief of a Mughal *tumān* (10,000 men); first wife of 'Umar Shaikh *Mīrān-shāhī;* mother of his second son, Jahāngīr who was two years the junior of Bābar.

Mems., 10, 14.

LVII. Fāṯīma Sulṭān *anaga* and Bībī. (No. 60.)

Mother of Raushan *kūka* and of Zuhra, wife of Khwāja Mu'aẓẓam. Bāyazīd *bīyāt* speaks of her as the *ōrdū-begi* of Humāyūn's *ḥaram,* a title which Blochmann translates 'armed woman.'

She was at Hindāl's marriage feast; she helped to nurse Humāyūn in 1546; and was an envoy to *Ḥaram* Begam for marriage negotiations; and she appears in Akbar's reign when her daughter is murdered.

Journal of the Royal Asiatic Society, October, 1898, art. Memoirs of Bāyazīd *bīyāt,* H. Beveridge.

Ṯabaqāt-i-akbarī, Elliot, V. 291.

Akbar-nāma, Bib. Ind. ed., *s.n.*.

Gul-badan, 26*a*.

LVIII. Fāṭima Sulṭān *Bāyqrā.*

Daughter of Sultān Husain Mīrzā *Bāyqrā* and of Mīnglī-bī *āghācha Uzbeg;* wife of Yādgār Muhamrnad Mīrzā *Shāh-rukhī* (died 875—1470-71). She was dead before 912H. (Mav, 1506).

Mems., 182.

Ḥabību-s-siyūr, 327 *et seq.*.

LIX. Fāṭima Sulṭān Begam.

A wife of Shāh Husain Beg *Arghūn,* and mentioned in the *Tārīkh-i-sind.*

LX. Fauq Begam. (No. 31.)

Ar. *fauq,* superiority, excellence.

Gul-badan, 25*b*.

LXI. Fīroza Begam. (No. 35.)

The princess of victory; Pers. *fīroz,* victorious, prosperous.

Gul-badan, 25*b*.

LXII. Fīroza Begam *Mīrān-shāhī.*

She was a granddaughter of Tīmūr, and married Mansūr Mīrzā *Bāyqrā,* Their son Husain was therefore a double Tīmūrid, fourth in descent through Mansūr and third through Fīroza.

Mems., 176.

LXIII. Gauhar-shād Begam and *āghā, Turkomān.*

The jewel of joy; Pers. *gauhar,* jewel, and *shād,* joy, delight.

Wife of Shāh-rukh, son of Tīmūr; sister of Qarā Yūsuf *Turkomān;* founder of the Masjid which bears her name in Mashhad, and, with her husband, of the Bāgh-i-zāghān (Ravens' Garden) at Harāt. Bābar saw her tomb (dated 861H., 1457) and her mosque in 1506.

Mems., 207.

Northern Afghānistān, C. E. Yate, *s.n.*

Tār. Rash., E. & K., 83 *n.*.

LXIV. Gauhar-shād Begam *Dughlāt.*

Daughter of Muhammad *Dughlāt Ḥisārī;* wife of Amīr Yār (*sic*)*;* son of Amīr Jān-wafā, who was *darogha* of Samarqand under Shaibāni in 906H. (1500) when Bābar took the city, and who was an intimate of Muḥammad *Ḥisārī,* and saved his life by a warning word, as a reward for which Gauhar-shād was given in marriage to his son.

Mems., 86, 88, 239.

Tār. Rash., E. & B., 193.

LXV. Gauhar-shād Begam *Mīrān-shāhī.* (No. 5.)

Daughter of Sulṭān Abū-saīd Mīrzā and paternal aunt of Bābar. She was at the Mjstic Feast.

Mems., 387.

Gul-badan, 11*a*, 24*b*.

LXVI. Gul-badan Begam *Mīrān-shāhī.* (No. 46.)

Cf. Biographical Introduction and her own *Humāyūn-nāma.*

LXVII. Gul-barg Begam *Barlās.* (No. 49.)

The rose-leaf princess; Pers. *barg,* leaf.

Daughter of Nizāmu-d-dīn ‘Alī *Barlās,* Bābar’s *Khalīfa;* niece, therefore, of Sultān Junaid *Barlās,* a brother-in-law of Bābar. (*Cf.* Shahr-bānū.) She may be the child of that Sulṭanam who received Gul-badan at Kūl-jalālī. *(*14*a)* She married, first, Mīr Shāh Husain *Arghūn,* in 930H. (1524). The alliance was not happy and a separation took place. She appears to have remarried Humāyun at some time before the defeat at Chausa (1539). She was with him subsequently in Sind, and from there went with Sulṭanam to Makka previous to 1543.

She was buried in Dihlī. Mīr Ma’sūm writes of her death: ‘She entrusted her soul to the guardians of the hour of death, and the leaves (*gul-barg*) of the rose-bush of her life were dispersed by the boisterous wind of mortality.’

Gul-badan, 21*a*, 25*b*, 29*b*, 30*b*, 49*b*.
Tārikhi-i-sind, Mīr Ma'ṣūm.
B. & H., I. 385.

LXVIII. Gul-barg, or - izar, or -rang, or -rukh *Mīrān-shāhī.*

By these various names is mentioned the mother of Salīma-sulṭān Begam. There are difficult points as to her descent which are discussed *s.n.* Salīma-sulṭān.

LXIX. Gul Begam. (No. 30.)

The rose princess.

She was at the Mystic Feast, and may be one of the various ladies of the rose who are entered *infra.*

Gul-badan, 255.

LXX. Gul-chihra Begam *Mīrān-shāhī.* (No. 45.)

The rosy-cheeked princess; Pers. *chihra,* face.

Daughter of Bābar and Dil-dār; their second child, and born between 1515 and 1517. She was full-sister of Gul-rang, Hindāl, and Gul-badan.

She married Bābar's first cousin (a son of his mother's brother Ahmad), Sultān Tūkhta-bughā Khān *Chaghatāī Mughal.* The marriage was arranged by Bābar, and took place in 937H. (end of 1530). She would then be about fourteen years old.

She was widowed *cir.* 940H. (1533), and nothing as to her remarriage is recorded until 956H. (1549), when she was over thirty years old. It is improbable that she remained a widow so many years. *(Cf.* App. *s.n.* Salīma-sultān.) In 956H. she entered upon what looks like a *mariage de raison* with 'Abbās Sultān *Uzbeg,* just before Humāyūn set out on his expedition for Balkh. The bridegroom came to suspect that the Tīmūrid army was about to act against his own people and ran away. Probably he did not take Gul-chihra with him. Her name next appears in the histories when she accompanies Gul-badan and Hamīda to India in 964H. (1557).

Gul-badan, 6*b*, 16*b*, 18*b*, 23*b*, 25*b*, 29*b*, 38*a*, 65*a*.
Akbar-nāma, Bib. Ind. ed., *s.n.*

LXXI. Gul-'izār Begam *Mīrān-shāhī.*

The rosy-cheeked princess; Pers. *gul,* rose, and *'izār,* cheek, face.

Daughter of Bābar and Gul-rukh; full-sister of Kāmrān and 'Askarī.

Gul-badan names no marriage for her, but she may have been the wife of Yādgār-nāsir.

Gul-badan, 6*b*.

Mems., 10.

LXXII. Gul-'izār Begam *Mīrān-shāhī.*

Daughter of Kāmrān Mīrzā; she accompanied Gulbadan Begam to Makka (983H., October, 1575). *(Cf.* App. *s.n.* 'Āyisha *Mīrān-shāhī.)*

Akbar-nāma, Bib. Ind. ed., III. 145.

LXXIII. Gul-nār *āghācha.* (No. 57.)

The red, red rose; Pers. *gul,* rose, and *nār (anār),* pomegranate, carnation red.

She was of Bābar's *ḥaram,* and may have been one of the two Circassian (Cherkis) slavēs (the other being Nār-gul) who were presented to the Emperor by Shāh Tahmāsp in 933H. (1526).

She was at Hindāl's wedding-feast, and shared in the conferences of Humāyūn and his family; and she was one of Gul-badan Begam's pilgrim band (983H., 1575).

Gul-badan, 25*b*, 30*a*, 35*a*, 38*a*.

Mems., 347.

Akbar-nāma, Bib. Ind. ed., III. 145.

LXXIV. Gul-rang Begam *Mīrān-shāhī.* (No. 44.)

The rose-hued princess.

Daughter of Bābar and Dil-dār and her mother's first child. She was born in Khost, probably between 1511 and 1515, during Bābar's exile from Kābul after the Mughal rebellion. She was given in marriage to Isān-tīmūr *Chaghatāī* Mughal, her father's first cousin, during the last days of her father's life and in 1530.

Isān-tīmūr is last mentioned in 1543, and of Gulrang there is no certain record after *cir.* 1534, when she was at Guālīār. (23*a*) (*Cf.* App. *s.n,* Salīma.)

Gul-badan, 66, 166, 186, 23*a*, 256, 296.

LXXV. Gul-rukh Begam (?) *Begchik Mughal.*

The rose-cheeked princess.

Wife of Bābar; mother of Kāmrān, 'Askarī, Shāh-rukh, Aḥmad, and Gul-'izar. Outside Kābul there was in 1545 the tomb of Gul-rukh Begam. (646) This may well have been hers.

She is perhaps a *Begchik.* This may be judged from the following notes:

(1) Kāmrān married a daughter of Sulṭān 'Alī Mīrzā *ṭaghāī.*[1] (Mems., 388.)
(2) Humāyūn married a daughter of Yādgār *ṭaghāī.* (Mems., 388.)

Amongst eontemporary *Begchik* amīrs are Sulṭān Alī Mīrzā and Yādgār Mīrzā.

If one follows the recorded incidents of Sulṭān 'Alī's life, one sees that Gul-rukh may be his sister.

(*a*) In 914H. (1508-9) he was ordered to drown Khalīl Khān.

---

[1] This is a difficult word to deal with. It has a wider use than its usual translation 'mother's brother.' It is used for the uncle, great-uncle, etc., in ascending line. In other words, the mother's brother, in at any rate distinguished families, of one generation remains the mother's brother, *ṭaghāī*, in the next and the next. Once a *ṭaghāī*, always a *ṭaghāī*. The numerous uncles on the mother's side who appear in the Memoirs and the *Tārīkh-i-rashīdī* as so-and-so *ṭaghāī*, might be described as brothers of the mothers of a king's or chief's children.

To found opinion of relationship on the unsupported use of the word is to court disaster. Great wariness is needed. A quite perplexing *ṭaghāī* is the Machiavelli of Mīrzā Ḥaidar's life, 'Alī Mīrzā *ṭaghāī* (*Dughlāt*). He is constantly on the scene, and the one fact not men-tioned which it is desirable to know is, whose brother was he? Only with much trouble can a surmise as to his parentage be hazarded.

(Tār. Rash., 183.) Having done so, he took refuge with Bābar in Samarqand. (*l.c.*, 265.)

(*b*) In 917H. (1511) he was with Sayyid Muḥammad *Dughlāt* in Andijān, apparently at Bābar's instance. *(l.c.,* 248.) In the same year he was sent by Sa'īd Khān who had reinforced Andijān under Bābar's orders, to Kāzan.

(*c*) In 920H. (1514) he accompanied Saīd in his conquest of Kāshghar, and at this date is named amongst the Begchik amīrs of the Kāshghar army. *(l.c,* 308, 326.)

(*d*) In 925H. (1519) he waited on Bābar, and is stvled *ṭaghāī* of Kāmrān. (Mems., 274.) Bābar says here: 'Sulṭān 'Alī Mīrzā, the maternal uncle of Kāmrān (Ilminsky, 311, *Kāmrān-nīnak ṭaghāī),* who in the year in which I passed over from Khost to Kābul had proceeded to Kāshghar, *as has been mentioned,*[1] waited on me here.'

Bābar must several times have passed from Khost (Andarāb) to Kābul. The *Tārīkh-i-rashīdī* fixes the occasion here alluded to as in 920H. (1514). This was Bābar's latest and last crossing of the northern passes to Kabul.

By thus bringing the statements of the Memoirs and the *Tārīkh-i-rashīdī* together, Sulṭān 'Alī Mīrzā *Begchik* is fairly-well identified with Sulṭān 'Alī Mīrzā, *ṭaghāī* of Kāmrān.'

(e) In 935H. (1528) Kāmrān married his daughter. (Mems., 388.) Mems., 274, 388.

Tār. Rash., 183, 248, 264, 265, 280, 308, 326.

LXXVI. Gul-rukh Begam *Mīrān-shāhī.*

Daughter of Kāmrān Mīrzā; wife of Ibrāhīm Husain Mīrzā *Bāyqrā;* mother of Muẓaffar Husain who married Sulṭān Khānam, Akbar's

[1] Something interesting as to the *Tūzūk-i-bābarī* (Turkī text of the Memoirs) may lie here. The period of Sa'īd's Kāshghar conquest fails in a gap of the *Tūzūk*. Bābar referred to an incident of that time as having been already mentioned. This suggests, as a cause of the gap, lost leaves, and not an omission of record. (*Cf. Tār. Rash.*, 247 n..)

eldest daughter, and of Nūru-n-nisa' who became a wife of Salīm (the Emperor Jahāngīr).

The story of her husband's rebellious pursuit and death (981H., 1573), and of her flight to the Dakhin with her son, is found at length in the histories.

She was living and visited by Jahāngīr in 1023H. (1614). *(Cf.* XIX. 'Āvisha-sulṭān.)

LXXVII. Gūn-war Bībī.

Wife of Humāyūn and mother of Bakhshī-bānū Begam.

Gul-badan, 39*b*.

LXXVIII. Habība Begam *Mīrān-shāhī.*

The beloved or desired princess.

Eldest daughter of Kāmrān Mīrzā and probably of the daughter of Uncle (*ṭaghāī*) Sulṭān 'Alī Mīrzā *Begchik* whom Kāmrān married in 935H. (1528). She married Yasīn-daulat (the Fair Sulṭān) *Chaghatāī Mughal,* a brother of Gul-badan's husband, Khiẓr, and her own second cousin. It may be that she married a second time after she was forcibly parted from Yasīn-daulat in 1551-52. (*Cf.* App. *s.n. Hājī Mīrān-shāhī.)* Gul-badan, 64*b*, 65*a*, 78*a*.

LXXIX. Habība-sulṭān Begam *Arghūn.*

The desired of the desired; Ar. *habība,* beloved, desired, and *sulṭān,* pre-eminence, sway.

'Brother's daughter of Sulṭān *Arghūn*' (? Muqīm, Shāh Shuja'a, or a brother of Zū'l-nūn); wife of Sulṭān Aḥmad Mīrzā *Mīrān-shāhī;* and mother of Bābar's wife, Ma'sūma. Bābar gave her a name of affection, *yanga. (Cf.* Index, *s.v..)*

Mems., 22, 23, 208, 238.

LXXX. Habība-sulṭān Khānish *Dughlāt.* (No. 21.)

Daughter of Muhamrnad Husain *Dughlāt* and Khūb-nigār *Chaghatāī;* full-sister of Mīrzā Ḥaidar; first cousin (maternal) of

Bābar; wife (1) of 'Ubaidu-l-lāh *Uzbeg,* and (2) of her cousin, Sa'īd Khān *Chaghatāī.*

She was taken captive as a child by Shaibānī *Uzbeg,* and she lived in his household until he gave her in marriage to his nephew, 'Ubaidu-l-lāh. Shortly before Shaibānī murdered her father (914H., 1508-9), 'Ubaidu-l-lāh asked for Ḥaidar (*ætat.* 11) to come to him and Habība in Bukhārā, and thus saved him from a general massacre of Mughal sulṭāns.

When' Ubaidu-l-lāh retreated to Turkistān (*cir.* 1511), Habība remained in Bukhārā. She then joined her uncle Sayyid Muḥammad *Dughlāt,* in Samarqand, and with him went to Andijān where he married her to her cousin Sa īd. She reared one of Sa'īd's children, Rashīd whose mother was a 'tribeswoman,' Makhdūm *Qāluchī,* but he certainly did her training no credit. She was widowed in 939H. (July 9th, 1533), so that Gul-badan may be wrong in saving that she was at the Mystic Feast in 1531. She may have been a wedding guest in 1537.

Tar. Rash., E. & R., 140, 192, 193, 206, 268, 451, 453.

Gul-badan, 24*b*.

LXXXL. *Hājī* Begam *Mīrān-shāhī.*

She was a daughter of Kāmrān, and accompanied Gul-badan Begam to Makka in 983H., but it is to be inferred that this was not the pilgrimage which gave her her title of *Ḥājī,* since she is so entered before the *haj* of 983H. (*Cf.* XIX, 'Āvisha-sulṭān.)

(*Ḥājī* Begam, Bega, *q.v.*)

(*Ḥājī* Begam, Māh-chūchak *Arghūn, q.v.*)

LXXXII. Hamīda-bānū.

Ar. *hamīda,* praised, laudable, and Pers. *bānū.*

Daughter of Sayyid Muhamrnad Qāsim. She died 984H. (1576-77), and was buried at Andakhui.

The above information is given by Captain Yate, and as Hamīda-bānū may be the daughter of one of Humāyūn's followers, I have inserted her name.

Northern Afghānīstan, Yate, p. 349.

LXXXIII. Hamīda-bānū Begam *Maryam-makānī.*

Posthumous style, *Maryam-makānī,* dwelling with Mary.

She was the mother of Akbar. There is difficulty in making precise statement as to her family rela-tions. She was of the lineage of Ahmad *Jūmī Zinda-fīl.*

(*a*) Gul-badan, whose long intirnacy with Hamīda invests her statement with authority, states that Mīr Bāba Dost was Hamīda's father, and that Khwāja Mu'azzam was her *barādar, i.e.,* brother undefined.

(*b*) The *Tārīkh-i-sind* states that her father was Shaikh 'Alī-akbar *Jāmī* who was one of the pillars of Mīrzā Hindāl. Nizāmu-d-dīn Ahmad says that 'Alī-akbar was father of Mu'azzam.

If the statements of paragraphs (*a*) and (*b*) stood alone, 'Bābā Dost' and "Alī-akbar' might be identified as the *petit-nom* and the name of one man.

There is a good deal to support this view, and there is something against it.

In favour of the identification of Bābā Dost with 'Alī-akbar are the following points:

(1) 'Bābā Dost' seems to be not a personal name, but a sobriquet of affection and domestic intimacy.

(2) Jauhar calls Hamīda the daughter of Hindāl's *akhund,* and Mr. Erskine (perhaps, however, inferentially) calls 'Alī-akbar Hindāl's preceptor.

(3) Mīr Bābā Dost was alive in 947H. (1540-41), the year preceding Hamīda's marriage, and was then with Hindāl. *(Akbar-nāma,* H. Beveridge, I. 360.)

(4) Nizamu-d-dīn Ahmad and *Badāyunī* contribute negative support to the identification by using the indefinite *khal,* maternal uncle, to describe the relation of Akbar and Mu'aẓẓam.

(5) *The Ma'āsiru-l-umara'* confirms the identification by use of the words *barādari-a'yānī,* full-brother. Its authority may not be of the best, but the choice of these words has some weight.

(6) ‘Alī-akbar was of the lineage of Aḥmad *Jāmī.* Humāyun had a dream which allowed him to know that the son prophesied in it by Aḥmad would be of the latter’s lineage. There is, I think, nothing said on this point of Mīr Bābā Dost, but saintly descent was claimed for Hamīda’s father.

(7) Gul-badan gives one the impression (it is little more) that Muazzam was younger than Hamīda. He calls his sister *Māh-chīchām,* which may be read as ‘Moon of my mother,’ but also as ‘Elder Moon-sister.’ *(Cf. 18b* n.) If he were Hamīda’s junior, and as Mīr Bābā Dost was alive in 1540-41, he could not have been an independent agent in 1543-44.

In opposition to the identification, there are two considerations:

(i.) *A* minor matter; two names are given by the sources: Mīr Bābā Dost and ‘Alī-akbar.

(ii.) The important fact that Abū’l-fazl calls Muazzam Hamīda’s *ukhuwwat-i-akhyāfī,*[1] which, according to Lane, must be rendered ‘uterine brother.’

Was, then, the name Bābā Dost a sobriquet of Shaikh ‘Alī-akbar?

Were Hamīda and Mu’aẓẓam full brother and sister? Were they the children of one father and two mothers, or were they uterine brother and sister?

Shaikh ‘Alī-akbar’s name I have not found in any passage except the one dealing with Hamīda’s parentage. Mīr Bābā Dost may be the man so named by Bābar (Mems., 262), and who was then with Humāyūn in the year of the birth of Hindāl (1519). He may also have gone with Humāyūn, Hamīda (? his own daughter) and Mu’aẓẓam (? his son) to Persia, the *bakhshī* in the little party of exiles. He is mentioned by Abū’l-fazl not only where already noted, but, we believe, also amongst Hindārs servants who were transferred to Akbar in 1551 (958H.).

---

[1] Steingass does not recognize the force of ‘uterine,’ since he renders *barādar-i-a’yārni* by ‘uterine brother.’

Two men with the name 'Alī-akbar are mentioned under Akbar, but neither appears to be a *Jāmī,* or to warrant identification with Hamīda's reputed father. (*Cf. Āīn-i-akbarī,* Blochmann, *s.n.* 'Alī-akbar.)

Whether there was any relationship more close than that derived from common descent from Aḥmad *Jāmī* between Māham Begam and Hamīda I am not able to say.

Hamīda was related to Bānū (Bābū) *āghā* who was the wife of Shihābu-d-dīn Aḥmad *Nishāpūrī* and a relation of Māham *anaga.* Bega (*Ḥajī*) Begam also had claim to descent from Aḥmad *Jāmī,* so that the saint's posterity was numerous in Akbar's court, and included the Emperor himself.

To Gul-badan's account of the discussion which preceded Hamīda's marriage, there may be added the following passage from the *Tazkiratu-l-wāqi'āt* of Jauhar. (I.O. MS. No. 221 and B.M. MS. Add. No. 16,711, f. 82.) After Humāyūn has asked whose daughter Hamīda is, he is told, perhaps by Dil-dār, that she is of the line of his Reverence the Terrible Elephant, Aḥmad *Jāmī,* and that her father, by way of blessing and benediction, has taught Mīrzā Hindāl, and that for this reason Hamīda is with the mīrzā's household.

The Persian (taken from the 1.0. MS.) is as follows: *Pidar-i-īshān do sili kalma ba jihat-i-tabarruk wa tayammun ba Mīrzā Hindāl sabq farmudand. Az ān jihat ba mā hamrā and.*

Erskine (II. 220) and Stewart (Jauhar, 31 n.) both say that Hamīda was married at fourteen years of age. The incidents of her wedded life are set down in Gul-badan Begam's book and in the *Akbar-nāma* and other sources; but having regard to her interesting personality, they may be enumerated here also.

She was married at Pāt early in 948H. (summer, 1541), and remained in Sind until she made with Humāyūn the terrible desert journey to 'Umrkut where Akbar was born (October 15th, 1542). About the beginning of the following December she and her baby went into camp at Jūn. after travelling for ten or twelve days. In 1543 she made the perilous journey from Sind which had Qandahār for its goal, but in course of which Humāyūn had to take hasty night from Shāl-mastān, 'through a desert and water-less waste.' She went with him, leaving her little son behind. She accompanied her husband to Persia, and it is recorded that on the way and at Sistān, its governor brought his mother and his wives to entertain her. With Humāyūn she made, amongst other pious visitations, one to Jām where was their ancestor Aḥmad's shrine. She was kindly treated by Shāh Tahmāsp and by his sister, and Gul-badan's details of the Persian episode can hardly have been learned from anyone but Hamīda. In 1544, in camp at Sabz-āwār, a daughter was born. She returned from Persia with the army given to Humāyūn by Tahmāsp, and at Qandahār would meet Dil-dār and Hindāl, her former protectors.

It was not until November 15th, 1545 (Ramzan 10th, 952H.) that she again saw her son, who recognized her. She had shortly after this to accept Māh-chūchak as a co-wife. In June, 1548, she and Akbar accompanied Humāyūn on his way to Tāliqān as far as Gul-bihār, and thence returned to Kābul. This may be the expedition made by the ladies and chronicled by Gul-badan, to see the *rīwāj.* When Humāyūn, in November, 1554, set out for Hindūstān, she remained in Kābul.

Bāyazīd *bīyāt* mentions that at this time he fell under her displeasure, and was reproved because he had not cleared out a house for one of her servants. He pleaded the commands of Mu'nim Khān, and was forgiven. Early in the reign of Akbar, Khwāja Mīrak, Nizāmu-d-dīn's grandfather and who was her *diwān,* was hanged by Mu'nim Khān because he had sided with Mīrzā Sulaimān.

She rejoined her son in the second year of his reign (964H., 1557), together with Gul-badan and other royal ladies. She is mentioned as in Dihlī in the fifth year, and she had a part in the plot for deposing Bairām Khān. She was closely associated with Gulbadan in Akbar's court and affection; together they interceded for Salīm with his father; together they received gifts from the Emperor; and their tents were side by side in his encampments. Hamīda was with Gul-badan in the latter's last hours.

Abū'l-fazl says that when long fasts came to an end, the first dishes of dressed meat used to go to Akbar from his mother's house.

Hamīda died in the autumn of 1604 (19th Shah-riyār 1013H.), sixty-three years after her wedding, and after almost fifty years of widowhood, passed as the proud mother of a great son. If she was fourteen in 1541, she must have been born in 1527 (*circa*), the year of Bābar's victory at Khānwa, and have been some seventy-seven years old at the time of death.

Gul-badan, 39*a*, 42*a*, 43*b*, 48*a*, 55*a*, 556, 58*a*, 59*b*, 62*b*, 66*a*, 74*a*, 786, 83*a*.

Akbar-nāma, Bib. Ind. ed., *s.n.*.

Aīn-i-akbarī, Aīn, 26, *Sufīyāna,* Blochmann, 61, 62.

Jauhar, *l.c.,* Nizāmu-d-dīn Aḥmad, etc.

Ma'āsiru-l-umara' Bib. Ind. ed., I. 618.

Journal of the Royal Asiatic Society, October, 1898, art.

Bāyazīd *bīyāt,* H. Beveridge, 16.

LXXXIV. *Ḥaram* Begam *Qihchag Mughal.*

Princess of the *Ḥaram*. Her name has been trans-literated by some European workers as *Khurram,* 'blossoming, cheerful,' and this seems the more probable name to bestow on a child. But some of the Persian texts support *Karam,* and the editors of the *Bib. Ind. Akbar-nāma* have adopted it. Gul-badan has *Ḥaram.*

Ḥaram Begam may be a sobriquet bestowed after the revelation of the facts of the bearer's character and dominance.

Daughter of Sulṭān Wais *Kulābī Qibchāq Mughal;* and sister of Chakr 'Alī and Ḥaidar Begs and of Māh Begam, a wife of Kāmrān. She married Sulai-mān Mīrzā *Mīrān-shāhī,* son of Khān Mīrzā (Wais). She had one son, Ibrāhīm (Abū'l-qāsim), and several daughters. Her children, through Shāh Begam *Badahhshī,* their paternal ancestress, claimed descent from Alexander the Great.

Most of the incidents of her career are given in the Introduction to this book, and her remarkable character is exhibited there. *Badāyunī* calls her *Walini'amat,* and says she was known by this name. This may be a tribute to her pre-eminence in character and action and also to the fact of her belonging to an older generation than Akbar's, under whom he wrote. The elder men of royal birth were Lords and the elder women Lādies of Beneficence in those days.

Gul-badan, 65*a*, 75*b*.

Akbar-nāma, Bib. Ind. ed., *s.n.*.

Badāyunī, Lowe, 61, 89, 90, 217.

Journal of the Royal Asiatic Society, October, 1898, art.

Bāyazīd *bīyāt,* H. Beveridge, 12, 16.

B. & H., *s.n.*.

Aīn-i-akbarī, Blochmann, *s.n.*.

Introduction, *supra.*

LXXXV. Hazāra Begam.

Princess of the tribe of the Hazāra. This is a title, and not a personal name.

She was the daughter of a brother of Khiẓr Khān *Hazāra* who was the chief of his tribe during the struggles for supremacy of Humāyun and Kāmrān. She married Kāmrān.

Gul-badan, 64*b*.

LXXXVI. Husn-nigār Khānam *Chaghatāī Mughal.*

The image of beauty; Ar. *husn,* beauty, and Pers. *nigār,* image. Daughter of Isān-būghā *Chagkatāī* and niece of Yūnas Khān; sister of Dost-muḥammad and wife of Abā-bakr *Dughlāt Mughal.*

Tār. Rash., E. & K., 89, 99.

LXXXVII. Isān-daulat Khānam and Begam *Qūclūn Mughal.*

Her name takes several forms. The *Bābar-nāma,* Turkī text (B.M. Or. Add. 26,324), has a clearly pointed *Ishān;* Ilminsky has *Isān passim.* An early Persian MS. (B.M. Or. 3,714) has *Isān* and *Isan.*

The Memoirs have *Isan* in all but two instances (p. 12), where *Ais* is used. But Mr. Erskine's Persian text (B.M. Add. 26,200), which is presumably his authority, can (I venture to think, after comparing the words he renders *Ais* with those he renders *Isan)* yield *Isan* in all places. Where he reads *Ais* (pp. 10 and 141) the *nūn* is not dotted; the letters closely correspond with those where it is dotted, and where he reads *Isan*.

The *Tārīkh-i-rashīdī* (B.M. Or. 157) writes *Isān*.

The weight of authority is in favour of *Isān*.

Isān-daulat was Bābar's maternal grandmother and a daughter of Mīr Shīr-'alī Beg *Ģūclūn (Kunjī)*, chief of the Sagharīchī *tumān* (10,000) of the Qūchīn Mughals.

She married Yūnas Khān *Chaghatāī Mughal* when he was forty-one years old. He was born in 818H. (1415-16), so that the date of her marriage is, approximately, 1456. At this time Yūnas was made Great Khān of the Mughals.

Isān-daulat bore three daughters, who were named Mihr-nigār, Qūt-līq-nigār, and Khūb-nigār. She had many brothers, of whom three, Shīram, Mazīd, and 'Alī-dost, took leading parts in Bābar's affairs. Her chief co-wife was Shāh Begam *Badakhshī*.

She shared the vicissitudes of her remarkable husband's remarkable career for some thirty years; nursed him through two years of paralytic helplessness till his death in 892H. (1487) at the age of seventy-four, and survived him about eighteen years. Four times at least she fell into the hands of an enemy:

(1) In Kāshghar, *cir.* 860H. (1455-56), when Mihrnigār was an infant at the breast and when she was returned in safety to her husband.

(2) In Tāshkand in 877H. (1472-73), when Yūnas had gone to buy barley at a time of dearth in Mughalistān. It was then that there occurred the well-known episode which shows Isān-daulat's high spirit and decision of character and which is briefly narrated in the Introduction (p. 68). She was returned with honour to her husband.

(3) In Andijān in 903H. (1497-98), when the town was taken from her grandson Bābar by his kinsfolk. She was sent after him in

safety to Khojand, and from there went on to the protection of her third daughter's home in Kāshghar.

(4) At Samarqand in 906H. (1500-1), when the town was taken by Shaibānī. She remained behind when Bābar left the place, and rejoined him in a few months with his 'family, heavy baggage, and a few lean and hungry followers.'

In the eighth year of her widowhood (900H.) she was guiding Bābar's affairs with decision and sense in Andijān. He says that few women equalled her for sagacity, far-sight and good judgment, and that many important affairs were carried out by her counsel.

News of her death reached Bābar in Kābul early in 911H. (June, 1505), during the forty days' mourning for his mother.

Two slight records of her remain for mention.

Desert-born and of a tribe which clamoured against settled life, she yet had a garden-house at Andijān. She reared a half-sister of Bābar, Yādgār, daughter of Aghā *āghācha.*

Mems., 10, 12, 16, 27, 58, 59, 100, 111, 169.

Tār. Rash, E. & R., 86, 94, 175, 197, 308.

B. & H., *s.n.*.

LXXXYIII. Jahān-sulṭān Begam.

The world-ruling princess; Pers. *jahān,* world, and Ar. *sulṭān,* sway. Probably a child of Humāyūn. She died in Kābul, aged two, in 954H. (1547).

Gul-badan, 70*a*.

LXXXIX. Jamāl *āghā.*

Grace; Ar. *jamāl,* grace, beauty.

Wife (1) of Sanīz Mīrzā *Dughlāt,* and by him mother of 'Umar and Abā-bakr and Jān (or Khān)-sulṭān Khānam.

(2) of Dost-muhammad *Chaghatāī* in 869 H.

(3) of Muḥammad Ḥaidar *Dughlāt,* and by him mother of Muḥammad Husain Mīrzā *Ḥisārī* (Ḥaidar's father) and Sayyid

Muḥammad Mīrzā.

Her third marriage was made by the Mughal custom of *yanga-lik, i.e.,* marriage by a younger brother of an elder brother's widow. *(Cf.* Khān-zāda *Mīrān-shāhl.)*

Tār. Rash., E. & R., 88, 89, 99, 102, 104.

XC. Jān-sulṭān Begam. (No. 32.)

The soul-ruling princess; Pers. *jān,* life, soul, and Ar. *sulṭān,* sway.

She was at the Mystic Feast in 1531.

Gul-badan, 256.

(Jūlī Begam, *Chūlī, q.v.*)

XCI. Khadīja Begam.

Presumably she was named after Muhammad's first wife.

She was first a slave[1] of Sulṭān Abū-sa'īd Mīrzā, and upon his death in 873H. (1469) she betook herself to Harāt and there became the wife of Sulṭān Husain *Bāyqrā.*

She had a daughter, known as Āq Begam, by Abū-sa'īd, and two sons, Shāh Gharīb and Muẓaffar Husain, by her marriage with Husain.

Hers is an instance where the conferring of a title is mentioned. Bābar says that Husain was passionately fond of her and that he raised her to the rank of begam; also that she managed him entirely. To her are attribuled the intrigues and rebellion which ruined Ḥusain's family. She acquired more influence than any other of his wives, and it was consequently round her surviving son Muẓaffar Husain, that adherents gathered after his father's death. She forced on the joint-kingship which excited Bābar's ridicule. Mīrzā Ḥaidar when speaking of the death of Jahāngīr *Mirān-shāhi,* said that he was generally reported to have been poisoned in his wine by Khadīja

[1] Turkī text (Ilminsky), ghancha-chī, which Redhouse translates a seller of rosebuds and a young and good-looking female slave. The Persian text has the same word ghuncha-chī. The interest of these details is the light they may cast on the use of such words as āghā and āghācha.

Begam after her old fashion.

In 912H. (1506-7) Bābar saw her in Harāt, and he was there unlawfully entertained by her at a wine-party. When Shaibānī conquered the city in 913H. she was cast down from her high estate and given up to be plundered, and was treated as one of Shaibānī's meanest slaves.

Mems., 179, 182, 183, 198, 204, 223.

Tār. Rash., E. & R., 196, 199.

XCII. Khadīja-sulṭān Begam *Chaghatāī Mughal.*

Fourth daughter of Sulṭān Aḥmad Khān *Chaghatāi.* After her father's death in 909H. (1508-4), Mīrzā Abā-bakr *Dughlāt* took possession of his capital, Aksu in Farghāna, and with it of Khadīja-sulṭān, then a child. He however, says Mīrzā Ḥaidar, treated her kindly and when she was of age, he gave her in marriage to his son Jahāngīr who was her second cousin. She accompanied her husband to her full-brother Sa'īd's court, shortly after 920H. (1514), and while in Kāshghar, Jahāngīr was murdered by an unknown hand, in Yangī-ḥiṣār. She then remained, respected and honoured, in her brother Sa'īd's family circle. In 923H. (1517) she was married to Shāh Muḥammad Sulṭān *Chaghatāi,* a grandson of Sulṭān Maḥmūd Khān, through Muḥammad, the only son of Maḥmūd who survived the massacre of sulṭāns by Shaibānī. The marriage of one of Khadīja's brothers, Aiman, was celebrated at the same time.

When Rashīd succeeded his father Sa'īd, in Kāshghar (939H.—July, 1533) Khadīja was badly treated by him. She was then ill and confined to bed, but Rashīd banished her and her children and made her start on the weary journey for Badakhshān. She died on the road after much hardship of travel. She left four children, Ismā'īl, Ishāq, Ya'qūb, and Muḥtarima. They went on to Kābul, and were there received with fatherly kindness by their uncle, Isān-tīmūr.

Tār. Rash., E. & R., 161, 329, 352, 382, 451.

XCIII. Khadīja-sulṭān Begam *Mīrān-shāhī.* (No. 6.)

Daughter of Sulṭān Abū-sa'īd Mīrzā *Mirān-shāhī* and paternal aunt of Bābar. I have not ascertained the name of her husband. She went to India in 934H. (1527), arriving in November, with Fakhr-jahān and their children. She planned to return with her sister and Bābar took leave of them both on Muharram 5th, 935H. (September 20th, 1528), but various business detained her and Bābar paid her another of his dutiful visits on October 9th. When or if she returned to Kābul is not said, but she was at the Mystic Feast in Āgra in 1531.

Gul-badan, 11*a*, 24*b*.

Mems., 374, 382, 387.

XCIV. Khāl-dār *anaga.*

The nurse with a mole; *khāl-dār,* mole-marked.

Mother of Sa'ādat-yār *kūka.*

Akbar-nāma, Bib. Ind. ed., I. 44.

XCV. Khānam Begam. (No. 18.)

Daughter of Āq Begam; granddaughter of Abū-sa'īd *Mīrān-shāhī,* The 'Khānam' may indicate that she is a Chaghatāī chief's child.

Gul-badan, 24*b*.

(Khānam, Muhtarima, *q.v.)*

XCVI. Khānish *āghā Klucārizmī.*

Daughter of Jūjūq Mīrzā *Khwārizmī;* wife of Humāyūn; mother of Ibrāhīm who died as an infant. Bāyazīd calls her child Muḥammad Farrūkh-fāl, but Gul-badan and Abū'l-fazl are against him. Farrūkh-fāl was the child of Māh-chūchak. Ibrāhīm was born on the same day as Muḥammad Hakīm, *i.e.,* Jumāda I. 15th, 960H. (April 19th, 1553).

Gul-badan, 71*a*, 71*b*, (?) 73*b*.

Bāyazīd (I. O. MS. 72*a*), *Journal of the Royal Asiatic Society,* October, 1898, art. Bāyazīd *bīyāt,* H. Beveridge, p. 14.

Akbar-nāma, Bib. Ind. ed., I. 331.

XCVII. Khān Sulṭān Khānam and Sulṭānam *Dughlāt.*
Both these names appear to be titles, and not personal.

Daughter of Sanīz Mīrzā *Dughlāt* and Jamāl *āghā;* full-sister of Abā-bakr.

She was a woman of life-long piety and devotion to good works. Perhaps for this reason her brother who seems to have been an incarnation of unjust cruelty, treated her with studied barbarity, as a consequence of which she died in torture and suffering.

Tār. Rash., E. & R., 88, 258.

XCVIII. Khān-zāda Begam *Bāyqrā.* (No. 16.)
The khān-born princess; Turkī *khān,* and Pers. *zāda,* born.

Gul-badan says she is a daughter of Sulṭān Mas'ūd Mīrzā *Mīrān-shāhī,* and through a daughter grandchild of Pāyanda Muḥammad (*sic*) Sulṭān Begam, paternal great-aunt of Humāyūn. Bābar names no such marriage of a daughter of Pāyanda. 'The second of the daughters [of Pāyanda] was Kīchak Begam [whose name is probably a sobriquet]. Sulṭān Mas'ūd Mīrzā was extremely attached to her, but whatever efforts he made, Pāyanda-sulṭān Begam, having an aversion to him, would not consent to the match. She was *after-wards*' (Turkī *sūngrā,* P. de C. *dans la suite*) 'married to Mullā Khwāja.'

A daughter of Husain *Bāyqrā* and of Bābā *āghācha,* whose name was Sa'ādat-bakht and title Begam Sulṭān, was married to Masūd after his blinding. Her daughter might be fitly described as of inferior rank to the great begams. Such a description is given by Bābar of 'Khān-zāda, daughter of Sulṭān Mas'ūd Mīrzā.' Husain and Pāyanda's daughter would certainly rank as equal in birth to the daughters of Abū-sa'īd, since she was a full Tīmūrid.

The 'extreme attachment' of Masūd to Kīchak fits Musalmān marriage better than Musalmān courtship. It may be that, spite of Pāyanda's opposition, Mas'ūd married Kīchak. The 'afterwards' of the Memoirs (*supra*) and the *de la suite* of Pavet de Courteille seem to demand some more definite antecedent than Masūd's attacbment. Moreover, this presumably persisted with his wish to marry Kīchak.

Did he marry Kīchak, and was she divorced after his blinding or at some other time, and then was Sa'ādat-bakht given to him?

Mems., 181, 182, 387.

Gul-badan, 24*b*.

XCIX. Khān-zāda Begam *Mīrān-shāhī.*

Daughter of 'Umar Shaikh Mīrzā *Mīrān-shāhī* and of Qūt-līq-nigār Khānam; full-sister of Bābar and five years his senior. Eldest of her father's daughters. She is recorded as thrice married: first, to Shaibānī in 1501 (907H.); secondly, to a man of inferior rank, Sayyid Hada; and, thirdly, to Mahdī Muḥammad Khwāja,[1] son of Mūsa Khwāja. One child of hers is recorded, Shaibānī's son, Khurram-shāh Sulṭān.

She was born *circa* 1478 (883H.). This is known from the statement of her brother that she was five years his senior. In 1501 (907H.) she was married by Shaibānī when he captured Samarqand from Bābar. Gul-badan makes the marriage a condition of Shaibānī's peace with Bābar; Ḥaidar says she was given in exchange for Bābar's life, and Khāfī Khān, as a ransom (*ba tarīq-i-faida*). She was in Shaibānī's power and could have been married without consent of Bābar. As in 1501 she was twenty-three years old, she had almost certainly been married before, possibly to Mahdī. Her marriage arrangements with Shaibānī might include the divorce which the Musalmān law requires. Bābar does not go into details as to the marriage; he says she fell into Shaibānī's hands. Presumably as himself of Tīmūrid birth, Shaibānī would treat a Tīmūrid woman with respectful forms even when she was spoil of battle. To marry Khān-zāda, he divorced her maternal aunt, Mihr-nigār *Chaghatāī*.

Khān-zāda's son by Shaibānī, Khurram-shāh, died a young man. Shaibānī divorced her because she leaned to her brother's side in disputed matters. He then gave her in marriage to a certain Sayyid Hada, who fell in the battle of Merv with Shaibānī himself (1510).

[1] *Cf.* Appendix B., Mahdī Khwāja.

In 1511 and at the age of thirty-three, she was returned to Bābar by Shāh Isma'īl. At what date she married Mahdī Muḥammad Khwāja I am not able to say. It is probable that the marriage would take place within no long time after her return. As Mahdī is never described by Bābar in any way (as is his custom when a new actor comes upon the scene of his Memoirs), it is probable that Mahdī's joining Bābar and his marriage with Khān-zāda took place in the decade 1509-19, of which no record is known to survive.[1] Mahdī was with Bābar in 1519 (925H.), and is frequently mentioned subsequently.

There are many references to Khān-zāda by Gulbadan who frequently calls her Dearest Lady (*āka-janām*). She died at Qabal-chak in 1545 (952H.), aged about sixty-seven years, and after a life full of sorrows and chagrins.

Gul-badan, 3*b*, 15*b*, 18*b*, 23*b*, 24*b*, 27*b*, 28*b*, 50*b*, 62*b*, 63*a*.
Mems., 10, 98, 241 (Supplement).
Tār. Rash., E. & R., 117, 155, 175, 196, 239, 400.
Ḥabību-s-siyār, under date 923H.
Khāfī Khān, I. 33 (here Khāna-zāda).

C. Khán-zada Begam *Mīrān-shāhī,*

Daughter of Sulṭān Maḥmūd *Mīrān-shāhī* and Khān-zāda Termiẕī II.; wife (1) of Abā-bakr *Dughlāt,* and mother by him of (?) Jahāngīr, Turāngīr, and Bus-tāngīr; (2) of Sayyid Muḥammad *Dughlāt* who married her in conformity with the custom of *yanga-lik.* (*Cf.* Jamāl *āghā.*)

Mems., 30.
Tār. Rash., E. & R., 330.

CI. Khān-zāda Begam Termiẕī.

Of the family of the Khāns of Termiz; wife of Sulṭān Aḥmad Mīrzā *Mīrān-shāhī.* She was a bride when Bābar was five, *i.e.,* in 893H. (1488) but, according to Turkī custom, was still veiled. Sulṭān

[1] There are some indications that a record of this decade once existed.

Aḥmad desired Bābar to pluck off the veil and run away, a little ceremony which it was supposed would bring him good luck when his time for marriage should come.

Mems., 23.

CII. Khān-zāda Begam *Termiẕī (a.).*

Daughter of the chief (*mīr-i-buzurg*) of Termiz; wife of Sulṭān Maḥmūd Mīrzā *Mīrān-shāhī;* mother of Sulṭān Mas'ūd Mīrzā. She died apparently early in her married life. The mīrzā was greatly afflicted at her death.

Mems., 29, 30.

CIII. Khān-zāda Begam Termiẕī ***(b.).***

Daughter of a brother of Khānzāda Termiẕī *(a.);* granddaughter of the chief of Termiz; wife of Sulṭān Maḥmūd Mīrzā *Mīrān-shāhī;* mother of Husain (who died, aged thirteen, before his father) and of five girls, Khānzāda, Bega, Āq, Āī, and Zainab.

Mems., 29, 30, 38, 128.

CIV. Khān-zāda Khānam.

'Épouse légitime 'of Muzaffar Mīrzā *Bāyqrā,* and illegally taken by Shaibānī.

Mems., 224.

Pavet de Courteille, II., 10.

CV. Khūb-nigār Khānam *Chaghatāī Mughal.*

The image of beauty. Here *khānam* has its full value, since Khūb-nigār was daughter of the *Khāqān,* the Khān emphatically.

Third daughter of Yūnas Khān *Chaghatāī* and Isān-daulat *Qūchīn;* wife of Muḥammad Husain *Dughlāt Ḥisārī;* mother of Ḥaidar and Ḥabība [1] She was a year older than her husband, and

[1] The translation of the Tārīkh-i-rashīdī (E. & R., 159) has the statement that Khūb-nigār bore six sons (farzandāri), and that two died at the breast and four survived. I believe it should read 'six children, of whom four died at the breast, and two survived her.'

was married in 899H. (1493-94). Bābar, writing in 907H. (1501-2) mentions the reception of news of her death. Her husband was murdered in 914H..

Mems., 12, 99, 218.

Tār. Rash., E. & R., 117, 118, 153, 156, 197.

CVI. Khurshed *kūkī.* (Nos. 55 and 64.)

Pers., the sun, sunshine.

Gul-badan, 26*a*.

CVII. Kīchak Begam *Bāyqrā.*

The small princess; Turkī, *kīchak,* small. The name is probably a sobriquet.

Daughter of Sulṭān Husain Mīrzā *Bāyqrā* and Pāyanda-sulṭān Begam *Mīrān-shāhī*; wife of Maulānā Khwāja who was of the family of Sayyid Atā one of her father's best vazīrs.

Khwānd-amīr reverses her marriage with that of her sister Bega, and makes her marry Bābar, son of Babfa.

Mems., 181.

Ḥabību-s-siyār, 327 *et seq.*.

CVIII. Kīchak Begam Termiẕī. **(No. 23.)**

Daughter of Mīr 'Alā'u-l-mulk Termiẕī and Fakhr-jahān *Mīrān-shāhī;* wife of Khwāja Mu'īn *Ahrārī;* mother of Mīrzā Sharafu-d-dīn Husain.

She went to Hiridustān with her mother, and was at Hindāl's wedding feast.

Mems., without names. *(Cf.* Fakhr-jahān and Shāh Begam.)

Gul-badan, 25*a*.

Akbar-nāma (lith. ed.), *s.n.*.

Aīn-i-akbarī, Blochmann, 322.

CIX. Kīchak māham. (No. 80.)

Cf. s.n. Māham for meaning of the word.

She is named as at Hindāl's wedding.

Gul-badan, 26*b*.

CX. Kilān Khan Begam.

This is clearly not a personal name. Pers. *kilān,* elder, great, and Turkī *khān,* a title.

Daughter of Sulṭānam Begam *Mīrān-shāhī* and granddaughter of Sulṭān Aḥmad Mīrzā. Which of Sulṭānam's three husbands was Kilān Khān Begam's father is not said; from her daughter's title, Tīmūr Sulṭān *Uzbeg* seems most probable.

Mems., 22.

Gul-badan, 24*b*.

CXI. Lād-malik *Turkomān.*

(?) Mistress of the Fort; Pers. *lād,* fortress, and Ar. *malik,* possessor, ruler.

Wife of (1) Tāj Khān *Sarangkhānī* and (2) of Shīr Khān *Sur* (935H., 1528-29).

B. & H., II. 131, 132, and authorities there cited by Mr. Erskine.

CXII. Lāl-shād Khānam *Chaghatāi Mughal.*

Perhaps, with a lip like the gleam of a ruby; Pers. *lāl,* ruby, and *shād,* gleam, happy.

Eldest daughter of Sultān Ahmad Khān *Chaghatāī* and of a 'slave' *(amm-i-wald).*

'Although she was outside the circle of distinction, she was finally married to Muhammad Amīr Mīrzā *Dughlāt.'*

Tār. Rash., E. & R., 161.

CXIII. Latīfa-sulṭān *āghācha.*

Of pre-eminent delicacy or gentleness; Ar. *latīfa,* delicate, and a jest, and Ar. *sulṭān,* sway.

Chār-shambihī, a Wednesday wife, of Sulṭān Husain Mīrzā *Bāyqrā;* mother of Abū'l-hasan and of Muḥammad Muhsin *(kepek,* round-shouldered).

The *Ḥabību-s-siyār* says she was a relation of Jahān-shāh (? *Turkomān* or *Barlās).* She was dead before 912H. (1506).

Mems., 179, 183.

CXIV. Latīf Begam *Duladāī Barlās.*

Granddaughter of Aḥmad Hājī Beg; wife (1) of Sulṭān Aḥmad Mīrzā *Mīrān-shāhī;* (2) of Hamza Sulṭān *Uzbeg,* and by him mother of three sons who fell into Bābar's hands at Ḥisār, and were released by him.

Both her grandfather Aḥmad and his paternal uncle, Janī Beg *Duladāī,* were amīrs of her first husband.

Mems., 23.

CXV. Māh-afroz Begam.

The princess who outshines the moon; Pers. *māh,* moon, and *afroz,* dazzling, illuminating.

She was a wife of Kāmrān and mother of *Hājī* Begam. Two of Kāmrān's wives are not known by their personal names, Hazāra Begam and the daughter of Uncle 'Alī Mīrzā *Begchik.* Māh-afroz may be one of these.

Gul-badan, 64*b*.

CXVI. Māham *anaga.*

Nurse of Akbar; wife of Nadīm *kūka;* mother of Bāqī and Adham *kā kas. Cf.* Bābū *āghā.* Much of her story is given in the Introduction to this volume.

CXVII. Māham Begam: *ākā* and *ākām* (lady and my lady).

The word Māham is explained by Mr. Erskine (who did not know Gul-badan's book) as Bābar's name of endearment for his favourite wife, and as meaning 'my moon.' Mr. Schuyler also translates it by the same words. He says that a woman who was shot for political offences in Bukhārā was known as 'My moon (Māham) of Keninghez.'

But many Māhams are chronicled, and not only Bābar gives the name to Humāyūn's mother; Gulbadan speaks frequently of 'my lady who was Māham Begam,' and Māham seems to be her personal name. It is used at least once as a man's. *(Akbar-nāma,* I. 320, Māham 'Alī Qulī Khān.)

Whether māham is to be classed with sulṭānam, khānam, begam, shāham, I am unable to say.

Sir Douglas Forsyth (Mission to Yarkand, 84) translates khānam and begam by *my lord* and *my chief.* But neither is a domestic word; both are in common use in the sources to designate, for general readers, the wives or daughters of khāns and begs, or princes. Sulṭānam also is a common title, and from Gul-badan's use of it does not appear to be a personal name, but to answer to sulṭān as khānam to khān, etc..

Against reading khānam as *my lady,* with a sense of possession or admission of superiority (as is done by Sir Douglas Forsyth), there are the Turkī words formed from it, viz., *khānam-alī,* honeysuckle, and *khānam-bājakī,* ladybird. Shāham, which has the appearance of being formed from shāh like the others by the suffix *am* or *im,* is used both for man and woman. Shīram occurs as a man's name.

Māham was a wife of whom it was said that she was to Bābar what 'Āyisha was to Muḥammad, and she was Humāyūn's mother. Gul-badan mentions her often, yet no one of the numerous sources I have consulted, sets down her family or the name of her father.

At one time it appeared to me probable that she was a Begchik Mughal, because Bābar calls Yādgār *Begchik, ṭaghāī* when speaking of him in connection with Humāyūn. Further consideration led to the abandonment of the theory.

Uncle Yādgār, Uncle 'Alī, and Uncle Ibrāhīm (*Chapūk,* slashed-face) are named as being three of the eight brothers or half-brothers of Gul-rukh, the mother of Kāmrān; and Bega (*Ḥaji*) Begam is the daughter of Uncle Yādgār.

Amongst these eight Begchiks I do not find one named Uncle Muḥammad 'Alī, and there is a good deal to lead one to regard a certain Khwāja Muḥammad 'Alī *ṭaghāī* as being Māham's brother.

He was associated with Khost, and it is on record that Humāyūn visited his maternal grandparents *(nanahā)* in Khost. The Begchiks do not seem to have been connected with Khost. Bābar speaLs frequently of Khwāja Muḥammad 'Alī as being employed in the government of Khost (925H.); as coming from Khost for orders, etc, and the *mīr-zādas* of Khost also are recorded as visiting the court. One of Māham's children was born in Khost.

Bābar frequently mentions an 'Abdu-l-malūk *Khostī,* and he may be a connection of Māham. He, however, appears as *Khostī, Khwastī, Ģastī, qūrchī, Qūrchīn,* and without a more complete good Turkī text no opinion can be formed as to his identity.

Gul-badan says that *Akā* (Māham) was related to the owners of the New Year's Garden in Kābul, and this was made by Ulugh Beg *Kābulī Mīrān-shāhī.*

Abū'l-fazl says Māham was of a noble Khurāsān family, related to Sulṭān Husain Mīrzā *(Bāyqrā),* and, like Hamīda-bānū Begam, was of the line of Shaikh Aḥmad *Jāmī (az dādman-i-a'yān wa ashrāf-i-Khurāsān and, wa ba Sulṭān Ḥusain Mirtā nisbat-i-khwesh dārand.* Perhaps *nisbat-i-khwesh*) implies blood-relationship on the father's side.

Gul-badan speaks of Māham's Mughal servants, but a Chaghatāī, a Begchik, a Qūchīn is also a Mughal, and Bābar often sinks the divisional tribe-name in the general one, Mughal (*e.g.,* Mems. 9 and 21).

Some considerations suggest that Māham was a *Dughlāt Mughal,* and of the family of 'Abdu-l-qadūs, but no valid opinion can be formed until a text as good as the Elphinstone is available for guidance.

Bābar married Māham in Harāt when he visited that city after Sulṭān Husain Mīrzā's death, and in 912H. (1506). Humāyūn was born on March 6, 1508 (Zū'l-qa'da 4th, 913H.). Four other children were born to her, and all died in infancy. They were Bār-bul, Mihr-jahān, Isān-daulat and Fārūq.

The events of her career are detailed in the Introduction to this volume and in Gul-badan Begam's book.

Mems., 250, 405, 412, 423, 428 n..

Gul-badan, 4*a*, 6*b*, 7*a*, 8*b*, 116, 136, 146, 16*a*, 16*b*, 17*a*, 18*b*, 21*a* and b, 22*a* and b, 23*a* and b, 24*b*.

Akbar-nāma, Bib. Ind. ed., and H. Beveridge, *s.n.* Māham and Māham 'Alī Qulī Khān.

Turkistān, Schuyler, 95 ff..

CXVIII. Māham *Kābulī.* (No. 81.)

At Hindāl's marriage feast.

Gul-badan, 26*a*.

CXIX. Māham Khānam *Chaghatāī Mughal.*

Second daughter of Sulṭān Aḥmad Khān *Chaghatāī* and full-sister of Mansūr Khān. Their mother was Sahib-daulat *Dughlāt,* sister of Mīr Jabār *Bardī Dughlāt.* Māham married Builāsh Khān *Uzbeg Kazāk,* son of Awīq.

Ḥaidar Mīrzā names her as a hostage given, with her mother, by her brother Mansūr to his half-brother Sa'īd at a time of their meeting in 1516. She had two other full-brothers, Bābājāk and Shāh Shaikh Muḥammad

Tār. Rash., N. E. & R., 160, 344.

CXX. Māh Begam *Qibchāq Mughal.*

The moon princess; Pers. *māh,* moon.

Daughter of Sulṭān Wais *Qibchāq Mughal* and sister of Ḥaram Begam; wife of Kāmrān Mīrzā.

Gul badan, 64*b*.

CXXI. Māh-chachaq *Khalīfa.*

She is mentioned by Bāyazīd as interceding for him with Hamīda-bānū. She may be a servant (*khalīfa*).

J. K. A. S., October, 1898, art. Bāyazīd *bīyāt,* H. Beveridge p. 16.

CXXII. Māh-chūchak Begam *Arghūn, Ḥajī* Begam.

The word *chūchak* presents difficulties. Ilminsky writes *chūchūq;* Bāvazīd. *chachaq;* Gul-badan, *chūchak* and *jūjak;* the Memoirs, *chūchak.* Mr. Blochmann and Mr. Lowe transliterate, *jūjak.* There is a Turkī word *jūjūq,* but its meaning of sweet-savoured is less appropriate for a woman't? name than a word which, spite of vowel variation it seems safer to take from the Persian; viz. *chachak,* a rose, and *chachak, chuchuk,* a lovely cheek, a mole.

Daughter of Mīrzā Muḥammad Muqīm *Arghūn* and of Bībī Zarīf *Khātūn;* wife (1) of Bābar's *kūkaltāsh* Qāsim; (2) of Shāh Hasan *Arghūn* of Sind (died 963H.); (3) of Īsā *Tarkhān Arghūn* of Tatta and Sind.

By Qāsim, she was mother of Nāhīd Begam and by Shāh Hasan of his only child, Chūchak or Māh-chūchak, Kāmran's wife.

She had an interesting story which Mr. Erskine tells at length. (B.& H., I. 348 *et seq..)*

On the death of ‘Īsā (975H.) his son and successor, Muḥammad Bāqī *Tarkhān,* who was a madman, ill-treated Mah-chūchak and Nāhīd who was then visiting her. This led to a plot against him, but in the end Māh-chūchak was imprisoned by him and starved to death. *(Cf s.n.* Nāhīd.)

Mems., 233.

B. & H., I. 348 *et seq..*

Tārikh-i-sind, Mīr Ma'sūm, in the account of Shāh Hasan's family.

Aīn-i-akbarī, Blochmann, 420.

Ihninsky, 273.

CXXIII. Māh-chūchak Begam *Arghūn.*

Daughter of Shāh Hasan and Māh-chūchak *Arghūn* and her father's only child; wife of Kāmrān; married 953H. (1546). Her wifely fidelity is commemorated by the historians. She went with Kāmrān to Makka after his blinding, and attended him until his death, October 5th, 1557. She survived him seven months.

Tārīkh-i-sind, Mīr Ma'sūm, in the account of Shāh Ḥasan's family.

CXXIV. Māh-chūchak Begam.

Sister of Bairām *Oghlān* and of Farīdūn Khān *Kābulī.*

She married Humāyūn in 1546. She had two sons, Muḥammad Hakīm (born 960H.—1553) and Farrūkh-fāl. Gul-badan says she had four daughters and then, with discrepancy frequently found in her writings. names three: Bakht-nisāʿ, Sakīna-bānū, and Amīna-bānū. The name of the best-known of her girls, Fakhru-n-nisāʿ, is omitted.

Māh-chūchak's story is told by her sister-in-law, in the Introduction of this volume, by Mr. Blochmann and by several Persian writers.

She was murdered by Shāh Abū'l-ma'ālī in Kābul in 1564.

Gul-badan, 71*a*, 716, 736, 786, 83*a*.

Jauhar, Mr. William Irvine's MS., Part II., Chapter II..

Bāyazīd, I.O. MS., 72*a*.

Nizāmu-d-dīn Aḥmad, 27th year of Akbar.

Badāyunī, Lowe, 54 *et seq*..

Āīn-i-akbarī, Blochmann, *s.n.*.

CXXV. Makhdūma *āghā.* (No. 59.)

The Lady *āghā;* Ar. *makhdūma,* lady, mistress.

Wife of Hindu Beg.

Gul-badan, 26*a*.

CXXVI. Makhdūma Begam *(Qarā-gūz).*

Wife of 'Umar Shaikh *Mīrān-shāhī;* mother of Ruqaiya, a posthumous child; she was married at the end of 'Umar's days; she was tenderly beloved, and to flatter him her descent was derived from his uncle, Manūchahr *Mīrān-shāhī.*

Mems., 10, 14.

CXXVII. Makhdūma-jahān.

The mistress of the world; Ar. *makhdūma,* mistress, and Pers. *jahān,* world.

Mother of Sulṭān Bahādur *Gujrātī.*

B. & H., II. 96.

CXXVIII. Makhdūma *Qāluchī.*

A wife of Sa'īd Khān *Chaghatāī;* a 'tribes-woman'; mother of Rashīd; sister of Suqār *Bahādur Qāluchī.*

Tār. Rash., E. & R., 140, 187, 309.

CXXIX. Makhdūma Khānam.

The Lady Khānam; Ar. *makhdūma,* lady, mistress.

Daughter of Shīr 'Alī Khān *Chaghatāī Mughal;* sister of Wais Khān; wife of Amāsānjī Taishī *Qālmāq;* mother of Qadīr, Ibrāhīm, and Ilyās.

Her marriage was a ransom for her brother Wais of whom it was commonly reported that he was routed sixty times by the Qālmāqs. On her marriage, Wais made Amāsānjī become a Musalmān, and Makhdūma continued the work of her husband's conversion and that of his tribe.

She named one of her daughters Karīm *Bardī* in affection and respect for the Dughlāt amīr of this name.

Mems., 409.

Tār. Rash., E. & R., 67, 91.

CXXX. Makhdūma-sulṭān Begam.

Daughter of Sulṭān Maḥmūd Mīrzā *Mīrān-shāhī* and Zuhra Begī *āghā Uzbeg;* elder sister of Sulṭān 'Alī Mīrzā. 'She is now in Badakhshān.' (Mems., 30.) The 'now' may be in the late twenties of 1500, and she may have been with Mīrzā Khān (Wais *Mīrān-shāhī*).

Mems., 30.

CXXXI. *Makhfī.*

Hid, concealed.

This is the poetical name (*takhalluṣ*) of Salīma-sulṭān Begam *Chaqānīānī,* Nūr-jahān Begam, and Zību-n-nisā', a daughter of Aurang-zīb.

CXXXII. Malika-jahān.

The world's queen; Ar. *malika,* queen, and Pers. *jahān,* world.

Elliot and Dawson, V. 81, 87, 88.

CXXXIII. Ma'sūma-sulṭān Begam *Mīrān-shāhī.*

The very chaste princess; Ar. *via'sūm,* chaste, innocent, and *sulṭān,* sway, pre-eminence.

Fifth and youngest daughter of Sulṭān Aḥmad Mīrzā *Mīrān-shāhī.* Her mother was Ḥabība-sulṭān Begam *Arghūn.* She married Bābar (her first cousin) in 913H. (1507), and from his account of the affair it was a love-match on both sides. She was half-sister of 'Āyisha, Bābar's first wife. She died in child-bed, and her infant received her name.

Gul-badan, 6*b*.

Mems., 22, 208, 225, 231, 429 Supplement.

CXXXIV. Ma'sūma-sulṭān Begam *Mīrān-shāhī.* (No. 43.)

Daughter of Bābar and Ma'sāma; wife of Muham-mad-zamān Mīrzā *Bāyqrā.*

Gul-badan. 6*b*, 23*a*, 255, 29*b*.

Akbar-nāma, s.n..

Mems., 22, 395, 429 Supplement.

CXXXV. Maywa-jān.

Fruit of life; Pers. *maywa,* fruit, and *jān*, life.

Daughter of Khazang *yasāwal* and a servant of Gul-badan Begam; an inferior wife of Humāyūn.

Gul-badan, 21*b*, 22*a,* 30*a*.

CXXXVI. Mihr-angez Begam. (No. 29.)

The princess who commands affection; Pers. *mihr,* affection, and *angez,* commanding, raising.

Daughter of Muẓaffar Husain Mīrzā *Bāyqrā;* granddaughter of Sulṭān Husain *Bāyqrā* and Khadīja.

She was accomplished after the fashion of gentle-men-at-arms and she played polo.

She was married by 'Ubaidu-l-lāh *Uzbeg* when Harāt was taken by Shaibānī (913H., June, 1507).

She was at the Mystic Feast in 1531.

Gul-badan, 24*b*.

Ḥabību-s-siyūr, 897 *et seq*..

CXXXVII. Mihr-bānū Begam *Mīrān-shāhī.* (? No. 27.)

The beloved; Pers. *mihr,* affection, and *bānū,* possessing.

Daughter of 'Umar Shaikh *Mīrān-shālī* and of Umīd *Andijānī;* full-sister of Nāsir and Shahr-bānū; born *cir.* 886H. (1481-82).

Gul-badan mentions a Mihr-līq Begam (No. 27.) who was a paternal aunt of Humāyūn, as being at the Mystic Feast. This may be Mihr-bānū. No aunt named Mihr-līq is mentioned elsewhere, and *līq* and *bānū* have the same sense.

Gul-badan, *25a.*

Mems., 10.

CXXXVIII. Mihr-bānū Khānam.

I think she is a relative of Bābar, and she may be the daughter of 'Umar Shaikh and Umīd, and thus Bābar's half-sister. (See *infra.)* From her title of Khānam, she is very possibly a Chaghatāī on her mother's side (Umīd was an Andijānī), or the style is due to her marriage with a khān. She appears to have married a man of high rank; perhaps Kūchūm (*Qūch-kunjī*) Khān who was Khāqān of his tribe from 1510 to 1530, or his son and successor (ruled from 1530 to 1533)· She had a son Pulād whom Bābar mentions as fighting with 'Qūch-kunjī' and his son Abū-sa'īd *Uzheg* at Jām (1528).

The Qūch-kunjī was the tribe of Isān-daulat.

Kūchūm, Abū-saīd, Mihr-bānū, and Pulād sent ambassadors and messengers to Bābar in the same year, and Bābar mentions his return gifts with quaint particularity. The envoys were entertained at a feast by him on December 12th, 1528 (935H.).

Mems., 10, 390, 395, 397, 399.

Tar. Rash., E. & E., *s.n.* Kuchum and Sulṭān and 206 n..

Muḥammadan Dynasties, Stanley Lane-Poole, 273.

CXXXIX. Mihr-jahān or -jān Begam *Mīrān-shāhī.*

Sun of the world or of life; Pers. *mihr,* sun, and *jahān,* world, or *jān,* life, soul.

Daughter of Bābar and Māham; born at Khost; died an infant.

Gul-badan, *6b.*

CXL. Mihr-nigār Khānam *Chaghatāī Mughal.*

The image of affection, or a very sun.

Eldest daughter of Yūnas Khān *Chaghatāī* and Isān-daulat (*Qūchīn, Kunjī*); born *cir.* 860H. (1455-56); wife of Sulṭān Aḥmad Mīrzā *Mīrān-shāhī;* first cousin of Bābar.

In 905H. (early in July, 1500) she was captured by Shaibānī and married by him. In 906H. (1500-1) she was divorced when he wished to marry Khān-zāda, her niece. She then stayed awhile in Samarqand. In 907H. (1501-2) she went to Tāshkand and joined the large family party which assembled there. (Mems. 99.) In 911H. (middle of 1505) she came to Kābul with other kinsfolk, soon after the death of her grandmother (Isān) and of her father, and during the ceremonial mourning of Bābar for his mother. 'Our grief broke out afresh,' he writes.

Mīrzā Ḥaidar gives a pleasant account of the welcome she accorded her generous and kindly nephew Bābar in 912H. (1506-7), when he put down Khān Mīrzā's (Wais) rebellion in Kābul: 'The Emperor leapt up and embraced his beloved aunt with every manifestation of affection. The khānam said to him: "Your children, wives, and household are longing to see you. I give thanks that I have been permitted to see you again. Rise up and go to your family in the castle. I too am going thither."'

In 913H. (1507), when Khān Mīrzā set out for Badakhshān with his mother, Shāh Begam, to try his fortunes in her father's ancient lands, Mihr-nigār also 'took a fancy to go. It would have been better and more becoming,' writes Bābar, 'for her to remain with me. I was her nearest relation. But however much I dissuaded her, she continued obstinate and also set out for Badakhshān.'

Mihr-nigār rued her self-will. She and Shāh Begam were captured on their way to Qila'-zafar by one of Abū-bakr *Dughlāt's* 'marauding bands,' and 'in the prisons of that wretched miscreant they departed from this perishable world.'

Mems., 12, 22, 99, 169, 232.

Tār. Rash., 86, 94, 117, 155, 196, 197, 200, 258.

CXLI. Mīnglī-bī *āghācha Uzbeg.*

A low-born wife (*ghūncha-chī*) of Sulṭān Husain Mīrzā *Bāyqrā.* The *Ḥabību-s-siyār* calls her a Turk and a purchased slave (*mamlūqa*) of Shahr-bānū Begam *Mīrān-shāhī* who brought her when she her self married Sulṭān Ḥusain, and presented her to him.

She was mother of three sons: Abū-tūrāb, Muḥammad Ḥusain, and Farīdūn Ḥusain; and of two daughters: Bairām (or Maryam) and Fātima.

Mems., 181, 182, 183.

Ḥabību-s-siyār (lith. ed.), 327 *et seq.*.

CXLII. Mīng-līq *kūkaltāsh.*

She escaped from Samarqand with Bābar's mother on its capture by Shaibānī in 907H. (1501).

Mems., 98.

CXLIII. Mubārika Bībī; *Afghānī āghācha.* (No. 56.)

Ar. *mubārika,* blessed, fortunate.

She was a daughter of Shāh Mansūr *Yūsufzai,* and was married by Bābar at Kehrāj on January 30th, 1519 (Muharram 28th, 925H.). The alliance was the sign and seal of amity between him and her tribe. *A* charming account of her and her marriage is given in the *Tāīākh-i-ḥāfiz-i-raḥmat-khāuī*, and Mr. Beveridge has translated it in full under the title 'An Afghān Legend,' so that it need not be reproduced here.

Gul-badan never gives the name Mubārika (Blessed Damozel) as that of the Afghān lady (*Afghānī āghācha*) whom she so frequently and pleasantly mentions. Hafiz Muḥammad (*l.c.*) savs that Mubārika was much beloved by Bābar, and this is borne out by the fact that she was one of the small and select party of ladies who were the first to join him in India. She went there, it is safe to infer, with Māham and Gulbadan in 1529.

She bore no child, and this misfortune Hafiz Muḥammad attributes to the envy of other wives who administered drugs to deprive her of motherhood and weaken her husband's affection.

She died early in Akbar's reign.

A brother of Mubārika, named Mīr Jamāl, accom-panied Bābar to Hindustān in 1525, and rose to high office under Humāyūn and Akbar. Hindāl had a favourite follower of this name who passed, on his death, into Akbar's service. He may well be the Yūsufzai.

Gul-badan, 8*a*, 25*b*, *30a,* 35*a*, 38*a*, 73*b*.

Mems., 250, 250 n., 251.

Akbar-nāma, Bib. Ind. ed., I. 315.

Asiatic Quarterly Beview, April, 1901, art. An Afghān Legend, H. Beveridge.

(Mughal Khānam, 'Ayisha, *q.v.)*

CXLIV. Muhibb-sulṭān.

The very loving khānam; Ar. *muḥibb,* a lover, one who loves, and *sulṭān,* pre-eminence.

Daughter of Sulṭān Husain Mīrzā *Bāyqrā* and a 'handmaid' *(ghūncha-chī).*

Mems., 30.

CXLV. Muḥibb-sulṭān Khānam *Chaghatāī Mughal.* (No. 20.)

Third daughter of Sulṭān Aḥmad Khān *Chaghatāī;* wife of Mīrzā Ḥaidar *Dughlāt.*

Gul-badan, 11*a*, 24*b*.
Tār. Rash., E. & R., 161, 280,[1] 341.

CXLVI. Muhtarima Khānam *Chaghatāī Mughal.*
The honoured khānam; Ar. *muhtarim,* respected, honoured.

Daughter of Shāh Muḥammad Sulṭān *Kāshgharī Chaghatāī,* and Khadīja Sulṭān *Chaghatāī;* wife (1) of Kāmrān, (2) of Ibrāhīm *Mīrān-shāhī,* the son of Sulaimān and *Ḥaram.*

She is occasionally spoken of simply as 'Khānam.'
Gul-badan, 62*b*.
Akbar-nāma, s.n..
Ain-i-akbarī, Blochmann, *s.n.*.
Tār. Rash., E. & R., 451.
Cf. Introduction.

CXLVII. Munauwar Sulṭān Begam *Bāyqrā.*
The illuminated princess; Ar. *munawar,* bright illuminated.

Daughter of Sulṭān Husain Mīrzā *Bāyqrā* and Bābā *āghācha;* wife of Sayyid Mīrzā of Andekhud who appears also to have married her niece. She was famed for her beauty. The Memoirs and Ilminsky's text do not give her name, and I have found it in the *Ḥahību-s-siyār.* From this same work is derived the information that Sayyid Mīrzā is a name given to a son of Ulugh Beg Mīrzā *Mīrān-shāhī.*

Mems., 182.
Ḥabību-s-siyār, 327 *et seq.*

CXLVIII. Nāhīd Begam. (No. 54.)
Pers. *Nāhīd,* the name of the mother of Alexander; a name for the planet Venus, *etc.*.

Daughter of Māh-chūchak *Arghūn* by her marriage as a captive of Bābar, with his foster-brother Qāsim; wife of Muhibb-'alī *Barlās.*

[1] There is some error here in the translation, as its statements do not agree with known facts.

When her mother, resenting her position in a mis-alliance, ran away, Nāhīd, then eighteen months old, remained in Kābul.

When her mother was imprisoned in Sind by Muhammad Bāqī *Tarkhān,* Nāhīd escaped to Bhakkar, and was protected, till her return to Akbar's court, by Sultān Mahmūd *Bhakkarī* (975H.).

She was at Hindāl's wedding feast. Much of her story is contained in the īntroduction of this volume.

Gul-badan, 4*a*, 26*a*.

Tārīkh-i-sind, Mīr Ma'sūm.

Bādshāh-nāma s.n. (fully used by Blochmann).

Aīn-i-akbarī, Blochmann, *s.n.*.

B. & H., I. 348, 351, 352, 385.

CXLIX. Nār-gul *āghācha.* (No. 58.)

(?) Red as a rose, pomegranate-red. For *nār* sce *infra.* Pers. *gul,* a rose.

She was perhaps one of two Circassian slaves, of whom Gul-nār may be the other and who were sent to Bābar by Tahmāsp in 1526.

Mems., 347.

Gul-badan, 25*b*, 35*a*, 38*a*.

CL. Nār-sulṭān *āghā.* (No. 77.)

Presumably Pers. *nār,* a pomegranate; but it might be Ar. *nār,* advice, counsel, or even fire, and *sulṭān,* pre-eminence, a high degree of what is expressed by the first word of the compound name.

Gul-badan, 26*a*,

CLI. Nigār *āghā.* (No. 76.)

Pers. *nigār,* a mistress, a sweetheart.

Mother of Mughal Beg.

Gul-badan, 26*a*.

CLII. Nizhād-sultan Begam *Bāyqrā.*

The princess of highly distinguished race; Pers. *nizhād,* family, high-born; Ar. *sultān,* pre-eminence.

Eldest daughter of Sultān Husain Mīrzā *Bāyqrā* and Bābā *āghācha;* wife of Sikandar Mīrzā, son of *Bāyqrā* Mīrzā who was her father's elder brother.

Mems., 182.

Ḥabību-s-siyār, 387 *et seq.*

CLIII. Pāpā (? Bābā) *āghācha.*

Mr. Erskine writes *Papa,* and Ilminskv, perhaps following him, *Pāpā. Bābā—i.e.,* darling—would seem a more fitting name for one who is said to have been much beloved.

She was a low-born wife of Sultān Husain Mīrzā *Bāyqrā* and foster-sister of Āfāq Begam. The mīrzā 'saw her and liked her,' and she became mother of seven of his children, *i.e.*, four sons, Muḥammad Ma'sūm, Farrūkh Husain, Ibn Husain, Ibrāhīm Husain; of three daughters, Nizhād-sulṭān, Sa'ādat-bakht, and a third whose name Bābar does not give.

Mems., 181, 182, 183.

CLIV. Pāshā Begam *Bahārlū Turkomān* of the Black Sheep.

(?) Turkī *Pāshā,* a lord, or Pers. *pecha,* chief, before.

The *Ma'āsir-i-rahīmī* writes *pāshā.*

Daughter of 'Alī-shakr Beg *Bahārlū;* wife (1) of Muhammadī Mīrzā of the Black Sheep; (2) in 873H. (1468-69) of Sultān Mahmūd Mīrzā *Mīrān-shāhī;* mother by Mahmūd of three daughters and one son, Bayasanghar (born 882H.).

Bābar does not give the name of any one of the three girls, nor does he mention that one of them was a wife of his own. One married Malik Muhammad Mīrzā *Mīrān-shāhī.* The *Ma'āsir-i-rahīmī* supplies the information that another was Sālḥa-sultān Begam and that she had a daughter by Bābar whose name was Gul-rukh; that Gul-rukh married Nuru-d-dīn Muḥammad *Chaqānīānī,* and had by him Salīma-sultān Bēgam. Abū'l-fazl says that a daughter of Pāshā by Sultān Mahmūd Mīrzā was married to Khwāja Hasan *Khivāja-zāda,* and that on account of this connection *Firdaus-makānī* (Bābar) married Mīrzā Nūru-d-dīn to his own daughter, Gul-barg Begam, and that Salīma-sultān Begam was the issue of this marriage.

(There are difficulties connected with the account here given of Sālha which are set forth under the name of her daughter, Salīma-sultān.)

Pāshā Begam was of the same family as Bairām Khān. (*Cf.* genealogical table *s.n.* Salīma-sultān.)

Mems., 29. 80, 31, 72.

Tār. Rash., E. & R., 93 n..

Ma'āsir-i-rahimī, Asiatic Society of Bengal MS. in year 1024H..

CLV. Pāyanda-sulṭān Begam *Mīrān-shāhī.*

(?) Of fixed pre-eminence; Pers. *pāyanda,* firm, stable, and Ar. *sulṭān,* pre-eminence.

Daughter of Abū-sa'īd Sulṭān Mīrzā *Mīrān-shāhī;* paternal aunt of Bābar; wife of Sulṭān Husain Mīrzā *Bāyqrā;* sister of Shahr-bānū whom Sulṭān Husain Mīrzā divorced; mother of Ḥaidar Mīrzā *Bāyqrā;* of Āq, Kīchak, Bega, and Āghā Begams.

When the Uzbegs took Khurāsān, 913H. (1507-8), she went to 'Irāq, where 'she died in distress.'

Mems., 30, 180, 181, 182, 204, 208 and n., 223.

Gul-badan, 25*a* (here a *Muḥammad* is inserted after Pāyanda in the name).

CLVI. Qadīr Khānam *Qālmāq.*

Daughter of Amāsānjī Taishī *Qālmāq* and Makhdūma Khānam *Chaghatāī,*

Tār. Rash., E. & R., 91.

CLVII. *Qarā-gūz* Begam *Bāyqrā.*

The black-eyed princess. *Qarā-gūz* is a sobriquet, and I have not found her personal name.

Daughter of Sulṭān Husain Mīrzā *Bāyqrā* and Pāvanda-sulṭān Begam *Mīrān-shāhī;* wife of Nāsir Mīrzā, Bābar's half-brother.

Mems., 181.
(*Qarā-gūz* Begam, Babī'a, *q.v.*)
(*Qarā-gūz* Begam, Makhdūma, *q.v.*)

CLVIII. Qūtūq *āghācha* and Begam.
Ilminskv writes *Qūtūq;* Mems., *Katak.*

Foster-sister of *Terkhān* Bēgam; wīfe of Sultān Ahmad Mīrzā *Mīrān-shāhī;* mother of four daughters: (1) Babī'a (*Jarā-gūz*), (2) Salīqa (Āq), 'Āyisha (wife of Bābar), (4) Sulṭānam.

She was married 'for love,' and Aḥmad was 'prodigiously attached' to her. She drank wine; her co-wives were neglected from fear of her. At length her husband put her to death, and 'delivered himself from his reproach.'

Mems., 22.

CLIX. Qūt-līq (Qutluq) Khānam *Chaghatāī Mughal.*
(?) The image of happiness; from Turkī *qūtla,* happy, and *līq,* endowed with.

Daughter of Sulṭān Maḥmūd Khān *Chaghatāī;* wife of Jānī Beg Khān *Uzbeg.*

Her marriage was a sequel of vietory by Shaibānī over her father. *Cf.* 'Āyisha (her sister).

Tār. Rash., E. & R., 160, 251.

CLX. Qūt-līq-nigār Khānam *Chaghatāi Mughal.*
Second daughter of Yūnas Khān *Chaghatāi* ancl Isān-daulat *Qūchīn;* chief wife of 'Umar-shaikh *Mīrān-shāhī;* half-sister of Maḥmūd and Aḥmad Khāns; mother of Khān-zāda and Bābar.

She accompanied her son in most of his wars and expeditions, and lived to see him master of Kābul. She died in Muharram, 911H. (June, 1505).

Mems., 10, 11, 12, 30, 90, 94, 98, 99, 104, 105, 134, 169.
Gul-badan, 4*a*.
Tār. Rash., s.n..
Akbar-nāma, s.n..

CLXI. Rabī'a-sulṭān Begam *Bāyqrā* and Bedka Begam *Bāyqrā.* These two names may indicate the same person.

The Memoirs (176 and 177) say that Sulṭān Husain Mīrzā *Bāyqrā* had two full-sisters, Āka and Bedka, and that Bedka married Aḥmad *Hājī Tarkhān*, and had two sons who served Sulṭān Husain.

These statements are contained also in the Turkī texts (B.M. Add. 26,324, and Uminsky), and also in a considerable number of good Persian texts in the British Museum and Bodleian.

There is, however, this difference of statement. The Turki texts write: *Bedka Begam ham mīrzā nīnak aīkā-chī sī aīdī.* P. de C. translates: *était aussi l'ainée du mīrzā.* The Persian texts have: *Bedka Begam ki khwāhar-i-khurd mīrzā būd;* and from this Mr. Erskine translates: . . . *the mīrzā's younger sister.*

The Turkī, it should be observed, uses of Āka precisely the same word as of Bedka, *aīkā-chī sī.*

It may be right to regard Bedka as the younger of the two sisters of the mīrzā, and not as the sister younger than the mīrzā.

To pass now to what has led me to make a tentative identification of Bedka with Rabī'a-sulṭān.

The Memoirs (181) mention Rabī'a-sulṭān as the younger sister of the mīrzā (Husain) and as having two sons, Bābar and Murād who were given in marriage to two daughters of Husain.

The Turkī texts do not describe Rabī'a-sulṭān in any way, or say that she was Husain's sister. They simply mention the marriages.

The Persian texts say of Husain's two daughters (Bega and Āghā): *ba pisarān-i-khwāhar-i-khurd-i-khudrā Rabī'a-sulṭān Begam, Bābar Mīrzā wa Sulṭān Murād Mīrzā, dādā būdand.*

The Persian texts which state that Rabī'a-sulṭān was Husain's own sister, have greater authority than most translations can claim for such additional information as is here given, because the Persian trans-lation of the *Tūzūk-i-bābarī* was made in a court circle and at a date when such additional statements were likely to be known to many living persons.

Husain *may* have had a younger and half-sister, but the words in the Persian texts which are used of Rabī'a-sulṭān are those used of Bedka, and they are more applicable to a full than a half sister.

The *Āka* of the passage in which Bedka is mentioned has no personal name recorded. Bedka may be a word of the same class as *āka, i.e.,* a title or sobriquet, and Rabī'a-sulṭān may be the personal name of Bedka. Perhaps the word *Bedka* is *Bega.*

The facts of Bedka's descent are as follows: she was a daughter of Mansūr Mīrzā *Bāyqrā* and of Fīroza Begam *Mīrān-shāhī,* and thus doubly a Tīmūrid. She was full-sister of Bāyqrā and Husain Mīrzās and of Āka Begam. She married Aḥmad Khān *Hājī Tarkhān,* and had two sons whose names (if Bedka be Rabī'a-sulṭān) were Bābar and Murād and who married two of her nieces, Bega and Āghā.

Mems., 176, 177, 181.

Ilminsky, 203, 204, 208.

B.M. Turkī Add. 26,234, f. 48*a* and *b;* 53.

Other texts under 911H..

CLXII. Rabī'a-sulṭān Begam *(Qarā-gūz)* *Mīrān-shāhī.*

Daughter of Sulṭān Aḥmad Mīrzā *Mīrān-shāhī* and Qūtūq (Katak) *āghācha* (Begam); wife (1) of Sulṭān Maḥmūd Khān *Chaghatāī* and mother of Bābā Sulṭān, and (2) of Jānī Beg *Uzbeg* who married her after the murder of her father and her son by his cousin Shaibānī in 914H. (1508).

Mems., 22.

Tār. Rash., E. & R., 114, 116.

CLXIII. Rajab-sulṭān *Mīrān-shāhī.*

Ar. *rajab,* fearing, worshipping. *Sulṭān* may here be a title.

Daughter of Sulṭān Maḥmūd Mīrzā and a concubine (*ghūncha-chī*).

Mems., 30.

CLXIV. Ruqaiya Begam *Mīrān-shāhī.*

Ruqaiya was the name of a daughter of Muḥammad, and conveys the notion of bewitching or of being armed against spells.

Daughter of Hindāl; first wife of Akbar; she died Jumāda I. 7th, 1035H. (January 19th, 1626), at the age of eighty-four. She had no children of her own, and she brought up Shāh-jahān. Mihru-n-nisāʿ (Nūrjahān) lived 'unnoticed and rejected' with her after the death of Shīr-afkan.

Āīn-i-akbarī, Blochmann, 309, 509.

CLXV. Rugaiya-sulṭān Begam *Mīrān-shālī.*

Daughter of 'Umar Shaikh *Mīrān-shāhī* and Makh-dūma-sulṭān Begam *(Qarā-gūz).* She was a posthumous child. She fell into the hands of Jānī Beg *Uzbeg, cir.* 908-9H. (1502-4), and bore him 'two or three' sons who died young. 'I have just received information that she has gone to the mercy of God.' The date of this entry in the Memoirs is about 935H. (1528-9).

Mems, 10.

CLXVI. Sa'ādat-bakht (Begam Sulṭān) *Bāyqrā.*

Of happy fortune; Ar. *sa'ādat,* happy, and Pers. *bakht,* fortune.

Daughter of Sulṭān Husain Mīrzā *Bāyqrā* and Papa (Bābā) *āghācha.* She was married to Sulṭān Ma'sūd after the loss of his eyesight.

Mems., 182.

Ḥabību-s-siyār, 327 *et seg.*

CLXYII. Sāhib-daulat Begam *Dughlāt.*

The princess of good fortune; Ar. *sāḥib,* enjoying, and *daulat,* fortune.

Sister of Mīr Jabār *Bardī Dughlāt;* wife of Sulṭān Aḥmad Khān *Chaghatāī;* mother of Mansūr, Bābājāk, Shāh Shaikh Muḥammad and Māham.

Tār. Rash., E. & R., 125, 344.

CLXVIII. Sakīna-bānū Begam *Mīrān-shāhī.*

The princess guardian of tranquillity; Ar. *salīna,* tranquillity of mind, and Pers. *bānū,* keeper.

Daughter of Humāyūn and Māh-chūchak; wife of Shāh Ghāzī Khān, son of Naqīb Khān *Qazwīnī* a personal friend of Akbar.

Gul-badan, 71*a*.

Blochmann, 435, 449.

CLXIX. Sālha-sulṭān Begam *Mīrān-shālī.*

Cf. Salīma-sulṭān *Chaqānīānī.*

CLXX. Salīma-sulṭān Begam *Chaqānīānī.*

Daughter of Mīrzā Nūru-d-dīn Muḥammad *Chaqā-nīānī* and of a daughter of Bābar, as to whose name the sources ring changes upon the rose. She appears as Gul-rang (B. and H. *s.n.),* Gul-barg, Gul-rukh. As her mother was a full Turkomān or Turk by descent, it has occurred to me that she may have borne a Turkī name, and that the various forms it assumes in the Persian may have their origin in this.

As to her maternal parentage there are difficulties. From the *Ma'āsir-i-rahīmī,* under 1024H., the following information is obtained. Pāshā Begam *Bahārlū Turkomān* married (873H, 1469) as her second husband, Sulṭān Maḥmūd Mīrzā *Mīrān-shāhī.* By him she had three daughters and one son: Bayasanghar (b. 882H., 1477). One daughter whose name was Sālha-sulṭān Begam, married Bābar and bore him a daughter, Gul-rukh (*sic*). Gul-rukh married Nūru-d-dīn Muḥammad *Chaqānīānī,* and their daughter was Salīma-sulṭān Begam who married first, Bairām *Khān-i-khānān,* and secondly, the Emperor Akbar.

Abū'l-fazl (*Bib. Ind.* ed., II. 65) adds the particular that *Firdaus makānī* gave his daughter Gul-barg *(sic),* to Nūru-d-dīn because a daughter of Maḥmūd and Pāshā had been given to Nūru-d-dīn's grandfather Khwāja Hasan, known as Khwāja-zāda *Chaqānīānī.* He also states that Salīma-sulṭān Begam was the issue of Gul-barg's marriage.

In the Memoirs, as we have them, there is no mention of Sālha-sulṭān nor of Nūru-d-dīn's marriage with a daughter of Bābar. Yet Abū'l-fazl states that *Firdaus-makānī* arranged Gul-barg's marriage. The first omission is the more remarkable because Bābar (Mems., 30) states that Pāshā had three daughters. He does not give their names, and specifies the marriage of the eldest only. On the same page he tells of his marriage with Sālha's half-sister Zainal and of her death. The omission is remarkable and appears to have no good ground, since he chronicles his other Tīmūrid marriages. Of Pāshā's daughters it may be noted here that one married Malik Muḥammad *Mīrān-shāhī,* another Khwāja Hasan *Chaqānīānī,* and the third, Bābar.

It appears to me tolerably clear that Bābar's marriage with Sālha-sulṭān took place at a date which fails in a gap of the Memoirs, *i.e.,* from 1511 to 1519. This is the period which contains the exile from Kābul after the Mughal rebellion.

Not only does Bābar omit Sālha-sulṭān's name and his marriage with her (Mems., 30), but Gul-badan is also silent as to name, marriage and child of Sālha-sulṭān. This silence is in every way remarkable. She enumerates her father's children and gives their mothers' names, and she enumerates some of his wives in more places than one. From her lists a Tīmūrid wife cannot have escaped, and especially one whose child became the mother of Gul-badan's associate Salīma-sulṭān.

An explanation of Gul-badan's silence and also of a part of Bābar's has suggested itself to me; it is conjectural merely and hypothetical. The absence of mention of Sālha-sulṭān and of her child suggests that she appears under another name in Gul-badan's list of her father's children and their mothers. She may be Gul-badan's own mother, Dil-dār Begam without undue wresting of known circumstantial witness.

The principal difficulty in the way of this identification is Abū'l-fazl's statement that Nūru-d-dīn's marriage was made by *Firdaus-makānī,* whereas Gulbadan states that her father arranged two Chaghatāī marriages for her sisters.

If we might read *Januat-āshyānī* (Humāyūn) for *Firdaus-makānī* much would fall into place; the marriage with Nūru-d-dīn could be a remarriage of Gul-chihra who was widowed in 1533, and of whose remarriage nothing is recorded until her brief political alliance with 'Abbas *Uzbeg* in 1549. It is probable that she remarried in the interval.

To pass on to recorded incidents of Salīma-sulṭān's life:

There is an entry in Hindāl's guest-list which may indicate her presence.

She accompanied Hamīda-bānū and Gul-badan to Hindūstan in 964H. (1557), and she was married at Jalindhar shortly after Safar 15th, 965H. (middle of December, 1557) to Bairām *Khān-i-khānān.* It is said that the marriage excited great interest at Court. It united two streams of descent from 'Alī-shukr Beg *Bahārlū Turkomān.* Salīma-sulṭān was a Tīmūrid through Bābar, one of her grandfathers, and through Maḥmūd, one of her great-grandfathers.

A few words must be said about her age at the time of her marriage, because the question has been raised through Jahāngīr's statement that she died at the age of sixty in 1021H., and commented upon by the *Darbār-i-akbarī.* If Jahāngīr gives her age correctly she must have been born in 961H., and this would make her a child of five when she married Bairām, and needs her betrothal by her father to Bairām to date from babyhood.

The *Darbār-i-akbarī* says that it is clear from Jahāngīr's statement of her age at death that she was married to Bairām *ætat.* 5, and that her memory is thus cleared from the reproach of two marriages!

Whatever is concealed in Jahāngīr's 'sixty,' nothing is said to indicate that he desired to bring Salīma-sulṭān into the circle of Hindū propriety. He may have had the wish; he was a Hindū mother's son. The comment of the modern author of the *Darbār-i-akbarī* witnesses to the Hindūizing action to which Moslim custom and thought have submitted. Adult remarriage was no reproach to Islām in Salīma's day.

It does not, however, seem correct to accept Jahāngīr's statement that Salīma-sulṭān was sixty only at death to have betrothed her as a baby and to have married her to a man of, at least, middle-age at five, is not in harmony with the Muḥammad custom of Humāyūn's day. Moreover, Jahāngīr himself speaks of her as married (*kad-khudā*) to Bairām. She is said by Abū'lfazl to have been betrothed (*nāmzād*) by Humāyūn, and married (*sipurdan*) by Akbar to Bairām Khān.

Badāyunī's words indicate adult and not child marriage; *sābiqā dar habāla-i-Bairām Khān Khan-i-khānān būd, b'ad azān dakhl-i-ḥaram-i-pādshāhī shūd.*

After the murder of Bairām in 968H. Salīma-sulṭān was married by Akbar. She was probably a few years his senior.

In 983H. she made her pilgrimage with Gul-badan. Particulars of the expedition are given in the Introduction to this volume.

Her name appears in the histories as a reader, a poet who wrote under the pseudonym of *makhfī,* and as pleading with Akbar for Salīm's forgiveness.

Her death is chronicled by Jahāngīr who heard of it on Zū'l-qa'da 2nd, 1021H. (December 15th, 1612), He gives particulars of her birth and descent, and of her marriages; and he states that she was sixty at the time of her death. By his orders her body was laid in a garden which she herself had made.

Jahāngīr praises her both for her natūrai qualities and her acquirements. She creates an impression of herself as a charming and cultivated woman.

Gul-badan, (?)26*a*.

Akbar-nāma s.n..

Badāyunī, Lowe, 13, 216, 389.

Tūzūk-i-jahāngīrī, Sayyid Aḥmad, Aligarh, 113.

Khāfī Khān, *Bib. Ind.* ed., I. 276.

Aīn-i-akbarī, Blochmann, *s.n.*.

Darbār-i-akbarī, 736.

The genealogical table on the next page illustrates Salīma-sulṭān's descent, and the following dates bear also upon the topic:

Pāshā married Maḥmūd......... 873H.—1469.

Bayasanghar born .... 882H.—1477.

Maḥmūd died .... 900H.—Jan. 1495

Bābar married Zainab, d. of Maḥmūd ... 910H.—1504.

Zainab died............. 913H.-914H.—1507-8.

Sālha's child, the wife of Nūru-d-dīn, was not born in 911H.—1511, because she is not in the list of children who left Kābul with Bābar in that year. (Gulbadan, 7*a.)*

CLXXI. Salīma Khānam *Chaghatāī Mughal.*

Daughter of Khiẓr Khwājā, but whether also of Gul-badan is not recorded.

She went with Gul-badan to Makka in 983H. (1575).

Āīn-i-akbarī, Blochmann, 441.

CLXXII. Salīqa-sulṭān Begam (Āq Begam) *Mīrān-shāhī.*

(Ilminsky, 25, reads Sālha.) The princess of excellent disposition; Ar. *salīqa,* of good disposiṭion, and *sulṭān,* pre-eminence.

Daughter of Sulṭān Aḥmad Mīrzā *Mīrān-shāhī* and Qūtūq (Katak) Begam; wife of her cousin Ma'sūd. The marriage was announced to Bābar in 900H. (1494) with gifts of gold and silver, almonds, and pistachios. She was captured by Abū-bakr *Dughlāt* with Shāh Begam and Mihr-nigār Khānam.

Mems., 22, 27.

CLXXIII. Sāmiḥa Begam *Barlās.*

The gentle princess; Ar. *sāmih,* gentle.

Daughter of Muḥibb 'Alī *Barlās* (son of Nizāmu-d-dīn 'Alī *Khalīfa),* and presumably of Nāhīd Begam; mother of Mujāhid Khān.

Mujāhid (who is named in the *Ṭabaqāt-i-akbarī* as commander of 1,000, but is not in the *Āīn)* was a son of Musāhib Khān, son of Khwāja Kilān (Bābar's friend).

GENEALOGICAL TABLE OF SALĪMA-SULṬĀN *CHAQĀNĪĀNĪ*.

Chaqānīān.
Khwāja 'Alā'u-d-dīn,
first successor of Khwāja
Naqshbandī.
|
Khwāja Ḥasan '*aṭṭār*.
|
Not named.
|
Khwāja Ḥasan, *Khwāja-zāda Chaqānīānī*. = d. [daughter of Sulṭān Maḥmūd Mīrzā and Pāshā Begam]
|
Mīrzā 'Alā'u-d-dīn Muḥāmmad.
|
Mīrzā Nūru-d-dīn Muḥammmad. = Gul-rukh, or -barg, etc. [daughter of Bābar and Salḥā-sulṭān Begam]
|
Salīma-sulṭān Begam. = Bairām *Khān-i-khānān*.

Black Sheep *Turkomāns.*
|
'Alī-shukr Beg *Bahārlū Turkomān.* — Pīr-'alī Bahārlū *Turkomān.*

'Alī-shukr Beg *Bahārlū Turkomān.*
|
Sulṭān Maḥmūd Mīrzā *Mīrān-shāhī.* = Pāshā Begam.
|
d. [= Khwāja Ḥasan] — d. = Malik Muḥammad. — Salḥā-sulṭān Begam = Bābar.

Pīr-'alī Bahārlū *Turkomān.*
|
Bīr-bal Beg.
|
Saif-'alī.
|
Bairām *Khān-i-khānān.*

CLXXIV. Sarv-qad and Sarv-i-sahī.

Straight as a cypress; Pers. *sarv,* a cypress, and *qad,* form, or *sahī,* erect.

Sarv-i-sahī, to use Gul-badan's word, was a singer and reciter. She belonged to the households both of Bābar and Humāyūn, and was subsequently married, with full *nisbat,* to Mu'nim *Khān-i-khānān.*

She acted as go-between of Mu'nim and Khān-i-zamān ('Alī Qulī *Uzbeg-i-sliaibānī)* during the rebellion of the latter—probably in the tenth year of Akbar, and Bāyazīd calls her a reliable woman and the *ḥaram* of the *Khāu-i-khānān.* She sang on the way to Lamghān by moonlight in 958H. (1551); she was with Mu'nim at the time of his death in Gaur (Safar, 983H., 1575), and in Rajab of the same year accompanied Gul-badan to Makka.

Gul-badan, 82*a* (inserted in the translation after 73*b*).

Bāyazīd, I.O. MS., 1226, 147*b*.

Akbar-nāma, Bib. Ind. ed., III. 145.

CLXXV. Shād Begam *Bāyqrā.* (No. 28.)

Daughter of Ḥaidar *Bāyqrā* and Bega *Mīrān-shāhī;* wife of 'Adil Sulṭān.

Gul-badan, 25*a*.

Mems., 180.

CLXXV *(a)*. Shād Bībī.

Wife of Humāyūn; lost at Chausa.

Gul-badan, 336.

CLXXVI. Shāham *āghā.*

(?) My queen; from Pers. *shāh,* king, ruler.

Of the *ḥaram* of Humāyūn. She went with Gulbadan Begam to Makka in 983H..

Aīn-i-akbarī, Blochmann, 441.

CLXXVII. Shāh Begam *Badakhshī.*

The princess of royal blood.

She was one of six daughters of Shāh Sulṭān Muḥammad, King of Badakhshān, the last of a long line of hereditary rulers of his country who claimed descent from Alexander of Macedon. Her mother was a sister of Sulṭān Sanjar *Barlās*.

She was given in marriage to Yūnas Khān *Chaghatāī* and was the mother of Maḥmūd and Aḥmad Khāns and of Sulṭān-nigār and Daulat Khānams. She was widowed in 892H. (1487), and survived Yūnas more than twenty years.

She dwelt in Mughalistān with her elder son, Maḥmūd, the then Khāqān of the Mughals, from the time of Yūnas' death until about 911H. (1505-6). Then 'base advisers provoked a quarrel between the mother and son—a son so obedient that he had never oven mounted for a ride without her permission. . . . They [the base advisers] decided to send Shāh Begam to Shāhī Beg Khān to solicit a country for herself, because she found living in Mughalistān distasteful. . . . Now, as the Begam was a very sensible woman, she went under this pretext, and thus left her son before those base advisers could bring about an open rupture, which would have caused endless scandal and reproach to herself. The rumour was that she had gone to entreat Shāhī Beg Khān while she was really enjoying in Samarqand the company of her children.' *(Tār. Rash,* E. & R., 180.)

Shāhī Beg did not permit her to remain in Samarqand but banished her to Khurāsān. From Khurāsān she went with other connections and relations to Bābar in Kābul. They arrived early in 911H. (June, 1505), during the ceremonial mourning for Bābar's mother, Shāh Begam's stepdaughter. With Shāh Begam was Ḥaidar Mīrzā's father and also Bābar's aunt, Mihr-nigār. Ḥaidar says that Bābar gave the party a warm welcome and showed them all possible honour; and that they spent some time in Kābul in the greatest ease and comfort.

Bābar's kindness fell on ungrateful ground, since in the following year, 912H. (1506-7), Shāh Begam fomented a rebellion against him in favour of her grandson, Mīrzā Khān. Ḥaidar says that during Bābar's absence in Harāt her motherly love (it was grandmotherly) began to burn in her heart, and persuaded her that Bābar was dead, and that room was thus made for Mīrzā Khān. The story of Bābar's magnanimity to her when he had put down the rising she had stirred, is well known and is detailed in the histories.

In 913H. (1507-8) she laid claim to Badakhshān, saying that it had been her family's hereditary kingdom for 3,000 years; that though she, a woman, could not attain to sovereignty, her grandson would not be rejected. Bābar assented to her scheme, and she set off for Badakhshān, together with Mihr-nigār Khānam and Mīrzā Khān.

The latter went on in advance to Qila'-zafar. The ladies and their escort were at once attacked and plundered by robber bands in the employ of the ruler of Kāshghar, Abā-bakr *Dughlāt,* and were by them conveyed to him in Kāshghar. They were placed in confinement, and 'in the prison of that wicked miscreant they departed from this perishable world' (cir. 913H.).

Mems., 12, 13, 22, 32, 60, 74, 99, 104, 105, 106, 169, 216, 217, 231.

Tār. Rash., E. & R., *s.n.*.

CLXXVIII. Shāh Begam Termiẕī. **(No. 24.)**

Daughter of Fakhr-jahān Begam and of Mīr Alā'u-l-mulk Termiẕī.

She may be 'Kīchak' Begam, and if not, is her sister.

She was the mother of Dil-shād Begam. If she be Kīchak, she was the wife of Sharafu-d-dīn Husain. *(Cf.* Kīchak.)

She was at the Mystic Feast.

Gul-badan, 24*a*.

CLXXIX. Shāh Khānam. (No. 17.)

Daughter of Badī'u-l-jamāl Begam.

Gul-badan, 24*b*.

CLXXX. Shahr-bānū Begam *Mīrān-shāhī.*

(?) Ar. *shahr,* the moon, the new moon.

Daughter of Sulṭān Abū-sa'īd Mīrzā *Mīrān-shāhī;* wife of Sulṭān Husain Mīrzā *Bāiyqrā,* and married to him before his accession in 873H. (March, 1469).

Bābar gives an entertaining detail about her married life. Once at Chekmān her husband was engaged in a battle with her brother Maḥmūd. All his ladies except herself alighted from their litters and mounted on horseback, presumably for rapid flight if the day went against Husain. Shahr-bānū, however, 'relying on her brother,' remained in her litter. This being reported to her husband, he divorced her and married her younger sister, Pāyanda-sulṭān.

Of her subsequent history nothing seems recorded. *(Cf.* Mīnglī-bī *āghācha.)*

Mems., 182.

CLXXXI. Shahr-bānū Begam *Mīrān-shāhī.* (No. 7.)

Third daughter of 'Umar Shaikh Mīrzā *Mīrān-shāhī* and Umīd *Andijānī;* half-sister of Bābar and eight years his junior; born *cir.* 1491; full-sister of Nāsir and Mihr-bānū; wife of Junaid *Barlās* (brother of Nizāmu-d-dīn 'Alī *Khalīfa)*; mother by him of Sanjar Mīrzā; widowed *cir.* 944H. (1537-38).

She seems to have gone to Sind with her nephew, Yādgār-nāsir Mīrzā, in 1540 and after the *débacle* in Hindūstān, for when Yādgār nāsir had fled from Sind to Kāmrān in Qandahār (a traitor cast aside by his employer, Shāh Husain *Arghūn),* Kāmrān sent ambassadors to Shāh Husain to request that the begam and her son might be returned to his charge. (Shahr-bānū was Kāmrān's paternal (half)-aunt and full-aunt of Yādgār-nāsir.)

She was at once started on her journey, but was insufficiently provided with necessaries for traversing the difficult desert tract which stretches towards the western mountain barrier of Sind. Numbers of her party perished before reaching Shāl (Quetta); and many died in that town from 'malignant fever.' Amongst its victims was Shahr-bānū, at the age of about fifty-one years.

Gul-badan, 24*b*.

Mems, 10.

Akbar-nāma, s.n..

B. & H., I. 526 and II. 253. (Here occur errors of statement, *i.e.*, that Shahr-bānū was Yādgār-nāsir's wife and Kāmrān's sister.)

CLXXXII. Shāh Sulṭān Begam.

(?) Wife of Abū-sa'īd Mīrzā *Mīrān-shāhī;* mother of 'Umar Shaikh Mīrzā.

The news of her death in Andijān reached Bābar in 907H. (1501).

Mems., 20, 99.

CLXXXIII. Shāh-zāda Begam and Sulṭānam Khānam *Safawī.*

The daughter of kings.

Sister of Shāh Tahmāsp of Persia. Her protection of the Emperor Humāyūn during his sojourn in Persia is named by many of the historians.

Gul-badan, *58a, 58b.*

CLXXXIV. Shāh-zāda Khānam *Mīrān-shāhī.*

Daughter of Sulaimān Mīrzā *Mīrān-shāhī* and *Ḥaram* Begam. She was betrothed to Humāyūn in 958H. (1551), but the affair went no further.

Journal of the Royal Asiatic Society, 1898, art. Bāyazīd *bīyāt,* H. Beveridge.

B. & H., II. 397.

Cf. appendix *s.n. Ḥaram* and Fāṭima.

CLXXXV. Sulṭānam Begam *Bayqrā.*

For meaning of *Sulṭānam, Cf.* app. *s.n.* Māham.

Daughter of Sulṭān Husain Mīrzā *Bāyqrā* and Chūlī Begam *Azāk;* her father's eldest girl and her mother's only child. She married, first, her cousin Wais, son of her father's elder brother Bayqrā, and, secondly, 'Abdu-l-bāqī Mīrzā *Mīrān-shāhī.* By her first marriage she had a son, Muḥammad Sulṭān Mīrzā, and a daughter who married Isān-qulī *Shaibānī,* younger brother of Yīlī-bārs Sulṭān. Through her son Muḥammad she was ancestress of those numerous rebel Bāyqrās whom history knows as 'the mīrzās.'

When the Uzbegs took Harāt in 1507 (913H.) she went to Khwārizm, and there her daughter was married. On April 12th, 1519 (Rabi' II. 12th, 925H.), Bābar records her arrival with her daughter in Kābul. He gave her the Garden of Retirement (*Bāgh-i-khilwat*) for her residence, and waited upon her with the cere-mony due to an elder sister. He bowed and she bowed; he advanced, they embraced; and having established this form of greeting, they kept to it.

Sulṭānam started from Kābul for India in 1527 with a grandson (her sons had six sons), but she died at the Indus and her body was taken back to Kābul for burial.

There are curious discrepancies of the texts in the passage about Sulṭānam which occurs at Mems., 181.

The first point to note is contained in the words: 'Her elder brother gave her in marriage to Sulṭān Wais Mirza, the son of Miangī Bāyqrā Mīrzā.' (Mems., 181.)

Barādar kilānash ba pisar miāngl Bāyqrā Mīrzā Sulṭān Wais Mīrzā dāda būd. (Waqi'āt-i-bābarī, Persian text, B.M. Or. 16,623, 1236.)

Aghā sī Bāyqrā Mīrzā nīnak ortānchī oghalī Sidtān Wais Mīrzāgha chīqārīb aidī. (Tūzūk-i-bābarī or *Bābar-nāma,* Turkī text, B.M. Add. 26,324, f. 526, and Ilminsky, 209.)

'Son frere ainé l'avait donnée en mariage à Sulṭān Wais Mīrzā, fils cadet de Bāyqrā Mīrzā.' (Pavet de Courteille, I. 375.)

Both the English and French versions make the elder brother of Sulṭānam give her in marriage. But she was an only child, and her father was living to act for her. The French version, here as in so many other places, appears to have relied upon Mr. Erskine. The Turkī text appears to yield something more probable, *i.e.,* 'His elder brother, Bāyqrā Mīrza's middle son, Sulṭān Wais Mīrzā. . . .'

Mr. Erskine has read *miāngl* as part of Bāyqrā's name. Comparison with the Turkī makes appear as the more probable reading: 'the middle son'—*pisar-i-miāngī.*

M. Pavet de Courteille's *fils cadet* lets slip the notion of *mīyān.* Bedhouse gives for the *ortānchī oghal* of the Turkī text, 'the middle son out of an odd number'—*e.g.,* the third out of five, the second of three, etc..

In the same passage the Memoirs have: 'Sulṭānam Begam set out along with her grandson. . . .' Here the Persian words *ba hamīn tārīkh* (Turkī, *ushbū tārīkh)* are omitted, with loss of precision, for they fix the date of her journey by conveying the information that it occurred at the time of her son's appointment to the government of Kanauj, *i.e.,* April, 1527.

Mems., 181, 190, 266.

Ḥabību-s-siyār, 327 *et seq.*.

Also the places mentioned in the notice above.

CLXXXVI. Sulṭānam Begam *Mīrān-shāhī.* (No. 12.)
Daughter of Sulṭān Aḥmad Mīrzā.

A Sulṭānam of this parentage is mentioned by Bābar (Mems., 22), by Ḥaidar (E. & R., *s.n.*), and by Gulbadan (24*b*). These appear to be at least two, and perhaps are three women. Their record is as follows:

(1). Sulṭānam, fourth daughter of Sulṭān Aḥmad Mīrzā. (Mems., 22.) She was the child of Qūtūq (Katak) Begam. She married her cousin Alī, son of Maḥmūd Mīrzā. 'Alī was murdered by Shaibānī *(Cf. s.n.* Zuhra) in 906H. (July, 1500), and his widow was taken to wife by Shaibānī's son, Muḥammad Tīmur. A third marriage is mentioned by Bābar, viz., to Mahdī Sulṭān. By this style the histories mention the Uzbeg chief who was associated with Hamza (Khamza) Sulṭān. But this Mahdī was put to death by Bābar in 1511, and Tīmūr was living in 1512 (918H.). Either Sulṭānam was divorced, perhaps to make marriage with some other kinswoman and later captive legal; or Mahdī Sulṭān may be the father of Adil Sulṭān; or he may be Mahdī Muḥammad Khwāja.

(2). Sulṭānam, daughter of Sulṭān Aḥmad Mīrzā, married Muḥammad Husain *Dughlāt* in the autumn of 1503. She was given to her husband by Khusrau Shāh who describes her as daughter of Sulṭān Aḥmad Mirzā *wa pādshāh-zāda-i-man,* by which Mr. Boss has understood that she was of Khusrau's 'family.' There was a son, issue of this marriage and named Abdu-l-lāh.

It is difficult to regard No. 1 and No. 2 as one woman, both because of their marriage dates and of the circumstance that No. 1 was an Uzbeg captive and No. 2 in Badakhshān. Bābar mentions no marriage of a Sulṭānam with Muḥammad Husain *Dughlāt. A* surmise—it is nothing more—has occurred to me, namely: No. 2 was married to the Dughlāt mīrzā shortly after the destruction of Tāshkend; Bābars wife 'Āyisha, third daughter of Sulṭān Aḥmad *Mīrān-shāhī,* had left Bābar shortly before that disaster. She might be Sulṭānam No. 2.

(3). Sulṭānam, or Sulṭāni, daughter of Sulṭān Aḥmad Mīrzā, was at the Mystic Feast in 1531. She is said to be the mother of Kilān Khān Begam. This title is not appropriate for the child of any of the marriages mentioned for No. 1 or No. 2. It is quite appropriate for the child of the marriage of Sulṭān Aḥmad and Qūtūq's firstborn daughter, Babī'a-sulṭān, because Rabī'a married Sulṭān Maḥmūd Khān who was the Elder Khān *(kilān)* and also the Great Khān *(Khāqān)* of the Mughals. Shaibānī murdered five of Maḥmūd's six sons, but probably his girls escaped because of their value as wives.

The above notes make for the opinion that Sulṭānam is a title, and not a name. *Cf.* app. *s.n.* Māham.

Mems., 22. Gul-badan, 246.

Tār. Rash., E. & R., 164, 170, 193.

CLXXXVII. Sulṭānam. (No. 52.)

Wife of Nizāmu-d-dīn 'Alī *Khalīfa.*

Gul-badan, 14*a*, 145, 26*a*, 50*a*.

CLXXXVIII. Sulṭān-nigār Khānam *Chaghatāī Mughal.*
Daughter of Yūnas Khān *Chaghatāī* and Shāh Begam *Badakhshī;* wife of Sulṭān Maḥmūd Mīrzā *Mīrān-shāhī;* mother of Sulṭān Wais (Khān Mīrzā); widowed in 900H. (January, 1495).

On Maḥmūd's death in Samarqand she joined her brothers in Tāshkand, going off 'without giving any notice of her intentions,' says Bābar. Later on she married Awīq (Adīk) Sulṭān *Jūjī,* the chief of the *Uzbeg Qazāqs.* Her story is somewhat confused in the Memoirs (13 and 14) by a double mention of her marriage to Awīq. Ḥaidar Mīrzā throws some light, and it seems that when Shaibānī had murdered her brother, Maḥmūd Khān, Awīq left him and joined the Uzbeg Qazāqs, his own people, and Sulṭān-nigār followed him into Mughalistān.

She had two daughters by Awīq, one of whom married 'Abdu-l-lāh *Qūchīn* and died a young wife, and the other married Eashīd Sulṭān *Chaghatāī.*

On Awīq's death, Sulṭān-nigār was married to his brother Qāsim, presumably in consonance with the Turkī custom of *yang-lik.*

With Qāsim's death, the khānship of the *Qazāqs* devolved on Sulṭān-nigār's stepson (*i.e.,* Awīq's by a co-wife) named Tāhir. 'He was,' says Ḥaidar, 'very much attached to her, and even preferred her to the mother who had given him birth.'

What follows is full of colour and feeling. Nigār-sulṭān showed her appreciation of Tāhir's affection, but petitioned him, saying: 'Although you are (as) my child, and I neither think of nor desire any son but you, yet I wish you to take me to my nephew, Sulṭān Saīd Khān. For I am grown old, and I have no longer the strength to bear this wandering life in the deserts of Uzbegistān. Take me where I may enjoy some quiet and repose.' She then offered to mediate for him and to obtain the support for him of the Mughal Khāqāns against his foes. Tāhir accordingly escorted her to the Mughalistān borders, and with her waited upon Sa'īd. 'The latter, from love of his aunt, rose, saying that although his rising to receive Tāhir was contrary to the rules of Chingīz (their common ancestor), yet that he did it out of gratitude because Tāhir had brought his aunt.'

Sulṭān-nigār died of a hemorrhage in the summer of 934H. (1528).

Mems., 13, 14, 30, 31, 99, 105.

Tur. Rash., E. & R , *s.n.*

CLXXXIX. *Tarkhān* Begam.

This is a title, and not a personal name.

In Bābar's time, according to Mr. Erskine (Mems., 24 n.), the ancient title of *Tarkhān* had come to belong to a particular family or clan. This may be well seen by consulting Professor Blochmann's *Āīn-i-akbarī,* 361, where the genealogical table of the Arghūns of Tatta shows the title to have become hereditary in their branch of the Arghūns.[1]

The Tarkhān Begam whose name stands above this notice was linked with these Tarkhān Arghūns in the way shown below. She married her first cousin, Aḥmad *Mīrān-shāhī,* and Qūtūq Begam was her foster-sister.

Mems, 22, 24.

Āīn-i-akbarī, Blochmann, 361.

B. & H., I. and II. *s.n.* Sind, Arghūn, etc.

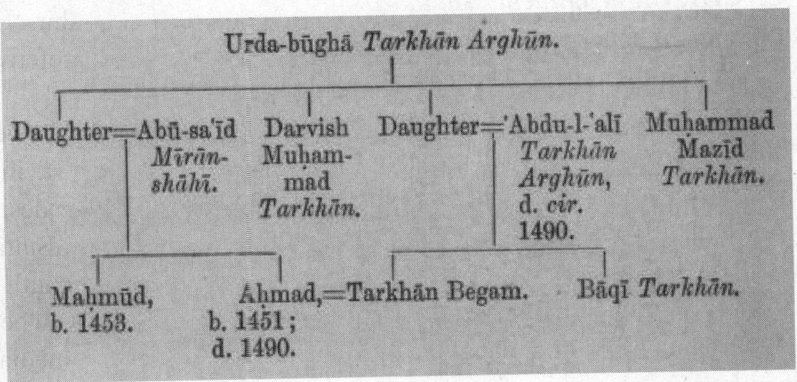

[1] Professor Blochmann (l c.) states that 'Abdu-l-'alī and five sons were murdered by Shaibānī, but Bābar and the Sind historians give no support to the story. It looks as though by some clerical error the account of the murder of Sultān Mahmūd Khān and his sons had crept in here. Shaibānī drove Bāqī out of his late father's government of Bukhārā.

CXC. *Tarkhān* Begam and Bega.

Gul-badan, 15*b*.

(Tarsūn-sulṭān, Yūn, *q.v.)*

CXCI. Ulugh Begam. (No. 10.)

Daughter of Zainab Sulṭān Begam; granddaughter of Sulṭān Abū-sa'īd; first cousin of Bābar.

Gul-badan, 24*b*.

CXCII. Ulūs (Anūsh and Alūsh) *ārihā Turkomān.* (? No. 53)

Turkī, *ūlūs,* tribe. Clearly a title.

Daughter of Khwāja Husain Beg *Turkomān* of the White Sheep, an amīr of 'Umar Shaikh *Mīrān-shāhī;* wife of 'Umar Shaikh; mother of a girl who died in infancy. She was removed from the *ḥaram* a year or eighteen months after her marriage. Gul-badan mentions a begam of this name as at Hindāl's wedding-feast; whether she is Ūlūs *āghā* promoted, I have no means of knowing.

Mems., 14. Gul-badan, 26*a*.

CXCIII. Ūmīd *āghācha Āndijāni.*

Pers. *ūmīd,* hope.

An inferior wife of 'Umar Shaikh Mīrzā *Mīrān-shāhī* whom she predeceased. She was the mother of Mihr-bānū who was two years older than Bābar and will have been born therefore in 1481; of Nāsir who was born in 1487; and of Shahr-bānū who was born in 1491.

Mems., 10, 14.

CXCIV. Umm-kulsūm Begam *Mīrān-shāhī.*

A. surname of Fāṭima, daughter of Muhamrnad: Ar. *umm,* mother, and *kuīsūm,* plumpness.

Granddaughter of Gul-badan Begam and a member of the Haj of 983H..

Akbar-nāma, III. 145.

CXCV. Ūzūn-sulṭān Khānam *Chaghatāī Mughal.*
(?) Pers. *auzūn,* or *ūzūn,* ample, increase.

Daughter of Shīr ʻAlī Khān *Oghlan Chaghatāi;* sister of Wais Khān and Makhdūma Khanām; paternal aunt of Yūnas Khān; wife of Amīr Sayyid ʻAlī *Dughlāt;* mother of Muḥammad Ḥaidar *Dughlāt* and great-grandmother of Ḥaidar Mīrzā, the historian.

She was widowed in 862H. (1457-58), and then, in conjunction with her son, received Kāshghar and Yangī-hisār from her stepson, Sāniz.

Tār. Rash., E. & E., 64, 87, 88.

CXCVI. Yādgār-sulṭān Begam *Mīrān-shāhī.* (No. 8.)
Pers. *yādgār,* remembrance.

Daughter of ʻUmar Shaikh *Mīrān-shāhī* and Aghā Sulṭān *āghācha;* half-sister of Bābar, and brought up by his grandmother, Isān-daulat. She was a posthumous child, and, if one may draw an inference from her example and others similar, is for this reason called Yādgār (Souvenir). Her father died Ramzan 4th, 899H. (June 9th, 1494). When a child of not more than ten, and in 908H. (1503), she fell into the hands of ʻAbdu-l-latīf *Uzbeg,* after the conquest of Andijān and Akhsī by Shaibānī, and in 91GH. (1511) Bābar's successes at Khutlān and Hisār enabled her to return to him and her own people.

I do not find any marriage mentioned for her by her name.

She is in the list of the guests at the Mystic Feast, and her mother is named (as such) as present at Hindā's wedding festivities.

Mems., 10.

Gul-badan, 24*b*, 26*b*.

CXCVII. Yūn (Tarsūn)-sulṭān *Mughal.*
Ilminsky, 15, writes *Ta.rsān.*

Inferior wife of Umar Shaikh, and married at the end of his life.

Mems., 14.

CXCVIII. Zainab-sulṭān Begam *Mīrān-shālīī.*

(?) From Ar. *zain,* adorning.

Fifth daughter of Sulṭān Maḥmūd Mīrzā and Khānzāda Begam *(b.)* Termiẕī; first cousin and wife of Bābar.

She was married at the instance of Qūt-līq-nigār, in the year of the capture of Kābul, *i.e.,* 910H. (1504-5), perhaps at the time that Jahāngīr Mīrzā, Bābar's half-brother, married her half-sister, Āq Begam. The marriage was not happy. Two or three years later Zainab died of small-pox.

Mems., 30.

CXCIX. Zainab-sulṭān Khānam *Chaghatāī Mughal.* (No. 19.)

Daughter of Sulṭān Maḥmūd Khān *Chaghatāl Mughal;* favourite wife of Sulṭān Sa'īd Khān *Kāshgharī,* her first cousin; aunt of Shāh Muḥammad Sulṭān whom Muḥammadī *Barlās* put to death; mother of Ibrāhīm who was born 930H. (1524), Sa'īd's third son and favourite child, of Muhsin, and of Maḥmūd Yūsuf.

On her husband's death in 939H. (July, 1533), she was banished by her stepson Rashīd, and went with her children to. Kābul where she met Ḥaidar Mīrzā and where she was under the protection of Kāmrān.

Gul-badan mentions her in the guest-list, and places her name as present at the Mystic Feast (1531), but this can hardly be right. She could easily have been at the marriage festivities in 1537.

tār. Rash., E. & E., 146, 375, 383, 467.

Gul-badan, 11*a,* 24*b*.

CC. Zainab-sulṭān Begam *Mīrān-shāhī.*

Gul-badan describes her as the paternal aunt or great-aunt (*'ama*) of Humāyīm. Bābar had no such sister, and no Zainab is mentioned by Gul-badan as a daughter of his grandfather Abū-sa'īd. An Āq Begam, however, is spoken of by her, and Zainab may be her personal name. Zainab had a daughter Ulugh Begam.

Gul-badan, 24*b*.

CCL. Zainab-sulṭān Begam.

There is a difficulty in identifying the begam of this name, whom Bābar mentions (Mems., 387) as coming to India. It will be seen by comparing the sources and their French and English interpretations:

Mems., 387. 'another, by name Zainab-sulṭān Begam, the granddaughter of Bikeh Chichām.'

P. de C, II. 355. 'et la petite-fille de Yenga-Tchetcham, autrement dite Zeineb-sulṭān Begam.'

B. M. Or., 3714, Pers., p. 482. *dīgar nabīra ijanga chichām ki Zainab-sulṭān Begam bāshad.*

Bodleian, Elliot, 19, f. 180*a*. *dīgar nabīra bega chichām ki Zainab-sulṭān Begam.*

Ilminsky, Turkī text, 447. *yana, yanga chichām hi Zainab-sulṭān Begam būlaghā'i nabīra sī kīlīb.*

It seems safer to take Zainab as the name of Bābar's relation (*i.e.,* the *yanga* of his *chicha*) than as that of the granddaughter (*nabīra*).

It may be observed here that the best authorities quoted above, *i.e.,* Ilminsky, behind whom is Kehr, and Or., 3714, have *ijanga* where Mr. Erskine and Elliot, 19, have *bega.* This exchange may occur in the case of other *begas* of this appendix. Until a good Turkī text more complete than that in the B. M. is found, this must be left an open question.

If *Zainab* be taken as the name of the *yanga,* she may be identifiable with one of the other women already entered in the appendix, but for deciding this point more examples are necessary of Bābar's application of the word *yanga.*

Mems., 387.

CCII. Zobaida *āghācha Jalāīr.*

The marigold; Ar. *zubaida.*

Granddaughter of Husain Shaikh Tīmūr of the Shaibān Sultāns. According to the *Ḥabibu-s-siyār,* she was a *Jalair.*

She was an inferior wife of Sulṭān Husain Mīrzā and the mother of 'Āyisha Begam. She predeceased her husband who died April, 1506.

CCIII. Zuhra Begī and Āghā *Uzbeg.*

Ar. *zuhra,* beauty, a yellow flower, the star Venus.

An inferior wife of Sultān Mahmūd Mīrzā; mother of Makhdūma-sultān Bēgam and of Sultān 'Alī Mīrzā.

She was married during the lifetime of Mahmūd's father, and therefore before Rajab 873H. (January, 1469), and was widowed Rabī II., 900H. (January, 1495). In 905H. (1499-1500) she entered into an intrigue with Shaibānī, a fellow-tribesman, of which the ultimate aim was dominance in Samarqand for her son 'Alī. A part of her scheme and offer was her own remarriage with Shaibānī. Bābar stigmatizes her action as 'stupidity and folly,' and says, further, 'the wretched and weak woman, for the sake of getting herself a husband, gave the family and honour of her son to the winds. Nor did Shaibānī Khān mind her a bit, or value her even so much as his other hand-maids, concubines, or women. Sulṭān 'Alī Mīrzā was confounded at the condition in which he now found himself, and deeply regretted the step he had taken. Several young cavaliers formed a plan for escaping with him, but he would not consent. As the hour of fate was at hand, he could not shun it. They put him to death in the meadow of Kulba. From his overanxiety to preserve this mortal and transitory life, he left a name of infamy behind him; and, from following the suggestions of a woman, struck himself out of the list of those who have earned for themselves a glorious name. It is impossible to write any more of the transactions of such a personage (? Zuhra), and impossible to listen any further to the recital of such base and dastardly proceedings.'

Mems, 29, 30, 31, 83, 84.

APPENDIX B

Mahdī Khwāja.

Nizāmu-d-dīn Aḥmad has included in his *Ṭabaqāt-i-akbarī* a story which he heard from his father Muḥammad Muqīm *Harāwī,* and of which the purport is that Bābar's *Khalīfa* (Nizāmu-d-dīn 'Alī *Barlās)* had at one time thought of placing a certain Mahdī Khwāja on the throne in succession to Bābar.

Two circumstances cast doubt on the story: (1) It was customary in Bābar's family for a son to succeed his father; (2) Bābar left four sons, the youngest of whom, Hindāl, was eleven years old.

Moreover, there were Tīmūrids both of the Bāyqrā and Mīrān-shāhī branches in India with Bābar whose claims to a Tīmūrid throne would be strongly enforced.

But Nizāmu-d-dīn Aḥmad has left us the story in circumstantial detail and it cannot be passed over unnoticed, and this the less because Gul-badan Begam throws some light on the identity of the Mahdī concerned, and also because in an important particular, *i.e.,* the relation of Mahdī to Bābar, I am able, through Mr. Beveridge's study of the *Ḥabību-s-siyār,* to give more accurate information than was at Mr. Erskine's disposal.

The story was old when Nizāmu-d-dīn set it down and it is not necessary to accept all its details as exact. It is sufficient to consider its minimum contents which are, that in the royal household there had been a rumour of a plan of supersession of Bābar's sons by Mahdī Khwāja at the instance of Khalīfa.

The question naturally arises, who was the man concerning

whom such intention could be attributed to the wise and experienced Khalīfa?

Nizāmu-d-dīn calls Mahdī Bābar's *damād,* and Mr. Erskine, amongst other translators, has rendered this by son-in-law. It is unnecessary to consider why any Mahdī Khwāja known in history should have been preferred to those sons-in-law who were of Bābar's own blood, because Gul-badan calls Mahdī Bābar's *yazna.* For this word the dictionaries yield only the meaning of 'brother-in-law' and 'husband of the king's sister.' Both these meanings are also attributed to *damād.* But the *Ḥabīb* settles the verbal question by a statement that Mahdī Khwāja was the husband of Khān-zāda Begam, Bābar's full sister.

It is not improbable that he had another close link with the Emperor, namely that of relationship to Māham Begam, but I am not yet able to assert this definitely.

Bābar never mentions Mahdī Khwāja's parentage. This is learned from Khwānd-amīr who states that he was the son of Mūsa Khwāja and grandson of Murtaẓa Khwāja. He was a sayyid; and from the circumstance that his burial-place was chosen as that of Sayyid Abū'l-ma'ālī Termiẕī, it may be inferred that he belonged to the religious house of Termiz. If so, he had probably Tīmūrid blood in his veins, since inter-marriage between the families was frequent.

Bābar mentions a Khwāja Mūsa who is perhaps Mahdī's father, in 914H., 1508. He immediately afterwards names Khwāja Muḥammad 'Alī, Māham Begam's brother, in suggestive sequence.

Bābar's first surviving record of Mahdī is made in 925H. (February, 1519) when 'Mīr Muḥammad Mahdī Khwāja' brings in a prisoner. It is in *cir.* 923H. (1517) that Khwānd-amīr speaks of the marriage of Mahdī and Khān-zāda, but this is probably a good deal after the fact, because Khān-zāda was returned to Bābar in 917H. (1511).

Mahdī Khwāja, as Bābar invariably calls him after his first appearance, went to Hindūstān with Bābar and is frequently mentioned. It is significant of his high position and presumably not only by marriage but by birth, that on military duty he is always associated with men of royal blood, either Tīmūrid or Chaghatāī. He is sometimes given precedence of them, and is never named last in a list of officers. Chīn-tīmūr *Chaghatāī,* Muḥammad Sulṭān Mīrzā *Bāyqrā,* Sulṭān Mīrzā *Mīrān-shāhī,* and 'Ādil Sulṭān are constantly associated with him. It seems clear that he was a great noble and ranked amongst the highest. Khāfī Khān calls him Sayyid Khwāja, and so does Khwānd-amīr. Whether the 'Khwāja' indicates anything as to his mother's marriage I am not able to say.

Khāfī Khān (I. 42) has a passage which *may* relate to him: *Sulṭān Mīrzā wa Mahdī Sulṭān binī a'māmrā* (of Bābar) *ki asīr-i-ān juma' būdand khalās sakht.* The date of the occurrence is *civ.* 1511, the year in which another Mahdī, *i.e., Uzbeg,* was killed by Bābar. Mr. Erskine appears to think that the two men, named here as released, were Hamza and Mahdī Sulṭāns *Uzbeg,* but the sources do not give the style of Mīrzā to either of these chiefs. They appear to have had marriage connections with Bābar in an earlier generation, and a son of Mahdī seems to have been 'Ādil Sulṭān (Mems., 363) who was father of 'Āqil Sulṭān *Uzbeg* (*Akbar-nāma,* I. 221).

A Mahdī Khwāja who was undoubtedly of Bābar's family, appears both in the *Tārīkh-i-rashīdī* and in Gul-badan Begam's *Humāyūn-nāma.* He is the son of Aiman, and grandson of Sulṭān Aḥmad Khān *Chaghatāī,* Bābar's mother's brother. But his age places him out of the question; he was about ten in 1530, and the hero of Nizāmu-d-dīn's story stroked his beard, and was either a *damād* or a *yazna.* Mahdī *Chaghatāī,* moreover, reached India after Bābar's death.[1]

---

1 The rough estimate of Mahdī Chaghatāī's age is made as follows: Aiman was married to Ḥaidar Mīrzā's cousin in 923H. (1517). (*Tār. Rash.*, E. and E., 144, 352.) He had five sons by this wife. (l. c. 144 and 401). Of these Ma'sūd is named as the eldest. The rest are Khiẓr (Gul-badan's husband) Mahdī, Isān-daulat (Habība's husband), and another. Khiẓr is inferentially the second son, but if Mahdī were the second, he could hardly have been born before 926H. (1520). This would make him about ten in 1530, but he may have been younger and the third son, as is indicated by the enumeration of Ḥaidar Mīrzā.

The *Ṭabaqāt* states that Mahdī Khwāja had long been connected with Khalīfa; the latter was himself a sayyid.

Nizāmu-d-dīn calls Mahdī a *jūwan* and Mr. Erskine has accentuated all the faults and characteristics of youth in his version of the story. But Gul-badan calls Hindāl an uninjurious youth at thirty-three, and there seems good ground to read often in *jūwan* the notion of vigour and strength rather than exclusively of fewness of years. In 1530 Mahdī had served Bābar eleven known years.

Like many other such small problems, that of the family connections of Mahdī Khwāja and the other men of his name may be solved by some chance passage in a less known author, or by a closer consideration of the personages of the Memoirs.

Mems., 255, 303, 305-307, 338, 340-342, 344, 345, 349, 352, 363, 370, 371, 401, 426.[1]

Akbar-nāma, s.n., 'Aqil Sulṭān and Mahdī.

Khāfī Khān, *Bib. Ind.* ed., s.n..

Ḥabibu-s-siyār, Khwānd-amīr, under date *cir.* 923H..

Cf. Index to this volume, *s.n.* Mahdī.

[1] At p. 424 Mr. Erskine has an entry of a Sayyid Mahdī who arrives from Guālīār in July, 1529. That this is a mis-reading for Mashhadī is shown by collation with other texts than his own.

INDEX
(OTHER THAN OF PLACES)

NOTE.—This index is full for the pages down to 201. It gives the Roman-numbered names only of Appendix A.

Reference to the Persian imprint is by folio numbering. This is reproduced accurately from the MS., in the Persian imprint, and as closely as the sentences permit in the translation.

Words in *'ain, ghain,* etc, are classed with their nearest equivalents.

INDEX OF PLACES

ACKNOWLEDGEMENTS

In the Fall of 2022, I was at the Jackman Humanities Institute in Toronto on a fellowship, placing final touches to my book *Vagabond Princess*. Jaya Aninda Chatterjee, my editor at Yale University Press, asked me if I would consider creating a compendium to *Vagabond Princess*. She suggested that a new translation of Gulbadan's memoir would make an attractive two book packet. Mesmerized by the audacious Gulbadan, I was also thinking about the work of Annette Beveridge at that time. Thanks to Jaya's invitation, I came to the decision that it is time to establish an intellectual genealogy that rings the gorgeous writing of Gulbadan. Annette had found a friend in the Princess. I have been obsessed with Gulbadan's work from the start of my history career.

So, Jaya, here is the compendium you asked for! Thanks for your reflections and diligent edits. Very special thanks to my agent, Bridget Matzie. I am grateful for your long-standing solidarity with my work of history. Thanks to Amanda Gerstenfeld for helping with all the steps of production. Warm thanks to Liz Pelton in the US, to Lucy Donchaster in the UK Yale office and to entire publicity team for their work. In India, warm thanks to Chiki Sarkar, Parth Mehrotra, Smita Mathur and the Juggernaut Books team.

I have lived with the spectacular work of Mughal Princess Gulbadan for over twenty years, the dynamic history that soaks it, the beauty of its content and language – and the magic of its disappearance. Writing about it in our times, I have learnt a great deal more about the spirit of history, the force of adventure and, above all, the power of friendship. For reading drafts of the introduction of this book, my gratitude to Bridget Matzie, Jaya Chatterjee, Parth Mehrotra, Gyan Pandey and Michael Fisher. For comments and conversations on early drafts, thanks to Sonya Mace, John Keay and Archana Venkatesh. For long years of intellectual care and immense solidarity, I am grateful to Daniel Weiss, Gyan Pandey, Gayatri Spivak, Allan Sealy, Lynne Huffer, Irina Dumitrescu, Molly Crabapple, Leslie Harris, Laurie Patton, Lois Reitzes, Max Kulyk, Sue Hunter, Lynda Hill, Rana Safvi, Ira Mukhoty, Alexis Wick, Meenakshi Alimchandani, Khushru Irani, Malaika Gutekunst, Sayali Bapat, Shyam Selvadurai, Linda Feng and Chet Van Duzer.

Only an utterly visual language can capture Gulbadan's itinerant world. For a number of years, I have gathered so much from the knowledge of my brilliant art history colleagues and friends. I am grateful to Sonya Mace, Molly Aitken and Cathy Benkaim.

Gratitude to the Emory librarian Gautham Reddy and the Uppsala University librarian Christina Swedberg for chasing obscure references. Special thanks to Sonya Mace at the Cleveland Museum of Art, and to Ursula Sims-Williams at the British Library, London. Warm thanks to Molly Crabapple for her superb, tent life painting.

For spectacles in prose and art that keep me alive, gratitude to Olga Tokarczuk, Patti Smith, Walter Benjamin and Teju Cole. And to the playful Mughal artists for the splendor of women's adventure they left behind.